CONCEPTIONS OF DEVELOPMENT

CONCEPTIONS OF DEVELOPMENT

Lessons from the Laboratory

Edited by

David J. Lewkowicz
Robert Lickliter

Psychology Press
New York • London • Hove

Published in 2002 by
Psychology Press
29 West 35th Street
New York, NY 10001

Published in Great Britain by
Psychology Press Ltd
27 Church Road
Hove, East Sussex, BN3 2FA

Psychology Press is an imprint of the Taylor & Francis Group.

Printed in the United States of America on acid-free paper.

10 9 8 7 6 5 4 3 2 1

Library of Congress Cataloging-in-Publication Data
Conceptions of development : lessons from the laboratory / David J. Lewkowicz & Robert Lickliter, ed[itor]s.
   p. cm.
  Includes bibliographical references and index.
  ISBN 0–86377–680–9 — ISBN 0–86377–681–7 (pbk.)
   1. Developmental psychology—Research. 2. Psychobiology—Research.
 I. Lewkowicz, David, J. II. Lickliter, Robert.

BF713 .C65 2002
115'.07'2—dc21

                                2002017836

Cover design: Jennifer Crisp
Cover image: Imagebank

CONTENTS

v

ABOUT THE EDITORS

David J. Lewkowicz is currently a senior research scientist at the New York State Institute for Basic Research, where for the past fourteen years he has been conducting research on the development of perception in human infants. By specifically focusing on the development of intersensory integration, he has attempted to gain greater insight into ways in which infants construct a unified perceptual picture of their world. Throughout his career he has also had an abiding interest in theoretical issues related to the development of behavior, and the current volume is, in part, a reflection of that interest.

Robert Lickliter is currently professor of psychology at Florida International University and research professor at the University of Miami Medical School. His research interests focus on the development of perception, with a particular emphasis on the relationship between prenatal experience and postnatal perceptual organization. His theoretical interests focus on the links between developmental and evolutionary theory.

CONTRIBUTORS

David J. Lewkowicz
NYS Institute for Basic Research
1050 Forest Hill Road
Staten Island, NY 10314

Robert Lickliter
Florida International University
Department of Psychology
Blacksburg, VA 24061

Myron A. Hofer
New York State Psychiatric Institute
Columbia University
1051 Riverside Drive
New York, NY 10032

Gilbert Gottlieb
Center for Developmental Science
University of North Carolina
Chapel Hill, NC 27599-8115

Celia L. Moore
Department of Psychology
University of Massachusetts, Boston
Boston, MA 02125

Meredith J. West
Indiana University
Department of Psychology
Bloomington, IN 47408

Andrew P. King
Indiana University
Department of Psychology
Bloomington, IN 47408

William A. Mason
Department of Behavioral Biology
California Regional Primate Research
Center
University of California, Davis
Davis, CA 95616

Rachel Keen Clifton
Department of Psychology
University of Massachusetts
Amherst, MA 01003

George F. Michel
Psychology Department
DePaul University
2219 N. Kenmore Avenue
Chicago, IL 60614-3504

Gerald Turkewitz
Department of Psychology
Hunter College
695 Park Avenue
New York, NY 10021

David F. Bjorklund
Department of Psychology
Florida Atlantic University
Boca Raton, FL 33428

Sandra E. Trehub
Department of Psychology
University of Toronto at Mississauga
3359 Mississauga Road North
Mississauga, Ontario L5L 1C6
Canada

Linda B. Smith
Psychology
1101 East 10th Street
Indiana University
Bloomington, IN 47405

Kurt Fischer
Harvard University
Graduate School of Education
Larsen 702
Cambridge, MA 02138

Zheng Yan
Harvard University
Graduate School of Education
Larsen 702
Cambridge, MA 02138

Richard M. Lerner
Tufts University
Eliott Pearson School—105 College
Medford/Somerville Campus
Boston, MA 02110

INTRODUCTION

Research is always personal, even if its results are not.
M. Mahner & M. Bunge
Foundations of Biophilosophy (1997)

This volume is about the process of scientific discovery. It began as a discussion between the editors after attending a conference on behavioral development. We were both struck by the fact that the scientific process is almost always portrayed as orderly and logical in both publications and presentations. Investigators are trained to present their approach to an issue or question as being conceived and pursued in a linear, somewhat formulaic manner—a set of problems is identified, research is designed and conducted to address the problems, and results are interpreted and applied. In contrast to this idealized view of the scientific process, we, like all practicing scientists, knew that this straightforward scenario is rarely the case. Scientific investigation typically involves unexpected twists and turns, a complex mix of struggles, blind alleys, and the occasional serendipity, insight, or discovery.

As we surveyed the available texts in the field of developmental science concerned with psychobiological development, we found that there was no ready source that a graduate student or practicing scientist could turn to for an accessible description of the process of scientific research and discovery. There was no obvious volume where one could examine how individual scientists come to formulate, modify, or even reject various conceptual frameworks regarding development over the course of their research careers. We concluded that the absence of such accounts is due not only to the constraints of usual publication formats, but also to the inherent difficulty of describing such a necessarily personal and abstract process. We also concluded that the richness of an individual's scientific pathway is typically lost or obscured through the very process of translation into the standard and acceptable formats for disseminating research findings. It seemed to us that making this personal process accessible could serve as a rich source of examples of how to think about development and a potential fountainhead for new ideas and new understanding.

In this light, we asked a number of senior scientists who have made important and lasting contributions to the field of developmental science to describe their own individual process of exploration and discovery. Our charge to them was to make their intellectual journey as explicit as possible, to show how their changing conceptual perspectives guided and transformed their research directions. In other words, we envisioned a forum for developmental scientists to remember and recount their personal pathways of scientific investigation and discovery. As our idea for this book project began to take shape, it become clear that what we were imagining was a volume that would differ markedly from the typical empirically based chapter collections. What we had in mind were chapters that focused on the intellectual *process* underlying the study of psychobiological development rather than a narrative-based autobiography (see Merrens & Brannigan, 1996 for an example of this type of approach). What we were looking for were personal perspectives on the processes and circumstances that led prominent investigators within developmental psychology and psychobiology to, both, devise the kinds of projects that they pursued over their research careers, and to formulate their particular conceptual views of the very process of development.

The chapters in this volume recount the intellectual journeys of thirteen prominent developmental scientists and document their individual struggles to better understand, describe, and explain various developmental phenomena. We asked each contributor to delineate the particular paths that led him or her to devise a systematic research program and to describe how the empirical results of such a program led to the formulation (and ongoing reformulation) of their particular view of development. We were particularly interested in getting them to provide a "behind-the-scenes" account of their process of scientific discovery and to reflect on the development of their ideas over the course of their research career. We believed that this effort would provide a unique contribution to developmental science, a more personalized view of scientific inquiry that could be of interest to both graduate students, investigators, and the wider public interested in lessons from the laboratory.

The core idea behind our charge to the authors was that development is a bidirectional process and that the process of scientific discovery is similar in this respect. In many ways, this was the most challenging aspect of our request: provide a personal slant on how your empirical work led to the formulation of your theoretical models of development and how these in turn further influenced your subsequent empirical work and ideas. We pointed out that the authors' existing journal articles and book chapters already provided detailed information regarding the specifics of the methods and results of their research and that this was not the primary interest or focus of this book. Rather, we asked the contributors to reflect on how their decades of empirical research had instructed, challenged, and modified their respective conceptions of development, and in turn, how their conceptions of development guided their empirical research.

We chose to conceptualize the volume in terms of the concept of bidirectionality in part because our own view of development is that it is a bidirectional process. That is, we view the various changes, improvement, and reorganizations in an individual's behavior over ontogeny as resulting from reciprocal, bidirectional interactions among organismic and contextual factors occurring over the course of individual development (Lewkowicz, 2000; Lickliter, 2000). This perspective is in contrast to the still widespread view of development as the unfolding of a predetermined or innate set of instructions, operating relatively independent of the activity, experience, or context of the individual. Interestingly, much of the empirical support for the conceptual shift to a more epigenetic or systems view of behavioral development has come from the laboratories represented in this volume. The collective efforts of our contributors over the last four decades have repeatedly challenged conventional assumptions of innate, predetermined, or hardwired behavior and in so doing changed the very nature of the questions now pursued in developmental science. Their contributions range across a variety of topics and disciplines, including physiological regulation, perception, motor skills, vocal learning, social development, memory, and language acquisition, to name but a few of the topics covered in the chapters to follow.

Several common themes emerge from the collected chapters. These themes appear in a variety of examples found throughout the volume and apply both to the process of scientific discovery and to the process of development. For example, many of the chapters make it clear that the scientific process (like the process of development) occurs "in medias res," in the middle of things. Paths taken, choices made, questions asked all depend on the context and circumstances available to the individual investigator. In other words, like life and development itself, the process of scientific discovery depends to a large extent on serendipity rather than on careful planning or design. Further, the scientific process (like the process of development) goes forward because of the individual's own activity and his or her experience with their surrounding context or milieu. The research issues undertaken, the type of data collected, and the interpretation of the findings all depend on the background, training, and developmental history of the individual investigator. Finally, equifinality, the notion that the same end point can be reached via different developmental pathways, is well illustrated by comparing the intellectual journeys and insights of the individual authors. Starting from very different initial conditions, each has reached remarkably similar or parallel conclusions regarding the developmental process, but often by very different routes or pathways.

Of particular interest is the fact that each author notes the conceptual obstacles to discovery and insight encountered along their individual journey. In their own way and in their own areas, each had to question and often struggle against the current "facts" or dogmas they encountered regarding the nature of behavior and its development. The chapters provide a flavor of this historical backdrop, of the prevailing "common sense" of their time, and its directive and constraining role in the formulation and eventual reformulation of each investigator's personal perspective and research strategy. These personal struggles led to some of the most influential theoretical and empirical contributions to be found in the current developmental psychobiology literature. The chapters of this volume provide the reader with a closer look at the birth and development of these "lessons from the laboratory."

In closing, we dedicate this volume to Robert Cairns, whose untimely death deprived the field of developmental science of one of its most creative and influential visionaries. Through his work on the development of aggressive behavior, Cairns built an integrated, process-oriented model that showed the complex interplay of genetic, physiological, and behavioral factors involved in the development of social behavior. Bob had agreed to contribute a chapter to this volume, and we deeply regret that it is missing the "behind-the-scenes" look into the creative process that went into the crafting of his distinctive vision of the developmental process. This vision will be missed.

☐ References

Lewkowicz, D. J. (2000). The development of intersensory temporal perception: An epigenetic systems/limitations view. *Psychological Bulletin, 126*(2), 281–308

Lickliter, R. (2000). An ecological approach to behavioral development: Insights from comparative psychology. *Ecological Psychology, 12,* 319–334.

Mahner, M., & Bunge, M. (1997). *Foundations of Biophilosopy.* Berlin: Springer-Verlag.

Merrens, M. R., & Brannigan, G. G. (1996). *The developmental psychologists: Research adventures across the life span.* New York: McGraw-Hill.

CHAPTER 1

Myron A. Hofer

The Riddle of Development

Ever since human beings have thought about themselves, they have argued about the origins of human nature. First religion and then evolution have provided answers to the ultimate sense of this question, answers that have satisfied some and infuriated others. The question has also persisted in a developmental rather than an evolutionary time frame. Here it exists today as a riddle, a trick question like one posed in ancient times by the sphinx, to the despair of travelers who attempted to answer it. For us the question takes the form: "Is our development shaped more by our genes or by our environment?" Despite all our attempts as developmentalists to answer this riddle by insisting that development always involves both elements and that it is the interaction of the two that should be the focus of our attention, the sphinx is not satisfied: the riddle persists—in the press, in public policy, and even in the back of our own minds. This persistence of the riddle is one of the reasons that I have found studying development so fascinating. In the course of the research I have done, my concept of development has been changed again and again. More recently, another question has gradually replaced the riddle in my mind and has led me to a different way to attempt to satisfy the sphinx, as I will relate below.

☐ Ignorance Is Bliss

My first interest in development came as a result of my clinical experience taking care of patients while a resident in internal medicine and in

5

psychiatry. What interested me most were the extraordinary differences between individuals in how they perceived their illnesses and the stresses in their lives, in the nature of the biological changes produced by the illness, and in how incapacitated they became. We were taught in medical school that these differences were due to some poorly understood combination of genetic and environmental influences, and most physicians left it at that. To some, patients were either endowed with good or poor "protoplasm." In my psychiatric training, however, I was taught how to understand my patients' illnesses in terms of the events of their childhood as they remembered them. Working with psychoanalytic developmental theory, I became adept at creating a "psychodynamic developmental formulation," but I knew it was more art than science. Nevertheless, I was left with a respect for the long-term shaping effects of early experience, the importance of the parent-child relationship, and the presence of stages and transitions in development. In the meanwhile, I read European ethologists, American learning theorists, and the reports of a handful of investigators who were beginning to study early behavior development experimentally in laboratory animals. Naturally, as a psychiatrist, I was most impressed by Harlow's (e.g., Harlow, 1961) and by Kaufman and Rosenblum's maternal deprivation studies (e.g., Kaufman & Rosenblum, 1967). Here, for the first time, was an animal model of psychiatric disease, I thought. However, I also read that simpler events such as food restriction, early handling, or changing ambient temperature could have significant long-term effects on rodent offspring behavior and physiology in adulthood.

From these studies, I saw the possibility of being able to construct, experimentally, a life history for an animal, one that resembled the early experiences my patients had told me about. In this animal model, I thought I could test some of the theories that I had been taught and even find out how my patients' early experiences had become translated into changed personality and behavior through development. My next step was postdoctoral training in the Department of Animal Behavior at the American Museum of Natural History with Ethel Tobach, while supported on a postdoctoral fellowship at Albert Einstein College of Medicine with Morton Reiser, and later a Research Scientist Development Award with Herbert Weiner as my mentor. I remember thinking at the time that although psychological development was still a mystery, the development of biological systems and behavior must be pretty well understood. I kept eagerly looking through papers and books in zoology and embryology. I went to two scientific meetings on early development with the expectation that someone would tell me how development was supposed to work.

But this never happened, and it finally dawned on me that nobody could give me a satisfactory explanation of the nature of development as a process, either at the level of biology or behavior.

Thus, the first way in which my concept of development was changed was to realize that I had to make do with a fragmentary, incomplete, and contradictory set of ideas. My concept of development would have to be a work in progress. This is not to say that I did not have any concepts *about* development. I had many of those, some of them assumptions that I probably was unaware of at the time. I didn't appreciate, then, the research advantages of not being committed to a particular viewpoint, but I did feel the excitement of setting out into uncharted territory.

☐ Development as a Research Tool

Today, as I read over my laboratory notebook and first NIH grant proposal from my present perspective some thirty years later, I am struck by what I might call my "attitude" toward development. I wanted to *use* developmental manipulations to answer questions I had about illness in adults. Could I devise a series of early and later life events in a rapidly growing laboratory animal, such as the rat, that would cause a major vulnerability to a particular life event in the adult animal? More specifically, I wanted to combine, longitudinally, a series of early life events that individually had been shown to increase adult physiological stress responses, so as to produce, by an additive or synergistic effect, a lethal vulnerability in autonomic cardiac control, a model of sudden death. More specifically, I proposed to crowd pregnant mother rats, socially isolate their offspring at weaning, and expose the unlucky progeny, when adult, to a forced swim-stress that had recently been shown to induce severe cardiac arrhythmias in a small minority of laboratory rats. Clearly, I had the idea that development was a process in which the effects of a series of stresses, occurring at various different ages, accumulate over time so as to produce a progressive increase in vulnerability to maladaptive responses in the adult. This linear, additive concept of development is still current and is easily discernible in clinical child development studies and animal model research today. Fortunately, I was also interested in finding out about the normal development of autonomic cardiac control, virtually unexplored territory at the time. In my doubts about my choice of a physiological, rather than a behavioral, variable to study, I was reassured by Ethel Tobach: "Remember, heart rate *is* a behavior."

☐ The Salutary Effects of Gathering Data

Notes in my laboratory book show a rapid shift in my ideas soon after I succeeded in developing a technique for recording heart rate from freely moving rat pups in their home cage environment. I soon found that the early development of autonomic cardiac control was anything but linear. In the first postnatal week, giving adrenergic and cholinergic receptor blocking drugs showed that resting sympathetic activity became increasingly evident under baseline conditions in the home cage litter situation. But then this faded in the second week, as growing parasympathetic activity slowed baseline heart rates throughout the second and third weeks. Phasic, sympathetically mediated cardiac rate increases in response to environmental stimuli were small and inconsistent in the first week, but became the typical response in the third week. Remarkably, although baseline cardiac rates showed virtually no tonic parasympathetic influence in the first and early second week, phasic vagal cardiac responses occurred as early as the first postnatal day (in response to gentle pressure over the mouth and face). Short episodes of bradycardia appeared spontaneously a few days later during active sleep, events that could be readily blocked by parasympathetic antagonists. To my further surprise, the most intense sympathetic cardiac acceleration occurred not in response to any of my stimuli, but as a spontaneous crescendo synchronized with the onset, and culminating at the height of, each face washing episode. Then I found that the cardiac rate response of the 10- to 12-day-old rat pup to being picked up from the home cage by the experimenter was not the expected increase in rate so characteristic of adult animals, but a vagally mediated decrease in cardiac rate during the first 1–2 minutes in the warmed test box. Four days later, pups responded to the same stimulus with a brisk cardiac acceleration, although their behavioral responses were quite similar at both ages. These results became the subject of my first developmental paper (Hofer & Reiser, 1969).

Even today, these findings seem to me to be an unusually clear illustration of a peculiar property of development, its complex and unpredictable patterning. We can give names to this property: "nonlinear," "epigenetic," and, more recently, "chaotic." Each somehow fails to capture its essence. However, I did find one cardiac stress response that did not vary substantially over the preweaning period, and I tried out my linear additive concept on it. I reasoned that the repeated elicitation of a stress response during infancy would increase the later vulnerability of the juvenile to the stimulus, as was thought to occur clinically with early traumatic experience. The relatively consistent stress response I had found was the sudden and prolonged bradycardia of the "dive reflex," which I could produce in young rats by facial compression and brief airway occlusion with a soft rubber membrane made from a surgical glove (Hofer, Engel, & Weiner, 1971). If response intensity failed to increase over time, it seemed possible that it would simply diminish with repetition, as in the habituation characteristic of adult responses. To my dismay, pups given this stimulus 3 times a day from day 2 to day 20 showed no discernible developmental change in any parameter of the response or in baseline cardiac rates at any age, when compared to normally reared controls (unpublished observations).

So much for the idea of a linear additive developmental effect of repeated stress! I remember going to my weekly meeting with Herbert Weiner, my research mentor, and grumbling about being wrong so often. Couldn't I be right for a change? He reassured me that this would eventually happen to me, but then he paused and said something that I have never forgotten. "The thing about science is that we're always wrong; either in a week, a year, or a hundred years, but we're always wrong; that's the wonderful thing about it." And he laughed and laughed.

☐ Serendipity Strikes

Next, I decided to work with an early experience that was known to have long-term effects—the daily brief handling of a litter of pups for the first 2 or 3 weeks of life. I thought I could improve on the standard experimental design if I handled only half the pups in a litter, leaving the other pups to be within-litter controls. If I had not made this change, I might have had a publication on the early effects of handling on autonomic cardiac responses (which remains to be done) and gone off in an entirely different direction in my research. However, what I found instead was that, although the daily handled pups did in fact show higher resting cardiac rates between days sixteen and twenty, the other pups that had been left with the mother each day showed the same effect (unpublished observations). Furthermore, in one litter, the mother became very disturbed, apparently as a result of an unauthorized change of shavings by the animal care personnel, and the pups were found the next morning to have abnormally low cardiac rates. Months earlier, a mother had escaped from the cage overnight and her pups had such low heart rates the next morning that I thought they must be sick or abnormal. Now I began to wonder: Could these rat pups be responding to maternal deprivation?

My notes show how much difficulty I had at the time believing that rat pups could show any response to maternal separation, and I raised the question in my lab journal as though it seemed almost absurd. Maternal separation, I thought, was something that only affected primates. How could a rat pup 'know' that its mother was gone? What possible reason was there to believe that the infant rat had the necessary affective-cognitive capabilities to form a social bond in the first place? This high degree of skepticism, in retrospect, was a crucial factor in my designing the kind of experiments that led to the discovery of hidden regulatory processes within the mother-infant relationship. I could not believe that the 40 percent decrease in cardiac rate that followed 24 hours of maternal separation was not an artifact of the procedure itself, a failure of experimental control. But I found that when I controlled for the effects of a novel environment, absence of littermates, body temperature loss, and starvation, by providing warmth and nutrient to groups of pups in their home cages, the cardiac rate response was unaffected (Hofer, 1970).

☐ Concepts as Constraints

In order to fit these results into my concept of early development I had to infer that the pups were showing a despair (Bowlby, 1969) or conservation-withdrawal (Kaufman & Rosenblum, 1967) response to rupture of an attachment bond with their mother. For the mother-infant relationship was at the time conceived solely in terms of the emotional responses generated, such as comfort, protest, or anxiety and despair. Environmental influences on the young, such as levels of stimulation, temperature, and the metabolic and growth-promoting effects of nutrient, were stored in my mind as a separate class of developmental process from those at work in the relationship between mother and infant.

Herbert Weiner suggested an alternative mechanism: that the rat mother might secrete some form of sympathomimetic (cardiac-rate-stimulating) substance in her milk that was not present in the cow's milk I had previously used to feed the pups every 4 hours during the 24-hour separation period. In the course of comparing rat and bovine milk on separated pups with low heart rates, I was surprised to find a rapidly acting, short-lived (2-hour) but intense cardiac acceleration in response to all kinds of milk, an effect that was blocked by beta-adrenergic antagonists (Hofer & Weiner, 1971; Hofer, 1971). I realized that in our initial separation study, in which we provided milk by gastric intubation (Hofer, 1970), although we had prevented weight loss and even produced a 4 percent average weight gain, we had not given milk frequently enough to fully replace the 10–15 percent daily weight gain of rat pups at this age. Herbert Weiner and I, with the assistance of Harry Shair, went on to find that glucose, protein hydrolysate, or fat (and not simple gastric distention) produced dose-related increases in cardiac rate, but only if given by the intragastric route, not if given intravenously (Hofer & Weiner, 1975). This response was blocked by low cervical spinal cord section, indicating a central neural, rather than a local or peripheral mechanism. The afferent signal appeared to involve paraspinal sympathetic afferents, rather than the vagus nerves.

Blood pressure remained unchanged after separation, due to alpha-adrenergic vasoconstriction (presumably in the mesentery supplying the nearly empty intestines), and arterial baroreceptors were found to mediate a substantial portion of the profound bradycardia of the separated infant (reviewed in Hofer, 1984). By supplying milk to separated rat pups through an indwelling gastric cannula, at rates sufficient to produce typical levels of weight gain, the profound bradycardia of separation could be entirely prevented. Separated pups could have heart rates between 500/min and 250/min, according to the rate of milk flow used (Hofer, 1973a).

These results gradually revealed that the cardiac rate of the infant rat was regulated by the milk the mother supplied, acting over neural pathways involving gastric interoceptors sensitive to nutrient components of milk. Meanwhile, as the cardiac studies were unfolding, we wanted to find out if there were behavioral effects of maternal separation as well. We soon found that whether or not warmth was supplied to a litter of pups, overnight maternal separation had powerful effects on the levels of locomotor, self-grooming, and rearing behavior shown by pups placed alone in a novel test area following the separation period. There was a marked increase in activity levels when separated pups were provided with sufficient heat under the home cage to maintain their normal pre-separation temperatures, whereas pups showed an equally impressive reduction in these behaviors and a decline when the litter was left in the home cage at room temperature, allowing their body temperature to fall 2–3°C (Hofer, 1973 a, 1973b, 1973c). The reduction in activity levels of the hypothermic pups seemed understandable, but the hyperactivity of normothermic pups was entirely unexpected. It was not affected by nutrient infusion, the size of the litter, or the familiarity of the separation environment. Hyperactivity could be reduced or eliminated, however, by some forms of tactile stimulation delivered to the pups throughout the separation period, but not by others. We provided this stimulation on schedules modeled after the nursing cycle and found that for the effective forms of stimulation, the effect on the pups' activity levels was graded, with more frequent or more intense stimulation having the greatest effect (Hofer, 1975a).

Gradually I was forced by these results to shift from thinking of separation as an imposed stress, to searching for what components of the mother-infant interaction the pup had lost when the mother was no longer present. If one of these components could be identified correctly and supplied experimentally, it appeared to regulate that physiological function or the behaviors specifically, either raising or lowering their level in a graded fashion. I realized that in maternal separation, all these maternal regulators must be lost at once, resulting in a complex pattern of rising and falling levels of different functions, creating the typical form of the separation response.

☐ Forced to Change

As these results came in, I was gradually forced into a major reorientation of my concept of the role of the mother-infant relationship in development, as well as of my concept of early separation responses. These changes in my ways of thinking did not come at once, but evolved slowly as I began to see more implications of the original regulator idea. For example, I realized that if the effects of maternal separation were the result of withdrawal of regulatory processes hidden within the mother-infant interaction prior to separation, then these same processes must be continuously active during normal development and in this way play a role in establishing and maintaining the normal levels of function characteristic of preweanling infants. The mother-infant interaction would thus be capable of regulating the development of a variety of processes throughout early development, and even have long-term effects extending into adulthood. It was as if the infants' homeostatic system extended to include the mother, until weaning gradually led to the primacy of the infant's intrinsic regulatory systems. Moreover, these maternal regulatory processes could apparently operate independently of each other, with different modalities of maternal stimulation acting over different afferent pathways and regulating different infant functions.

The independence of the different regulatory effects and the way that specific aspects of the mother-infant interaction could be linked to specific physiological and behavioral systems was an entirely different way of thinking about how patterns of mothering could affect development. These processes seemed to underlie what I had previously considered to be essentially emotional interactions and suggested that they could be understood at a different level than that of inferred affective states. In looking over my early papers and my lab notes at the time, I was apparently having such difficulty in coming to a new understanding of maternal separation that at first I paid little attention to the implications that the discovery of these regulatory processes had for development. Initially, I tended to see nutrient regulation of cardiac rate as somehow outside the normal mother-infant relationship and I did not immediately connect the effects of experimentally applied heat on separated pups' behavior to the warmth supplied by the mother during normal development. I first used the word "regulate" in a 1971 paper on the effects of milk on cardiac rate in separated pups (Hofer, 1971), but it was not until I had studied several other systems in separated pups, and discovered other regulatory interactions, that I began to appreciate their likely role in shaping normal development. Even then, it was not easy. I wrote, in the following somewhat labored sentence, "It does not seem overly speculative to conclude that the mother conveys specific information (in the broad sense of the term) to the infant over several discrete sensory pathways, and that this information has important developmental consequences for the infant" (Hofer, 1975b, p. 153). I remember well the mental sensation of struggling to work out these new ways of thinking, and then, having realized the implications, wondering why I had had such difficulty seeing them earlier.

☐ Following the Implications

The clear-cut effects of acute maternal separation and the idea that maternal regulatory interactions might have long-term effects on development led next to a series of studies on the long-term effects of early weaning. Sigurd Ackerman, Herbert Weiner, and I (1975) began a series of studies on the developmental origins of later vulnerability to gastric erosions under immobilization stress, a stress effect that had recently been shown to be enhanced in adult rats by premature weaning as juveniles. Because published studies varied in the age used for adult testing, we decided to do a cross-sectional study to determine when the most consistent and severe vulnerability occurred in our Wistar strain. This study was very time-consuming but unexpectedly revealed something that has greatly influenced my concept of development. Weanling pups permanently separated from their dams when 15 days of age showed no gastric erosions after immobilization two days later, nor did 17-day-old pups remaining with their mothers. But as the early weaned juveniles developed, they became progressively more vulnerable to immobilization stress, so that 90 percent or more showed gastric erosions at 30 days of age, often more extensive and deeper than in adults, with penetration into the muscle layers and accompanying hemorrhage that in some cases was fatal. Rats weaned more normally at day 21 or 25, in contrast, showed a very low rate of ulceration when immobilized at 30 days of age (early adolescence). The vulnerability of normally reared animals increased throughout adult life, rising to a peak of 50 percent incidence in midlife at 200 days of age. Surprisingly, these normally weaned adults were now actually *more* vulnerable than the early-weaned animals of the same age whose vulnerability had fallen to its lowest level (22 percent) at this age of testing.

As this data began to emerge, we knew we were on to something. First, we had found a powerful early-experience effect, one that could produce a lethal vulnerability. This was important because it provided one of the first demonstrations that a disturbance in an early social relationship could produce severe and even fatal organ pathology, not simply altered behavior, physiological change or transient tissue damage, as in previous 'stress ulcer' studies. Secondly, as we looked at the two very different developmental trajectories of gastric ulcer vulnerability over time, the graphic data display seemed to literally paint a picture of how early experience can powerfully shape the trajectory of subsequent development. The vulnerability that normally appeared only in mid-adulthood and increased with age, had been shifted in time so that it now peaked in early adolescence and then declined with age, rendering older early-weaned adults less vulnerable than the normally weaned.

This property of development, to alter selectively the timing of expression of an individual trait, is called *heterochrony* and has attracted considerable recent interest as one of the primary mechanisms of major evolutionary change (McKinney & McNamara, 1991). In evolution by heterochrony, mutation in a single gene that determines the *timing* of its expression relative to other genes, is thought to exert widespread effects on subsequent morphology and function, allowing rapid adaptation to extreme environmental changes. I had heard of heterochrony at the time

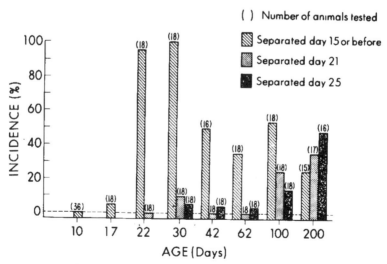

FIGURE 1.1. Incidence of immobilization-reduced gastric ulceration in rats at different ages as influenced by the age at which they were permanently separated from their dams. Different separation age groups are indentified and numbers of animals tested at each age are indicated in the key on the graph.

of these early-weaning studies, and recalled reading about it in Steven J. Gould's (1977) landmark analysis of the late-nineteenth-century "ontogeny and phylogeny" debate. But I never expected to encounter it outside the realm of fossils and geologic time. In our case, heterochrony seemed to be revealed by a single environmental event, not a single mutation in a gene.

We spent the next years finding out what we could about how this altered pattern of life-course vulnerability to stress was produced, and learned how difficult it is to unravel such a developmental change (Ackerman, Hofer, & Weiner, 1978 a, 1978b; Ackerman, 1980; Greenberg & Ackerman, 1989). Even the adult pathogenesis of this form of experimental gastric ulcer is complex in itself, and not yet well understood. But the early results have left in my mind to this day a mental picture of development as a network of different trajectories over time, each curve representing change in a structural or functional property of the organism with age. The shape of each individual curve is different, and it is the combination or interaction of these hills and valleys that determines the animal's age-specific characteristics. I don't know how useful such a mental picture might be to anyone else, or how limiting it may be to me, but I am stuck with it, and try to remember that it is simply a creation of my imagination and not a vision of the true nature of development.

☐ The Pleasures of Being Wrong

Soon after our early studies on gastric erosion vulnerability, a graduate student presented us with an idea that had occurred to him in the course of his clinical training. He wondered whether the experience of being weaned early might impair the later maternal behavior of the females, thereby creating conditions similar to early weaning for their offspring. In this way the vulnerability might be passed from mother to infant. Although this idea seems plausible to me today, my initial response to this proposal at the time was that it represented just the sort of anthropomorphic thinking and reliance on fanciful psychosomatic hypotheses that would be least likely to translate successfully into "animal model" research. On further reflection, however, I was persuaded that a well-designed study along these lines, with a clear negative result, might make this point clearly and even be publishable. Only the last proved to be true.

Not only did early weaning cause the females, as adults, to spend less time with their litters and lick them less, as predicted, but their normally weaned offspring were much more susceptible to gastric ulceration at 30 days of age! We could not believe the results, and insisted on a replication, using a different technician and close supervision of all stages of the experiment. While doing this, we thought it would be a good idea to run two additional groups in which infants were cross-fostered at birth between dams that had been early-weaned and others that had been normally reared. In case the result could be replicated, we would then be able to distinguish a prenatal from a postnatal origin of any maternally transmitted effect. This time we were more convinced, in part because the results did not follow the original hypothesis so perfectly. The pups that were born to normal mothers, and were immediately cross-fostered to the "pathological" mothers that had been early-weaned as infants, showed no ill effects. However, the pups that were born to dams that had themselves been early weaned developed a substantially increased vulnerability to gastric ulceration in early adolescence (30 days of age), even if reared by normal mothers and weaned normally at 21 days. Clearly it was some unknown alteration of the prenatal maternal environment, not the altered differences in postnatal mother-infant interaction, that was responsible for the transgenerational effect of early weaning.

These experiments (Skolnick, Ackerman, Hofer, & Weiner, 1980) joined a small number of other studies showing heritable effects of early experience (reviewed in Pollard, 1984) that remain to be understood in terms of their basic mechanisms. Although transmission of the trait was through the biological parent, there need be no alteration in genetic function of maternal germ cells. Early weaning is likely to act instead through an alteration of the maternal intrauterine environment, acting on her offspring at a very early developmental stage somewhere between zygote and preterm fetus.

Now my mental image of development was altered again. I imagined a folding of the development of one generation onto the development of the subsequent generation, a period of interaction between developmental histories, lasting throughout the relationship of parents with their offspring. This linkage of the development of the parents with the development of the young extends the impact of events that occur in one generation into the next and provides a biological analog to cultural evolution. In this way, I began to think about the relationship of developmental to evolutionary processes, a theme that will emerge again later in this chapter.

☐ Right at Last

Although the experiments on ulcer vulnerability involved early separation rather than changes in an ongoing mother-infant interaction, a clear implication of the earlier discovery of hidden regulators was that differences in "qualities" of parenting, acting throughout the preweaning period, could shape the development of characteristics of the young, with lasting effects persisting into adulthood. With this new concept in mind, I was looking for a likely possibility to test it experimentally. A few years later, Michael Myers, Susan Brunelli, and others in our lab found substantial differences between the mean blood pressures (BP) of different litters of adult rats of the homozygous SHR (spontaneously hypertensive) rat strain and also differences in pup retrieval and other maternal behaviors between mothers of the SHR and the Normotensive Wistar Kyoto (WKY) progenitor strain (Myers, Brunelli, Shair, Squire, Schindeldecker, & Hofer, 1989). This suggested that a causal link between spontaneous variations in maternal behavior and later offspring BP might be found within each genetically identical strain as well as between strains. And so we began the time-consuming task of observing litters of both strains every day from birth to weaning.

We found that naturally occurring variations in 3 of the 11 maternal behaviors correlated significantly with mean adult BP of their litters within both strains (Myers, Brunelli, Shair, Squire, & Hofer, 1989). High levels of the maternal behaviors in the preweaning period meant higher BP levels in adulthood. This correlation could not have a genetic origin, since all animals within each strain were genetically identical. Further, the two strains differed significantly from each other on mean levels of these 3 behaviors, with the SHR showing higher levels, as predicted by their higher adult BP. Meanwhile, McCarty and his colleagues had shown that cross-fostering of SHR pups to WKY dams significantly reduced their adult BP as predicted, but SHR dams did not raise the BP of WKY offspring (McCarty, Cierpial, Murphy, Lee, & Field-Okotcha, 1992). A possible explanation for this latter "failure" of cross-fostering was suggested by another study by Myers's group (reviewed in Myers, Shair, & Hofer, 1992). He had studied the F1 offspring of cross-bred SHR and WKY strains. These hybrid animals are genetically identical but can be born and reared by mothers of either strain, depending on the strain chosen for each parent. We found that these offspring did *not* differ in adult BP according to which strain of mother reared them, although the correlation between maternal behavior and litter BP was replicated in the sample as a whole. Observations of mother-infant interactions in these litters showed that when mothers of the two strains were rearing genetically identical F1 pups, they no longer differed in their maternal behavior.

These results showed us that the long-term effects of different foster mothers did not simply depend on the previously observed patterns of maternal behavior in a particular strain, but were mediated by an interaction between maternal and pup characteristics. I had not anticipated that rat mothers would be capable of responding differently to such closely related pups, or if this did occur, that the change in this interaction could eliminate the long-term effect of these mothers on offspring BP. I was also amazed to see such clear differences between individual litters of genetically identical homozygous strains reared in closely similar environments, and this led me to the next phase in the development of my thinking.

☐ The Enigma of the Innate

Most of our results to this point had led me to conceive of development primarily in terms of the contribution of the environment in regulating its course. I had come to realize that for early development in a mammal, its mother is its environment, and that the effects of this first social relationship could be understood for the first time, in terms of its basic behavioral and developmental processes. The results of some new studies, however, opened my eyes to the fact that questions about how genes produce their effects on behavior could be just as interesting. Harry Shair and I had been trying to learn how rat pups developed the contact quieting response (a rapid reduction of ultrasonic calling rates to near zero induced in isolated pups by littermates and familiar adults, as well as their own dam). This "comfort" response did not occur fully when isolated pups interacted with other kinds of contoured objects, or samples of furry texture, or home cage shavings, even when each of these was warmed to body temperature. We set about to discover how the relatively specific comfort response, expressed only to littermates or mother, was acquired. After finding that pups reared as singletons for a week prior to testing showed an undiminished contact quieting response to their now unfamiliar littermates (Hofer & Shair, 1987), we decided to artificially rear pups without *any* social contact and then add various kinds of daily social experiences in order to find which were most effective in restoring the contact quieting response. I assumed that artificially reared pups would not show contact quieting, but worried that they might also fail to show any "isolation calling" response after being reared alone in a plastic cup, a situation closely resembling the isolation test chamber. Perhaps, I thought, the isolation calling response itself was acquired through previous experience in the litter situation.

To my great surprise, 2-week-old pups that had had no experience with dam or littermates since the first few postpartum hours, not only called at high rates in response to the test chamber, but also showed consistent contact quieting responses to the dam that had been absent since the day of their birth (Hofer, Shair, & Murowchik, 1989). Their calling response, rather than being less intense, was nearly twice normal for their age, and the magnitude of the contact quieting response as a percentage of isolation response rates could not be distinguished from that of normally reared pups. When I presented this study at the annual meeting of the International Society of Developmental Psychobiology, I remember one colleague congratulating me on my demonstration of the role of "inapparent" environmental influences in the developmental process. Of course I knew he was right, and I had made the point in my presentation that there are no behaviors that are "simply genetic." Nevertheless, the results gave me a vivid reminder that even in mammals, behavioral responses to a conspecific *can* develop and be fully expressed on the animal's first encounter, despite the absence of prior opportunity for practice of the response, and even without any prior postnatal experience with that animal (e.g., Takahashi, 1992).

This important characteristic of development became more salient for me and at the same time more intriguing when Susan Brunelli and I videotaped the complex social play (or "play-fighting") interactions of pairs of these artificially reared pups when they were 25–30 days old, and compared the tapes with others showing normally reared pups of the same age in the same test chamber. To our great surprise we could not distinguish the isolation-reared pups from the normals. We never went on to quantitative analysis of their play interactions, so there may have been differences that went undetected in these unpublished pilot observations, but they nevertheless raised troublesome questions in my mind. How could juvenile mammals, without any interaction with conspecifics since the day of birth, show apparently normal movement patterns, postures, interactional timing, reciprocal cueing, and appropriate responses in the rapid-fire sequences characteristic of social play in young rats? What possible developmental processes could be imagined to account for this? If this is development, how can we also include, within a single concept, the consistent long-term effects of small variations in the mother-infant interaction patterns described above?

☐ From Development to Evolution and Back Again

The questions raised above seem most compelling to me at the present time, and I am searching for ways to begin to answer them. I am involved in two long-term projects that have few results as yet, but I find that in reading, discussions, grant writing, and thinking about what they might tell us, my way of thinking about development is changing.

In one approach, I have been collaborating with Dani Brunner, Jay Gingrich, and Rene Hen to study the development of behavior in mice with single-gene deletions, so-called knockout mice (e.g., Brunner, Buhot, Hen, & Hofer, 1999). As a result of deletion of a gene, the developing animal has none of the protein that only that gene can produce, in any of its cells, from zygote to adult. At this molecular level, there *is* a form of genetic determinism. But how the genome and the developing organs of the animal respond to the absence of that protein are not determined, but are subject to the many interactions that constitute the developmental process. Regulatory changes can occur in the expression of other genes, in the adaptive intercellular signaling of other cells, and in the timing of development of various systems as a result of the absence of the roles that the particular protein would have played in development. Some of these changes appear to compensate for the absence of the lost gene; others simply make the animal function differently. The extent of such "secondary" or "downstream" effects is not predictable at present, but they do not generally prevent knockout mice from showing the majority of behavioral and/or physiological defects that were predicted from the results of more standard (e.g., pharmacological) methods. New putative roles for genes are frequently discovered by molecular geneticists using these techniques, but loss of the specific gene product must always be distinguished from the possible effects of "secondary" adaptations of the experimental alteration of gene function.

In learning something about this new method, I have already revised my ideas about how gene changes initiate changes in behavior. I now think of genes and their protein products in some of the same ways I think of parents and their offspring. What happens after the gene-product is made is subject to the vicissitudes of a complex, changing intra- and intercellular world, in the same way that offspring go out into the larger environment after weaning. In addition, new mechanisms are discovered almost weekly by which gene actions influence the expression of other genes. The word "genomics" suggests to me a vision of genes operating in an environment as complex and interactive as an economy or a society. I find myself wondering if some of the interactive principles we have worked out for environmental effects on early behavior development might be found to operate at the level of the early expressions of gene activity.

For the moment, gene knockout technology in the study of behavior is being used to test specific hypotheses about brain mechanisms derived from the more indirect methods of the past, and to generate new testable hypotheses. Whether it can be used to unravel the many steps in the normal or abnormal development of behavior is another question. At the level of cellular, tissue, and organ structure development, gene knockout strategies have their clearest application, and in this rapidly advancing area of developmental biology we may find principles that will be useful for the study of behavior development.

The second project, one that Susan Brunelli and I embarked on several years ago, has stretched my concept of development the most and has linked my questions about developmental processes to questions about evolutionary processes (for review see Brunelli & Hofer, 2001). It began with the idea of using selective breeding for high and low isolation calling rates in infant rats as an efficient way to identify the relevant neural structures and the neurochemical basis of this early behavior. By creating strains that differ widely in levels of only one behavior, differences between strains in regional receptor density and neuromodulator activity should be limited to the specific neural circuitry mediating that behavioral difference. Thus by screening with neuroanatomical mapping techniques for a number of different receptors and neuromodulators, we should be able to rapidly identify the brain areas and neurochemical systems primarily involved in the regulation of isolation calling rates from among all the others with less direct influence on the response.

As we began to think more about this approach and to talk with colleagues, we came to realize that this was not just a technique for revealing neural mechanisms, but that it might also be a novel means of studying evolutionary as well as developmental processes, as will be discussed below. Furthermore, there do not appear to have been any previous published studies on selective breeding for an *infantile* trait, so that we are in unexplored territory. Yet in nature, selection operates at all ages, and particularly severely early in development. Infant isolation calling is thought to be a behavior with variable risk/benefit ratios, depending on ecological circumstances, because calls can attract predators as well as maternal responses.

From a developmental perspective, one of the first questions anyone would like to ask about our study is whether selection for this infantile trait alters adult behavior. If juvenile isolation calling rates reflect the intensity of a separation anxiety state, could we find some forms of adult anxiety responses that would also differentiate the two strains? Or would no continuity be found between infant and adult responses, the selection being age-specific rather than affecting a lifelong developmental trajectory? Within the much shorter preweaning period, would selection at 10 days of age act by displacing forward and/or backward in time the developmental course of the isolation calling response as we had seen with ulcer vulnerability? Normally, isolation calling begins in the first 2 days after birth and rises to a peak at 5–7 days in the strain we are using for selective breeding, and then gradually declines and disappears at 18–20 days (Brunelli, Keating, Hamilton, & Hofer, 1996). Alternately, would the strain difference be limited to the day or two around the age of testing (10 days postnatal)?

The more questions occurred to us, the more they seemed to center on one central question: What, exactly, is selection acting upon? For example, were we selecting for one motor pattern out of the several re-

sponses elicited by isolation, or were we selecting for an underlying organized central response state, isolation calling being an indicator of the
intensity of that state? In the former case, we would have altered the
communicative display without affecting the central anxietylike state. In
the latter case, other emotional behaviors such as defecation/urination,
autonomic and adrenocortical responses should also differ in the two
strains. It even seemed possible that our selection for this communicative
behavior would alter the mother-infant interaction into patterns that facilitated or compensated for the development of high or low calling rates
in the young. Since writing this chapter, our study has provided some
answers to these questions (Hofer, Shair, Masmela, & Brunelli, 2001).

Embarking on these two genetic approaches led me to think about development in a new way. We developmental psychobiologists have, for
many years, studied behavior development by experimentally altering
the environment at a particular age. Now it is beginning to be possible to
alter experimentally the organism's genome with the same precision and
control as we have over its environment. We can alter not only a specific
gene but, with selective breeding for behavioral traits, we may be able to
alter the developmental timing of the expression of the (unknown) genes
predisposing to those traits, and then go on to identify them. Contem-
plating these genetic manipulations of the time course of developmental
processes awakened my dormant interest in the relationship between
evolution and development.

At about this time, I read *The Beak of the Finch*, a remarkable book by
the science writer Jonathan Weiner (1995), describing, in an eminently
readable form, the work of Peter Grant and his colleagues in the Galápagos
Islands over the previous decades (Grant, 1986). For the first time, evolution has been observed as it occurred, something I had not thought possible. I immediately realized that this meant that we could now do much
more than just theorize about the role of development in evolution. Our
selective breeding study, and all the questions that it raised, now took on
a new dimension. We were actually going to be able to watch how the
evolutionary processes of variation and selection alter the course of behavior development. I realized that I needed to know how evolutionary
biologists think about development and what I might be able to learn
from this different perspective.

☐ A Simple Principle?

As I set out into this new area, I recalled a memory from an international
meeting more than ten years ago in Cambridge, England. At dinner, after
some very good wine, I was asked by an Italian graduate student, "If one

wish could be granted, what would you most want to discover in your research?" At first I was totally at a loss. All I could think of was a sentence I had once seen inscribed on a plaque in Ethel Tobach's laboratory at the American Museum of Natural History: "If we knew what we wanted to discover, it wouldn't be research, would it?" Before I started to explain to the student that she was asking me the wrong question, I found myself saying, "I'd like to discover a simple principle that explains development, the way natural selection explains evolution." My impulsive answer keeps turning over in my mind and I have come to realize that it represents a (possibly unrealistic) direction in my current concept of development: that all the apparent heterogeneity and complexity might be explained by some simple principle. Although frequently I told myself that this is a ridiculous idea, more recently I have thought that perhaps I should change the level at which I have been viewing development—I needed an evolutionary perspective. As I began to read in the field of evolutionary biology, I realized that I did not know the answers to some simple questions about how development evolved. How and when did an appreciable period of development evolve within the life cycles of primitive organisms, and what was its survival value? How did development convey an increase in fitness and thus become shaped by natural selection over time? I was not prepared for the sheer number of new books on evolution published in the last decade, and I have had to be selective in my reading. Thus at this point my concept of development has enlarged and is in the midst of a period of change, so I can only offer a concept in progress.

I realized that I had not thought much about the fact that development itself is a product of evolution, although I knew that it appeared hundreds of millions of years ago, soon after single-cell organisms had evolved the capacity to form aggregates or colonies during their simple life cycle. Bonner (1993) points out that the next step, multicellular forms, required a series of stages for their construction, and thus development evolved as the growth phase of the life cycle. He goes on to suggest that the advantages conveyed by multicellularity and a developmental phase lay in their capacity to produce new forms that were both larger and more differentiated in function, allowing them to occupy and utilize niches in the environment that no other organisms had been able to colonize and exploit. The selective advantages of increased size and complexity, Bonner argues, are responsible for the trends evident in the fossil record showing the appearance of ever larger and more complex organisms over the past several hundred million years. Bonner's perspective provided an answer to a question that had troubled me for some time: why are there so many different patterns and processes in development? Why is it so complicated? The answer may simply be that the evolution of a wide variety of adult forms came about through a wide variety of developmental paths and processes. Many of these different processes were retained as more complex forms evolved, and are now represented in the heterogeneity of developmental processes in animals we study today.

In the history of evolution, its products have often come to play a role in facilitating and shaping subsequent evolution. A prime example is the cellular process of meiosis and the sexual reproduction it made possible. So how might development facilitate and shape subsequent evolution? Asking this question has led me to think about development in a new way and may even provide a simple developmental principle of the sort I wanted to find. It appears to me that in addition to facilitating increased size and complexity in evolution, development has provided a means for enhancing the range of potentially "useful" variation that natural selection can act upon. Variation, which was as important as natural selection in Darwin's formulation (see Darwin, 1868), has been relatively neglected in evolutionary studies ever since genetic mutation and recombination were discovered several generations ago. These two genetic mechanisms are generally considered to be quite sufficient to account for heritable variation in traits, so that attention has centered on the many ways by which natural selection acts upon this source of variation. But mutation and recombination act in a random manner, producing many traits that may not be of use in the animals' particular environment. Indeed, the capacity of random events alone to produce existing biological structures so perfectly adapted to their environment has often been questioned. The advent of a long period of development in the life cycle, in which the young organism grows and is changed by its interaction with its environment, allows the production of wide variations in traits that are thus well adapted to specific characteristics of the changing environment in which evolution is taking place. The problem with this mechanism for generating new phenotypes, of course, is that traits acquired through experience during development are generally considered not to be heritable, and thus cannot play a role in evolution. For an important exception to this view see Gottlieb (1997).

Thus, although development may allow the fine-tuning of adaptations to the environment in one generation, it cannot produce the heritable variation required for it to be considered as a major contributor to evolution. Or can it? Let's look back in this paper to some of the results of our experiments. The experience of early weaning in the mother's infancy, we found, transmits her acquired stress ulcer vulnerability to her offspring, where it is no longer acquired, but inherited. Maternal behavior plays a role in the heritable transmission of hypertension in a genetically vulnerable strain. Many years ago (1963) Victor Denenberg and Arthur Whimbey described transgenerational effects of infantile handling on emotional behaviors, and very recently Michael Meaney and his associates have described in detail the transmission of acquired changes, in maternal behavior, in emotional responses, and in the development of hypothalamic adrenocortical system regulation, to offspring in the next two generations (Francis, Diorio, Liu, & Meaney, 1999).

We can identify the point of origin of these transgenerational effects according to the period of development in which they take place: prenatal in the case of vulnerability to gastric ulceration, and postnatal in the case of hypertension, emotional behavior, and adrenocortical responsivity. These behavioral/physiologic mechanisms can now be added to the better-known examples of the transgenerational effects of malnutrition and of maternal drug addiction. In another more familiar process, traits acquired by social learning are certainly heritable through the well-known process of cultural transmission that we have recently come to realize extends to a much wider variety of animal species than was previously supposed (Frank, 1998).

Finally, there are two other mechanisms for the heritability of acquired developmental changes that are well established in evolutionary biology and experimental genetics, but not widely appreciated. The first of these is the role of acquired changes in behavior development in exposing potential (but hitherto latent) genetic variability to natural selection. As described by Ernst Mayr many years ago, "A shift into a new niche or adaptive zone is, almost without exception, initiated by a change in behavior. The other adaptations to the new niche, particularly the structural ones, are acquired secondarily. With habitat and food selection— behavioral phenomena—playing a major role in the shift into new adaptive zones, the importance of behavior in initiating new evolutionary events is self-evident" (Mayr, 1963, p. 604). Here, the mechanism for the heritability of developmental change is a combination of classic genetics and novel behavioral responses to the environment during development.

The last mechanism for the heritability of developmentally acquired variation that I will discuss is of potentially broad applicability, although I have been able to find only a few published experimental demonstrations. It was first proposed a century ago by J. M. Baldwin (1896) and is thus known as the Baldwin effect. Scientists at the time were attempting to account for the evolution of adaptive traits without resorting to the inheritance of acquired habits, since Weisman had recently shown (1893) that germ line cells are formed very early in embryonic development and thereafter are isolated from changes occurring in response to experience. Baldwin proposed that if a population is enabled to survive for a number of generations through an acquired response to enduring environmental change, this will eventually result in the accumulation of hereditary germ cell changes that then become independent of the original environment. Unfortunately, no mechanism could be suggested for this accumulation process, until C. H. Waddington's experiments fifty year later (1956).

Waddington became intrigued by an environmental effect on the development of the characteristic vein pattern of the fruit fly wing that mimicked a rare genetic trait in the population. He termed this novel vein pattern, produced by brief heat shock during larval development, a "phenocopy," as contrasted to the standard genocopy. This effect, which occurred in about half the early heat-shocked flies, was of course not passed on to their normally reared progeny. At this point he did an inspired thing. He selectively bred a line of flies from those that showed the heat-shock phenocopy (HSP+), and another line from those that did not (HSP-). In the HSP+ line, the proportion of offspring showing the phenocopy rose to 90 percent after 15–20 generations, and in the HSP- line it fell to 10–15 percent. Thus the HSP- line had evolved through selection to be highly resistant to heat shock, and the HSP+ line to be highly sensitive. But the totally unexpected result was that when he stopped giving heat shock to the HSP+ line, some of the subsequent matings produced the trait in the absence of the environmental event. And these individuals then regularly produced offspring with the trait. Waddington explained this transformation from an acquired to a hereditary character in classical genetic terms. He proposed that in the process of selection for sensitivity to the heat shock, alleles favoring this response accumulated in the HSP+ line (as regularly occurs in selective breeding) to the point that an intially very rare allelic combination, in which the trait spontaneously appeared, now occurred with some regularity, and when males and females both had this combination, the trait predominated in the population. An environmental response had become a heritable trait.

It seems to me that the mechanism for what Waddington called "genetic assimilation" could have played an important role in the evolution of complex behavioral responses that are adapted to specific features of the environment but do not require prior experience with those features for their development. This could help explain our observations, described above, in which we found that the contact comfort response and play interactions developed normally in rats reared without social companions. It also seems possible that in this way, a response that is initially learned can gradually come to evolve into a heritable trait requiring minimal prior developmental experience through repetitive selection for those individuals with particularly strong predispositions to learn that response.

Thus, in summary, my recent research has led me to a simple principle that helps me organize the disparate processes and changing concepts described in this paper: Development is a source of nonrandom variation on which natural selection acts. Development converts random genetic variation into adaptive traits shaped by the environment, and can then, under certain circumstances, transmit these to the next generation. This principle also provides a new perspective on the old riddle of development: is it Nature or Nurture? For it appears to me that evolution has given us a spectrum of developmental processes that vary in their nature for different traits. These variants range from processes that allow developing organisms to anticipate highly predictable environmental conditions and respond appropriately at their first experience with them (by utilizing relatively closed developmental systems) to other processes that have been selected in more variable ecological conditions, where it may have been advantageous for more open developmental systems to evolve. These open systems depend upon organism's prior interaction with its particular environment to shape the emergence of individual traits in each generation. Relatively open or closed developmental systems will be more or less effective for a given trait and a given set of ecological conditions, and will be selected in evolution accordingly. Thus, the balance present today in the development of any given trait between those processes that are relatively independent of specific external environmental influences and other that are relatively sensitive to life experience will depend in this way upon the evolutionary history of that trait.

□ Acknowledgments

This research was made possible by the long-term support of the National Institute of Mental Health through project grants and a Research Scientist Development Award, from 1968 to the present. I would also like to thank the New York State Psychiatric Institute and The Sackler Institute of Developmental Psychobiology for their more recent support.

□ References

Ackerman, S. H. (1980). Early life events and peptic ulcer susceptibility: An experimental model. *Brain Research Bulletin*, Vol. 5, Suppl. 1, 43–49. ANKHO International Inc.

Ackerman, S. H., Hofer, M. A., & Weiner, H. (1975). Age at maternal separation and gastric erosion susceptibility in the rat. *Psychosomatic Medicine, 37,* 180–184.

Ackerman, S. H., Hofer, M. A., & Weiner, H. (1978a). The predisposition to gastric erosions in rat: Behavioral and nutritional effects of early maternal separation. *Gastroenterology, 75,* 649–654.

Ackerman, S. H., Hofer, M. A., & Weiner, H. (1978b). Early maternal separation increases gastric ulcer risk in rats by producing a latent thermoregulatory disturbance. *Science, 201,* 373–376.

Baldwin, J. M. (1896). A new factor in evolution. *American Naturalist, 30,* 441–541.

Bonner, J. T. (1993). *Life cycles: Reflections of an evolutionary biologist.* Princeton, NJ: Princeton University Press.

Bowlby, J. (1969). *Attachment and loss. Vol. 1: Attachment.* New York: Basic Books.

Brunelli, S. A., & Hofer, M. A. (2001). Selective breeding for an infantile phenotype (isolation calling): A window on developmental processes. In E. Blass (Ed.), *Handbook of behavioral neurobiology.* New York: Plenum.

Brunelli, S. A., Keating, C. C., Hamilton, N. A., & Hofer, M. A. (1996). Development of ultrasonic vocalization responses in genetically heterogeneous National Institute of Health (N:NIH) rats. Parts I and II. Influence of age, testing experience and associated factors. *Developmental Psychobiology, 29,* 507–516 and 517–528.

Brunner, D., Buhot, M. C., Hen, R., & Hofer, M. A. (1999). Anxiety, motor activation and maternal-infant interactions in 5HT$_{1B}$ knockout mice. *Behavioral Neuroscience, 113,* 409–640.

Darwin, C. (1868). *The variation of animals and plants under domestication, volumes one and two.* Reprinted 1998. Baltimore and London: The Johns Hopkins University Press.

Denenberg, V. H., & Whimbey, A. E. (1963). Behavior of adult rats is modified by the experiences their mothers had as infants. *Science, 142,* 1192–1193.

Francis, D., Diorio, J., Liu, D., & Meaney, M. J. (1999). Nongenomic transmission across generatioins of maternal behavior and stress responses in the rat. *Science, 286,* 1155–1158.

Frank, S. A. (1998). *Foundations of social evolution.* Princeton, NJ: Princeton University Press.

Gould, S. J. (1977). *Ontogeny and phylogeny.* Cambridge, MA: Harvard University Press.

Grant, P. R. (1986). *Ecology and evolution of Darwin's finches.* Princeton, NJ: Princeton University Press.

Greenberg, D., & Ackerman, S. H. (1989). Energy expenditure during stress ulcer formation in vulnerable rats. *American Journal of Physiology, 256* (Regulatory Integrative Comp. Physiol. 25), R403–R407.

Harlow, H. F. (1961). The development of affectional patterns in infant monkeys. In B. M. Foss (Ed.), *Determinants of infant behaviour* (vol 1., pp. 75–88). London: Methuen.

Hofer, M. A. (1970). Physiological responses of infant rats to separation from their mothers. *Science, 168,* 871–873.

Hofer, M. A. (1971). Cardiac rate regulated by nutritional factor in young rats. *Science, 172,* 1039–1041.

Hofer, M. A. (1973a). The role of nutrition in the physiological and behavioral effects of early maternal separation on infant rats. *Psychosomatic Medicine, 35,* 350–359.

Hofer, M. A. (1973b). Maternal separation affects infant rats' behavior. *Behavioral Biology, 9,* 629–633.

Hofer, M. A. (1973c). The effects of brief maternal separations on behavior and heart rate of two week old rat pups. *Physiology & Behavior, 10,* 423–427.

Hofer, M. A. (1975a). Studies on how early maternal separation produces behavioral change in young rats. *Psychosomatic Medicine, 37,* 245–264.

Hofer, M. A. (1975b). Infant separation responses and the maternal role. *Biological Psychiatry, 10,* 149–153.

Hofer, M. A. (1984). Early stages in the organization of cardiovascular control. *Proceedings of the Society for Experimental Biology and Medicine, 175,* 147–157.

Hofer, M. A., Engel, M., & Weiner, H. (1971). Development of cardiac rate regulation and activity after neonatal immunosympathectomy. *Communications in Behavioral Biology, 6,* 59–62.

Hofer, M. A., & Reiser, M. F. (1969). The development of cardiac rate regulation in preweanling rats. *Psychosomatic Medicine, 32,* 372–388.

Hofer, M. A., & Shair, H. N. (1987). Isolation distress in 2 week old rats: Influence of home cage, social companions and prior experience with littermates. *Developmental Psychobiology, 20,* 465–476.

Hofer, M. A., Shair, H. N., Masmela, J. R., & Brunelli, S. A. (2001). Developmental effects of selective breeding for an infantile trait: The rat pup ultrasonic isolation cell. *Developmental Psychobiology, 39,* 231–246.

Hofer, M. A., Shair, H. N., & Murowchik, E. (1989). Isolation distress and maternal comfort responses of two-week-old rat pups reared in social isolation. *Developmental Psychobiology, 22,* 553–566.

Hofer, M. A., & Weiner, H. (1971). Development and mechanisms of cardiorespiratory responses to maternal deprivation in rat pups. *Psychosomatic Medicine, 33,* 353–362.

Hofer, M. A., & Weiner, H. (1975). Physiological mechanisms for cardiac control by nutritional intake after early maternal separation in the young rat. *Psychosomatic Medicine, 37,* 8–24.

Kaufman, I. C., & Rosenblum, L. A. (1967). The reaction to separation in infant monkeys: Anaclitic depression and conservation withdrawal. *Psychosomatic Medicine, 22,* 548–576.

Mayr, E. (1963). *Animal species and evolution.* Cambridge, MA: Belknap Press.

McCarty, R., Cierpial, M. A., Murphy, C. A., Lee, J. H., & Field-Okotcha, C. (1992). Maternal involvement in the development of cardiovascular phenotype. *Experientia, 48,* 315–322.

McKinney, M. L., & McNamara, K. J. (1991). *Heterochrony: The evolution of ontogeny.* New York: Plenum.

Myers, M., Brunelli, S. A., Shair, H. N., Squire, J. M., & Hofer, M. A. (1989). Relationships between maternal behavior of SHR and WKY dams and adult blood pressures of cross-fostered F1 pups. *Developmental Psychobiology, 22*(1), 55–67.

Myers, M. M., Brunelli, S. A., Squire, J. M., Shindledecker, R., & Hofer, M. A. (1989). Maternal behavior of SHR rats in its relationship to offspring blood pressure. *Developmental Psychobiology, 22*(1), 29–53.

Myers, M. M., Shair, H. N., & Hofer, M. A. (1992). Feeding in infancy: Short and long-term effects on cardiovascular function. *Experientia, 48,* 322–333.

Pollard, J. W. (1984) Is Weismann's barrier absolute? In M.-W. Ho & P. T Saunders (Eds.), *Beyond neo-Darwinism.* London, Orlando, San Diego, New York, Toronto, Montreal, Sydney, Tokyo: Academic Press.

Skolnick, N. J., Ackerman, S. H., Hofer M. A., & Weiner, H. (1980). Vertical transmission of acquired ulcer susceptibility in the rat. *Science, 208,* 1161–1163.

Takahashi L. K. (1992). Developmental expression of defensive responses during exposure to conspecific adults in preweanling rats (Rattus norvegicus) *Journal of Comparative Psychology, 106,* 69–77.

Waddinton, C. H. (1956). Genetic assimilation of the bithorax phenotype. *Evolution, 10,* 1–13.

Weiner, J. (1995). *The beak of the finch.* New York: Vintage Books.

Weismann, A. (1893). *The germ-plasm: A theory of heredity.* London: Scott Publishing Co. Ltd.

Emergence of the Developmental Manifold Concept from an Epigenetic Analysis of Instinctive Behavior

When I completed my doctoral dissertation on experimental studies of the critical period for imprinting in ducklings, during the oral defense of my dissertation, one of my professors noted that even at the height of the critical period not all of my ducklings followed the maternal model, and he asked whether that would happen in nature. The answer was that I did not know, because imprinting was a laboratory phenomenon discovered when Douglas Spalding, in 1873, hatched chicks in an incubator and observed that they took him to be their mother and followed him around as they would their parent under natural conditions. When Spalding took his young charges for a stroll through town, astonished onlookers thought that he was endowed with mysterious powers and had cast a spell over the chicks! When the ethologists Oskar Heinroth and Konrad Lorenz rediscovered the imprinting phenomenon by hatching goslings and ducklings in incubators, they also did not extend their observations to what happens in nature when hatchlings interact with their maternal parent and take leave of the nest.

So, after getting a job as a research scientist at Dorothea Dix Hospital in Raleigh, North Carolina, with the generous and much-needed assistance of my wife, Nora Lee Willis Gottlieb, I began to tape-record and photo-

31

graph nest activities in the hole-nesting wood duck and the ground-nesting mallard duck in nature. In our first experience observing a mallard hen on the nest with her eggs and, subsequently, with her hatchlings in Bath, N.C., my wife and I took turns manning the recording equipment 24 hours a day because we did not know if the hen might lead her young from the nest during the night or during the day. In this particular case, we were about seventy-five feet from the hen and could not see her, so we did not take photographs as we would later on. I lack what is known in Yiddish as *sitzfleisch*, so it was my wife's perseverance and encouragement that carried the day with this seemingly unending eavesdropping. With our new Nagra tape recorder, on June 19, 1962, we got some excellent recordings of the hen's call during the exodus from the nest, and that vocalization provided the basis of my experimental work with mallard ducklings for the next thirty-three years.

What we discovered with the observations of the mallard brood was that during the hatching process, even before her young hatched, the hen uttered a distinctive vocalization that she continued to utter after hatching and during the exodus from the nest. Several years later, with prompting from Professor Mark Konishi, we termed this species-characteristic vocalization the maternal assembly call. The young are highly attracted to it, so it gives the hen a great degree of social control over the behavior of her immature hatchlings, helping to get them out of the nest and keeping her young close by and out of harm's way. Laboratory experiments had emphasized the visual side of the imprinting phenomenon, so we were unprepared for the apparent importance of the auditory component as evidenced not only in the hole-nesting wood duck, in which there was reason to believe in the importance of the hen's call because of the hole-nesting situation described below, but also in the fact that Peter Klopfer (1959) had shown that wood ducklings could learn artificial sounds whereas ground-nesting ducklings did not.

We were somewhat prepared that the mallard hen might use a special vocalization in enticing her young from the nest, because we had previously observed the nest exodus in wood ducks at Hester's Pond, in Wendell, North Carolina, through the kind courtesy of Dr. Eugene Hester, son of the pond's owner and a zoologist at North Carolina State College at the time. Wood ducks lay their eggs in deep cavities in which the young have no opportunity to see their hen when she prompts them to follow her example—she must call to them to entice them to leave the nest. When the hen is deliberately flushed from the nest, the young make no attempt to climb out of the nest box to follow her. It is only when she calls to them that they quickly climb to the exit hole and bravely jump to the ground or water below, with nonfunctional wings aflutter and shrieking their heads off with excitement.

When we first embarked on studying imprinting in nature, my wife and I would drive miles to any locale where we knew ducks to be nesting. To make things more manageable and convenient, I obtained permission to start an Animal Behavior Field Station on the farm ponds at Dorothea Dix Hospital.

We erected wood duck nest boxes on posts in the water. This was often a precarious two-person operation and we enjoyed the encouragement of the mental patients who used the area for recreational outings. They also got treated to seeing one or the other of us fall into the water when the ladder we used to fasten the boxes to their posts would give way on the soft pond bottom. Since it was a warm-weather activity, no harm was done, except to our slightly bruised egos (the patients would laugh quite uproariously whenever we hit the drink).

Several years later Nora and I purchased a home in the countryside outside Raleigh, and we were able to have yet another field station there as well, because it came with a small farm pond. We were now able to collect wild duck eggs for our laboratory experiments at several locations, as neighbors permitted me to erect wood duck nest boxes on their ponds. We used the field station at home to continue to make observations of nesting activities in wood ducks, mallards, and other species, and it was there that we reared the ducklings that served in our laboratory experiments. We reared them to flight stage in pens and then released the birds to the wild. We attached U.S. Fish and Wildlife numbered leg bands to the birds when we released them at about eight weeks of age, and we were delighted when some of the females would come back to our area to nest in the spring of the following year. (I must admit that we were less delighted to get the leg bands back from the U.S. Fish and Wildlife Service telling us where the birds were killed by hunters.) We also learned about other predators and were constantly in competition with raccoons, opossums, and black snakes for the eggs of the species that were now needed to fill the incubators for our experiments in the laboratory at Dorothea Dix Hospital.

I mentioned earlier that the mallard and wood duck hens uttered a species-characteristic maternal assembly call to entice their young from the nest (exodus call), and they used that same vocalization while leading their broods once off the nest. All mallard hens utter the same basic call (with individual variations) while calling their young from the nest. The acoustic features of the mallard assembly call across all the hens are recognizably the same to the human ear, even with the individual variations. And the same can be said for the wood duck call. This is what is meant by the term "species-typical" or "species-specific." Each species has its own distinctive call, which is stable across hens within each species, and different between the species.

Since both mallard and wood duck hens begin uttering their respective assembly calls during and after the hatching process prior to the exodus from the nest, I, at that time armed with the concept of auditory imprinting, thought it was likely that the ducklings in each species were learning the distinctive acoustic features of their species maternal call by being exposed to it before leaving the nest. I was in for quite a surprise. When I incubated mallard and wood duck eggs in the laboratory and then gave them choice tests between their maternal call and the maternal call of another species, mallard ducklings chose the mallard maternal call and wood ducklings chose the wood duck maternal call. Since by now I had acquired the maternal assembly calls of various other species (mandarin duck, pintail duck, junglefowl and their domestic counterparts, barnyard chickens), I could offer the incubator-hatched birds a variety of choice tests, and they invariably chose their own species maternal call. I extended these observations to chickens and junglefowl and they, too, invariably preferred their own species maternal call to that of other species. I had inadvertently discovered an instinct! The mallard and wood ducklings didn't have to be exposed to their mother's assembly call in order to be attracted to it—they were already attracted to it! What was happening inside the nest prior to the exodus was the learning of their particular mother's version of the species maternal call, the basis for the ducklings to recognize the particular acoustic features of their mother's call: individual auditory recognition, as I later documented in laboratory experiments (Gottlieb, 1988). Before those experiments, I was much more interested in getting at the basis of this auditory instinct, a difficult problem that would take many more years than I would have thought to work out in an entirely satisfactory manner.

What does it mean to say that a behavior is instinctive? The usual defining features are that it is genetically determined, unlearned, has survival value (i.e., is adaptive), is exhibited by all members of the species without explicit training (another way of saying it is unlearned), and that it is behavior emitted in response to social or physical signals uniquely provided by other members of the species. Thus, the "built-in" attractiveness of the maternal assembly call fits this definition because it would appear to be unlearned, has survival value, does not require explicit training, all members of the species exhibit it, and it is called forth by the species-specific acoustic features of each species maternal call. The attractiveness of the maternal call enables the parent to maintain social control over the behavior of her highly active young at a time when the ducklings are particularly susceptible to such hazards as cold and predation. The hen can call her young out of the nest and gather them to her promptly anytime danger threatens. In the wild, ducklings are apt to get separated from their mothers in swamps and marshes. When that happens, the young can use the parent's call to locate her. The adaptive significance of the "built-in" responsiveness to the maternal call is thus clear.

☐ Nonobvious Prenatal Experience?

The possible developmental basis of the adaptive behavior of newborns is often written off when it is said to be instinctive or innate, meaning that it has no basis in the prenatal experience of the fetus (mammal) or embryo (bird). While it is reasonable to think that the species-typical or species-specific behavior of the newborn that is crucial to its survival has no *obvious* prenatal experiential basis, that does not rule out that prenatal experience may be playing a nonobvious role. This is a risky supposition but is one I embraced early in my career, having been encouraged by the writings of Z.-Y. Kuo and his intellectual descendants, T. C. Schneirla and his student Daniel S. Lehrman. Kuo (1976) did not actually present experimental evidence on this point, but his observations of the behavior of the chick embryo were suggestive that the motor movements involved in pecking in the chick hatchling had their roots in embryonic experience, based on his observations that the various components of pecking were in evidence in the embryo. It is very difficult to do the obvious embryonic motor deprivation experiments to prove the point, because even short-term paralysis induces severe structural abnormalities in the chick embryo. In the case at hand, I was luckier in that I was able to do the necessary sensory deprivation and sensory replacement studies that are easier to do in embryonic stages than are motor deprivations having to do with the pecking response.

Namely, I was in the position to ask whether the embryos' experience of their own vocalizations in the last few days of the embryonic period somehow sensitized them to the acoustic features of the maternal assembly call of their own species. Each species has a characteristic maternal assembly call that is acoustically different from the assembly call of other species, and in each species the embryos begin vocalizing several days before hatching. To the human ear there is no similarity between the embryonic vocalizations and the respective maternal calls, so this was indeed confronting the question of a nonobvious relationship between the acoustic features of the embryos' calls and that of their species' maternal call.

Figure 2.1 shows the auditory choice test arena in which the ducklings were tested. For ease of presentation, I will describe the research with only one species (mallard ducklings), one of the two species in which the story is complete. If the reader is interested in the research on the other species or in further details, they can be found in my 1997 monograph

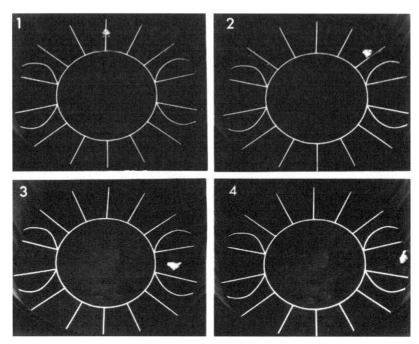

FIGURE 2.1. Simultaneous auditory choice test arena. (1) Duckling placed equidistant between two speakers (not visible), in front of which are painted elliptical approach areas. (2) Duckling on its way toward approach area. (3) Duckling in approach area. (4) Duckling snuggling to curtain and orienting to nonvisible speaker broadcasting maternal call of its own species.

Synthesizing Nature-Nurture, in which all of the procedures and test results are described in greater detail.

Since the incubator-hatched ducklings were able to choose the mallard assembly call over the assembly calls of other species within 24 hours after hatching, I devised a behavioral and physiological procedure to test them as embryos prior to hatching to see if they were already selectively responsive at that time. By affixing tiny electrodes to the body of the embryo several days before hatching, we were able to obtain two behavioral measures (bill-clapping and vocalization) and one physiological measure (heart rate).

The procedure was to record the rate of bill-clapping, vocalization, and heart beat for five minutes before exposing the embryo to a one-minute recording of the mallard assembly call or the call of another species, and to determine whether the behavioral and physiological rates changed during exposure to the call. The behavioral measures changed only in response to the mallard maternal call, whereas heart rate changed in response to all of the calls, thus indicating the species-specificity of the behavioral response. So the instinctive response was in place already before hatching.

In order to determine if the embryo's vocalizations somehow supplied the crucial acoustical information that allowed them to respond so specifically to the mallard hen's assembly call, it was necessary to devise a surgical procedure to take away the embryo's ability to vocalize before hatching and then test the devocalized ducklings' selective preference for the mallard call after hatching. If the devocalized ducklings were as selective as the vocal ducklings, then obviously the embryonic vocalizations were playing no role in that auditory selectivity. On the other hand, if the devocalized ducklings were less selective, then the exposure to their own vocalizations was playing a role.

As shown in Figure 2.2, the mallard duck embryo begins to move into the airspace of the egg early on day 24 of incubation. They respire through their lungs at that time and they begin to vocalize, albeit infrequently and feebly, at that point. So we would have to devise a procedure that would preclude their vocalizing but not be otherwise harmful to them so that they could be tested as healthy ducklings after hatching. This was no small order; it took more than eighteen months and the help of my zoologist colleague John Vandenbergh to solve this problem.

As can be seen in Figure 2.3, the voicebox (syrinx) is located in the chest cavity of the embryo. To render the embryo mute, it was necessary to make a small incision in the skin to gain access to the internal tympaniform membranes below the syrinx. When strong rushes of air from the lungs pass over the tympaniform membranes, they vibrate, thus causing the embryo to vocalize. If we could somehow prevent the membranes from vibrating, the embryo would be mute. We tried a number of ways of stilling the membranes without otherwise harming the embryo,

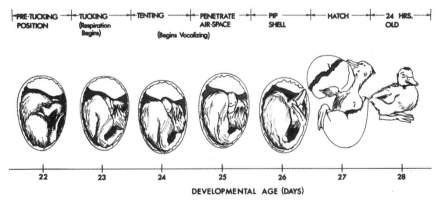

FIGURE 2.2. Late embryonic and early postnatal stages in mallard duckling. (Devocalization takes place in tenting stage early on day 24.)

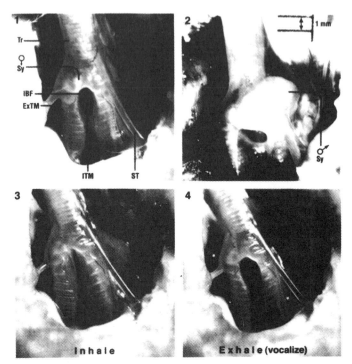

FIGURE 2.3. Ventral aspect of vocal apparatus of mallard ducklings. (1) Female syrinx (voicebox). (2) Male syrinx. (3) and (4) Expansion and constriction of internal tympaniform membranes during inhalation and expiration (with vocalization), respectively. Tr, trachea; Sy, syrinx; IBF, interbronchial foramen; ExTM, external tympaniform membrane (bilateral); ITM, internal tympaniform membrane (bilateral); ST, sterno-trachealis muscle (bilateral).

but these were for nought until my neurologist colleague George Paulson suggested we try Collodion, a nontoxic glue used to suture wounds during surgical procedures with humans. Collodion worked like a charm. As the birds grew in the first week or so after hatching, they would usually slough off the Collodion and regain their voice, but we could do our experiments in the 24–72 hours after hatching, when the birds were still mute, so this was a choice procedure that would allow us to answer the experimental question.

Since the hit rate on complete devocalization is about 90 percent, it was necessary to devise individual soundproof incubator chambers so that if an embryo was incompletely devocalized its completely devocalized "sibs" would not be able to hear its voice and could thus be tested without having heard their own or others' vocalizations. Finally, we were ready to go!

When we tested the muted birds after hatching, we discovered that

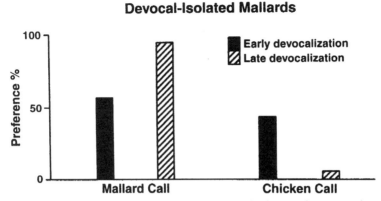

FIGURE 2.4. Devocal-isolated ducklings muted early do not show a preference for mallard call over chicken call after hatching, whereas devocal-isolated ducklings muted late do show the normal preference for mallard call over chicken call.

their selective response to the mallard maternal call had indeed been disrupted. As shown in Figure 2.4, their normal preference for the mallard call over the chicken call was no longer in evidence: they were as likely to select the chicken call as the mallard call. Now, since these birds had sustained an operation as embryos, we did a number of control experiments to show that what caused their poor performance was not the trauma of the operation itself but the failure to hear their own vocalizations. The best proof of this came in an experiment in which we had miscalculated the age of the birds at devocalization: they had been in the airspace from 15 to 23 hours before we had scheduled them for devocalization. We went ahead with devocalization as usual and when we tested these birds their preference for the mallard call over the chicken call was normal (Fig. 2.4).

Thus, it was not the trauma of the operation but their inability to hear their own vocalizations that caused the perceptual deficit in the original devocalized group.

In the service of finding out just what "information" the exposure to their own embryonic call supplied about the maternal call, we next embarked on a long series of experiments with vocal birds to determine which acoustic features of the mallard call were critical to their preference. With this information in hand, we would be in a position to specify why the muted ducklings found the chicken call as attractive as the mallard call. The idea was that, in the absence of normal auditory experience, the muted birds' perception of the critical acoustical features of the mallard call was dulled and that the chicken call must have a less precise version of those critical characteristics and thus was attractive to the muted duck-

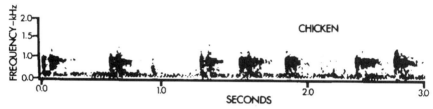

FIGURE 2.5. Sonagrams of mallard and chicken maternal calls.

lings. If one looks at Fig. 2.5, it is immediately obvious that the acoustic features of the chicken call depart from those of the mallard on these attributes: repetition rate (2.3 notes/sec vs. 3.7 notes/sec); low frequencies but not high frequencies as in the mallard; and the frequency modulation of the notes (the notes of the chicken call are a "blob," whereas the notes of the mallard call are modulated).

It turned out in our experiments with vocal birds that repetition rate and high frequencies (>1000 Hz) were the critical features. If we sufficiently degraded these features away from the normal mallard call, the birds would not respond to the degraded call.

For the sake of simplicity, I will first describe our experiments showing that the repetition rate preference of the muted birds is broader than usual (including the rate of 2.3 notes/sec of the chicken call), and then explore the high-frequency insensitivity of the muted birds at the neurophysiological level of analysis. All of this is in the service of finding out whether the experience of their embryonic contact call, the most often repeated vocalization of embryos, is essential to normal auditory perceptual development.

To explore whether the repetition rate preference of the muted birds broadened so as to include the 2.3 notes/sec of the chicken call, we spliced in blank pieces of tape between the notes of the normal (3.7 notes/sec) mallard call to make a mallard call at 2.3 notes/sec. This would hold all other acoustic features constant between the calls and thus show a broadening of repetition rate preference in the muted birds.

As can be seen in Fig. 2.6, when the muted birds are placed in an audi-

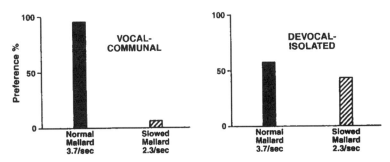

FIGURE 2.6. Vocal-communal and devocal-isolated ducklings' preferences in choice test between normal and slowed mallard maternal calls.

tory test with the normal mallard (3.7 n/s) versus the slowed mallard (2.3 n/s) calls, they perform exactly as they did in the test with the mallard and chicken calls: no preference. The vocal birds show a clear preference for the normal mallard call.

☐ Documenting the Specific Embryonic Experiential Requirements for Normal Auditory Development: First Behavioral Evidence for the Developmental Manifold Concept

Since the repetition rate of the mallard call is a critical acoustic feature as far as the ducklings are concerned, and hearing their own embryonic vocalization appears to be crucial in the development of the ducklings' perception of repetition rate, with the assistance of my doctoral student Richard Scoville, I next examined the repetition rate of the embryos' contact call to see how well it matched the repetition rate of the normal mallard call (~4 notes/sec). While the embryos do produce contact calls at 4 n/s, as shown in Figure 2.7 their production of contact calls before hatching is highly variable, ranging from 2 n/s to 6 n/s (Scoville, 1982). In order to see if the embryos' preference for the 4 n/s mallard maternal call was a straightforward consequence of learning, we exposed some devocalized embryos to a 4 n/s contact call and others to the naturally occurring variation in the contact call (2, 4, 6 n/s) and later tested them for their preference for the normal mallard maternal call (3.7 n/s) versus the slowed mallard maternal call (2.3 n/s).

As can be seen in Figure 2.8, the mute birds that were exposed as embryos to the 4 n/s contact call did not show a preference for the normal mallard maternal call, whereas the mute birds exposed to the variable

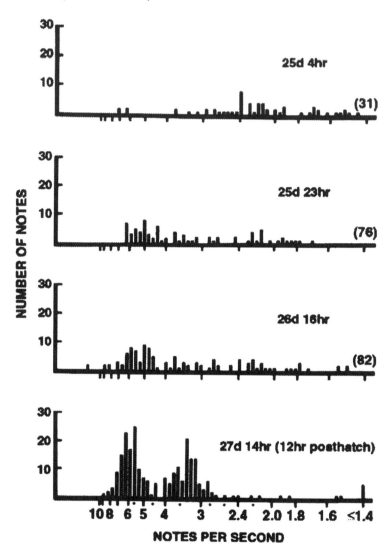

FIGURE 2.7. Repetition rate of calls of mallard embryos and hatchlings. (Modified from Scoville, 1982, Fig. 2.4, p. 49, unpublished.) Prior to hatching (day 25, 4 hr to day 26, 16 hr), approximately 90% of the notes are contact calls. After hatching, the ducklings produce distress calls (~2–4 n/s) as well as contact calls (~5–8 n/s).

rate contact calls did show a preference for the normal mallard maternal call. This result is particularly significant because it shows that, in order for their perceptual development to be normal, the embryos must be exposed to the range of repetition rates that they would ordinarily experience in the usual course of embryonic development. In order to get an

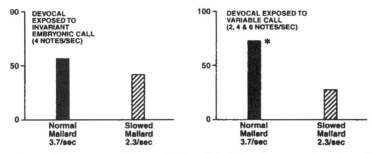

FIGURE 2.8. Preferences of devocal-isolated ducklings for normal or slowed mallard maternal calls as a consequence of being exposed as embryos to 4 notes/sec contact call or variable rate contact call.

even finer fix on this point, we exposed mute embryos to just part of the normal range of repetition rate variation, either 2–4 n/s or 4–6 n/s.

As shown in Figure 2.9, the mute embryos exposed to only a portion of the normal variation in the repetition rate of the contact call did not show the normal preference for the mallard maternal call at 3.7 n/s. Since the embryos only produce the 2, 4, 6 n/s variation in the contact call before hatching (after hatching their contact call narrows to around 5–8 n/s), we exposed muted birds to the variable 2, 4, 6 n/s embryonic contact call after hatching instead of before hatching, and, much to our surprise, the birds exposed to the fully variable contact call after hatching did not show the species-typical preference for the normal mallard maternal call over the slowed mallard maternal call.

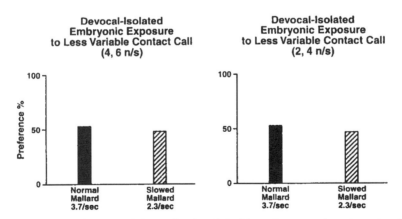

FIGURE 2.9. Preference of devocal-isolated ducklings for normal or slowed mallard maternal calls as a consequence of being exposed as embryos to less variable contact calls.

Thus, for their perception of the mallard maternal call to develop normally, the birds must not only be exposed to their usual repetition-rate variation of the embryonic contact call, but they must be exposed to that variation before hatching, which is the period when they produce the full variation of repetition rates.

To see if the embryos needed to be exposed to the frequency modulated (FM) signal of their contact calls or whether white noise pulsed at the appropriate rate would be effective, we exposed muted embryos to such calls and found that the white-noise call was ineffective in promoting the preference for the normal mallard maternal call. Thus, for their perceptual development to be normal, the embryos must not only hear the usual variation in repetition rate but must also be exposed to the usual FM signal of their contact call. In summary, the highly specific experiential requirements for normal auditory perceptual development in mallard ducklings exposed to their own or sib contact calls:

1. Must be embryonic (not duckling) contact call;
2. Must be exposed in the embryonic state, not postnatally;
3. Must be exposed to the full range of repetition rate variation (2–6 n/s, not 2–4 or 4–6 n/s);
4. Must be the natural frequency modulated signal, not unmodulated white noise.

This remarkable degree of specificity of the experiential input requirements led me to the notion that natural selection has operated on the entire developmental manifold (the developing organism and its typical early experiential context) and not merely on the genetic, organic, or organismic aspects of the developing system. A major, often unrecognized, force in development is the experiential canalization of species-specific behavior that brings about the necessary maturation of the underlying neural structures and functions only under species-typical timing and environmental (experiential) conditions (i.e., the total developmental manifold).

The concept of *experiential canalization* has two components to it. Exposure to the embryonic contact call is necessary not only (1) to promote normal auditory responsiveness to the mallard maternal call, but that experience may also (2) buffer the embryo from becoming responsive to the maternal calls of other species. If the second component is correct, if devocal-isolated embryos were exposed to a recording of the chicken maternal call, they would prefer it to the mallard maternal call after hatching. Whereas, if vocal embryos were exposed to a recording of the chicken maternal call, they would be unaffected by such exposure and would show the usual preference for the mallard call over the chicken call when

TABLE 2.1. Conditions Favoring Canalization or Malleability of Species-Specific Preference

| | Predicted preference | |
Condition	Mallard	Chicken
1. Vocal-communal	X	
2. Vocal-isolated	X	
3. Devocal-isolated	X - - - - - - - - - - - -X	
4. Devocal-isolated, exposed to chicken call		X
5. Devocal-isolated, exposed to chicken call (30 min/hr) and embryo contact call (10 min/hr)	X	

Note. X = preference; X- - - - - - -X = no preference.

tested after hatching. The table above sets out the full design and predictions of an experiential canalization experiment. The predictions are that devocal-isolated embryos would be malleable in the absence of hearing their own and sib contact calls and thus come to prefer the chicken call, whereas vocal-isolated embryos, having been exposed to their own and sib contact calls, would not develop a preference for the chicken call.

The stimulated birds were exposed to the chicken call for 30 min/hr from day 24 of embryonic development to 48 hr after hatching, at which time they were tested for the first time in the mallard versus chicken test. To determine the persistence of the preference shown at 48 hr, the birds were retested at 65 hr with no further exposure to the chicken call. To approximate normal brooding and incubation conditions in Group 5 in Table 2.1, in addition to vocal-isolates that heard only their own contact call, another group (5b) was exposed to a recording of the embryonic contact call for 10 min/hr after each 30 min/hr exposure to the chicken call. This amount of "sib stimulation" would be well below the amount that would be received under natural conditions, in which the birds would be exposed to the vocalizations of as many as 8 to 13 conspecific siblings.

As can be seen in Table 2.2, the vocal-communal and vocal-isolated (VI) birds showed, as expected, a unanimous preference for the mallard call over the chicken call, whereas the unstimulated devocal-isolated (DI) birds did not show a preference. Furthermore, as predicted, the DI birds exposed to the chicken call showed a preference for the chicken call over the mallard call at 48 hr and continued to show that preference at 65 hr. Also, as predicted, the VI birds exposed to the chicken call did not develop a preference for it. The buffering effect of the contact call was even more clearly in evidence in the VI birds that received explicit exposure to the contact call, as well as the chicken call: these birds preferred the mal-

Table 2.2. Preferences of Mallard Ducklings in Mallard (M) – Chicken (C) Choice Test

	Predicted	Obtained
1. Vocal-communal	M	M
2. Vocal-isolate	M	M
3. Devocal-isolated	None	None
4. Devocal-isolated, exposed to chicken call	C	C
5a. Vocal-isolated, exposed to chicken call	M	None
5b. Vocal-isolated, exposed to chicken call (30 min/hr) and embryonic calls (10 min/hr)	M	None, M

Note. Mallard ducklings in groups 4 to 5b were exposed to chicken maternal call for two days before hatching and two days after hatching and then tested at 48 hours and retested at 65 hours after hatching. Results obtained in groups 1 to 5a held for both tests; group 5b went from no preference to preference for mallard in retest.

lard over the chicken call in the retest. Thus, self-stimulation alone (Group 5a) can block the preference for the chicken call, but, to maintain the species-typical preference for the mallard call in the face of exposure to the chicken call, exposure to contact calls produced by siblings is required (Group 5b). The last VI group (5b) heard the broadcast of only one sibling's calls, which would be considerably less than would occur under normal incubation and brooding conditions in nature.

Thus, exposure of mallard ducklings to their variable-rate embryonic contact call not only fosters species-specific perceptual development (i.e., ensuring selective responsiveness to the maternal call of the species), it also buffers the duckling from becoming responsive to social signals from other species. In the absence of exposure to the contact call, the duckling is capable of becoming attached to the maternal call of another species even in the presence of its own species call (in simultaneous auditory choice tests).

When thinking about evolution, canalizing influences account for developmental stability, so that what we think of as normal or typical for a species repeats itself generation after generation (as a consequence of the developmental manifold). For evolution to occur, through genetic change or otherwise, the canalizing influences associated with the developmental manifold must be overcome. Canalization is thus a conservative feature of individual development that prevents evolution from occurring in a ready fashion. Substantial changes in behavior can occur when the developmental manifold is changed, thus paving the way for evolutionary change (Gottlieb, 1992).

☐ The Requirement of Species-Typical Embryonic Auditory Experience for Normal Neural Maturation

The possibility of taking the developmental analysis to the brain level arose when Dr. Lubov Dmitrieva, of the former Soviet Union, joined my laboratory as a research associate in the early 1990s. Dr. Dmitrieva, shown at her console in Figure 2.10, had considerable experience in recording brain-stem auditory-evoked responses (BAERs) from young, small song-birds, so she did not find recording from duck embryos an exceptional challenge.

The experimental setup for recording BAERs from duck embryos and hatchlings is shown in Figure 2.11. Since the BAER measures the threshold sensitivity of the auditory system to pure tones, that allowed us to analyze the muted ducklings' responsiveness to the other critical acoustic feature of the mallard maternal assembly call: frequency (Hz) sensitivity.

Our prior behavioral results with mute embryos indicated that, in the absence of hearing the frequencies (1500–2500 Hz) of their embryonic contact call, the ducklings were relatively insensitive to these frequencies in the mallard maternal call when tested after hatching. (The correspondence of the Hz range of the embryonic contact call to the higher Hz in

FIGURE 2.10. Lubov Dmitrieva seated at clinical audiometer with an auditory-evoked response (BAER) from a day-24 embryo on the screen.

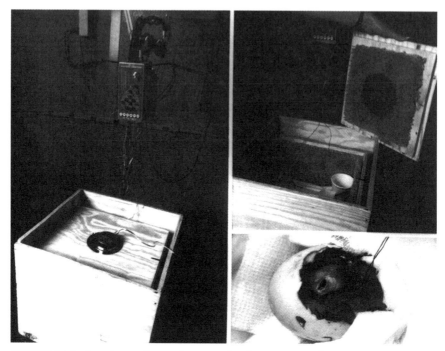

FIGURE 2.11. Experimental setup for recording brain-stem auditory-evoked responses (BAERs) from embryos and hatchlings (left and upper right). The setup was in a soundproof chamber adjacent to a room (Fig. 2.10) that housed a large computer (clinical audiometer), which delivered pure tones and recorded the BAERs.

the mallard maternal call is shown in Fig. 2.12.) To be more specific, when we tested muted embryos after hatching with the normal mallard maternal call vs. the same call with the high Hz (over 825 Hz) filtered out, the muted birds showed a significantly weaker preference (70 percent) for the normal call, whereas the vocal ducklings showed a stronger preference (90 percent) for the normal over the filtered call at 24 hours after hatching. This suggested that in the absence of hearing their own high Hz (1500–2500 Hz) the muted birds were less sensitive to the presence of these Hz in the maternal call. To directly test this possibility at the level of the brain, Dr. Dmitrieva recorded the BAER of muted and vocal embryos and hatchlings at three ages: on day 24 of embryonic development prior to vocal-auditory experience, at hatching (after approximately two days of embryonic auditory experience in the vocal birds), and at 48 hours after hatching.

As shown in Figure 2.13, complete auditory deprivation in the muted birds virtually arrested neurophysiological auditory development beyond day 24 of embryonic development. On day 24, prior to vocal-auditory

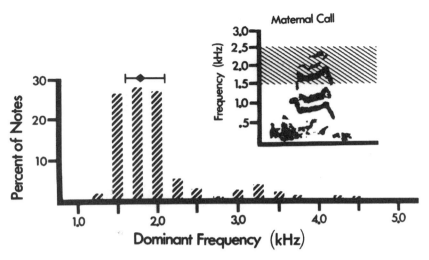

FIGURE 2.12. Dominant frequency of 444 call notes recorded from mallard duck embryos on days 25 and 26 of development. Because embryos emit few alarm-distress calls, and those calls have a higher dominant frequency (most of their energy above 3.0 kHz), approximately 90% of the notes in this sample are contact notes (i.e., notes whose dominant frequency is between 1.5 and 2.5 kHz). Inset shows a note from the mallard maternal call and its fit with the dominant kHz of the embryonic contact call. (From Scoville, 1982, Fig. 2.9, p. 69, unpublished.)

experience, the embryos are most sensitive to 1000, 1500, and 2000 Hz, and after day 24 their threshold drops only slightly in the absence of normal auditory experience. On the other hand, as can be seen in Figure 2.14, when vocal birds are exposed to their own and sib vocalizations between day 24 and day 26–27, their thresholds plunge to their most mature levels in the 2–3 days prior to hatching and show no further improvement in the 2 days after hatching. These results fit beautifully with the embryonic critical period described earlier in connection with the behavioral experiments on repetition rate. In addition, they show a virtual arrest of auditory neurophysiological development of high Hz sensitivity in the absence of normal auditory experience, a similar kind of arrest also being suggested in the behavioral experiments with repetition rate. Thus, if auditory neural maturation is to be normal, the mallard duck embryo must be exposed to the vocalizations that it would hear during the normal course of embryonic development.

The higher frequencies in the mallard maternal assembly call fall in the range from 1.5 to 2.5 kHz (i.e., 1500–2500 Hz). As noted earlier, when mallard ducklings are devocalized and reared in auditory isolation, they are less sensitive than vocal birds to the absence of the higher frequencies

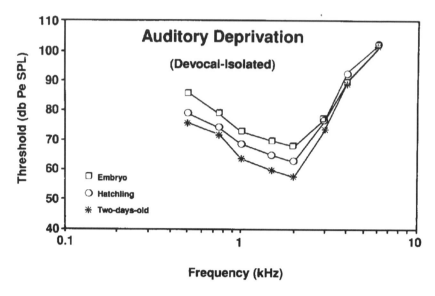

FIGURE 2.13. Threshold of BAER in aurally deprived day-24 embryos, hatchlings, and 2-day-old ducklings. (Data from Dmitrieva & Gottlieb, 1994.)

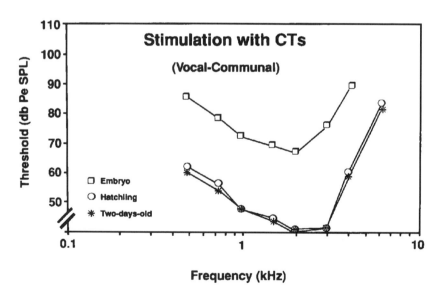

FIGURE 2.14. Threshold of BAER in aurally experienced day-24 embryos, hatchlings, and 2-day-old ducklings. (Data from Dmitrieva & Gottlieb, 1994.)

(1500–2500 Hz) of the mallard assembly call when tested with the normal mallard assembly call versus the same call with the higher Hz removed. Given the present neurophysiological results concerning the aurally experienced and inexperienced embryos' thresholds for pure tones in the 1500–2500 Hz region, it comes as almost startling support for the development manifold concept that it is in the embryonic period that the vocalizations of the embryos are just where they are needed: primarily in the range of 1500–2500 Hz. As shown in Figure 2.15, in the postnatal

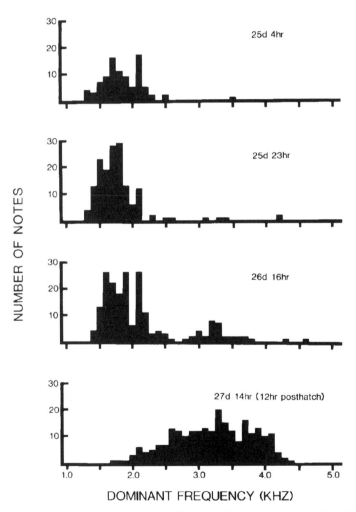

FIGURE 2.15. Dominant frequencies (kHz) in the vocalizations of mallard duck embryos (day 25, 4 hr; day 25, 23 hr; day 26, 16 hr) and hatchlings (day 27, 14 hr = 12 hr after hatching). (From Scoville, 1982, Fig. 2.5, p. 51, unpublished.)

period the ducklings' vocalizations shift upward to a predominance of notes at 2500 Hz and above (bottom of Figure 2.15). These findings also correspond to those with repetition rate: in the embryonic period the repetition rate of the embryos' vocalizations are in the range that is essential to their species-specific perception of the repetition rate of the maternal call, whereas after hatching the repetition rate of the contact call is above that range (Figure 2.7).

☐ Summary and Conclusions

When one reads the older literature on the evolution and development of species-specific or instinctive behavior, it's common to read that such behavior is an outcome of heredity. That is, natural selection favored animals whose genes dictated adaptive behavior:

Genetic Activity → Species-Specific Behavioral Development

As it became clearer that the genes must be specifying the neural development underlying the behavior rather than the behavior as such, the progression was envisaged as:

Genetic Activity → Neural Maturation → Species-Specific Development

Then in the 1950s with the discovery that normally occurring sensory experience was necessary to at least *maintain* already developed nerve cells and neural connections (synapses), the picture became:

Genetic Activity → Neural Maturation → Experience → Species-Specific Development

The present results suggest an even greater importance of normally occurring sensory experience, not merely a maintenance role but an essential *constructive* function of such experience:

Genetic Activity ↔ Neural Maturation ↔ Experience ↔ Species-Specific Development

In this latter view, the nervous system does not develop fully or normally without the benefit of normally occurring experience. Thus, experience in this case plays a constructive role in the development of the nervous system and species-specific behavior. This is a significant departure from the notion that normally occurring experience only comes into play once the nervous system has been fully constructed by the activity of the genes. In the present view, the normal activity of the genes themselves is dependent upon signals arising from the internal and external environment during the course of normal development (evidence presented in Gottlieb, 1998). That is why there are arrows going back to genetic activity in the diagram above. That diagram presents the essence of probabilistic epigenesis, a topic that I have been working on since 1970. In the research described in this chapter I was able to take the bidirectional analysis across three of the four levels (species-typical development, experience, neural maturation). I was frustrated in taking the analysis to the genetic level by an event early in my career and one late in my career.

From the beginning of my work in the early 1960s I was eager to include the genetic contribution and seized upon an early opportunity to collaborate with two neurologists, one of whom (George Paulson) was adept at brain dissection in birds, and the other of whom (Stanley Appel) was running a laboratory in which protein synthesis in the nervous system was being studied. According to what was then already known, protein synthesis was the result of messenger RNA activity, and mRNA activity was a consequence of DNA activity (DNA $\rightarrow$ mRNA $\rightarrow$ protein). So, protein synthesis could be used as an indirect measure of genetic activity. Accordingly, I prepared two groups of duck embryos for Paulson and Appel by exposing them for several days before hatching to tape-recorded sib vocalizations or to extra visual stimulation by incubating them in a lighted incubator. The control group was incubated in the dark and in acoustic isolation from other embryos. The point of the experiment was to look for enhanced protein synthesis in the auditory and visual parts of the brain in the treated groups.

Subsequently, Appel told us that both experimental groups showed an enhancement of protein synthesis in the synaptic regions of the brain stem, in which the auditory nuclei are located, and in the optic lobes of the brain, which mediate auditory as well as visual stimulation. This was a clear indication that the extra auditory and visual stimulation had enhanced gene expression in the embryo. This, of course, implied a bidirectional relationship all the way to the genetic level during the embryonic period, and it meant that genetic activity could be influenced by normally occurring exteroceptive sensory stimulation and thus result in an enhancement of neural maturation. The experiment was completed in 1965, and Paulson and I pleaded with Appel to complete the data analysis so we could share the results with interested colleagues by publishing them. Alas, overly hectic research, clinical, and other duties took precedence in

Appel's life, so Paulson and I were frustrated in our desire to see this work to completion in the form of publication in a refereed journal. At the time there was only one other study in the literature implicating exteroceptive influences on genetic activity, a study involving the influence of vestibular-mediated learning on changes in nuclear RNA base ratios in vestibular nerve cells in rats (Hydèn & Egyhàzi, 1962). It was not until 1967 that Rose published a study showing enhanced RNA and protein synthesis in the visual cortex of rats as a consequence of visual stimulation.

The second disappointment in taking the analyses to the genetic level was the consequence of an unknown technical mistake. In the early 1990s, after getting the positive results with the aurally experienced embryos showing enhanced neural maturation, I made contact with a laboratory that was routinely doing c-fos studies of neural tissue. C-fos is a gene whose expression is activity-dependent (e.g., it can be activated by sensory stimulation). We prepared two groups of brains paralleling the auditory experience or inexperience of the embryos that Dr. Dmitrieva and I had studied earlier and took them to the c-fos laboratory, where they were sectioned and further prepared for analysis. I knew from other work in the literature that c-fos would react to auditory stimulation, so this would not be a discovery but only represent the satisfaction of having been able to traverse all the levels of analysis in my own research program. Unfortunately, there was a problem with the way we prepared the brains, because we got no evidence of c-fos activity in the auditory system of these birds. Otherwise, as I look back on over thirty years of research activity, I thank my lucky stars for having had the continuing personnel and financial support that provided the empirical evidence for the developmental manifold concept and probabilistic epigenesis. I am also indebted to some younger colleagues, Meredith West and Andrew King, for their much fuller elaboration of the developmental manifold concept in their concept of the ontogenetic niche (West & King, 1987), and to Richard Lerner for so usefully integrating probabilistic epigenesis into his notion of developmental contextualism (Lerner & Kauffman, 1985).

In the rather long intervening period since this chapter was originally written, several publications in developmental and evolutionary biology have appeared that are consonant with, and significantly extend, the developmental manifold idea. These articles represent a move away from the nondevelopmental genocentric tradition of biology expressed so succinctly in the following quotation: "Traditionally, evolutionary biologists have viewed mutations within individual genes as the major source of phenotypic variation leading to adaptation through natural selection, and ultimately generating diversity among species" (Ochman & Moran, 2001, p. 1096).

The developmental manifold holds that natural selection operates on outcomes of development that include genes but that development is not controlled or determined by genes in the sense of genes providing a blueprint or program for development. Evelyn Fox Keller (2000), in her book, *The Century of the Gene*, has shown not only the conceptual but the empirical inadequacy of genetic blueprints or programs for development. She advocates replacing the genetic program idea with a developmental program. Jason Scott Robert (2001) has taken Keller's notion to a further degree of refinement in his critical analysis of the role of the ubiquitous homeobox genes in development and evolution, in this case moving from a genocentric view of development and evolution to a developmental systems view of gene action and evolution. Among other things, the developmental systems view holds that selection acts directly on phenotypes not genotypes. This idea itself is not new and can be traced back to Mivart (1871), who pointed out that adaptations arise *before* they are selected for, that is, they are the product of development. What Mivart could not have known in advance of experimental studies of embryology and developmental genetics was the absolute importance of developmental (epigenetic) conditions in recreating the changed phenotype generation after generation. This idea has been significantly elaborated by Newman and Müller (2000), and by Weiss and Fullerton (2000), who point out that, during the course of evolution, the genes associated with a given morphological outcome (phenotype) may change while the evolved outcome is kept stable by *epigenetic* mechanisms, a conclusion consonant with the developmental manifold idea but one that certainly goes beyond it. Not to claim too much, this particular view (developmental systems thinking), as pointed out by Robert, Hall, and Olson (2001), has not yet permeated the thinking of evolutionary developmental biologists. Nonetheless, it is gratifying to see that the evolutionary implications of research on instinctive behavioral development is consonant with the most recent thinking about morphological evolution. Certainly, a change is in the wind in the way development is now being invoked in relation to evolution (see True & Haag, 2001).

☐ Acknowledgments

The author's research and scholarly activities are supported in part by NIMH Grant P50–MH–52429 and NSF Grant BCS–0126475. This chapter is a much abbreviated and somewhat modified version of material that appeared in G. Gottlieb, *Probabilistic Epigenesis and Evolution* (Worcester, MA: Clark University Press, 1999).

☐ References

Dmitrieva, L. P., & Gottlieb, G. (1994). Influence of auditory experience on the development of brain-stem auditory-evoked potentials in mallard duck embryos and hatchlings. *Behavioral and Neural Biology, 61,* 19–28.

Gottlieb, G. (1988). Development of species identification in ducklings: XV. Individual auditory recognition. *Developmental Psychobiology, 21,* 509–522.

Gottlieb, G. (1992) *Individual development and evolution: The genesis of novel phenotypes.* New York: Oxford University Press.

Gottlieb, G. (1997). *Synthesizing nature-nurture: Prenatal roots of instinctive behavior.* Mahwah, NJ: Erlbaum.

Gottlieb, G. (1998). Normally occurring environmental and behavioral influences on gene activity: From central dogma to probabilistic epigenesis. *Psychological Review, 105,* 792–802.

Hydèn, H., & Egyhàzi, E. (1962). Nuclear RNA changes of nerve cells during a learning experiment in rats. *Proceedings of the National Academy of Sciences USA, 48,* 1366–1373.

Keller, E. F. (2000). *The century of the gene.* Cambridge: Harvard.

Klopfer, P. H. (1959). An analysis of learning in young Anatidae. *Ecology, 40,* 90–102.

Kuo, Z.-Y. (1976). *The dynamics of behavior development: An epigenetic view* (enlarged ed.). New York: Plenum.

Lerner, R. M., & Kauffman, M. B. (1985). The concept of development in contextualism. *Developmental Review, 5,* 309–333.

Mivart, St. G. (1871). *On the genesis of species.* London: Macmillan.

Newman, S. A., & Müller, G. B. (2000). Epigenetic mechanisms of character origination. *Journal of Experimental Zoology, 288,* 304–317.

Ochman, H., & Moran, N. A. (2001). Genes lost and genes found: Evolution of bacterial pathogenesis and symbiosis. *Science, 292,* 1096–1098.

Robert, J. S. (2001). Interpreting the homeobox: metaphors of gene action and activation in development and evolution. *Evolution and Development, 3,* 287–295.

Robert, J. S., Hall, B. K., & Olson, W. M. (2001). Bridging the gap between developmental systems theory and evolutionary developmental biology. *BioEssays, 23,* 954–962.

Rose, S. P. R. (1967). Changes in visual cortex on first exposure of rats to light: Effect on incorporation of tritiated lysine into protein. *Nature, 215,* 253–255.

Scoville, R. P. (1982). Embryonic development of neonatal vocalizations in Peking ducklings (*Anas platyrhynchos*). Unpublished doctoral dissertation, University of North Carolina at Chapel Hill.

True, J. R., & Haag, E. S. (2001). Developmental system drift and flexibility in evolutionary trajectories. *Evolution and Development, 3,* 109–119.

Weiss, K. M., & Fullerton, S. M. (2000). Phenogenetic drift and the evolution of genotype-phenotype relationships. *Theoretical Population Biology 57,* 187–195.

West, M., & King, A. (1987). Settling nature and nurture into an ontogenetic niche. *Developmental Psychobiology, 20,* 549–562.

CHAPTER

Celia L. Moore

On Differences and Development

One simple way to describe development is "qualitative transformations during an individual life span." Development is fundamentally about becoming different from a previous condition, and the job of a developmental scientist is to figure out how this happens. But on what dimension should difference be assessed? On appearance? function? underlying mechanism? external stimulus or milieu? Is it possible to remain similar on one or more dimensions, yet become different on a third? How do the different dimensions interweave as development progresses? At some point during my graduate student days, I became fascinated by these related puzzles. The fascination continues.

Sexually reproducing organisms like ourselves begin life as a zygote. This single cell, newly formed by the fusion of egg and sperm, is provoked by that act to begin a series of divisions. The daughter cells do not disperse, but remain interconnected in an adhesive matrix, where their numbers continue to increase and the entire collective takes shape as an individual organism. Newly divided cells, which are identical to parental cells, change over time to take on new forms and new functions. The direction of change differs from one group of cells to the next, leading to discrete populations of mature cells. *Differentiation* is the term used by developmental biologists to label this fundamental developmental process at the cellular level. However, transformation is not confined to cells. Whole organisms also undergo development, changing in form and function over time. Again like cells, they may also become different from one another during the course of development. Some individual differences are minor fluctuations in a common pattern, but others are predictable divergences that lead to identifiably different populations of individuals.

Differences between males and females, which have come to occupy a lot of my thought, provide good examples of predictable divergences in development. The language we commonly use to talk about sex differences creates some difficulties. The phrase *sexual differentiation* is commonly used to mean both the intraorganismic differentiation of structures used in sexual function (differentiation in the cellular sense as used by embryologists) and the divergent development of male and female organisms. My conceptual development has been spurred by an effort to sort out concepts suitable for thinking about both developmental change within organisms and the emergence of differences between organisms. I confess that I have not always understood that these were two separate goals. In the remainder of this essay, I will attempt to trace the steps that have led to that eye-opening realization and to the particular conception of development that I now hold.

☐ Seeds from the Institute of Animal Behavior

Development is constrained by the raw materials available at each stage, is rarely linear, and is often nudged in one direction or another by historical contingencies. My conceptions of development took their initial adult shape in graduate school, at the Institute of Animal Behavior of Rutgers University in Newark, New Jersey, amid the social turmoil of the second half of the 1960s. I arrived at the Institute primed by courses that I took with R. K. Selander to think about evolutionary biology and the exciting new field of ethology and by courses that I took with E. J. Capaldi to think about learning and comparative psychology. Professor Capaldi also sponsored my first intensive research experience, which involved running rats in mazes, and introduced me to the possibility of graduate study by inviting me into his graduate course and to a speaker series. Daniel Lehrman was one of the speakers to visit the University of Texas that year. I was thrilled.

For reasons that are obscure to me and in any event irrelevant, I became interested in animal behavior—most particularly hormones and reproductive behavior. I applied to study with two giants in the field, Daniel Lehrman and Frank Beach, and was accepted at both universities. I chose Lehrman and Rutgers, Newark and all.

The Institute of Animal Behavior was an astonishing place during my graduate student days. Its location in a run-down building in the middle of a large, noisy, and run-down city made an unlikely backdrop for the serious study of animals, yet the resident faculty and students, the constant stream of top scientists from around the world, and the charismatic enthusiasm of Lehrman as director formed an unparalleled intellectual microclimate for this purpose. I incorporated much from this rich and heady mix of raw materials into my own conceptual development as a student and took much away to chew on later. The broadest and most inclusive influence was a theoretical persuasion that evolutionary and developmental concepts must be integrated, as they were in the Schneirla-Lehrman theoretical framework on which the Institute was founded (Lehrman, 1953, 1970; Schneirla, 1956, 1957) and in the developmentally sophisticated revisions of classical ethological theory (Bateson, 1966; Hinde, 1966). A major component of the Schneirla-Lehrman theory was that development results from bidirectional interactions between the organism and its environment. Although this in now accepted as mainstream thought within developmental psychobiology, at the time it had fierce competition from instinct theories that were built on conceptions of endogenous maturation impervious to outside influence and unidirectional biological causes in development (Lorenz, 1957). Indeed, these competing ideas still flourish within much of psychology (Michel & Moore, 1995). In a lasting influence on my own thought that has made me forever skeptical of instinct theory in all guises, I saw bidirectional interaction made specific and empirical in two research programs that were going on all around me at the Institute: Lehrman's work with ring dove reproductive cycles (Lehrman, 1965), and J. S. Rosenblatt's work with maternal behavior in rats (Rosenblatt, 1967).

☐ Lessons from Rats, Laughing Gulls, and Ring Doves

My more general theoretical ideas about development have many diverse sources: all those pioneering theorists and experimentalists who fed the streams that have merged into modern developmental psychobiology (Michel & Moore, 1978, 1995). There was also the preparation to think in theoretical terms by my mentors; of these, Colin Beer had a major hand in developing a taste for the history and philosophy of biology, psychology, and their interdisciplinary commerce. But the general theoretical framework I use does not explain fully the more specific dimensions of my own work and thought. Why have I found certain concepts critically important and certain research strategies most compelling? As I reflect on the concepts that have been most central to the main body of my work, I find myself going back to my first immersion in research to give them flesh and bones. Because the lessons I learned from working with rats, laughing gulls, and ring doves during these early years have so colored the meanings of the developmental concepts I most use, I will introduce them here as I met them then.

Bidirectional Causation

Ring doves taught me many things. They are forthright and unambiguous beasts: their lessons were always crystal clear. One of their lessons was that external stimulation can have profound and often enduring changes on an organism. With help from Lehrman, of course, they made it clear that causal arrows run in two directions. Although many seemed to find the idea of bidirectional organism-environment interactions subtle at best, I found it hard to miss when confronted by pictures of huge oviducts in female ring doves who had simply spent a few days observing a courting male through a glass window, and the shrunken oviducts in females separated from the male by an opaque partition (Lehrman, Wortis, & Brody, 1961).

There are equally striking changes in crop morphology that result from the stimulation of sitting on eggs (Hansen, 1966; Michel & Moore, 1986). Ring doves and pigeons have an unusual method of feeding their young by regurgitating the epithelial cells that are shed from their crops, which begin to thicken rapidly as hatching approaches. Ring dove crop growth was the standard way to measure prolactin secretion before radioimmunoassays were developed, and avian oviducts were known to be stimulated by ovarian hormones. These were no fleeting behavioral responses or hypostatized memory traces, but substantial physiological and anatomical changes in the organism from an external stimulus, mediated through known neuroendocrine mechanisms. The changes were also correlated with major behavioral reorganizations, for example, from a bird that showed no incubation behavior to one that did (Lehrman, 1965), which suggested that the nervous system could be affected as well. It seemed to me likely, but much more difficult to establish, that if the endocrine state and peripheral morphology could be so readily changed by external stimulation, so could the nervous system. It took me some time to get around to testing this idea for sex differences in the nervous system (Moore, Dou, & Juraska, 1992), but I began to think about it long ago.

Organism as Whole Body

I also learned from ring doves of the profound effects that hormones can have on behavior, sometimes through unexpected routes. There is perhaps nothing remarkable in the observation that physiological condition can affect behavior. That is, after all, the mainstream message of physiological psychology. However, the field was then, even more than today, focused almost entirely on the effects of the brain on behavior. The fact that hormones, including gonadal steroids arising far from the brain, were important determinants of behavior meant to me that the whole body has to be taken into account. Furthermore, I was in addition much influenced by Lehrman's (1955) hypothesis that prolactin exerts its effects on parental feeding behavior through what he called a peripheral tension in the crop, an organ that becomes engorged with crop-milk as a result of the prolactin. Lehrman found that local anesthetic applied to the crop region, but not to other parts of the parental dove's body, reduced feeding responses. Although it was subsequently determined that crop engorgement is not necessary for regurgitation feeding behavior and that peripheral tension cannot, therefore, be the whole story (Hansen, 1966), Lehrman's analysis of the mechanism underlying prolactin's effect on the behavior was my introduction to the potential importance of the much-overlooked periphery. There were a few other islands of research on the periphery in a sea of brain studies—for example, Beach and Levinson (1950) on genital morphology and rat sexual behavior and Hinde (1965) on brood patches and canary nest building. This work prepared me to stay on the lookout for potential peripheral mediators and indirect pathways of hormone action, which I have since found in no short supply in my own study system.

Nature of Experience

The Institute of Animal Behavior of the 1960s, like the American Museum of Natural History that gave rise to it, was a center of opposition to Lorenzian instinct theory. Through the force of his 1953 paper—and his personality, which could so readily fill rooms and cross continents—Lehrman became its most effective critic. A central postulate of instinct theory is that reproductive and other naturally occurring behavior develops from innately given blueprints, without need of individual experience. Lehrman thought this was nonsense best ignored by anyone really wishing to understand the process of development. As he put it in that famous 1953 critique:

> The use of "explanatory"categories such as "innate" and "genically fixed" obscures the necessity of investigating developmental *processes* in order to gain insight into the actual mechanisms of behavior and their interrelations. The problem of development is the problem of the development of new structures and activity patterns from the resolution of the interaction of *existing* structures and patterns, within the organism and its internal en-

vironment, and between the organism and its outer environment. At any stage of development, the new features emerge from the interactions within the *current* stage and between the *current* stage and the environment. The interaction out of which the organism develops is *not* one, as is so often said, between heredity and environment. It is between *organism* and environment! And the organism is different at each different stage of its development" (Lehrman, 1953, p. 345; emphases in original).

Lehrman's ring doves were important allies in the efforts to get this message across. From instinct theory, one would predict that ring doves will incubate when put in the right hormonal condition and stimulated with a nest and eggs. Yet they only do so after they have had previous reproductive experience (Lehrman & Wortis, 1960). So, how do ring doves manage their first cycle? They don't practice as adolescents or learn from watching their elders, and they don't have innate devices that can be switched on by hormones. The answer to the riddle came from rejecting the dichotomous formulation and asking questions about the raw materials from which ring doves can build incubation behavior. Ring doves incubate when they have their first clutch of eggs because they have woven together the experiences of courting and nest building and internal physiological changes to make this behavioral state just as surely as they have woven together straws to make their nest (Lehrman, 1965).

The ring dove work was not alone. There were other contemporaneous experiments exploring the nature of experience and its role in the development of "instinctive" behavior. Of these, Rosenblatt and Aronson's (1958) work on the development of sexual behavior in male cats and Hailman's (1967) work on the development of gull chick pecking had the most influence on my own thinking. I took several things from all this work that became an enduring part of my conceptual makeup. Perhaps the most important are a broad definition of experience and an understanding of how it becomes incorporated into the maturing organism.

Equifinality

My first really intensive research experience was with maternal behavior in rats. With all the hormonal changes of pregnancy and lactation, it seemed likely to many that hormones were involved in its development and maintenance. But which hormones? The answer was unknown at the time, and it turned out to be hard to come by (Rosenblatt & Siegel, 1981). The study I helped with as a first-year graduate student in Rosenblatt's lab was meant to find out whether the pituitary hormones prolactin and oxytocin were involved in its maintenance. So pups were removed from dams, some of which then got hormone treatment over a period of several days, while others did not. Then pups were returned to see whether the treated females remained maternal. It turns out that they were no more likely to be maternal than were controls. However, the interesting finding was that the nonmaternal dams gradually became maternal as a result of exposure to the pups. Rosenblatt (1967; Rosenblatt & Siegel, 1981) later studied this phenomenon in its own right. He found that even female rats that had never been mated would become maternal as a result of experience with pups. They would do so even when ovariectomized or hypophysectomized. They did not even have to be females: males, which do not even have nipples in rats, would perform maternal behavior after adequate pup stimulation. On the basis of this and other work, Rosenblatt concluded that maternal behavior could develop through two different routes: the usual one for parturient dams, which involves hormone action; and one that involves no hormones.

This work was my introduction to the developmental concept of equifinality. There can be more than one path to the same developmental endpoint. This concept has obvious relevance for the study of sex differences: it should be borne in mind that males and females can sometimes reach the same outcome through different means. As it turns out, this is how it works for parental care in at least some mammalian species where both mother and father care for the young (Lonstein & deVries, 1999). Some differences that lie beneath the skin—even differences in brain structure—are in the service of the same behavioral outcome.

Development from, Not Toward

The process view of development moves forward, starting from material precursors and actions from which organisms can build new states, mechanisms, or actions. It eschews developmental analyses that start from an outcome and attempt to imagine developmental steps leading to that outcome, on the grounds that you are likely to get out of such an analysis only what you put in. This is a central problem with nativistic conceptions of development, such as those found in Lorenz's instinct theory and, in more modern times, with those in sociobiology, "evolutionary" psychology, and some cognitive developmental theories. As a corollary to this problem, there is a need to recognize that both surface appearance and function, derived as they are from the final state, are unreliable guides for the study of development.

The first experiment I ever planned and finished on my own gave substance to that caution (Moore, 1975). Laughing gulls build nests before laying eggs in them and incubating. Ethologists were then much concerned with displacement activities, in which behavior inappropriate to a given functional state could be expressed when appropriate ones were somehow frustrated. Nest building during the incubation period was interpreted by some as such a displacement. Beer (1963) had made the case that such an interpretation was unnecessary, because nest building was correlated with a rising and settling incubation pattern throughout the entire cycle from nest construction through incubation. Following his lead, I reasoned that displacement nest building should not be regulated by the condition of the nest, but be randomly distributed. So I cut pieces out of the nest rims of incubating birds and found that they built nonrandomly to repair the nest. Nest building was nest building, even when it occurred under the functionally defined condition of incubation.

My doctoral dissertation (Moore, 1976a, 1976b) also played with the dissociations among form, function, and mechanism. Ring doves incubate and brood their young squabs using identical motor patterns. From surface appearance, it seems that there has been no developmental change in behavior from one stage to the next. However, if the doves are given a choice between sitting on a nest with eggs and one with squabs, a definite developmental transition is revealed. Doves going through their first cycle prefer eggs to squabs until their own young hatch, at which time they switch choices; doves in their second cycle also show preferences to eggs early in incubation but switch to squabs shortly before hatching. The transition to squabs is facilitated either by injecting prolactin, a hormone associated with late incubation and hatching, or by giving them squabs. This facilitation is greater in naive birds. I learned from these studies that some developmental transitions were hidden by similarity in surface appearance, making experimentation necessary to determine both this fact and the nature of antecedent conditions that shape the transition.

I also learned that clues to these antecedents could be found by attending to the natural history of the animal, construed with respect to development to include those aspects of its surround and internal conditions that are reliably present during the developmental process. For cycling ring doves, this certainly includes hormones such as prolactin, the mate, the nest, the eggs, the squabs, and prior experiences with these agents and stimuli. I came to adopt this conceptual approach to the study of development as a more reliable guide to likely mechanisms than similarities in appearance or functional outcome.

☐ Protesting the Organizational/Activational Theory of Sexual Differentiation

Shortly after completing my degree, I took a position as an assistant professor at the University of Massachusetts Boston, a branch that was still new enough in the early 1970s to be in rented space downtown. I had an office in the Statler-Hilton (now Park Plaza) hotel, which gave me a private washroom in a wonderful location, but no laboratory. While waiting for the campus and my laboratory to be built, I found myself with time on my hands. The ring doves got me in trouble.

Writing seemed an obvious thing to do under the circumstances, and one of the things on my mind was the organizational/activational theory of sexual differentiation (Phoenix, Goy, Gerall, & Young, 1959; Goy, 1970). It was of course a hot idea in hormones and behavior during the early 1970s, shaping most of the literature in the field. I thought it had some serious problems. The very concept of organization was itself a problem. This was the idea that gonadal steroids circulating during early development—prenatally or early postnatally, depending on the species—act directly on the brain to organize it for the performance of specific behavioral patterns. I had seen naive ring doves, pumped up with progesterone, standing for hours in a cage with nest and eggs, looking even more perplexed than usual, while their experienced counterparts, all business and no nonsense, sat on the nest within minutes. I was not prepared to believe that hormones contained instruction packets.

The theory also seemed far too quick to assume that any enduring effects of early steroids on behavioral outcomes would necessarily be located in the brain. I remembered the ring doves and their enlarged crops. I thought Beach (1971) had it right: consider the periphery, consider species differences, consider the great overlap of behavior in the two sexes, consider some restraint in hypostatizing brain structures. Beach's critique of the hormone organization theory appeared in the same year that Raisman and Field (1971) published their report of a sex difference in the ultrastructure of the rat preoptic area. His paper went against the grain of the times and was widely dismissed. Instead, the first observation of sex differences in brain anatomy fed a frenzy to find more, and these differences were called upon to bear a large explanatory burden (e.g., Goy & McEwen, 1980).

Having been steeped in the need to study development step-by-step, I was skeptical that the organizational/activational research strategy could reveal that much about the developmental process. It was typical of the paradigm to treat an animal with hormones prenatally and measure outcomes in adulthood *without looking at any intervening stages*. This left lots of unexplored territory and many possible pathways, perhaps convoluted ones, from the early hormones and end points of interest. It seemed to me possible that early hormones set all manner of processes into motion that could converge on behavioral differences days, weeks, months, or years down the road. What about those canines developing in young male rhesus monkeys? What about size differences resulting from early hormones? What about the genitalia? or odors, or other socially important cues? If such a research strategy had been used to study ring dove parental behavior, we would never have learned of the importance of courtship for the development of nest building, of nest building for the development of incubation, of incubation for the development of care of young (Lehrman, 1965; Cheng, 1979). The ring dove reproductive cycle would have seemed a series of instincts activated in sequence by a string of hormones and not the complicated, progressive interweaving of internal and external factors that it is.

Thus, I was disturbed by the undercurrent of nativism that ran through organizational/activational theory. This was most obvious in its account of development in female mammals. Testosterone, it was said, is secreted in young males, where it organizes the brain according to masculine specifications so that the animal can do male things when called upon to do so later in life. There is no comparable hormone in females, and no comparable organizational period. Therefore, it was concluded, female brains develop to do female things according to intrinsic mammalian instructions (e.g., Gerall, 1966). Their brain organization and behavior, it would seem, needed no explanation, at least within the theory. The language used to make this point was often blunt: "masculine differentiation is an active process, female differentiation a passive one" (Hutt, 1972, p. 62); "The principle of differentiation somewhat simplified seems to be: add androgen and obtain a maleadd nothing and obtain a female" (Money & Ehrhardt, 1968, p. 32). I found the nativism a surprising part of the theory, particularly since its architects had done distinguished work on the role of experience in the development of sexual behavior.

I was also surprised that no one seemed to have noticed this nativistic core. Given the large number of people working in the field of hormones and behavior who had joined forces during this era to criticize the nativism in instinct theory, why had no one worried about the nativistic aspects of organizational/activational theory?

I was a graduate student during a time of great social upheaval and protest, of active questioning of social roles and expectations. I read the feminists of the day, and was particularly influenced by Dorothy Dinnerstein. I sat in on her course while she was developing the ideas that later became *The Mermaid and the Minotaur* (1977). I became sensitive to the blind spots that develop from overly familiar arrangements. In the end, I decided that blind spots arising from familiar sexual arrangements and beliefs about sex differences had a lot to do with the flaws in the organization/activation theory and the fact that they were left unnoticed and uncorrected.

So it happened that while waiting for a laboratory in which to continue my ring dove research, I wrote a long paper to tell the world my concerns, in the hope that people would stop multiplying demonstrations of early hormone effects on sex differences and begin to study how the development works. In 1974, I submitted the paper to the *Psychological Bulletin*, where it received very positive reviews but was rejected by the editor as too controversial for a journal intended for archival purposes. (I'm sure his hereditarian views had nothing to do with it.) Given the paucity of outlets for papers of this type at the time, I put it in a drawer and decided that I needed to make my points empirically. Much later, after the field had matured and the ideas in the paper were, or so I thought, no longer so controversial, I gave the manuscript a major update and overhaul. I submitted it once more to the *Psychological Bulletin*, now with a different editor. This time the reviews were negative. One was eight pages long, pointedly signed by a contributor to the development of organizational/activational theory. I gave up on the *Bulletin* and published the paper in a new journal, where it has been read by a few people (Moore, 1985). But I knew I was on to something.

☐ Differentiation, Differences, and Development

It turns out that I had not gone far enough in the thinking that went into the 1974/1985 paper. Even though I had rejected—rightly, I still believe—organization and activation as inadequate concepts for capturing what was happening developmentally, I had retained the muddled concept of differentiation. I had been blinkered by the all-too-familiar linguistic and conceptual devices that we use to talk and think about sex and gender. Several more years passed before I noticed this mistake.

Sexual Differentiation as Making of Sex Differences

The original Phoenix, Goy, Gerall, and Young (1959) report was very deliberate in drawing a parallel between the "organizing" effects of prenatal testosterone on sexual behavior in guinea pigs and the effects of this hormone on the differentiation of genital tissues. The title of their report referred to the "tissues mediating mating behavior." Thus, they kept the embryological meaning of *sexual differentiation* as development from an undifferentiated state of pluripotentiality to one differentiated for sexual function, but extended its scope from the internal and external genitalia to include sexual behavior and its underlying tissues, presumed to be neural. The organizing effects of hormones referred to their specific and enduring effects on the process of sexual differentiation during early critical periods. The embryological origins of *organization* and its specific variants, *masculinization* and *feminization*, were made plain throughout the early literature. For example, Goy (1970) devoted a long discussion to whether the external genitalia, with a single bipotential primordium that develops in one of two directions, or the internal genitalia, with its two independent primordia that develop (or regress) separately, made the best model for sexual behavior.

Somewhere along the way, with no one taking notice, *sexual differentiation* came loose from these embryological moorings and became neither *sexual* nor *differentiation*. The organizational hypothesis was tested across a broad spectrum by manipulating early gonadal steroids, and we soon had sexual differentiation of birdsong; of play; of personality; of liver function; of psychosexuality generally; of the brain both generally and in its particular regions, whether or not sexual function was known or even anticipated; etc. What was meant, of course, was that sex differences in outcome had been found that could be manipulated by early hormone treatments. *Sexual differentiation* became the making of individual (male/female) differences.

In retrospect, it would have been useful had people talked about sex differences in sexual differentiation when sexual behavior and its mechanisms were meant. That would have been accurate, but it probably would have seemed redundant, even in the beginning. The sexes do, after all, typically diverge during the course of sexual differentiation. Masculine sexual behavior does not as a general rule develop to the same extent in males and females; nor does feminine sexual behavior. (How many nonsexual, but sexually divergent, outcomes come about as incidental by-products of sexual differentiation is an open question.) Male/female divergence and sexual differentiation are correlated. But they are not the same thing. One refers to individual differences in outcome; the other to a developmental process within an individual organism. I underscore this point because I think it is an important one. And because it took me a long time to see it.

Meanwhile, the field of hormones and behavior was flourishing in response to the excitement generated by the developmental findings. As studies multiplied, people began to investigate not just whether, but how, hormones affected neural and behavioral development in a variety of species and systems. This led to complications in and modifications of the organizational/activational model of hormone action (e.g., Yahr, 1988). The mechanisms of hormone action during putative organizational and activational stages were found to overlap (Arnold & Breedlove, 1985; Tobet & Fox, 1992); females were found to undergo an active, hormone-dependent developmental process (Döhler, 1978); a significant role for afferent input during the putative organizational period was described (Beyer & Feder, 1987); and the periphery was found to be involved (Breedlove,

1992). There were other developments. Two particularly important ones were the great increase in comparative studies and the increasing sophistication and mainstreaming of the early hormone studies within neuroscience (Tobet & Fox, 1992). For many working in the field, *organization* and *activation* have come to be used loosely as synonyms for early and late hormone action, or have been dropped in favor of less loaded or more precise terminology. In recognition of this evolution in meaning, I used a rather soft, descriptive definition of *organization* in a 1990 paper: "When hormones present at one developmental stage contribute to changes in the organism that endure beyond the secretory period into later stages, they are said to have *organizing* effects" (Moore, 1990, p. 281; emphasis in original).

For most who work in the area, sexual differentiation now means the study of sex differences, or sexual dimorphisms, as they are often called. Open any book with "sexual differentiation" in the title and you will find a lot about divergence in two sexual populations—and perhaps nothing about sex.

Maternal Contributions to Sex Differences—Or Is It Sexual Development?

I have taken some space to give a thumbnail sketch of the organizational/activational model and the research it generated because my own research program on sexual development in rats began as a reaction to it. I did not begin this program with a fascination for sex differences: I had worked primarily with monomorphic birds who do not arouse this curiosity, and I held the personal belief that human sex differences were grossly exaggerated. My long-range goals were to set up a ring dove colony and dig more deeply into the concept of experience and initiate a project with the gulls and terns on the Boston Harbor islands. But I decided to postpone that agenda and spend a couple of years making a point about the development of sex differences, motivated by the events that had happened to come my way at that stage of my career, no doubt leavened by feminist politics and plain dogged persistence.

I think I was primarily concerned about the simplistic and damaging way that some ideas about hormone action were being imported into human developmental psychology and the popular media. This work was used to feed the opposition of social and biological explanations of sex differences. When "organizational" effects of hormones were found, many seized on them to argue for hardwired, biological determinants of sex differences. So I thought that I would find out whether there were sex differences in socially provided input during the putative critical period for sexual differentiation and, if so, whether I could relate this input to hormonal condition of pups on the one hand and to the development of their sexual behavior on the other. I deliberately chose rats, not just for their convenience, but because most would see them as a hardwired kind of animal, making any positive results more compelling. Thus, the research was designed as a challenge to the nativism that I saw to be inherent in the theory and that so many thought to be the take-home message of the animal literature.

As it happened, I did find a maternal bias that could be manipulated with pup hormonal condition and, eventually, consequences for sexual development that could not be attributed to direct effects of hormones on the developing pups (Moore & Morelli, 1979; Moore, 1992). Predictably perhaps, my interest in the developmental questions was quickly emancipated from its reactive beginnings and took on a life of its own. The brief detour on the way to my birds expanded into a project that could fill the comparative developmental framework that I had assimilated through my early research experience. It grew to include studies meant to relate development to evolution and function as well as studies to explore the mechanisms and processes underlying sexual development.

Throughout all this experimentation, up until 1987 or 1988, I saw myself as working on the development of sex differences or sexual differentiation, terms that I used just as interchangeably as others in the field. Then, as I was pulling together some material for a talk, I suddenly realized that I didn't care about the difference between males and females: what I cared about was the behavior. This was true both for evolutionary function and for development. It mattered, for example, whether a male was good at removing the sperm plugs of his competitor. Whether his sister was also good at this, or completely incapable of it, was entirely beside the point. It mattered to find out how the developmental mechanisms worked, whether or not they worked the same way in males and females. Of course, I had been working on these functional and developmental questions all along, even though I had muddled sex differences and sexual development during my reflections on the work.

☐ Differences, Development, and Systems

Developmental scientists are a variable lot who differ on many theoretical dimensions, but perhaps the sharpest conceptual distinction is between those who focus on individual differences in outcome and those who focus on processes that lead up to the outcome: development to versus development from. Those who focus on individual differences will seek to isolate and identify originating factors and will feel their work is done when the difference that made a difference is found. Those who seek to unravel developmental processes will take note of the difference-making factor, but will see it as one among many threads.

I knew which of these types I thought I was—or wanted to be—and began to think my way through the sex divergence/sex development conflation that had gone on in my head as in the field at large. I found a little book by Bull (1983) on sex-determining mechanisms very helpful. He was very careful to distinguish *sex determination* from *sex development*. A sex-determining mechanism is one that determines whether an individual will be male or female: it "refers to the earliest elements in ontogeny common to one sex that distinguishes it from the other sex, including environmental and genetic effects acting in parents or zygotes that differentially influence the probability of producing or becoming male/female" (p. 8). He went on to underscore the distinction with sex development (or its synonym, sex differentiation): "Sex development refers collectively to the various molecular, genetic, and physiological processes that produce a male or a female from a zygote of a given genotype and parents in a given environment" (p. 8). Sex determination is the difference that makes a difference; sex development is the process. Knowing how one works gives you no clue about the other.

Of the many wildly varied sex determining mechanisms Bull describes, the mechanism used by map turtles has become my example of choice. There are no genetic differences between males and females. A zygote will become a male if it develops in sand kept cool by the shade of plants and a female if it develops in warm, unshaded sand. Few would feel that sexual development had been explained by saying that the sand did it. So it is—or should be—with sex differences in exposure to early hormones: this very likely will turn out to be the difference that made the difference if indeed sex differences in phenotype are found, but the hormone exposure is just the "earliest element in ontogeny common to one sex that distinguishes it from the other" (Bull, 1983, p. 8).

I knew this all along, but not with clarity and consistency. The work I did for my chapter in Dewsbury's *Contemporary Issues in Comparative Psychology* (1990) was my effort to achieve this clarity. "Identification of a sex-determining factor does little to explain the development of sexual function, because it specifies only what initially tips the course of development into somewhat different directions for males and females. A developmental analysis would explain how an organism progresses from early stages with neither male nor female sexual capacity to later stages of sexual competence. This is the process of *sexual differentiation*" (Moore, 1990, p. 280, emphasis in original). "The sex differences that arise during the course of sexual differentiation are often secondary to the development of masculine or feminine sexual function. . . . I will use *differentia-*

tion to refer to the development of sexual function, in a sense parallel to that used to refer to the development of vision or ingestion, with no necessary implication of differences between the sexes" (Moore, 1990, p. 281). I have attempted to be consistent in separating the question of divergence from that of development in my subsequent work (e.g., Moore, 1995).

By removing any focus on the individual (sex) difference question, I could concentrate on sorting out the many ways in which hormones and experience become interwoven during the long process of sexual development in rats. I introduced three concepts to describe how I saw this process: levels of organization; cascading effects of hormones, where changes at one stage set in motion internal and external events that shape the next; and webs, where heterogeneous internal and external elements that have nothing in common on functional or formal criteria are joined to become the mechanisms that underlie sexual behavior (Moore, 1990). In these concepts, for they are not original, it is easy to see the tracks of ring doves and their reproductive cycles and quite a lot of other work that has come to characterize modern developmental psychobiology (Michel & Moore, 1995).

☐ Individual Differences as Tools for Exploring Development

I have been critical of starting a developmental analysis by focusing on individual differences in outcomes. This approach can lead to simplistic notions of development causation, with phenotypes explained by genes for them, and cognitive achievements explained by hypostatized devices for them. In the microcosm of my research area, it can puff undue importance into sex differences that may be nothing more than meaningless secondary effects. But individual differences, perhaps especially sex differences, can be useful as tools for digging into developmental process.

Naturally occurring, "instinctive" behavior is often defined these days as behavior that develops without obvious experience, which means without instruction, example, or practice. How can one even make a start with the nonobvious? One approach is to change criteria for what makes an obvious candidate to test in a developmental experiment. There are two related attitudes that have been used very effectively by many developmental psychobiologists to generate such studies (Michel & Moore, 1995). One is to adopt the mind-set of a naturalist and explore what is there in the organism's world; another is to think in terms of antecedents, the raw materials out of which new capacities might be built, rather than in terms of the final state.

The maternal environment is most of a young rat's natural world, as it is for mammals generally, so I have found that an obvious place to start. And, since I want to understand the development of masculine sexual behavior, for which there are some sex differences in outcome, I have found it useful to look for sex differences in steps along the way. This has revealed many aspects of the organism and its surround that might serve as raw materials for sexual development, including pup odor, maternal stimulation of the perineal region, and the size of peripheral nerves that carry afferent input from this region (Moore, 1992, 1995; Gans, White, & Moore, 1996). The observed sex differences point the way to developmental experiments, through which pieces of the puzzle can begin to be assembled. Once a start is made with this strategy, other factors that may not be different for the two sexes will be suggested for test. Maternal odor is one such obvious candidate, even though it is there equally for males and females.

So I now think of sex differences primarily as tools for exploring development. During the past thirty years, I have gone from thinking of sex differences as the object of study, to a muddled state in which I seemed to be studying sex differences and sexual development in parallel, to a distinction between studying divergence and development and, finally, to thinking of sex differences as tools for the study of development.

☐ Concluding Comments

Conceptual development, like other development, is growth from one stage to another achieved through organism-environment interaction. I have attempted to trace my conception of development beginning with gains during early research experiences in graduate school. These concepts, now incorporated into my thinking, were used to act on a new research domain. They shaped how I approached that task so that I saw the field differently from those who came from different origins. But what was in the field had an effect on me as well. Prevailing conceptions of sex differences and sexual differentiation shaped my thinking, initially through reaction and then through partial incorporation. My most recent conception of sexual development is a reformulation based in part on an effort to reconcile what I came to see as an inconsistency in my conceptions of individual differences and individual development.

Development is a process of building from what is available, including functionally unrelated materials. Even in the intentional world of human thought, there are unplanned and unexpected factors that enter into the picture. I've included a few biographical details to identify some of the contingent factors that have played a critical role in my conceptual development.

The mind is a messy thing, and I'm sure this reconstruction of my own mental development is more orderly than reality. There were many other things on my mind during the past three decades than what I have written about here. Some things I've left out to make a manageable narrative; others I've left out because I don't know what they are.

It is an exciting time to be working in the developmental sciences: genetics and evolution have both undergone recent revolutionary change by the inclusion of developmental concepts; much of the astonishing growth of neuroscience has been focused on development; and developmental psychobiology has put the organism, with its multiple levels and surrounding environment, back into the center of behavioral study. There is much more to come. Even though I have been asked to reflect on my own conceptions in this essay, I have come away with a very clear understanding that the study of development is a huge community enterprise that spans generations and many disciplines. Its concepts and its theories build from what came before, perhaps forming something a little new, perhaps honing the old for new tasks. As in evolution and organismic development, there will be, from time to time, with a little luck, an emergent leap.

☐ References

Arnold, A. P., & Breedlove, S. M. (1985). Organizational and activational effects of sex steroids on brain and behavior: A reanalysis. *Hormones and Behavior, 19,* 469–498.

Bateson, P. P. G. (1966). The characteristics and context of imprinting. *Biological Reviews, 41,* 177–220.

Beach, F. A. (1971). Hormonal factors controlling the differentiation, development, and display of copulatory behavior in the ramstergig and related species. In E. Tobach, L. R. Aronson, & E. Shaw (Eds.), *The biopsychology of development* (pp. 249–296). New York: Academic Press.

Beach, F. A., & Levinson, G. (1950). Effects of androgen on the glans penis and mating behavior of castrated male rats. *Journal of Experimental Zoology, 114,* 159–171.

Beer, C. B. (1963). Incubation and nest-building behaviour of black-headed gulls. IV. Nest-building in the incubation and laying periods. *Behaviour, 21,* 155–176.

Beyer, C., & Feder, H. H. (1987). Sex steroids and afferent input: Their roles in brain sexual differentiation. *Annual Review of Physiology, 49,* 349–364.

Breedlove, S. M. (1992). Sexual dimorphism in the vertebrate nervous system. *Journal of Neuroscience, 12,* 4133–4142.

Bull, J. J. (1983). *Evolution of sex determining mechanisms.* Menlo Park, CA: Benjamin/Cummings.

Cheng, M.-F. (1979). Progress and prospect in ring dove research: A personal view. In J. S. Rosenblatt, R. A. Hinde, C. G. Beer, & M.-C. Busnel (Eds.), *Advances in the study of behavior* (vol. 9, pp. 97–129). New York: Academic Press.

Dinnerstein, D. (1977). *The mermaid and the minotaur.* New York: Harper Colophon.

Döhler, K.-D. (1978). Is female sexual differentiation hormone-mediated? *Trends in Neuroscience, 1,* 138–140.

Gans, S. E., White, R. H., & Moore, C. L. (1996, November). *Testosterone reverses sex differences in the sensory pudendal nerve.* Paper presented at meeting of International Society for Developmental Psychobiology, Georgetown, DC.

Gerall, A. A. (1966). Hormonal factors influencing masculine behavior of female guinea pigs. *Journal of Comparative and Physiological Psychology, 62,* 365–369.

Goy, R. W. (1970). Experimental control of psychosexuality. *Philosophical Transactions of the Royal Society of London B., 259,* 149–162.

Goy, R. W., & McEwen, B. S. (1980). *Sexual differentiation of the brain.* Cambridge, MA: MIT Press.

Hailman, J. P. (1967). The ontogeny of an instinct. *Behaviour,* Supplement XV. Leiden, Netherlands: E. J. Brill.

Hansen, E. W. (1966). Squab-induced crop growth in ring dove foster parents. *Journal of Comparative and Physiological Psychology, 62,* 120–122.

Hinde, R. A. (1959). Unitary drives. *Animal Behaviour, 7,* 130–141.

Hinde, R. A. (1965). Interaction of internal and external factors in integration of canary reproduction. In F. A. Beach (Ed.), *Sex and behavior* (pp. 381–415). New York: Wiley.

Hinde, R. A. (1966). *Animal behaviour: A synthesis of ethology and comparative psychology.* New York: McGraw-Hill.

Hutt, C. (1972). *Males and females.* Middlesex, UK: Penguin.

Lehrman, D. S. (1953). A critique of Konrad Lorenz's theory of instinctive behavior. *Quarterly Review of Biology, 28,* 337–363.

Lehrman, D. S. (1955). The physiological basis of parental feeding behavior in the ring dove (*Streptopelia risoria*). *Behaviour, 7,* 241–286.

Lehrman, D. S. (1965). Interaction between internal and external environments in the regulation of the reproductive cycle of the ring dove. In F. A. Beach (Ed.), *Sex and behavior* (pp. 355–380). New York: Wiley.

Lehrman, D. S. (1970). Semantic and conceptual issues in the nature-nurture problem. In L. R. Aronson, E. Tobach, D. S. Lehrman, & J. S. Rosenblatt (Eds.), *Development and evolution of behavior: Essays in memory of T. C. Schneirla* (pp. 17–52). San Francisco: Freeman.

Lehreman, D. S., & Wortis, R. P. (1960). Previous breeding experience and hormone-induced incubation behavior in the ring dove. *Science, 132,* 1667–1668.

Lehrman, D. S., Wortis, R. P., & Brody, P. (1961). Gonadotrophin secretion in response to external stimuli of varying duration in the ring dove (*Streptopelia risoria*). *Proceedings of the Society for Experimental Biology and Medicine, 106,* 298–300.

Lonstein, J. S., & De Vries, G. J. (1999). Sex differences in the parental behaviour of adult virgin prairie voles: Independence from gonadal hormones and vasopressin. *Journal of Neuroendocrinolgy, 11,* 441–449.

Lorenz, K. (1957). The conception of instinctive behavior. In C. H. Schiller (Ed. and Trans.), *Instinctive behavior* (pp. 129–175). New York: International Universities Press. (Originally published 1937.)

Lorenz, K. (1965). *Evolution and modification of behavior.* Chicago: University of Chicago Press.

Michel, G. F., & Moore, C. L. (1978). *Biological perspectives in developmental psychology.* Monterey, CA: Brooks/Cole.

Michel, G. F., & Moore, C. L. (1986). Contributions of reproductive experience to observation-maintained crop growth and incubation in male and female ring doves. *Animal Behaviour, 34,* 790–796.

Michel, G. F., & Moore, C. L. (1995). *Developmental psychobiology: An interdisciplinary science.* Cambridge: MIT Press.

Money, J., & Ehrhardt, A. A. (1968). *Man and woman, boy and girl.* Baltimore, MD: Johns Hopkins University Press.

Moore, C. L. (1975). Nest repair in laughing gulls. *The Wilson Bulletin, 87,* 271–274.

Moore, C. L. (1976a). Experiential and hormonal determinants affect squab-egg choice in ring doves (*Streptopelia risoria*). *Journal of Comparative and Physiological Psychology, 90,* 583–589.

Moore, C. L. (1976b). The transition from sitting on eggs to sitting on young in ring doves, Streptopelia risoria: Squab-egg references during the normal cycle. *Animal Behaviour, 24,* 136–145.

Moore, C. L. (1985). Another psychobiological view of sexual differentiation. *Developmental Review, 5,* 18–55.

Moore, C. L. (1990) Comparative development of vertebrate sexual behavior: Levels, cascades, and webs. In D. A. Dewsbury (Ed.), *Contemporary issues in comparative psychology* (pp. 278–299). Sunderland, MA: Sinauer.

Moore, C. L. (1992). Effects of maternal stimulation on the development of sexual behavior and its neural basis. In G. Turkewitz (Ed.), *Developmental psychobiology. Annals of the New York Academy of Sciences* (vol. 662, 160–177).

Moore, C. L. (1995) Maternal contributions to mammalian reproductive development and the divergence of males and females. In P. J. B. Slater, J. S. Rosenblatt, C. T. Snowdon, & M. Milinski (Eds.), *Advances in the study of behavior* (vol. 24, 47–118). New York: Academic Press.

Moore, C. L., Dou, H., & Juraska, J. M. (1992) Maternal stimulation affects the number of motor neurons in a sexually dimorphic nucleus of the lumbar spinal cord. *Brain Research, 572,* 52–56.

Moore, C. L., & Morelli, G. A. (1979). Mother rats interact differently with male and female offspring. *Journal of Comparative and Physiological Psychology, 93,* 677–684.

Phoenix, C. H., Goy, R. W., Gerall, A. A., & Young, W. C. (1959). Organizing action of prenatally administered testosterone propionate on the tissues mediating mating behavior in the female guinea pig. *Endocrinology, 65,* 369–382.

Raisman, G., and Field, P. M. (1971). Sexual dimorphism in the preoptic area of the rat. *Science (Washington, D.C.), 173,* 731–733.

Rosenblatt, J. S. (1967). Socio-environmental factors affecting reproduction and offspring in infrahuman mammals. In S. A. Richardson & A. F. Guttmacher (Eds.), *Childbearing—Its social and psychological aspects* (pp. 245–301). Baltimore: Williams & Wilkins.

Rosenblatt, J. S., & Aronson, L. R. (1958). The influence of experience on the behavioral effects of androgen in prepuberally castrated male cats. *Animal Behaviour, 6,* 171–182.

Rosenblatt, J. S., & Siegel, H. I. (1981). Factors governing the onset and maintenance of maternal behavior among nonprimate mammals: The role of hormonal and nonhormonal factors. In D. J. Gubernick & P. H. Klopfer (Eds.), *Parental care mammals* (pp. 13–76). New York: Plenum.

Schneirla, T. C. (1956). Interrelationships of the "innate" and the "acquired" in instinctive behavior. In P.-G. Grassé (Ed.), *L'Instinct dans le comportement des animaux et de l'homme* (pp. 387–452). Paris: Masson and Cie.

Schneirla, T. C. (1957). The concept of development in comparative psychology. In D. B. Harris (Ed.), *The concept of development* (pp. 78–108). Minneapolis: University of Minnesota Press.

Tobet, S. A., & Fox, T. O. (1992). Sex differences in neuronal morphology influenced hormonally throughout life. In A. A. Gerall, H. Moltz, & I. L. Ward (Eds.), *Handbook of behavioral neurobiology. Vol. 11: Sexual differentiation* (pp. 41–83). New York: Plenum.

Yahr, P. (1988). Sexual differentiation of behavior in the context of developmental psychobiology. In E. M. Blass (Ed.), *Handbook of behavioral neurobiology. Vol. 9: Developmental psychobiology and behavioral ecology* (pp. 197–243). New York: Plenum.

Meredith J. West
Andrew P. King

The Ontogeny of Competence

ABF Notes, Morrill Hall, Cornell, August 1968. New graduate students waiting for first teaching assignment. Practically first sentence of APK to MJW, "What is your theory of learning?" MJW thought it an odd opening; APK did not.

☐ Prologue: Animal Behavior Farm: Mission and Lifestyle

At a recent national meeting, after a paper session on the development of mate choice, someone stopped MJW and asked about her "feminist political agenda." MJW asked for clarification, not aware of having so grand a thing as an agenda. The questioner said, "Well, it's just you keep asking the speakers what the animals were doing, what they could see or hear . . . you know . . . little stuff, stuff not related to mate choice." The questioner had done a good job of characterizing the behavior she had seen, but did not have enough information to understand the underlying reason for MJW's curiosity, the "agenda" as it were. Although we are interested in the big question of the process of development, we are also truly fascinated by the particulars of developmental systems. For us, development is in the details. As a result, we tend to ask concrete questions of others and ourselves. Examples of such questions include the diet of study animals, the specifics of their housing, how often animals are observed, and most importantly, what animals do when humans say the animals are "choosing" or "preferring" or "interacting." In this chapter, we discuss our approach to the study of development. The specific domain for our work has been birdsong. The study of birdsong is often touted as a model system for the study of learning, maturation, and experience. While we do not dispute this general view, we will argue that the study of song learning has much more to offer by considering development in context, development as it occurs in the everyday life of organisms.

The editors asked the contributors to this book to frame their scientific journeys in terms of their own life history and development. We puzzled about how to capture our journey. The strategy we chose, as introduced above, was to include brief notes about life in our laboratory over the years as we chronicle the course of our research. These notes were chosen because they capture or caricature distinctive features of our approach. We hope they shed a more personal light on our scientific style. The accuracy of the memories is about p < .10.

The chapter contains four sections. First, we outline the theoretical context present when we began our work. Second, we show how our ideas evolved as we studied brown-headed cowbirds. Third, we describe the new approaches we are using to study of the pragmatics of song learning. Finally, we discuss some of the implications of this new knowledge for the general study of development and, in particular, the need to shift from an individual to a social perspective about developmental processes.

☐ Cultivating Behavior Down on the Farm

ABF notes, Liddell Farm, August 1973. Students just returned from 72-hr vigil in barn, had been camping out for days to see what happens to baby cowbird when foster mom sees it is a cowbird . . . hot and humid in the barn amidst cows, pigs, chickens, mosquitoes, and so on. Finally, the object of interest appeared . . . baby cowbird emerged on rafter, fluttered, flapped, and floated right into the mouth of a pig. . . . Students return hot, dirty, heart-broken; pig pretty chipper.

Our students call our lab "the farm." We are not sure who started this practice but we like it. In the Midwest, farmers grow corn, wheat, or beans. We grow behavior. We create circumstances allowing us to see young birds living in different social settings. For example, some birds may live with adult conspecifics, others only with other juveniles. These social arrangements produce what can loosely be called behavioral strains. We then evaluate the strains in different ways to assess the behavioral yield of the particular social conditions (West & King, 1994). As in all farming, we have had good years, not-so-good years, and never-in-a-million-years years.

We did not realize we were becoming farmers until it was probably ridiculously obvious to everyone else. There certainly were many clues.

For the past twenty-five years, we had lived and worked in laboratories only steps away from where we lived. We began in a rental house, which we outfitted with large birdcages in the garage and sound-attenuating chambers in the living room. Did we mention there were baby birds at our wedding? At the present, our laboratory is located on 90 acres of old field and forest edge. It consists of several lab buildings, nine outdoor-indoor aviaries, and two homes—one for us, and one for students, postdocs, and two parrots left scholarships by their now deceased Indiana University alumnus.

While we may not ourselves have hit on the analogy to farmers with respect to our research, we knew from the start that we wanted to study animals in social settings, that is, settings containing fundamental parts of the natural environment. We also knew we wanted to watch the growth of behavior as it was occurring. We had entered psychology at a time when watching animals was not a high priority. With some outstanding exceptions, coming primarily from the "Rutgers or American Museum of Natural History" group (Lehrman, 1970), description was not as high a priority. Inattention to descriptive work seems ironic in that research on early experience was thriving. But it was the outcome, not the process, of early experience that was valued; observing and documenting the "experience of early experience" was not so valued.

At the same time frame, the shadow of Harry Harlow and colleagues eclipsed interest in normal development (Harlow & Harlow, 1962; Harlow, Harlow, & Hansen, 1963). The dark side of development—what happens to animals when raised in impoverished conditions—was the dominant paradigm. We were not interested, however, in what happened to animals living a life no member of their species had ever encountered. Perhaps such conditions were useful to create eye-catching models of psychopathology, but we wanted examples of normal ontogeny. We wanted to study animals as they developed the necessary skills for survival, a positive ontogenetic perspective, emphasizing "learning what comes naturally" (Kaufman, 1975).

We began our work in the pre–Gary Larson cartoon era, a time when scientists perhaps found it easier to maintain the illusion that they were in charge of a lab animal's experiences (Larson, 1984). Few worried about how animals perceived the experimental task (but see Breland & Breland, 1961). We had had a memorable lesson on the topic of animal/experimenter discrepancies in perspectives early on. It came during a brief stint observing ongoing studies of learned helplessness in dogs. The dogs lived in kennels a few rooms away from the testing room in which they were exposed to inescapable or escapable shock. The dogs provided no way to predict shock appeared to give up. They did not attempt to escape to the safety of the other side of the apparatus. These studies, and many more to come, contributed to a heuristic model of human depression, focusing on the emotional consequences for people of undergoing experiences they can not control (Seligman, 1968, 1975).

But, when not inside the testing room, some of the dogs seemed far from helpless or depressed: some resisted being taken out of their cage, while the others walked toward the testing room with tails wagging. But, once near the testing room, their behavior changed. Anyone who has observed dogs at the vet has seen examples of such transitions: happy dogs frown and strong dogs whimper. Returning to the behavior of the dogs in the lab, our question was, when did the experiment begin and end from the animal's point of view? We do not dispute that the different testing conditions had vastly different experimental outcomes, but we wonder if enough appreciation was being given to comparing behavior inside and outside of the testing room. The memories of these dogs have remained with us over the years as a lesson in evaluating tasks from the animal's and experimenter's perspective. More than once, we have found that the tables had been turned on us.

Thus, to summarize, we wanted to study development in a system in which the animals' behavior was visible and amenable to thorough description; we wanted the object of development to be a skill with ecological relevance; and we wanted to be able to follow development over time. The behavior we chose was the ontogeny of birdsong. To set the stage, we first discuss the theoretical zeitgeist regarding birdsong circa 1970 and then how brown-headed cowbirds (*Molothrus ater*) became the focus of our inquiries. In reality, the interests in song learning and cowbirds co-occurred, but we will start with the theory.

☐ Birdsong: The Model Behavior

ABF notes, 1972, Liddell Farm. Cowbird egg # 62 hatches, . . . the nestling thrives, first one to do so in 62 tries! Turns out to be a female . . . APK/MJW perplexed . . . what to do with a female who cannot sing?

If birdsong had not existed, Niko Tinbergen would have invented it (Tinbergen, 1963). Birdsong is the perfect example of his definition of integrative study, requiring attention to cause, function, development, and evolution of behavior. With respect to one of these topics—development—Colin Beer captured the way to categorize early approaches to the study of song ontogeny. He stated that "what developmental study [of song] looks for depends on what is thought to be there to find, which depends on how the social communication system is viewed in its syntactic, semantic, and pragmatic aspects" (Beer, 1982, p. 300).

With respect to this study of birdsong in the 1970s, the search for syntax ruled. Researchers such as Thorpe and Marler had established that song structure (a less anthropomorphic term than syntax) was learned in songbirds (Marler, 1970a, 1970b; Thorpe, 1958). Songbird species also showed remarkable continuity from generation to generation in the reliable transmission of song structure. Thus, the fact of learning or plasticity as part of "what was there to find" was not an issue. But, from our point of view, those studying birdsong did not seem comfortable with the idea of plasticity in models of birdsong. The fact of learning was, in some sense, a problem to which a solution had to be found. Concern stemmed from the dangerous side of learning: that is, what mechanisms keep birds from learning the wrong thing (Kroodsma, 1982)?

The ethologists' fears were, in part, an understandable reaction to behaviorism's quite grandiose claims that animals could learn all sorts of strange things by means of conditioning. But the concern also related to the foundations of ethology, that is, the belief that behavioral traits of animals are reliable enough to be used in taxonomic decisions. Although most of us associate ethology with a "back-to-nature" philosophy, questions about phylogeny and the classification of species by ancestry represent its most important contribution (Lorenz, 1970). Until ethology, and even after, the classifying and reclassifying of species relied solely on the identification of morphological characters such as the shape of a bird's beak. For an ethological trait, that is, a behavior, to be taken seriously, its reliable transmission from one generation to the other had to be established. With respect to song, mechanisms were needed to explain how developmental programs fostered stable transmission by restricting learning to the "right" song for the "right" species. Such a view favored innate explanations of transmission, that is, developmental programs closed to learning. How else to guarantee accurate transmission? Or, if song learning was not entirely closed, as appeared to be the case for song, what mechanisms were there to modulate exposure to social or vocal influence?

The question of limits on learning overlapped with interest in the concept of critical or sensitive periods. The idea of critical periods suggested fail-safe mechanisms or safety nets to protect young learners from the vagaries of the environment by controlling the timing of vulnerability to environmental influence. The question of protected learning for songbirds was of evolutionary consequence. The adaptive risk, for example, was that sparrows of one subspecies would copy and retain songs of a second subspecies. Such copying could then affect mate selection and thus potentially affect speciation (Marler, 1960).

The search for guided learning was also motivated by a different view of the construct of learning itself: was it a meta- or subcategory of behavior? In the hands of psychologists, learning was accepted as a superordinate category, a tool of general use in many behavioral domains. Ethologists, on the other hand, preferred to think of learning as simply another type of adaptation such as nest building. In the words of James Gould (1982):

> Animals are perhaps in some sense molded and shaped by their environments and experiences, but within a set of complex, species-specific rules that do not at all fit the model that classical behaviorists maintained. Learning . . . is one of the standard, off-the-shelf programming tricks available to evolution and despite the usual dichotomy; this kind of learning is the epitome of instinct (p. 275).

Thus, song learning was considered domain-specific plasticity. That view was also apparent when looking at how song learning was studied in the laboratory. If it can be said that life imitates art, methods must imitate theory. The general method involved housing young birds under conditions of controlled exposure to species-typical stimulation. The kinds of experimental conditions used to study songbirds in the 1970s emphasized physical compartmentalization and the isolation of nature and nurture. The goal was to reveal the developmental "blueprint" for vocal ontogeny, the syntax or acoustic structure present in the absence of exposure to conspecifics. In general, these studies confirmed that songbirds housed with no exposure to conspecifics, that is, isolate birds, did not develop typical song structure (matters of semantics and pragmatics were, as noted earlier, typically not addressed). The songs of isolates generally bore a resemblance to the species' song(s), but lacked important details. The songs of isolates were thus considered to represent the innate blueprint for song upon which experience would build (Marler, Mundinger, Waser, & Lutjen, 1972; Thorpe, 1961).

☐ Windows for Development Analyses

ABF notes, 1984, North Carolina home. Five-year-old son of APK/MJW is stunned to learn that he does not have 23-year-old brother . . . Try to explain to him that student he sees each day in kitchen, bathroom, and outdoors is not sibling but academic offspring . . . question of adoption raised.

We began studies of song learning against this developmentally conservative backdrop: plasticity was dangerous. We chose from the start to tinker with basic methods. We did not want to raise young birds alone, but instead with social companions. Moreover, we wanted to study syntax, semantics, and pragmatics concurrently. These goals stemmed from a positive view of learning and an open, or liberal, view of developmental processes. Harlow's research and much of the research on early experience seemed off-center to us, as they focused so much on negative outcomes. Our positive thinking came about in large part from immersion in ecological/Gibsonian psychology (Gibson, 1969; Gibson, 1966). We saw ourselves as part of a "performatory" school of thought about development, learning, and perception. To understand how animals develop, we had to measure what James J. Gibson had called "performatory" feedback, that is, multimodal feedback obtained by acting or behaving in an environment rich in potential information. Thus, for us to understand ontogenetic mechanisms of perception and learning required that we create constructive developmental contexts. We needed to see animals in action, animals with behavioral options in environments with something to offer.

In looking at our own thinking at the time, perhaps the single most important difference in our view of development, compared to others studying song, was that we did not believe there was a neutral zone or holding pattern for developmental systems. Moreover, we did not accept that experience was passively delivered to young organisms, as emphasized in Gould's statement cited earlier. Thus, animals in isolation were still in environments and they could shape such environments and obtain feedback. These environments represented biased living conditions (sensu E. J. Gibson, 1969). Our job was to find out how the bias affected the process and outcome of development.

Our first attempts to design new contexts now seem awfully timid. First, we chose simply to use larger cages so those animals could be housed socially and so that we could see them. Later, we used enclosures that eventually outgrew the size of most labs, culminating in the construction of indoor-outdoor aviaries. These housing changes intersected with laboratory procedures, as we needed to find ways to measure what animals actually do with one another. If one were to look at the major change in the style of our research over the years, that is, kinds of treatments, kinds of questions, the trend would be toward more detailed social analyses carried out in socially more complex settings (West & King, 1994).

☐ The Cowbird: An Unlikely but Timely Choice

ABF Notes, 1973, kitchen, Freeville, NY. APK/MJW eating dinner with birdcage on table housing 15-day-old baby cowbird and 30-day-old cardinal. We beg for a 15-minute break to eat our dinner. Cowbird objects, cheeping at rate of 10 chips/msec at 90 dB. Finally, cardinal takes control . . . finds a stray piece of burlap and shoves it down cowbird's throat.

We have saved our inadvertently most brilliant move to the last, our choice of cowbirds (*M. ater*). We did not know at the time that the species would thrive in the laboratory or be exceptionally tolerant of inquisitive humans. We also did not know how important female cowbirds, who do not sing, would be to our story. We had had the cowbird urged upon us, in some sense, by the writings and words of Lehrman. He pointed out that a brood parasite like the cowbird should have a very different developmental program to handle early experience than should a nonparasitic species like its near relative, the red-winged blackbird (*Agelaius phoenecius*) (Lehrman, 1974). Brown-headed cowbirds do not raise their own young—the female lays her eggs in the nest of many other songbird species (Friedmann, 1929). How then do young cowbirds get to know other cowbirds and how do they avoid misdirected learning? Why doesn't a cowbird raised by a vireo sound like a vireo or try to mate with vireos?

In our exuberant state, we charted a course to study all seven species of cowbirds, from those in North America to those in South America. Not all cowbird species display brood parasitism, with the southernmost cowbird in Argentina, the bay-winged cowbird, being completely nonparasitic. We would trace how dependence on early experience changed as reliance on brood parasitism changed. As of this writing, we are still engrossed with the North American species and still puzzling about developmental contexts applicable to it. We could never have anticipated the ontogenetic riches we were about to uncover. The beginnings of our interest in the species were also auspicious. Cowbirds were no farther away than our front walk. We still use slides today that came from photographing our "first" cowbirds on our sidewalk in 1971.

When Lehrman drew attention to the cowbird, little was known about its development. In the next decade, we would learn that the cowbird's song ontogeny is exceptional, but not in ways that anyone had predicted (West, King, & Eastzer, 1981a). There is plasticity at individual and populational levels, there is sensitivity to social context, and there are really three interrelated stories—one for males, one for females, and one for the natural unit of the social group.

In our initial work, we used a modified version of acoustic deprivation to look at song development. We found that when acoustically naive male cowbirds were housed socially with nonsinging females or members of other species but deprived of hearing adult song, they, like all passerines studied to date, produced atypical vocalizations. This finding was at the time somewhat surprising, as cowbirds had been expected to manifest an entirely closed program for development to avoid learning the songs of their foster parents (Mayr, 1963, 1974). Acoustically naive females, on the other hand, appeared to respond exclusively to conspecific song with no prior experience.

But, even more surprising than the male's plasticity, however, was the finding that naive females responded more to playbacks of the songs of naive, as opposed to wild, male cowbirds. To test the functional properties of songs, we had played back songs to females living in sound chambers with other females but no males. Females responded with twice as many copulatory postures to the songs of isolates compared with those of normally reared males (King & West, 1977; King, West, & Eastzer, 1980; West & King, 1980).

We now have many new thoughts about the meaning of that first study (see West & King, 2001). But, as a way to bootstrap a research program, there was no better way to start. First, we had discovered an important new assay, testing of song function by playback to females. No longer did we have to rely only on sonograms of song structure, pictures that sometimes were misleading, as human eyes could not discern what avian ears found most stimulating. We also had an anomaly, a Kuhnian gift to motivate our work. Why would the songs of isolated males be better than those of wild males? We reasoned that the naive songs might have been more arousing because the males had been denied access to adult males whose influence might have suppressed the song's potency. Cowbird song is sung not only to females during mating, but also to males during mate competition, an experience that we now know changes song content.

The seemingly superior function of isolate song was also puzzling, as cowbirds are not acoustically deprived during song development but live in large flocks. What then did these data say about the effects of isolation from adult males on cowbirds? Briefly, the data told us although the young males lacked an adult model, they had been given a captive and noncompetitive audience in the form of females or nonconspecific companions. Isolation had conferred on males by default the status of a dominant male. And like dominant males in a normal group, they could sing songs highly attractive to the female with less risk of attack by other males. When we allowed adult males to spend winter with only females, we found the same effect: the experience improved the perceptual potency of their songs on playback females.

Another set of studies clarified further the nature of the "experience" of isolation, namely, that its most obvious facet, lack of auditory exposure, was not responsible for the functional outcome obtained, songs attractive to females. We maintained males in a common auditory environment but exposed them to different social experiences: some males lived in a group of males and females; others lived with only females but could see the group; and others lived with females with only auditory access to the other birds. The results replicated those of the first study: the birds in visual isolation from other males but housed with females developed highly effective songs, whereas the males in a group or the males witnessing the group's interactions sang less effective songs (West & King, 1980). Cowbird song was thus highly dependent on a male's perception of the *social* consequences of singing. And that was indeed what isolation had biased, the performatory consequences of singing.

☐ Expanding the Developmental Range

ABF Notes, Summer 1982, South Aviary. Have spent winter tutoring male cowbirds to sing local North Carolina song and foreign Texas cowbird song . . . Males became bilingual, a first, we think . . . now will test what NC and TX females think. Check aviary one day and find no birds but one very robust black snake . . . only bilingual cowbirds in the cosmos now in his gut. By next day, he digests our efforts and returns leg bands.

We next considered the idea that deprivation revealed the "innate" or "inherited" components of song production, as discussed earlier. Examination of the acoustic structure of isolate songs revealed that they contained "generic" structures for cowbird song, a cowbird-biased alphabet soup. The mix perhaps partly reflected the design of males' vocal morphology and syrinx and also sound preferences, perhaps acquired in flocks with adults and juveniles when they were quite young (King & West, 1988). Some isolates managed by chance to string together effective combinations, others quite strange ones. To learn more about the building blocks and building process for cowbird song, we expanded our studies to new geographic populations. The ones of most interest here were birds from North Carolina (NC) and Texas (TX).

Comparisons of these populations uncovered more male plasticity and little female plasticity. NC females responded most to NC songs, TX females to TX songs. But we found that juvenile NC males became bilingual (singing clear renditions of both NC and TX variants) when exposed to adult TX males (West, King, & Harrocks, 1983). In contrast, adult NC males did not learn TX song when housed only with TX males, but they did do so when housed with TX males *and* females (West & King, 1985).

Maybe the handwriting had been on the wall since our first study in which we used females as companions for some of the males . . . maybe females affect song content? We tested this proposition directly by investigating the female's influence on naive juvenile males. Thus, hand-reared, acoustically naive NC males were housed in acoustic isolation from other males but maintained in one of three conditions: individual housing with other species; with NC females; or with TX females for their first fall, winter, and spring. The three groups of males developed significantly different vocal phenotypes, although none had ever heard cowbird song and all presumably had the same templates. Analysis of their first-year songs revealed that males housed with other species showed intermediate performance on acoustic and geographic measures of song content, while NC males housed with NC females sang no TX song, and NC males with TX females included TX-specific song structures. Moreover, the two groups of males with females show non-overlapping distributions on critical acoustic measures (King & West, 1983). However the females effected this change, they did not do it by singing. And however the males learned, it was not accomplished by imitation, the only mechanism proposed to explain birdsong learning.

We were also led to consider the role of females from other studies using naive males whose social experiences were supplemented by hearing tutor tapes of normal male songs. When tutored with local songs, NC males housed with canaries copied significantly more of the tutor songs than did males individually housed with NC females (West & King, 1986). Thus, although all the males had access to the same "innate" program and the same tutoring regime, their repertoires differed reliably by group from very early in development. Furthermore, although the males with NC females learned the tutored copies, as did the males with canaries, they subsequently went on to improvise and change the material enough so that the original songs were no longer easily matched. The males with canaries did not deviate from the tutor songs. Thus again, female cowbirds appeared to provide a different learning environment than nonconspecifics.

☐ Measuring the Sounds of Silence

ABF Notes, March 1984. APK/MJW reviewing videotapes of female cowbirds being sung to by young male cowbirds . . . female has put on her psychoceramic makeup, no facial muscles moving. Then we see male levitate off perch and move toward her . . . we rewind tape to discover her moving her wing and covering it up with a wing stretch right before male had risen off the perch . . . male delirious . . . he has found chink in her armor . . . sings hundreds more songs in next hour.

We used several contexts to explore female influence. First, we studied a winter flock. Did juvenile males have access to females during the time of year that their songs undergo the most rapid and extensive changes? The answer was yes—juvenile males associated quite closely with females, much more closely in fact than with adult males (King & West, 1988). Juvenile males were captured with females in all eight banding sessions, yielding a higher ratio of juveniles to females than adult males to females. Thus, the access was there.

We also exploited a laboratory setting of males and females individually housed together in the same enclosure to videotape interactions between males and females during the time period when flocks begin to disperse and males and females return to prospective breeding grounds. We found that most of the time, well over 90 percent, females appeared to do very little when a song occurred; it was often hard to tell from her behavior that she had heard a song. The clue to what was happening between the male-female pairs came from watching the males: every once in a while, when a male sang, he would suddenly change the pace of his singing, as well as sometimes abruptly move toward the female. With videotape, we retraced the males' movements (West & King, 1988). We found that such changes in the males' behavior were preceded by wing actions by females—movements we called wing strokes; if a bird could point, a wing stroke would qualify. Wing strokes occurred infrequently. In general, males had to sing 100–200 songs between wing strokes. The data suggested to us that female cowbirds used a gestural signal system to communicate about an acoustic signal system: a visual system within a vocal system. Thus, the task confronting the young males was a multimodal one; they had to look as well as listen.

To find the functional value of wing strokes, we employed a playback test during the breeding season to see if females would adopt copulatory postures to songs that had elicited wing strokes as opposed to ones that had not. The answer was yes—wing stroke song elicited significantly more copulatory postures from a different set of females, who knew no more about the singer than his song (West & King, 1988). And thus, we concluded that wing stroking was a form of positive reinforcement, dispensed on a partial schedule, serving to shape the males singing toward more female-preferred signals.

Before turning to the studies of the 1990s, let us bring together what we had found thus far. Early in our development, we had rejected the idea that species-typical deprivation provided a baseline or blueprint for song. In cowbirds, naive males deprived of hearing adult males showed atypicalities in their song, but the origin of the difference could not be attributed solely to what was *not* there, but to social influences from what was there. Our data showed how important social effects were. Some have tried to dismiss or qualify our data as idiosyncratic because the data came from a species with a very different life history. To that charge, we countercharged that other species had not been studied as our cowbirds had been studied. What would happen in "traditional" species if the social context were rich but still uninformative about song structure? The results to date show that social context affects basic features of song ontogeny including the timing of sensitive periods and the kinds and quantity of songs copied from tutors (Baptista & Gaunt, 1994; Baptista & Patrinovich, 1984; Slater, 1989). Some of these effects have been subsumed under the name of "action-based" learning—recognition of the role of social reinforcement in the selective attention to species-typical stimulation and in the attrition of song material (Marler, 1991; Nelson & Marler, 1994).

During the 1980s, we had also carried out parallel studies, not described here, asking about the function of song for mating and the consequences of learning neophenotypic variants such as NC males learning TX song [(West, King, & Eastzer, 1981b) West & King, 1988]. These data helped us understand relationships among aspects of communication. The data showed that males in aviaries who were successful in courting and copulating with females produced songs that playback females (who heard only their song) responded to at high levels. Mate-choice experiments also showed that bilingual males' success depended on the perceptual preferences of the females. In general, females-preferred natal song variants and thus mate success correlated with the amount of female preferred song in a male's repertoire. These data fit nicely with the data from studies of song development where we had shown that naive males biased their emergent repertoire toward the songs matching their female companions' natal preferences. Thus, the story about structure fit well with the story about function (the analog to semantics). But we still had not achieved our goal of incorporating the third part of a communicative system—pragmatics. That step consumed the 1990s.

☐ Studying Song Use: What Do Males Know and Do They Know They Know It?

ABF notes, Summer 1983, South Aviary. Have new group of bilingual and monolingual males. One of monolingual birds, male 2G, put in aviary with females who like the other variant of song. His songs get him nowhere . . . contrives new plan . . . sits in corner of aviary and waits for another male to induce female to adopt copulatory posture . . . male 2G then zooms in and knocks off the singer and copulates . . . true avian finesse.

In the 1990s, we now wanted to see song and singing in a competitive social context. In retrospect, there were several reasons why we had not taken this step sooner. In the 1970s and 1980s, we had focused almost exclusively on the male cowbird's song and the female's perception of it. Although we had looked at courtship in wild-caught males, we had never considered looking at courtship in the neophenotypes we had created. Other labs had also not looked at the behavior of birds housed under such impoverished conditions. The simplest reason was that there did not seem to be much to study. Like Harlow's motherless monkeys, hand-reared, companion-poor songbirds exhibited fear, stereotypy, and stress when placed in open environments. What probably deterred researchers the most from such studies was that the birds' vocalizations were the true targets of inquiry, as it was assumed that acoustic structure held the key to understanding song ontogeny. The state of the isolate bird's song, not the state of the bird, was of theoretical concern.

The growing use of playback techniques to learn about song function also mitigated against further investment in looking at the behavior of socially and acoustically naive birds. These techniques worked well in many species to differentiate the functional properties of songs from males with different developmental histories (Searcy, 1992). If song structure could be connected to song function via playback, there seemed to be sufficient basis to conclude that the song functioned to affect female choice. The idea of connections between the production and perception of mating signals fit preconceptions of what one "ought to see" when studying the components of a communication system, that is, intrinsic coupling of sender/receiver behavior. The ethologists' diagrams of stickleback courtship with a set of arrows connecting male behaviors to female behaviors seemed applicable to many species (Morris, 1970). Lorenz too had speculated that primary, innate programming automatically allowed animals to perform species-typical behaviors at just the right time and to the right receiver (Lorenz, 1965).

All of us know that naming a behavior does not explain its function, that is, a nominalist fallacy. But could there also be a "connectionist" fallacy, that is, an automatically triggered assumption in humans that behaviors humans link together are also linked together by the animals being observed. All researchers implicitly adopt a connectionist mind-set to relate what they are seeing and what they think it means. But, in the case of cowbirds, were we projecting our intuitions about linkages between behaviors without sufficient testing of animals' abilities to link acts together?

Thus, we undertook the study of the translation of capacities into competencies. As we carried out the studies to look at song and singers in context, we discovered another reason why such work had not been done. It was hard! Figuring out ways to get cowbirds to assume social roles such as tutor or receiver and to perform these roles for young naive males or females took orchestration. At times, we felt more like the directors or producers of a summer play than researchers. We describe one such study below in detail to demonstrate the complexity of arranging social circumstances in which to watch our subjects and the considerable payoff of such efforts.

The first study featured wild-caught juvenile male cowbirds (*M. a. artemisiae*) from an ancestral part of the cowbird's range, South Dakota

(Freeberg, King, & West, 1995). In the study, we combined controlled social housing, playback tests, and measures of courtship to obtain a year-long look at social and vocal outcomes. To begin, we housed the South Dakota (SD) individually with canaries (*Serinus canaria*) or female cowbirds from the same SD site. Thus, we were using housing conditions we had used many times before. But instead of stopping the study when the males' songs were fully mature, we initiated new means of assessment to see what the males would do if allowed to interact with female cowbirds, nonconspecific companions, or each other in new social contexts. We also used playback of the males' songs to SD females to relate male courtship success to the potency of the male's vocalizations. And we recorded the males' vocal production throughout the year to trace changes in the structure of their songs.

Briefly, the experimental design was as follows: first, the young males were housed with the pairs of female cowbirds or canaries, with whom they lived for the next nine months, the time frame in which they develop song repertoires. In May, to initiate the new phases, we moved the males to flight cages by group; thus, the canary-housed (CH) males were in one cage, and the female-housed (FH) males in another. After several weeks, we moved the birds to large aviaries containing many potential social companions, including female cowbirds from South Dakota, Indiana, and North Carolina, as well as canaries and starlings. And waiting backstage were adult male cowbirds from the same geographic locations. They would play a role in the final act. Our general question was, what would our naive males do when given so many social options?

Observations of the FH and CH males after they emerged from the enclosures and were placed in their respective flight cages suggested that the aviary plans might be premature. The birds were in fragile social states (even though they had had companions throughout the year, and thus were not true isolates). The day that the males were removed from their female or canary companions, even the most naive observer would have been able to tell that these cowbirds were different. Noise in the laboratory room, especially unexpected sounds such as a human sneeze, produced frantic flying and hovering as the birds attempted to locate a perch unoccupied by another male (there were many perches to choose from and burlap cloth to hide behind). Observers reported the birds to be frozen in place for long periods. Even seemingly so simple an act as flying to the floor of the cage to eat involved problem-solving—the males would make several tries before actually landing and eating or drinking if another male was already there. For the first five days, we did not see two males sharing a perch, nor did we see two birds eat or drink at the same time. The CH males appeared to be the more fragile group: they were even slower to show social interactions with each other.

But the cowbirds' singing resumed quickly, much sooner than other social behaviors. The first vocalizations occurred the day after emergence and included typical cowbird sounds, as well as some odd imitations and improvisations such as the sounds of female rattles and imitations of canary calls. The manner in which males delivered their song was, however, different from that of wild males. The songs were not accompanied by the typical song spread display. The display begins with the male raising the feathers on his head and chest, lifting and spreading the wings while bowing forward, sometimes to the point that his beak reaches the perch or ground (Lowther, 1993). The displaying male then wipes or rubs his beak against a perch. Song co-occurs with the display, although song can also occur without it. The CH and FH males sang, but without the concurrent bowing actions. Most vocalizations were also not directed to other individuals. The birds often sat down on the perch while generating vocalizations, with little sign of responsiveness to events around them. The singing looked more like reflexive hiccuping than communicating.

During emergence, we saw social deficiencies, but some of these lessened considerably as the birds settled into their new surroundings. Within a week to ten days, the males had changed considerably. They were singing and displacing one another from perches, foraging as a group, and in the case of the CH males, "guarding" the cage wall and singing through the wire to a new group of canaries in the next cage (not their former companions).

But the subsequent events of that summer greatly revised our thinking about learning to connect socially. First in a large flight cage, then in a large aviary, we watched as the CH males chased and sang to new canaries. Had these males been displaying these behaviors to female conspecifics, we would have labeled it "courtship." Even more striking was the inattention of the CH males to female cowbirds. The female cowbirds, in breeding condition, were generally ignored by the CH males. The CH males' persistence was striking and the canaries' patience admirable. But even when the canaries retreated, and even when the female cowbirds approached and solicited with copulatory postures, the CH males quickly resumed their canary pursuits. It was as if they were on a behavioral spring: the female cowbirds could pull the males toward them with active displays, but after a while the spring could be stretched no more, flinging the males back to their canary pursuits.

The FH males did vocalize to female conspecifics in the flight cage tests and ignored the canaries, behaviors that made sense to us. But what did not make sense was what happened in the aviaries. The FH males had little success courting female cowbirds in the more open and complex setting. The major failure was that they did not direct their vocalizations to female cowbirds. They devoted the majority of their time to interactions with other males, singing many more songs to each other than to females. At least the CH males showed the kind of energy and drive breeding male cowbirds usually display; they just chose inappropriate targets. But the FH males seemed lifeless by comparison, content to sing to one another or just to themselves.

After documenting the behavior of the young males with several sets of females, we brought on adult males. Would they court the females effectively and would young males learn something by watching them? The introduction of the adults had an immediate and salutary impact on the females. Until that time, they had showed little interest in the FH and CH males, who, in turn, had paid little attention to them. The day the adults arrived, we saw more females and more social activity than at any time prior. The adults successfully courted and copulated with females. But their success did not change the behavior of the FH or CH males, except perhaps to suppress what little courtship we had seen. Thus, learning on the job did not appear to work.

By the end of the breeding season, we knew something about the playback females' opinions of the songs of the FH and the CH males. The females had responded significantly more often to the songs of the FH males compared to the CH males. In a second playback test, we found that the playback females responded as much to the songs of the FH males as they did to recordings of wild males from South Dakota. Thus, the lack of success of the FH males was not a result of having ineffective songs. The lack of concordance between the reactions of the playback females compared to the aviary females gave us more evidence that what was wrong with the FH males was not song-related, but skill-related.

Taken as a whole, these data challenged several long-held assumptions. In past studies, we had assumed that playback females could recognize effective songs, but we had also assumed that males could recognize *when to sing* such songs. Clearly, we were wrong. As we thought about it, the new findings suddenly cast song playback methods in a new light. When we carried out playback work, we did more than playback songs. We were borrowing skills naturally used by successful males. We were engineering links by our actions and technology, links we assumed were second nature to the birds themselves. We chose the song, its playback level, the time, and the distance of the recipient to the speaker. The new data suggested that if we left those actions to the FH males, the playback procedure would not have worked. It had never occurred to us that we had been supplying vocal skills for the male whose song we had recorded.

Throughout the entire aviary task, observers had also found themselves trying to instill vocal skills. They silently coached the birds on what to do to court successfully. When an FH male would sing to a female, an observer might say, "Okay, now sing another song, wait . . . don't leave, look at her, look her in the eye, follow her, ignore that male, keep on her tail."

In the following two years, we repeated the experiment with a new population of cowbirds, birds from Indiana (West, King, & Freeberg, 1996). We obtained essentially the same results. Although cowbirds from Indiana were not as persistent in "courting" canaries, neither the CH or FH males showed much courtship skill with female cowbirds. We also carried out studies to rehabilitate the CH and FH males over the next year. We found they could be highly successful at courting if exposed to males one year older than themselves. Exposure to other same-aged males did not improve courtship ability.

To summarize, these experiments revealed the multiple layers of learning needed to connect behaviors we had not known could be dissociated by social manipulation. Five lessons stood out. First, the CH males' orientation toward canaries made clear that species recognition is not a sure thing in cowbirds; neither innate programming nor early learning guarantee attention or recognition of mates. Had we stumbled on an imprinting-like process? The data from the FH males argued against imprinting in that they should have shown strong mating affiliations toward female conspecifics, and they had not. Second, the cage and aviary tests revealed the need to consider physical space as not simply an issue of animal well-being, but as a social variable in and of itself. Differences in the social and physical setting lead to different levels of competence (or lack thereof). Had we stopped our studies after observing the CH and FH males in the confines of their flight cage, we would have concluded that FH males showed appropriate recognition and attention to potential mates, and we would have been wrong. Only in the aviaries setting did we see that FH males did not seek out females. In the confines of a small cage, such seeking was not necessary.

The failure to find correlations between vocal function as tested by playback and vocal uses as tested by aviary performance was the fourth lesson, calling into question the continued acceptance of a sound-centered view of courtship. While the data indicated a definite role for vocal behavior (we saw no consortships or copulations unaccompanied by singing), the data suggested that we had placed too much emphasis on the song. In the subsequent replicates, we also found that not only did song potency fail to correlate with performance within years, it also did not correlate across years, suggesting that the social contexts exert effects after the first year. Thus, song structure, in and of itself, could not withstand the burden of explanation required to connect signal production and perception to successful reproduction. This was the assumption that had sustained us during the 1980s. We knew now that social influence must be considered as part of initial and subsequent conditions in which learning and assessment occurs (Payne & Payne, 1993).

Finally, the studies showed that new tools were needed to confront the multidimensional nature of social influences. Songs can be recorded and analyzed and matched on objective acoustic criteria. In contrast, the quality and timing of song overtures, a male's ability to maintain proximity to a female, her willingness to be close to him, his persistence in following her, and his tendency to guard her from other males would require new social metrics.

☐ Promoting Culture in Cowbirds

ABF notes, Summer 1990, West Aviary. Top male, YDB, in aviary hurts himself somehow and loses his voice, air sac hurt we guess. Suddenly, he can only squeak . . . whole aviary takes a break from courting to diagnose him and then exploit him, amount of male singing triples . . . YDB's 2 female mates look elsewhere . . . he resumes singing a week or so later . . . female mates profess fidelity . . . all eggs really his . . . YDB orders DNA tests.

In these studies, we had focused on contexts that brought out incompetence—failures to court. It is always easier to break down a system than put one together. Our view of development as a constructive process demanded, however, that we find evidence that social contexts could facilitate the formation of functional behavioral connections. In Hubel and Wiesel's (1962) original work and much that followed, they showed that the cells in the cortex of kittens could develop new receptive properties as a function of biased visual rearing. Could we show new communicative properties by biased social rearing?

Powerful testimony about the constructive properties of development came from studies of mate preferences carried out in our lab. In a two-year-long study, Freeberg studied the mate preferences of young male and female SD juveniles, exposed to one of two cultures (Freeberg, 1996, 1998). The first culture (natal) consisted of juvenile SD birds housed in aviaries with adult SD males and females. The second (novel) culture was composed of SD juvenile male and females housed with adults from an Indiana population. All of the juvenile SD birds had had experience with conspecifics before being captured, and continued throughout the experiment to live with other juveniles from their capture site. Moreover, as the study took place in spacious aviaries, the young birds were not forced by physical constraints to be near the adults or the other juveniles. Moreover, they could hear and see wild birds outside of the aviary.

Under these conditions, Freeberg found that mate preferences were predicted by social or cultural experience, not by natal background. Looking at the data from the female perspective was the more crucial test, as females should have been more resistant to altering mate choice. Although the females all came from the same local population, social experience significantly biased courting and copulating. But the critical assay of the robustness of the cultural transmission followed. Freeberg tested whether the differences in preferences could be transmitted to a new generation of young males and females, also captured in South Dakota. Their models were the former pupils from the original study, the experiential F1s. The answer was yes, social experience again predicted mate assortment in the F2s.

Freeberg's work provided the evidence we needed to show that postnatal social experience could build new preferences. Second, the data again showed that the early experiences of cowbirds with other cowbirds are not sufficient to prevent further learning. Moreover, the data showed a positive outcome: social experience during a young cowbird's first year influenced subsequent courtship. Given that cowbirds from South Dakota would not typically begin life or travel to breeding grounds containing cowbirds from Indiana, the guided learning would be beneficial.

The work also had special meaning to us because, after many years of trying, these data were the first to show considerable plasticity in female cowbirds. Up to this point, female preferences had proved hard to move around. We had tried to do so by housing females for almost an entire year with males from another cowbird population in sound-attenuating chambers, thinking massive exposure would increase the chances of inducing malleability. We found little evidence of malleability in song preferences as tested by playback. And so, finding malleability when females were faced with a seemingly more complex setting containing many options was an important breakthrough. These data also made us wonder if failures in other species to find malleability reflected hitherto unrecognized inhibitory effects of standard isolate housing, such as higher levels of stress. Maybe males profit from one-on-one time with females, but maybe females do not?

The malleability Freeberg found should not be taken as evidence of fragility of the connected system as a whole or of misguided learning; in nature, SD males and females would be tutored by adult SD males and females. Most theorists believe that one has to build a genetic safety net for each individual in a species. We are coming to believe the opposite: social learning affords a collective safety net, and that net only emerges in a social setting. This view relates to our earlier statement that there were at least three stories to understand—the ones pertaining to the different needs of the two sexes, and the compound and synergistic story of their lives together. In that social environments typically provide stable and useful information, it becomes difficult to approach the study of vocal learning only as an individual adaptation.

Before turning to the summary, we should make clear that even in overly simplified environments, social learning is a systemic force. Recently, we looked at interactions throughout the year of young males individually housed with two adult females. Some males were housed with adult females from their local region to maximize synchrony between the two sexes with respect to local song preferences and timing of breeding. Some males were housed with adult females from a distant population, females with different song preferences and a different time course for breeding readiness. We predicted that different patterns of social and perceptual compatibility would lead to measurable differences in song development.

The results show that the actions of adult females were associated with different rates of progress throughout the stages of vocal development. Young males housed with local adult females developed stereotyped song earlier, reduced motor practice earlier, and produced more effective playback songs than did males with females from the distant population. The males with the "distant" females showed slower growth and more variable song well into the spring. Longitudinal observations of social interactions showed that the two groups of females differed reliably in social responses to males. The major difference in the nature of the social interactions was that the local females stayed when males sang instead of flying away, whereas distant females flew, sometimes even before the song was finished. Female proximity gave males an opportunity to receive more social feedback to individual songs and, conversely, gave females more chances to shape content by more subtle cues such as wing stroking or beak movements (Smith, King, & West, 2000). Moreover, the amount of female proximity was correlated with playback song potency and the rate of progression to stereotyped song.

The importance of proximity even in such small enclosures ($1m^3$) relates back to the observers' coaching of the FH males in the aviary setting. Much of observers' advice focused on maintaining proximity. We think that one of most important pragmatic skills facing cowbirds is learning how to sing while close to a female. He must have the social versatility necessary to deal with male competition and female attraction at the same time.

Proximity manipulation now seems to be one of the most basic lessons for young males and is the subject of our work in progress. In these studies, we are looking at how large groups of cowbirds aggregate when given lots of physical space, and we are also comparing patterns of aggregation and interaction in social groups with different compositions, such as juveniles with only adult males or only adult females. From what we can tell so far, the matter of being able to get close and remain close is essential in learning among males and between males and females. Different patterns of proximity produce different opportunities for singing, listening, and receiving feedback.

☐ **Developmental Harvest**

ABF Notes, Indiana University, Spring 1996. Discussed authorship in ethics class: students suggested new authorship format modeled after movies, with titles and credits for producer, director, actors, and so on. Studies of canary- and female-housed males fit the bill. Maybe the review would read:

> "The play's the thing" (ABF productions). A gripping story of the summer of 1992 for young males coming of age after sheltered childhoods. Red Green steals the show in his attempt at genetic suicide as he rejects his own kind for a life with canary sidekicks. Unfortunately, rated PG: too little sex or violence, but some profanity especially from Southern females. Musical score uneven. Sequel in the works.

Years living and working with cowbirds have not changed many of the basic beliefs we held as we began our work. Social animals need a social context to show how they learn and develop. Development is not a passive unfolding or stamping of information onto a helpless young animal. And methods reinforce assumptions. It is easy to maintain the scientific fiction that development is not dynamic, synergistic, flexible, and active if the settings in which one studies development are static, compartmentalized, rigid, and passive.

Our new beliefs rest on the idea of a "social gateway" as the logical starting point in ontogenetic research. The "social/cultural gateway" refers to the settings and sequence of events through which organisms obtain access to information for learning. We begin with the rationale that many young animals do not have control over access to potentially important stimulation. Although young animals may create that access by means of interaction with their natal social setting, the nature of the setting may impose constraints. In young mammals, it is through the action of their mothers, stimulated in part by their own behavior and that of their siblings, that thermal, acoustic, visual, tactile, and olfactory cues and their multimodal manifestations become available for learning.

Nor do many young organisms have direct control over proximate reinforcement systems that may consolidate and shape perceptual and attentional processes. In many species, it is only through the species-typical group that fundamental opportunities for developmental growth of knowledge take place. Such knowledge resides within the social gateway, where older organisms or peers facilitate or limit sensory exposure and its timing and duration. The gateway may also "set" or "prime" learning and the opportunity to use newly acquired information in settings containing critical feedback mechanisms. For example, nondominant animals may not get to use what they have learned or may have to modify it further as a function of a social hierarchy; animals in the periphery of a group may not hear, see, smell, or sense the same level of sensory cues. Also, natural social aggregations create synergistic environments and kinds of stimulation not possible if done by individual animals. When we were kids, certain incompetencies between kids were explained by saying that "so-and-so must have been behind a tree when God gave out talent for hitting baseballs or [fill in the blank]." The gateway is meant to capture the idea that not all animals, even if in the "same" environment, profit in the same way.

We would further argue that the social gateway has been bypassed in most laboratory research, not only in development, but in perception, cognition, and neuroscience, and so on. Animals are brought through the laboratory door and stripped of any social gateway. Thus, how they naturally learn and how they are manipulated to learn may differ. Hamsters, for example, can be taught after many shaping trials to use a fishing technique to obtain food; their young can learn the same behavior in one trial if just allowed to watch mom and given access to the materials (Previde & Poli, 1996). Which kind of learning has been favored by natural selection and had thus shaped cognitive and neural processes? We also wonder if some of the failures of animal models to predict human actions stem from the reality that humans come with gateways. Whether the animal-to-human application is a new drug or a new theory of memory, its success, or lack thereof, may be due to the differences in the nature of organisms living inside or outside the gateway.

The new fields of computational modeling propose distributed systems of intelligence. What we propose are distributed systems of information access. The idea of a distributed system opens up new ways to think about the delivery and potential use of information and forces us to recognize the inherent social dependencies that probabilistically control the spread and dissemination to individual and groups in individuals (Bar-Yam, 1997). In cowbirds, a young male's opportunity to learn song from other males or to receive feedback from females depends on their actions as well as his behavior. In ongoing studies of social groupings, we have found that young males do not have automatic access to adults. Indeed, the willingness of adult males to interact with the young males appears to be a critical parameter. That willingness, however, is also a function of just how active and exploratory the young male is. In turn, a female's attention to a young male appears to depend on prior interactions by that male with adult males. We are far from being able to describe the structure of distributed opportunities, but we know the structure is there. The idea that gateways exist has many implications. First, it suggests that, for many animals, the idea of the world of an individual animal may not be a useful construct. Many researchers have argued that the organism/environment bond is a fundamental consideration in developmental theory. But the idea of a gateway goes a step further toward the idea that social contexts are logically the first mechanism to be understood in studying development or learning.

So too, we may have to rethink whether behaviors represent individual or team efforts. For a male cowbird to be successful, many other actions by other conspecifics are required, including cooperation from females, a history of successful competition with other males, the presence or absence of other males with superior abilities, and a little luck. We would liken his success at courtship to an RBI in baseball. A hitter cannot get an RBI without the cooperation of the hitters before him, the skills of the pitcher and opposing fielders, and a manager smart enough to know which batting order will work. Baseball is a distributed system for success or failure, a fact often obscured by stunning individual performances such as hitting 70 home runs (and McGwire's team did not get to the playoffs).

Looked at from an evolutionary point of view, social gateways also have relevance. Terkel has done fascinating studies of the black rat (*Rattus rattus*) in Israel (1996). The species has learned to strip pinecones to secure a new food source. The behavior is culturally transmitted from mother to offspring; the young do not seem to be able to learn it simply by handling partially opened pinecones or watching each other. The black rats' use of this food source is very new, and other species now live near the same Jerusalem pine trees, trees only there in the last quarter century. What is to prevent new species from learning how to eat cones? The constraint may be that they cannot gain access to the black rat social system unlocking the key to pinecone use. Researchers report that they find no partially stripped cones lying about the forest floor: the only route to such learning tools is the adult, mother rat, from whom babies do snatch pieces of cone. Work on filial imprinting has also shown important differences in learning when exposure to an unfamiliar imprinting stimulus is filtered through the system of sibling interactions (Lickliter, Dyer, & McBride, 1993). There it seems that siblings are attractive enough to one another that their mother may have to compete with them to be the one imprinted on. Removing an animal from the socially distributed network of opportunities for learning may mean that we see only backup systems for modifying behavior, not the systems that define species/environment niches.

☐ Final Thoughts

ABF Notes, May 1991, Indiana Farm. Son's first-grade class coming to visit . . . what to do about facts of life? What if cowbirds show off mating skills? Son saves the day . . . when it happens, son turns to classmates and says, "See, that's how cowbirds populate."

We suppose the question we hear most often is, "How can you study the same species for so many years?" The answer is that it is not the same species year after year. As we learn new things, cowbirds transform before our eyes into ever more interesting and ever more complex subjects. Perhaps one of the most special experiences for us takes place in late winter, when Indiana is gray and depressing. Migrating birds begin to return, among them some of the cowbirds we have released, recognizable by their lab leg bands. A few are now five or six years old. Seeing a former subject induces the crazy feeling to tell Male RGR or Female G-G what has happened in the lab or what we know about cowbirds that we did not know when they left. But then we remember, they already know. . . . We are the ones who still have the learning to do.

☐ References

Baptista, L. F., & Gaunt, S. L. L. (1994). Historical perspectives: Advances in studies of avian sound communication. *Condor, 96,* 817–830.

Baptista, L. F., & Patrinovich, L. (1984). Social interaction, sensitive periods, and the song template hypothesis in the white-crowned sparrow. *Animal Behaviour, 36,* 1752–1764.

Bar-Yam, Y. (1997). *Dynamics of complex systems.* New York: Addison-Welsley.

Beer, C. G. (1982). Conceptual issues in the study of communication. In D. E. Kroodsma & E. H. Miller (Eds.), *Acoustic communication in birds* (pp. 279–310). New York: Academic Press.

Breland, K., & Breland, M. (1961). The misbehavior of organisms. *American Psychologist, 16,* 681–684.

Freeberg, T. M. (1996). Assortative mating in captive cowbirds is predicted by social experience. *Animal Behaviour, 52,* 1129–1142.

Freeberg, T. M. (1998). The cultural transmission of courtship patterns in cowbirds, Molothrus ater. *Animal Behaviour, 56,* 1063–1073.

Freeberg, T. M., King, A. P., & West, M. J. (1995). Social malleability in cowbirds (*Molothrus ater artemisiae*): Species and mate recognition in the first 2 years of life. *Journal of Comparative Psychology, 109,* 357–367.

Friedmann, H. (1929). *The cowbirds: A study in the biology of social parasitism.* Springfield, IL: C. C. Thomas.

Gibson, E. J. (1969). *Principles of perceptual learning and development.* New York: Appleton-Century-Crofts.

Gibson, J. J. (1966). *The senses considered as perceptual systems.* Boston: Houghton-Mifflin.

Gould, J. L. (1982). *Ethology: The mechanisms and evolution of behavior.* New York: W. W. Norton.

Harlow, H. F., & Harlow, M. K. (1962). Social deprivation in monkeys. *Scientific American, 207,* 136–146.

Harlow, H. F., Harlow, M. K., & Hansen, E. W. (1963). The maternal affectional system of rhesus monkeys. In H. L. Rheingold (Eds.), *Maternal behavior in mammals* (pp. 254–281). New York: Wiley.

Hubel, D. H., & Wiesel, T. N. (1962). Receptive fields, binocular interaction and functional architecture in the cat's visual cortex. *Journal of Physiology, 160,* 106–154.

Kaufman, I. C. (1975). Learning what comes naturally: The role of life experience in the establishment of species-typical behavior. *Ethos, 3,* 129–142.

King, A. P., & West, M. J. (1977). Species identification in the N.A. cowbird: Appropriate responses to abnormal song. Science, 195, 1002–1004.

King, A. P., & West, M. J. (1983). Female perception of cowbird song: A closed developmental program. *Developmental Psychobiology, 16,* 335–342.

King, A. P., & West, M. J. (1988). Searching for the functional origins of cowbird song in eastern brown-headed cowbirds (*Molothrus ater ater*). *Animal Behaviour, 36,* 1575–1588.

King, A. P., West, M. J., & Eastzer, D. H. (1980). Song structure and song development as potential contributors to reproductive isolation in cowbirds. *Journal of Comparative and Physiological Psychology, 94,* 1028–1036.

Kroodsma, D. E. (1982). Learning and the ontogeny of sound signals in birds. In D. E. Kroodsma & E. H. Miller (Eds.), *Acoustic communication in birds* (pp. 1–24). New York: Academic Press.

Larson, G. (1984). *Hound of the far side.* Kansas City, MO: Andrews, McNeal, and Parker.

Lehrman, D. S. (1970). Semantic and conceptual issues in the nature-nurture problem. In L. R. Aronson, E. Tobach, D. S. Lehrman, & J. S. Rosenblatt (Eds.), *Development and evolution of behavior: Essays in memory of T. C. Schneirla* (pp. 17–52). San Francisco: Freeman.

Lehrman, D. S. (1974). Can psychiatrists use ethology? In N. F. White (Ed.), *Ethology and Psychiatry* (pp. 187–196). Toronto: University of Toronto Press.

Lickliter, R., Dyer, A. B., & McBride, T. (1993). Perceptual consequences of early social experiences in precocial birds. *Behavioural Processes, 30,* 185–200.

Lorenz, K. (1965). *Evolution and modification of behavior.* Chicago: University of Chicago Press.

Lorenz, K. (1970). *Studies in animal and human behavior,* volume I (Robert Martin, Trans.). Cambridge, MA: Harvard University Press.

Lowther, P. E. (1993). Brown-headed cowbird (*Molothrus ater*). In A. Poole & F. Gill (Eds.), *The birds of North America, no. 47* (pp. 1–24). Washington, DC: Academy of Natural Sciences.

Marler, P. (1960). Bird songs and mate selection. In W. E. Lanyon & W. N. Tavolga (Eds.), *Animal sounds and communication* (pp. 348–367). American Institute of Biological Sciences.

Marler, P. (1970a). Birdsong and speech development: Could there be parallels? *American Scientist, 58,* 669–673.

Marler, P. (1970b). A comparative approach to vocal learning: Song development in the white-crowned sparrows. *Journal of Comparative and Physiological Psychology Monographs, 71,* 1–25.

Marler, P. (1991). Song-learning behavior: The interface with neuroethology. *Trends in Neuroscience, 14,* 199–206.

Marler, P., Mundinger, P., Waser, M. S., & Lutjen, A. (1972). Effects of acoustical deprivation on song development in redwing blackbirds (*Agelaius phoeniceus*). *Animal Behaviour, 20,* 586–606.

Mayr, E. (1963). *Animal species and evolution.* Cambridge, MA: Harvard University PRess.

Mayr, E. (1974). Behavior programs and evolutionary strategies. *American Scientist, 62,* 650–659.

Morris, D. (1970). *Patterns of reproductive behaviour.* New York: McGraw-Hill Book Company.

Nelson, D. A., & Marler, P. (1994). Selection-based learning in bird song development. *Proceedings of the National Academy of Science, 91,* 10498–10501.

Payne, R. B., & Payne, L. L. (1993). Song copying and cultural transmission in indigo buntings. *Animal Behaviour, 46,* 1045–1065.

Previde, P., E., & Poli, M. D. (1996). Social learning in the golden hamster (Mesocricetus auratus). *Journal of Comparative Psychology, 110,* 203–208.

Searcy, W. A. (1992). Measuring responses of female birds to male song. In P. K. McGregor (Eds.), *Playback and studies of animal communication* (pp. 175–189). New York: Plenum Press.

Seligman, M. E. P. (1968). Chronic fear produced by unpredictable electric shock. *Journal of Comparative and Physiological Psychology, 66,* 402–411.

Seligman, M. E. P. (1975). *Helplessness: On depression, development and death.* San Francisco: Freeman.

Slater, P. J. B. (1989). Bird song learning: causes and consequences. *Ethology Ecology & Evolution, 1,* 19–46.

Smith, V. I., King, A. P., & West, M. J. (2000). A role of her own: Female cowbirds influence male song development. *Animal Behavior, 60,* 599–609.

Terkel, J. (1996). Cultural transmission of feeding behaviors in the Black rat (Rattus rattus). In C. M. Heyes & B. G. Galef (Eds.), *Social learning in animals: The roots of culture* (pp. 17–48). San Diego: Academic Press.

Thorpe, W. H. (1958). The learning of song patterns by birds, with especial reference to the song of the chaffinch, *Fringilla coelebs. Ibis, 100,* 535–570.

Thorpe, W. H. (1961). *Bird song.* London: Cambridge University Press.

Tinbergen, N. (1963). On the aims and methods of ethology. *Zeitschrift für Tierpsychologie, 20,* 410–433.

West, M. J., & King, A. P. (1980). Enriching cowbird song by social deprivation. *Journal of Comparative and Physiological Psychology, 94,* 263–270.

West, M. J., & King, A. P. (1985). Social guidance of vocal learning by female cowbirds: Validating its functional significance. *Ethology, 70,* 225–235.

West, M. J., & King, A. P. (1986). Song repertoire development in male cowbirds (*Molothrus ater*): Its relation to female assessment of song. *Journal of Comparative Psychology, 100,* 296–303.

West, M. J., & King, A. P. (1988). Female visual displays affect the development of male song in the cowbird. *Nature, 334,* 244–246.

West, M. J., & King, A. P. (1994). Research habits and research habitats: Better design through social chemistry. In E. F. Gibbons Jr., E. J. Wyers, E. Waters, & E. W. Menzel Jr. (Eds.), *Naturalistic environments in captivity for animal behavior research* (pp. 163–178). Albany, NY: SUNY Press.

West, M. J., King, A. P., & Harrocks, T. H. (1983). Cultural transmission of cowbird song: Measuring its development and outcome. *Journal of Comparative and Psychological Psychology, 97,* 327–337.

West, M. J., King, A. P., & Eastzer, D. H. (1981a). The cowbird: Reflections on development from an unlikely source. *American Scientist, 69,* 57–66.

West, M. J., King, A. P., & Eastzer, D. H. (1981b). Validating the female bioassay of cowbird song: Relating differences in song potency to mating success. *Animal Behaviour, 29,* 490–501.

West, M. J., King, A. P., & Freeberg, T. M. (1996). Social malleability in cowbirds: New measures reveal new evidence of plasticity in the Eastern subspecies (*Molothrus ater ater*). *Journal of Comparative Psychology, 110,* 15–26.

West, M. J., & King, A. P. (2001). Sciences lies its way to the truth . . . really. In E. M. Blass (Ed.), *Handbook of behavioral neurobiology* (pp. 587–613.). New York: Plenum.

CHAPTER 5

William A. Mason

The Natural History of Primate Behavioral Development: An Organismic Perspective

It seems I have always been fascinated with development as a natural phenomenon. Like most children in the small town where I grew up, I was constantly encountering examples of animals growing, changing, becoming something new and different from what they were. I collected caterpillars and watched them become butterflies, saw tadpoles turn into frogs, naked nestlings become fully feathered and fly around on their own, and kittens transformed from blind and helpless creatures to playful juveniles, finally to become adults, sometimes friendly and eager for human contact and sometimes indifferent and aloof. I enjoyed the spectacle of natural development and occasionally wondered about what was going on in these animals as they changed and grew. Also as many children do, I fell in love with dogs. We had several as pets when I was growing up, and I was given one of my own to care for and train when I was ten or twelve years old. We learned from each other.

Watching these animals grow, observing the changes in their behavior, interacting with them—these were simple and absorbing pleasures that, like many other young people, I encountered early in life. I was curious about what animals did and why they did it. The discovery of something new provided a small thrill, whether the novelty occurred spontaneously or in response to a situation I had arranged. Although these early interests and activities were not "scientific" in the usual sense, they had an abiding influence on my view of development as an aspect of a species's natural history.

☐ Received Views

I found little in my first years of formal training in psychology to nurture my interest in the natural history of development. The period was the late 1940s and early 1950s. The dominant approaches to development covered a broad range of theoretical possibilities, but scarcely ever referred to the specific details of behavioral development in real animals. The mechanistic approach of strict Watsonian behaviorism, exemplified during my student days by Hull, Skinner, and their many supporters, was probably the most widely accepted. The essential model presupposed a passive organism whose development was shaped by the interdependent relations between stimuli, responses, and reinforcements, which were thought of as the critical elements producing behavioral change. Although animal research provided the foundation of this approach, its adherents believed that the ideas applied equally as well to humans as to rats. Freud and the psychoanalysts offered an alternative model that was also popular. The psychoanalytic model focused exclusively on human beings, emphasizing the intense and mainly unconscious strivings of the developing individual to satisfy its primordial needs and longings within the family circle. In spite of his historical role in the development of psychoanalysis, Jung was not much discussed, although I found his ideas about biologically based archetypes intriguing. The theoretical perspectives of Piaget and the Gestalt psychologists were less prominent in the intellectual ambience of that time than either of the first two approaches. They were also presented as focusing on human development, which was viewed as a process of the unfolding of cognitive abilities and functions according to predictable stages of psychological growth (Langer, 1969); they had no serious impact on my thinking.

These different views of development were interesting at a purely academic level, but they were not inspiring. At the time I did not perceive their relevance to my youthful experience with the natural phenomena of development and was more strongly attracted to approaches that viewed animal behavior within a more explicit biological framework (Beach, 1950; Harlow, 1953; Hebb, 1953; Lashley, 1949; Nissen, 1951, 1953, 1954; Schiller, 1952; Schneirla, 1949, 1952; Scott, 1954). Because of its emphasis on diverse species and their natural behavior, I was particularly intrigued by ethology, which was being introduced to English-speaking audiences at about this time (Lorenz, 1952).

☐ Primate Development: The Phenomena

I had just finished my Ph.D. and was in the process of learning about these refreshing new approaches to animal behavior when I was offered a position at the University of Wisconsin primate laboratory supervising a developmental project with infant rhesus monkeys. The program was just getting under way, and I participated in all aspects of the work, including taking occasional night shifts in the monkey nursery. It was a first step in the formation of my ideas about primate behavioral development, and the beginning of a lifelong educational experience.

In the following years I became acquainted in varying degrees with individuals from other primate species, including gibbons, chimpanzees, orangutans, and gorillas, as well as several species of Old World and New World monkeys. I was able to watch animals when they were engaged with the world and behaving freely and spontaneously, to observe the development of individuals from many of these species informally in various contexts besides research settings, and to make casual as well as systematic comparisons between different species. I was also instructed in countless ways by my own children. The strong impression I gained from these experiences of basic similarities as well as important differences among species was amplified and confirmed in many careful accounts of primate development, going back more than a hundred years. (For reviews see Mason, 1964, 1965a; Mason, Davenport, & Menzel, 1968.)

The amount and quality of naturalistic and experimental data were sufficient to warrant an attempt at synthesis, and I began working toward a developmental model that aimed to stay close to the facts of primate development, while helping to organize a diversity of findings. What I wanted was a rational conceptual framework that had four general attributes: (1) It would emphasize behavior patterns that were part of the primates' natural repertoire (species-typical), particularly patterns relating to social development. (2) It would explicitly recognize that developmental changes in the organization of these patterns were always the outcome of influences originating within the organism acting conjointly with elements in its environment. (3) It would offer a plausible adaptive-evolutionary interpretation of phylogenetic similarities and differences in the organization of natural behavior patterns. (4) It would attempt to link distinctive primate attributes of motivation, temperament, and cognition to developmental processes. My purpose in this chapter is to provide an overview of such a model.

☐   A Model of Primate Development: Basic Features

The model that emerged, shown schematically in Figure 5.1, is mainly descriptive. The most complete version appeared in the early 1970s (Mason, 1971a, 1973). This was after several years of intensive experience with captive rhesus monkeys and chimpanzees, relatively brief exposure to free-ranging howler monkeys and rhesus monkeys and combined field and laboratory research on New World monkeys (Mason, 1971b). I have been surprised at the durability of the basic framework and its ability to accommodate new information.

The model views development from the standpoint of two major adaptive problems or "tasks," that the developing primate confronts, each characterized by a distinct developmental trend. One task is to make an effective adjustment to the maternal niche ("filial" in Figure 5.1), and the other is to respond effectively to the demands and opportunities of the nonmaternal environment ("exploitative" in Figure 5.1). The trends relating to each of these tasks appear early in ontogeny, follow different developmental trajectories, and are present throughout life. They lay down the principal functional dimensions along which preadult psychological development proceeds.

The behaviors associated with each trend are distinguished by differences in their form, their functions, and their relations to level of *arousal*. The concept of arousal is treated as a hypothetical psychophysiological state that is correlated with the intensity of perceived stimulation, which in turn is correlated with *dispositions* to engage in certain classes of behavior (Berlyne, 1967; see also Schneirla, 1959). Its role in the model presented here is principally to summarize relations between developmental status, motivational state, and behavior (Mason, 1971a, 1973).

Momentary changes in arousal have predictable *affective consequences*. Immature primates operate according to the pleasure principle. A given level of arousal is experienced as pleasant or unpleasant and establishes a disposition to engage in certain patterns of behavior. These behaviors act on the prevailing level, either to raise or to lower it. Behaviors that reduce arousal from aversive levels or increase it from levels that are too low are affectively positive and become attractive and potentially rewarding. Contrariwise, activities that increase arousal when it is already at aversive levels are disruptive and tend to be avoided; reductions in arousal when the levels are already unpleasantly low are also avoided (Mason, 1967, 1970b). Together the reciprocal relations between arousal-increasing and arousal-reducing behaviors constitute a kind of *hedonic homeostatic "system"* that enables the immature primate to exercise a degree of control over its own affective state.

Whether a change in arousal level is experienced as pleasant or unpleasant depends on the developmental status of the individual (which affects the "preferred" level of arousal), the existing level, and the direction of change. As a corollary to Figure 5.1, it is assumed that at earlier stages of development, low levels of arousal are preferred, tolerance for conditions that increase arousal is weak, and even modest increments are likely to cause distress. The behaviors most prominently associated with this aspect of development tend to reduce arousal and maintain it at low levels. As development proceeds, tolerance for conditions that augment arousal gradually increases, modest increments are attractive and rewarding, and arousal-increasing behaviors become more frequent. Very high levels of arousal are aversive, however, and interfere with many forms of cognitive activities, particularly those that draw on refined attentional and perceptual processes (Mason, 1970a, 1970b). The changes in the relative frequencies of arousal-reducing and arousal-increasing behaviors are progressive until the individual enters maturity, when the preference for arousal-increasing activities tends to decline. Despite these changes in the relative frequencies of arousal-reducing and arousal-increasing behaviors, they retain their early regulatory effects on arousal throughout life and occasionally appear in fully mature individuals, a phenomenon that in humans is often characterized as "infantile," "childish," "playful," or "regressive." Pleasure continues to be influential, of course, although as the individual approaches maturity, simple hedonism is sometimes overridden by emerging adult motivations and activities, particularly those relating to reproduction, and the formation and maintenance of social groups.

From a functional standpoint, it makes sense that infant primates usually respond negatively to increases in arousal. Monkeys and apes have never acquired the practice of using dens or nests where offspring can be left while their parents go about their daily routines. Infant survival depends on maintaining physical contact with a caregiver, on the capacity to find the nourishment it needs, typically with only modest assistance, and on being able to signal to the caregiver when things go awry. The three main avenues through which these ends are achieved are clinging; rooting, oral grasping, and sucking; and "distress" vocalizations. The first developmental trend is inferred from these contact-seeking behaviors. Virtually any disturbance in equilibrium—for example, noise, hunger, sudden loss of support—can activate contact-seeking behaviors, and their performance, particularly clinging, reduces arousal, an event that probably contributes to the formation of an emotional attachment to a specific individual. Other contact-seeking behaviors that seem to reduce arousal (although probably less effectively than clinging) include being groomed, stroked, held, and rocked (Berkson, 1968; Mason, 1965b, 1967; Yerkes &

Tomlin, 1932). Tolerance for high levels of arousal increases with age, and this is accompanied by a corresponding decline in the frequency of arousal-reducing activities, although they can be reinstated under conditions of extreme arousal.

It also makes functional sense that the developing infant becomes more tolerant of increases in arousal, as Figure 5.1 is meant to suggest. The trend associated with this task is the principal avenue through which the individual is led to interact with its nonmaternal environment. It is inferred from a progressive increase in affectively positive activities that augment arousal, such as exploration, object and motor play, and other "exploitative" or "stimulus-seeking" activities. The disposition to engage in exploitative behaviors is likely to be evoked by modest increments in arousal when the level is not already high (Welker, 1961). The initial response to objects or events that elicit exploitative behaviors may indicate ambivalence. Barring aversive consequences, this tends to decline with repeated exposures, is eventually superseded by attraction, and the object or event becomes rewarding until its efficacy gradually diminishes, thereby enhancing responsiveness to other forms of novelty (Sackett, 1965; Menzel, Davenport, & Rogers, 1961). Thus, in this fashion the exploitative trend is a primary agent leading the infant away from its caregiver and familiar surroundings toward more extensive and varied interactions with the larger environment. It becomes prominent later in development

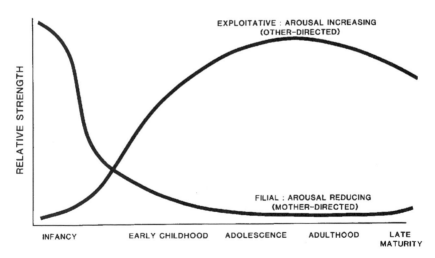

FIGURE 5.1. Idealized model representing developmental changes across the life span in relative strength of tendencies to engage in behaviors that increase arousal above normal levels (arousal-increasing) and reduce it below normal levels (arousal-reducing). The curves are also presumed to reflect developmental changes in degree of tolerance/preference for these two classes of behavior.

than the first trend, eventually overrides it, and continues to rise into late adolescence.

In my experience, the basic framework of the model applies to diverse species of primates. The form and function of mother-directed behaviors are essentially the same in monkeys and apes from all parts of the world, in spite of wide differences among species in ecology and social organization. I have also found that the relationship to eliciting conditions and the developmental course of exploitative behaviors are similar among these species (Mason, 1965a; Mason & Mendoza, 1998; Mason, Davenport, & Menzel, 1968; Mayeaux & Mason, 1998; see also Rosenblum, 1968). The easy accommodation of so many different taxa within the same conceptual framework reflects the strong descriptive bias of the model and its focus on the anthropoid primates, a biological group in which species share many attributes, including essential features of parental behavior and infant development.

☐ Primate Development: Interspecies Differences and Trends

Beyond the broad similarities among diverse species, monkeys and apes also differ from each other in many aspects of their development. As a comparative psychologist I was particularly intrigued by evidence that the living primate species, in contrast to most mammalian orders, constitute a graded series that *approximates* an evolutionary trend (Clark, 1960). I perceived this as providing a rationale and an incentive for a comparative-evolutionary approach to primate behavior (Mason, 1968a; 1968b). A striking attribute of this trend is that the time required to reach reproductive maturity increases systematically. In the words of the distinguished physical anthropologist Adolph Schultz; "In regard to all parts of postnatal life one can recognize a clear trend toward prolongation, beginning in monkeys, as compared with lemurs, more pronounced in gibbons, still more in all three great apes and by far the most marked in man. For instance, general growth, at least in length, is completed in only 3 years in prosimians, in 7 years in Old World monkeys, such as macaques, in not over 9 years in gibbons, in 11 years in the large man-like apes, and in as much as 20 years in recent man. Other ontogenetic events, such as the onset of menstruation or the completion of the dentition, show closely corresponding gradual postponements reaching their extremes in man" (Schultz, 1956, p. 890). As might be expected, correlated differences also exist in behavioral development: for example, the average age at which individuals achieve such developmental milestones as walking independently, beginning to eat solid foods, and starting to engage in social play.

Along with the trend toward the prolongation of growth, I find it particularly significant that the *organization* of early behavior patterns appears to change systematically, at least among humans, chimpanzees, and rhesus monkeys, the species for which comparative data are most complete (Mason, 1968a). Rooting, oral grasping, sucking, clinging, and the righting reflex are present in the neonates of all three species, but they are performed more promptly, reliably, vigorously, and efficiently in rhesus monkeys compared to chimpanzees, and in chimpanzees compared to human infants (Mason, 1965a). It was evident from my experience with these species that the contrasts are not instances of developmental "arrest," but changes in the organization of behavior that are evident throughout ontogeny, for example, in the loosening and elaboration of motor patterns displayed during investigatory activities and play of young animals and in the complexity and flexibility of adult behavior. That a comparable change has occurred in motivational factors that govern behavior is most likely.

Over the years the how (evolution) and why (adaptive value) of the trend toward prolongation of primate behavioral development have received much attention. For me the most exciting hint of answers to both the how and the why questions came while I was participating in a field study of howler monkeys on Barro Colorado Island in Panama in 1959 and happened upon the concept of *neoteny* (de Beer, 1958; Mason, 1968a, 1979). As to the how question, phylogeny is generally believed to be due to modifications in ontogeny across generations. An important way in which this happens is through changes in the temporal order or sequence of developmental events, a phenomenon called heterochrony (Gottlieb, 1987). Neoteny is a form of heterochrony in which immature ancestral characteristics are retained by sexually mature animals, usually as the result of differential slowing of developmental rates. Compared to members of a precursor species, the neotenous individual not only develops more slowly but is able to breed while in many other respects it remains immature.

The physical evidence for neoteny within the primates, correlated with the trend toward the prolongation of immaturity, is persuasive, at least for selected species. For example, in such traits as brain weight, the feeble development of the brow ridges, the sparseness of hair over most of the body, and the small size of the canine teeth, the mature human resembles the young chimpanzee more than the adult animal (de Beer, 1958). Within the chimpanzee genus, the bonobo (*Pan paniscus*) is physically neotenous compared to the common chimpanzee (*Pan troglodytes*) (Shea, 1983), and the common chimpanzee is neotenous compared to the macaques.

As to the why question, it is easy to imagine the adaptive benefits that might result from neoteny. Reproductively mature neotenous animals would be more playful, affectionate, inquisitive, and innovative compared to like-age adults of a less neotenous species, and as a corollary, more capable of coping with changing circumstances. In general, this is a fair characterization of the differences between humans, apes, and macaques. On the other hand, the more open organization of behavior in neotenous animals and the infusion of immature qualities into the adult repertoire might also be manifested in greater intra- and interindividual variability in important adult activities, for example, mating and parental care, and this also seems to be true within the human, ape, and macaque series. Comparative data for the New World cebus and squirrel monkeys likewise suggest that prolonged immaturity is associated with a looser organization of early behaviors, correlated with greater plasticity, complexity, and adaptability of adult performance (Elias, 1977; Fragaszy, Baer, & Adams-Curtis, 1991). Thus, one might hypothesize that slowing down development and the associated changes in the organization of behavior reflect an evolutionary tradeoff in which the comparatively rapid development of tightly organized and relatively stereotyped behavior patterns becomes less reliable and predictable, while concurrently becoming less rigid and more capable of adapting to current circumstances (Mason, 1968a, 1968b, 1979).

☐ Primate Behavioral Development: Proximate Influences

The concept of neoteny provides a helpful framework for thinking about the evolution and adaptive significance of systematic differences between species in the complexity and plasticity of performance, although it does not address the nature of the specific variables within the organism and in its environment that produce these effects. This issue of proximate influences on development is a fundamental part of understanding the natural history of primate behavioral ontogeny, and it has been an abiding theme in my research.

It is widely known that ontogeny begins at conception, and that by the time it leaves the birth canal the mammalian neonate is already richly equipped with organized behaviors that facilitate its adjustment to the outside world. In monkeys and apes these patterns relate both to the model's arousal-reducing developmental trend, for example, clinging, rooting, oral grasping, and sucking, and to the arousal-increasing exploitative trend, which is focused on more general features of the environment, for example, the tendencies to respond selectively to different patterns of visual and tactile stimulation, to manipulate conspicuous objects, and to react positively or negatively to certain sounds and visual gestalts

(Berkson, 1963; Fantz, 1958; Foley, 1934; Hines, 1942; Jacobsen, Jacobsen, & Yoshioka, 1932; Mason, Harlow, & Rueping, 1959; Mason, 1961a, 1985; Mowbray & Cadell, 1962; Rosenblum & Cross, 1963).

Many of these early behavior patterns are identifiable by their species-typical form. Although they superficially resemble *reflexes* or *fixed action patterns*, they are more flexible and more responsive to variations within the individual and its environment than these concepts usually imply. They are hedonically resonant and capable of generating affective responses whose valence and intensity vary with the environmental context and the individual's existing motivational state. Moreover, while the basic form of the behaviors remains recognizable as development proceeds, the details of their organization are characteristically altered; the frequencies with which they occur also change and their functions are often expanded. These modifications contribute to and characterize the two major trends depicted in Figure 5.1. Almost certainly experience is not the primary cause of these changes, although its influence is powerful and pervasive. It can be discerned in the organization of motor patterns (for example, nonnutritive sucking of finger or toe instead of the mother's nipple), in the effective stimuli for eliciting and sustaining behavior (for example, clinging to an inanimate object instead of the mother's body), and in the processes intervening between stimulus and response (for example, the perceived significance of objects and events, effects of basal levels of arousal).

These early patterns are properly viewed as basic species-typical structures that assimilate and act on information. They are fundamental units in behavioral development and I refer to them as *schemas* (Mason, 1970a). My use of the concept owes much to Lashley, Hebb, and especially, Piaget. Lashley recognized that the brain "has definite predilections for certain forms of organization and imposes these upon the sensory impulses which reach it," and he suggested that in "its functional organization the nervous system seems to consist of schemata or basic patterns within which new stimuli are spontaneously fitted." (Lashley, 1949, p. 35). A few years later Hebb presented his highly influential ideas about the effects of early experience on the formation of *cell assemblies* and *phase sequences*, hypothesized to exist within central nervous system (Hebb, 1949). Although Piaget did not delve into the workings of the brain, his early training in biology is reflected in many aspects of his thinking about psychological development, including his ideas about schemas, a concept that occupied a fundamental place in his theories (Flavell, 1963; Furth, 1969; Piaget, 1970, 1971).

Schemas are dynamic structures that can be modified during development in several ways. A schema can be changed by use or repetition, it can be changed through the complementary processes of *assimilation* of incoming information within an existing schema and *accommodation* of the schema to the new information, and it can be changed by one schema joining another (usually several others) to form a higher-order functional unit (Piaget, 1970; Hunt, 1961). These properties are inferred from observed modifications of behavior. Modifiability is a matter of degree, of course, a quality that may be described as *openness*. Openness is influenced by multiple variables, including the functions of the schema, as well as species-typical attributes. As previously described, the more slowly developing and more neotenous primate species appear in general to be more open (i.e., more sensitive to experiential influences) compared to more rapidly developing species.

Principle of Component Schemas

One of the most important changes in early schemas during primate behavioral development, in my opinion, is their incorporation and integration as components in the formation of higher-order, biologically meaningful functional units. This is a dialectic and probabilistic process in which the individual participates actively and opportunistically in the development of major biological systems. The evidence suggests that primitive schemas create biases and dispositions that lead the immature organisms to respond differentially and selectively to certain features of the objects it encounters in its environment, based on how adequately they correspond physically and psychologically to critical aspects of major functional systems in the biology of the species. The outcome of this "best fit" process is that selected objects eventually emerge as perceived "goals" or "ends" to which the relevant early schemas become "means." In this fashion the individual forms new concepts or categories based on the attributes of the selected objects. These emergent conceptual objects and their perceived equivalents (i.e., similar objects that fall within the same psychological domain) acquire the ability to motivate and reward behavior in a manner suggesting that they have become *functionally autonomous* (Allport, 1937). The essential idea is that primitive schemas that initially guide development eventually lead to the emergence of higher-order units—classes of objects ("goals") and activities ("consummatory responses")—that are no longer closely tied to the schemas that were their historical source.

According to this conception, some degree of affinity exists initially and throughout development among the component schemas participating in the formation of a given higher-order functional unit, although the linkage among these components is loose and variable rather than fixed and unchanging. Consequently, because the emerging higher-order functional "system" is never completely independent of the influence of the participating schemas, it is only *semi-autonomous*; because its actions are never completely determined by any specific schema or configuration of participating schemas, however, its organization is only *quasi-coherent*; and because it is only semi-autonomous and quasi-coherent such a system is inherently *open*—that is to say, its functioning is in some degree susceptible to and most likely dependent on the individual's personal experience.

To illustrate the process through which schemas become components in the development of higher-order, semi-autonomous, quasi-coherent functional systems, I will draw mainly on data from rhesus monkeys and, to a lesser extent, chimpanzees and other primates. The examples revolve around the development of filial attachment (from the subject's standpoint the central organizing concept is "mother"), appetite for solid foods (central organizing concept: "edibles"), sex behavior (central organizing concept: "sex partner"), and parenting (central organizing concept: "infant"). The emergence of such semi-autonomous categories ("goal objects") is a prominent feature of primate ontogeny, and may well be a general phenomenon in the development of goal-directed behavior in warm-blooded mammals (Berridge, 1996; Dickinson & Balleine, 1995; G. Hall, 1996; W. Hall, Arnold, & Myers, 2000; Hunt, 1961; Lorenz, 1970; Schneirla & Rosenblatt, 1961).

Filial Emotional Attachment

The specific schemas that are the basis for the initial adjustment to the mother soon lose their reflexlike quality and begin to work together as loosely coordinated elements in a larger pattern relating to feeding, comfort, and security, all normally provided by the biological mother. In the process of forming an emotional attachment clinging is of primary importance. Although the schemas associated with feeding (rooting, oral grasping, sucking, swallowing) are facilitated if the infant has something to grasp and support itself, their contributions to attachment are minor compared to the effects of clinging to a soft, warm, and claspable body (Harlow & Zimmerman, 1959; Hoffman, Mendoza, Hennessy, & Mason, 1995). In the initial stages of attachment formation the visual properties of this object are unimportant.

The transition from indiscriminate clinging to any claspable object that an infant happens to encounter to an emotional attachment selectively directed to a specific "maternal" entity is a developmental process that requires time to complete and follows a predictable course. We have investigated the formation and expression of attachment in a variety of species, in various age groups, and in animals raised in different environments with widely different attachment figures. As might be expected, all these factors can influence the rate at which an attachment develops. Nevertheless, based on similar methods and comparable behavioral and physiological measures we have found the essential phenomena of emotional attachment to be remarkably consistent (Hill, McCormack, & Mason, 1973; Hoffman, Mendoza, Hennessy, & Mason, 1995; Mason, 1965b, 1967; Mason & Capitanio, 1988; Mason, Hill, & Thomsen, 1971, 1974; Mason & Kenney, 1974; Mendoza & Mason, 1986). A reasonable conclusion from these findings is that filial attachment is founded on a psychoneuroendocrine core that is a basic feature of the biology of all primates and probably most mammals (Kraemer, 1992; Mason & Mendoza, 1998).

While the genesis of an emotional attachment to a specific figure draws upon primitive behavioral and biological dispositions—the schemas mediating the initial adjustment to the mother—it also creates the possibility of establishing a *relationship* with the attachment figure. This relationship is based theoretically on the total history of psychologically relevant experiences with the object of attachment, and it can carry the individual into a new functional level with greatly extended developmental possibilities. The central feature of this change is that the "mother" (real or artificial) emerges as a conceptual "object," a distinct and abiding entity with multiple attributes. Obviously, the process is heavily influenced by experience. The attachment figure is eventually recognized at a distance and from various angles of regard, is preferred over others of similar appearance, and is perceived as an individual with diverse qualities (Mason & Capitanio, 1988; Mason, Hill, & Thomsen, 1971, 1974; Mason & Kenney, 1974).

A relationship with a specific attachment figure also creates the possibility of major motivational changes, with important developmental implications. Most obviously, this figure quickly acquires the ability to control the infant's immediate behavior and emotional state. It is the focus of the infant's attention. Its absence causes distress and its presence alleviates it. By various behavioral means it is able to administer rewards (e.g., being present in a stressful situation, active nurturant behavior) and punishments (e.g., indifference to comfort-seeking attempts, abandonment, rejection). These effects are present, of course, whether or not the object of attachment is aware of how they are produced.

Without doubt the most important feature of relationships with attachment figures is their ability to *potentiate* new forms and levels of psychobiological functioning. By "potentiate" I refer primarily to the fact that some attributes of the relationship lead to stable changes in broad aspects of behavior such as are usually referred to as traits, coping strategies, cognitive styles, categorical knowledge, temperament, and the like (Capitanio,

1999; Clarke & Boinski, 1995; Rumbaugh, Savage-Rumbaugh, & Washburn, 1996; Schusterman, Reichmuth, & Kastak, 2000; Terrace, 1984). The possibility that social factors early in development were likely to produce such effects was suggested by my original comparisons of wild-born and nursery-reared monkeys, although I found few clues as to what their precise nature might be (Mason, 1960, 1961a, 1961b; Mason & Green, 1962). I later learned that potentiation may occur even with relatively simple attachment figures, and that their long-range consquences may be impossible to predict.

The first clear evidence of potentiation I encountered emerged from a study carried out with Gershon Berkson using mobile and stationary artificial mothers to investigate the genesis of habitual stereotyped body-rocking. This behavior intrigued us because it is common in monkeys and apes raised apart from the mother but extremely rare in mother-reared animals. It is also interesting because it appears frequently in very similar form among blind, autistic, and severely mentally defective humans, although the etiology is probably different for each of these groups from that for nonhuman primates (Berkson, 1967). To examine the effects of maternal mobility we raised two groups of rhesus monkeys with identical cloth-covered surrogates, except that for one group they were mechanically driven to move up and down and around the cage on an irregular schedule and for the other they were stationary. In all other respects the animals experienced identical conditions. The surrogates were permanently removed when the monkeys were about ten months of age and they continued to live in identical conditions until the research ended. As predicted, mobility prevented the development of stereotyped body-rocking. None of the nine monkeys raised with mobile surrogates ever rocked habitually, whereas all but one of the ten monkeys raised with stationary surrogates did so (Mason & Berkson, 1975).

Tests conducted outside the living cage clearly suggested that mobility had potentiated broad changes that we had not anticipated in the monkeys' responses to environmental stimuli. Animals raised with mobile surrogates more readily entered a novel room, more frequently contacted and made more varied responses to an unfamiliar stimulus-person, spent more time looking at other monkeys, and were more sensitive to differences among them in appearance and behavior (Anderson, Kenney, & Mason,1977; Eastman & Mason, 1975; Mason & Berkson, 1975). Many of these tests were carried out after the animals were permanently separated from their surrogates, suggesting that the effects of rearing conditions were general and persistent.

There were reasons to suspect that from a functional standpoint the mobile surrogate was doing a great deal more than just carrying the infant about the cage. Based on our observations of the monkeys in their living cages it seemed we had unwittingly created a social substitute that was capable of simulating some of the generic attributes of social interaction. Its movements were not entirely predictable: it could withdraw from the infant without warning; sneak up behind it and deliver a gentle rap on the head; its comings and goings demanded adjustments that were not required of the monkeys raised with a stationary surrogate. These qualities probably explain why play behavior, which appeared in both groups in the second month of life, quickly became much more frequent in the monkeys raised with mobile surrogates (Mason & Berkson, 1975). The interactive properties of the mobile surrogates may also have contributed to other unanticipated effects.

The case for potentiation by attachment figures was strengthened in subsequent research in which we compared rhesus monkeys raised with either a living substitute mother (a female mongrel dog) or an inanimate one (a "fur"-covered hobby horse). We chose dogs because preliminary findings indicated they were effective substitute mothers (Mason & Kenney, 1974). We wanted an attachment figure that would be fully social, yet would not present the special features of the biological mother, shaped by natural selection to guide offspring behavioral development along species-typical paths. In contrast to real mothers, dogs did not respond maternally to the monkeys, their behavior was not undergoing developmental changes concurrently with those in the monkeys, and throughout the study—which covered the first several years of life—they remained tolerant and highly social companions.

In both rearing conditions the animals lived with their attachment figures in sheltered outdoor kennels. They had frequent visual contact with dogs, other monkeys, people, and a variety of other ongoing and occasional events. In addition, they were routinely exposed in the presence of their surrogates to five complex outdoor environments, each containing a variety of toys, puzzles, and climbing devices. We wanted to minimize the usual problems of imposing general restrictions on the experience of our monkeys.

The consequences of being raised with a living attachment figure were profound. Effects on behavior and physiology were evident in the expression of filial attachment and in the monkeys' basic stance toward the environment. Compared to individuals raised on hobby horses, dog-raised monkeys were more attentive to their surroundings, more sensitive to novelty and change, more manipulative in their social interactions, and more likely to perform successfully in problem-solving situations (Capitanio, 1984, 1985; Capitanio & Mason, 2000; Mason, 1978; Mason & Capitanio, 1988; Mason, Mendoza, & Moberg, 1991; Wood, Mason, & Kenney, 1979).

The source of these differences, as in the study with mobile surrogate mothers, relate to the element of animation of the attachment figure, although precisely how it does so is unknown. I suspect that the major effective variable is *response-contingent stimulation* (Mason, 1978). The importance of this factor in early human development has been emphasized by Lewis and Goldberg (1969) and illustrated in a series of classic studies by Watson and associates (e.g., Watson & Ramey, 1972). Its relevance to the socioemotional development of nonhuman primates has also been demonstrated by Mineka et al. in a study with rhesus monkeys (Mineka, Gunnar, & Champoux, 1986).

Appetite for Solid Foods

Before I started working with infant macaques it never occurred to me that they would have to acquire an appetite for solid foods. I thought that upon reaching a certain age an infant monkey would be ready and eager to eat grapes, bananas, apples, oranges—all those things that adult monkeys like so much and are willing to work for, even when they are not deprived of food. I soon discovered I was wrong. Nursery-reared infants do not recognize solid foods as such.

An early study of first encounters with solid foods indicated that appetite develops slowly and appears to be led by primitive schemas, principally the tendency to grasp any small, conspicuous, portable object and carry it to the mouth. Each day for 40 days we tested two groups of laboratory-reared infants starting when they were 20 days of age with small pieces of banana, identical except that for one group the bananas were multicolored with food dyes and for the other they were uncolored. Hand and mouth contacts with the food were increasingly more frequent with the colored bananas. Results for a third group tested with arrays of mixed foods (banana, orange, bread, apple, grape) were indistinguishable from those for the monkeys tested with multicolored banana. Not all individuals actually swallowed the food, and the number that did varied with the experimental conditions. Of the ten animals in each group, the number consuming food during at least one session was nine, seven, and three individuals in the mixed, multicolored, and uncolored groups, respectively. Consumption varied with the quality of the specific items. It was surprising, however, that the avidity for food characteristic of adults was displayed by few if any of these infants (Mason & Harlow, 1959).

This study was prompted by the practical difficulties of getting infant rhesus monkeys to accept and work for solid foods. In more naturalistic settings opportunities such as watching older animals eating and being able to sample similar foods within easy reach could make for a smoother and unremarkable transition. Nevertheless, Lashley and Watson's thorough longitudinal study suggests that the basic process is essentially the same in the more normal circumstances of an infant rhesus monkey living socially with its mother and other animals (Lashley & Watson, 1913).

The results of this simple study helped shape my view that early behavioral schemas (in this case, grasping, lifting, mouthing conspicuous objects, preferences for specific taste qualities) contribute to the formation of higher-order semi-autonomous "systems" (in this instance, appetite) that are able to exert powerful control over behavior. Although I am convinced that hedonic qualities play a part, precisely how the transition from "pleasure" to "appetite" comes about is an open question. As Berridge writes in his recent review of the brain substrates involved in food reward, "The sight of food has no intrinsic motivational value. It is merely an aggregation of visual shapes and colors, like the sight of any object. It is not an incentive until value becomes attached to it by experience. . . . The question is—what must be done by the brain to a perception or representation to transform mere information into an attractive, riveting and desired incentive?" (Berridge, 1996, p. 15).

Development of Sex Behavior

Sex behavior is a prime example of early schemas becoming integrated as components of higher-order functional systems. In rhesus monkeys the species-characteristic components of copulatory behavior are readily recognized in both male and female. In the typical male sequence, he approaches, orients his body toward the partner's perineum, places both hands on her hips, stands with both feet clasping her rear legs, and thrusts. The complementary pattern of the female is to stand on all fours while she orients her hindquarters toward the partner, holding her tail above or to one side of the perineal area, and bracing while the partner mounts. Sex may be initiated by male or female. Although the forms of male and female sex behavior are quite distinct, both patterns are shown by either sex and may be directed toward partners of either sex.

Contrary to a common assumption at the time, my initial comparisons of wild-born and nursery-reared adolescent rhesus monkeys indicated that the integration of these component schemas into the functionally effective, species-typical patterns of sexual behavior was dependent on experience. Nursery-reared animals of both sexes were incapable of the normal patterns of copulatory behavior for their age and species (Mason, 1960). The deficiencies were particularly conspicuous in males. Inexperienced males were often sexually aroused in the presence of another monkey, but even though they displayed most of the components of the normal sequence in easily recognizable form, the elements did not constitute an integrated, species-typical, biologically effective pattern. The orientation toward the partner was often inappropriate and independent of the partner's posture. Consequently, grasping the partner and thrusting were misdirected. Although males occasionally tried to clasp the partner's legs with their feet while mounting, only one male ever succeeded in doing so with both feet in the characteristic manner, and this occurred infrequently. Nursery-reared females were also aberrant. They usually failed to make appropriate postural adjustments in response to their partner's mounting attempts, and their sexual presentations were variable and often misdirected (Mason, 1960). These deficiencies were confirmed in subsequent research and found to persist indefinitely, in spite of a variety of efforts at amelioration, such as placing nursery-reared adolescent males and females together on a small island, pairing laboratory-reared estrous females with sexually experienced males, and pairing laboratory-reared males with sexually experienced females. Although some females eventually mated with experienced breeding males, few males ever mated successfully even after many opportunities (Harlow, 1965; Harlow, Joslyn, Senko, & Dopp, 1966; Senko, 1966).

The sexual competence of both male and female chimpanzees is also affected adversely by atypical early experience. Chimpanzee copulatory behavior is similar to that of the macaques. Either sex may initiate sexual behavior, their roles are complementary, and successful copulation requires coordination between partners. As in rhesus monkeys, the basic pattern in the common chimpanzee (*P. troglodytes*) is dorsoventral, although the double foot-clasp of the partner's legs is not typical; copulatory behavior is also less stereotyped. Chimpanzees raised in social isolation for the first three years of life or restricted to extensive contact with humans during infancy and early childhood were found to be sexually incompetent even after many opportunities for normal socialization during and after puberty. In contrast to similarly raised rhesus monkeys, however, most of the isolation-reared chimpanzees eventually learned to copulate with sophisticated partners, an achievement that the authors suggest reflects the greater overall complexity of chimpanzee behavior and their less rigid and stereotyped sexual performance (Rogers & Davenport, 1969).

Why do these pubescent and adult monkeys and apes either fail to develop the normal patterns of copulatory behavior or require recourse to extraordinary procedures to overcome their copulatory incompetence, even when seemingly appropriate opportunities are provided? It is not that the relevant schemas are missing, for there are clear indications that they are present in both species in early infancy. Moreover, young animals normally display the typical adult form well in advance of reproductive maturity (Bingham, 1928; Goy & Wallen, 1979; Hines, 1942; Southwick, Beg, & Siddiqi, 1965). Bingham's observations of sexual behavior in immature chimpanzees clearly convey the idea that component schemas are incorporated into the development of higher-order functions: "Such phenomena as clinging, embracing, mouthing, manipulation, pelvic pushing and erections, all appear in diverse conditions in advance of recognizable copulatory behavior. Their assemblage in novel sexual adjustments seems, after review of their genesis, to be largely an old story with the details more or less rearranged" (Bingham, 1928, p. 95).

While the precise causes of normal and deviant sexual behavior probably vary with gender and with species, based on my observations of socially deprived adolescent rhesus monkeys I suspected that the disruptive effects of high arousal and lack of early opportunities to develop appropriate communicative and other cognitive social skills were important. In particular, intense rough-and-tumble play by highly aroused males and their strong aggressive tendencies evoked negative reactions in females that were already somewhat fearful, creating a situation that was not consistent with effective copulation (Mason, 1960, 1961b; 1965a). In support of this proposition, eliminating negative reactions from the partner seems to move the deprived male's sexual behavior somewhat closer to species-typical norms. In a study by Deutsch and Larsson (1974) two adult male rhesus monkeys that had been raised with cloth surrogates were tested with a cloth model of a monkey standing quadrapedally in approximation of the normal sexual presentation posture. Each animal grasped and mounted the model in the appropriate orientation, with at least one foot clasping the model's leg, and thrusted against it. One male actually achieved ejaculation. When tested with mother-reared females, however, both males remained completely inadequate sexually.

The most informative observations on rearing conditions conducive to adult sexual competence is provided in a series of studies by Goy, Wallen, and associates. Their research emphasized the foot-clasp mount in male rhesus monkeys, a crucial element in the successful copulatory pattern of this species. The prinicipal rearing variables they examined were the amount and duration of experience with age mates, with the mother, and the conditions in which these experiences occurred (Goy & Goldfoot, 1974; Goy, Wallen, & Goldfoot, 1974; Goy & Wallen, 1979; Wallen, Bielert, & Slimp, 1977; Wallen, Goldfoot, & Goy, 1981).

The general outcome of their research is consistent with my early suspicion that high arousal and poor communication impair the early development of sexual competence. They found that augmenting the amount of exposure to peers strongly increased the incidence of foot-clasp mounting, and that the most effective condition was being raised with continuous access to the mother and to age mates. The frequency of fearful and aggressive behaviors was also much lower in the groups having continuous access to the mother and to peers (Goy & Goldfoot, 1974; Wallen,

Bielert, & Slimp, 1977), which may be viewed as evidence that the presence of mothers during interactions among peers modulated arousal and encouraged the development of basic communicative skills and positive social relations.

Parental Behavior

Parental behavior provides the final illustration of my thesis that component schemas appear early in ontogeny and become loosely joined in the development of higher-order, semi-autonomous, quasi-coherent functional systems. As with sexual behavior, schemas for parental behavior are present in infancy, they appear in the same form in both sexes, and they continue to be accessible throughout life. That is not to say that males and females do not differ, of course, for it is clear that well in advance of reproductive maturity they begin to display a bias toward specific patterns that are appropriate to their sex.

Again, the most complete data are available for the macaques, particularly rhesus monkeys. The major behavioral elements in the caregiving activities of an adequate mother rhesus monkey during the first few weeks following the birth are clasping the infant to her ventral surface, carrying it as she goes about her daily routine, restraining it if it attempts to leave and she is unwilling to have it do so, and retrieving it when it is at a distance or signals that it is in a state of distress. Ordinarily, adult male rhesus monkeys do not participate in infant care, although instances have been reported in which an adult male has assumed the role of caregiver (Breuggeman, 1973). And of course, such behavior is commonplace in other macaque species such as the Japanese monkey and Barbary macaque (*M. fuscata, M. sylvana*) (Mitchell, 1969).

The relatively discrete purposive acts that make up the bulk of the parental repertoire are common elements in the behavior of developing rhesus monkeys of both sexes. Actions such as cuddling, carrying, retrieving, and protecting are directed toward infants and yearlings of both sexes by all age classes of males and females, including infants that are themselves scarcely strong enough to carry another infant (Breuggeman, 1973). Presumably these activities help to form the concept or category "infant monkey" which has powerful control over the behavior of adult monkeys of both sexes. Several lines of evidence suggest that, as in the other examples considered here, this process of integrating component schemas within a higher-order parental "system" is dependent on appropriate opportunities early in development and takes time to complete. For example, in spite of their attraction to infants, young monkeys are often clumsy in handling them and seem to improve with practice

(Lancaster, 1971). Other indications of the effects of experience include reduced maternal competence in monkeys that were not mothered themselves, monkeys that were deprived of contact with peers, monkeys that have had no prior exposure to infants, and even normally socialized monkeys that are experiencing motherhood for the first time. Deficiencies range from clumsiness and uncertainty to outright abuse (Arling & Harlow, 1967; Harlow, Harlow, Dodsworth, & Arling, 1966; Holman & Goy, 1980; Maestripieri & Carroll, 1998a, 1988b; Seay, Alexander, & Harlow, 1964). Even the most severely impaired females, the "motherless mothers" of the Wisconsin studies, show considerable improvement in maternal competence after their first infant, although they are probably never on a par with normally socialized females (Champoux, Byrne, DeLizio, & Suomi, 1992; Ruppenthal, Arling, Harlow, Sackett, & Suomi, 1976).

Patterns of parental behavior of rhesus monkeys are not necessarily the same in other species. For example, many New World monkey infants always ride on the caregiver's back and even during nursing are not cradled against the mother's belly in the characteristic manner of virtually all Old World anthropoids (Kohda, 1985). The father's role also varies widely, from lack of recognition of their own offspring in most primates to extensive involvement in caregiving of their young by a few species, such as the New World titi monkey, *Callicebus* (Mendoza & Mason, 1986).

In spite of these differences, in keeping with the principle of component schemas, two features that appear to be shared by all species of anthropoid primates are a dependence on experience in the development of parental behavior and a tenuous association among the component schemas usually included in a species's parenting "system." Although experience and strength of association among elements are related, they are conceptually and functionally distinct. Experience may improve parenting by modifying schemas or strengthening associations among them, but it is also clear that experience does not always result in improved performance. Even within the same species, behavioral tendencies associated with the qualities of maternal protectiveness, rejection, abusiveness, and neglect appear to vary independently. For example, the same mother may show high levels of contact-promoting and nurturant behaviors (approaching, making contact, restraining, grooming) while also displaying a strong tendency to reject, break contact, and leave her infant (Fairbanks, 1996). A mother may also show extreme forms of physical abusiveness (dragging, stepping on, biting, hitting their infants), while at the same time maintaining close proximity and protectiveness (Maestripieri & Carroll, 1998b; Troisi & D'Amato, 1984; Troisi, D'Amato, Fuccillo, & Scucchi, 1982). Such behaviors have been noted in mothers born and raised in social groups and living in seemingly optimal conditions. Some of these effects may be modified by experience; others, apparently not (Maestripieri & Carroll, 1998b).

Our titi monkeys, maintained as a breeding colony for more than thirty years, created a special opportunity to observe some of the complexities of the relations between experience and component schemas. In the wild and in captivity this species shows a sharp division of parental labor in which the father carries the infant at virtually all times when it is not nursing. The mother is a willing participant in this arrangement and appears eager to have him do so; in fact both she and the infant (for whom the father is the principal attachment figure) are stressed if he becomes separated from them (Hoffman, Mendoza, Hennessy, & Mason, 1995; Mendoza & Mason, 1986). As always, however, there are exceptions. Occasionally, parental behavior does not conform to the species-typical pattern. Some fathers have refused to have any contact with their infants and some mothers (not all) are apparently willing to take on all caregiving responsibilities. These grossly atypical behaviors are usually seen only with firstborn infants and disappear with later offspring. We suspect, however, that performance of parents as individuals and as a "team" (whose coordinated efforts are critical to reproductive success) continues to improve with experience across several generations of young. From a purely practical standpoint, we came to regard some individuals as parental "champions" who could be counted on to succeed, with virtually any partner, whereas others were predictably mediocre and seemed to need a competent helpmate. So too, we perceive some pairs to behave as if they understand what nature intends, and year after year produce a healthy, viable infant who receives excellent care. From a strictly personal, non-scientific standpoint, which is, after all, where my interest in development began, I view these small histories as examples of the importance of a proper environment, the right genes, and, of course, a large measure of good luck.

☐ Conclusions

In this essay I have tried to convey a sense of my conception of the natural history of primate behavioral development as it has emerged over decades of working with a variety of primate species in a diversity of settings. The bedrock of my approach is description of the behaviors of individual animals, whether acting alone or in social groups. In addition to my own experience, I have relied extensively on the reports of many other qualified observers. My long-standing aim has been to organize the complex phenomena of primate behavioral development within a rational conceptual framework. This essay presents my most recent attempt along these lines.

Conceptions of development are theoretical, of course, and need to be evaluated critically. This is what I propose for this final section. I will focus on major ideas that have become part of my conception of behavioral development. Be advised, however, that my concern is less with pointing out the shortcomings of the theoretical constructs that I have favored than examining their utility in organizing empirical findings.

The most important and enduring construct in my conception of primate development is *arousal*, a motivational concept. Its theoretical role is to accommodate an array of seemingly disparate findings within a common framework. To summarize those findings briefly: immature primates relate to the environment according to the pleasure principle. For the neonate any disturbance in its normal state of equilibrium is unpleasant, and it responds with agitation or distress. A return to equilibrium is experienced as pleasurable. Early in the postnatal period infants show the beginnings of a progressive trend toward greater tolerance for and attraction to stimulation, and they respond to modest increments as pleasant and rewarding. Whether increases in the general level of stimulation are experienced as pleasant or aversive depends on the individual's existing state. In relaxed circumstances increases in stimulation are pleasant and may elicit behaviors that further increase the level, such as social play, exploratory behavior, or gross motor activities. However, if the individual is in an existing state of high excitement, uncertainty, fear, and the like, further increases in stimulation are experienced as unpleasant or aversive and produce avoidance or distress. Developmental changes in the effects of age, experience, forms of stimulation, and the current state of the organism on behavioral responsiveness have been amply demonstrated. The principal value of the arousal concept in my view of development has been as a tool for organizing and clarifying the complex and dynamic relations among these variables.

Another important theoretical construct in my conception of development is *schema*, an information-processing concept. It is abundantly clear that the newborn monkey or ape enters the outside world equipped with a sizeable repertoire of behaviors that help it to adjust to the kind of environment it is likely to encounter. Many of these early behaviors are part of organized information-processing units (schemas). The most significant schemas for behavioral development are responsive to variations in the environment and in the individual's state, and they are potentially modifiable by experience. In the terms of a familiar paradigm, their structure may be portrayed as S (stimulus)–O (organism)–R (response)–F (feedback). The presence of feedback in these schemas provides an extremely important function that distinguishes them from schemas that lack this attribute and consequently are more rigid, reflexlike, and less open to the influences of experience.

Schemas that respond to feedback meet an important conceptual need in my view of behavioral development by providing structures that are capable of *mediating dynamically* between the developing individual and its environment, thereby contributing an idiographic quality to the organization of its development. The developing monkey or ape is an active and opportunistic participant in a process that usually moves it toward the functional endpoints that are characteristic of its species. It is clear, of course, that this progression is neither automatic nor random, but flexibly organized and probabilistic. Schemas are important contributors to this process.

The most consequential schemas for the long-term development of behavior are highly motivated, affectively charged, and able to generate feelings of pleasantness and unpleasantness. They are present in the neonate and continue to appear as development proceeds. The likelihood that a given schema will be manifested on any given occasion varies with the perceived situation, the individual's developmental status, and its momentary state of arousal. Figure 5.1 is a coarse attempt to depict some of these relationships. The evidence indicates that actions and stimuli that reduce arousal from aversively high levels or increase it from unpleasantly low levels can act as rewards. Based on such observations I suggest that the hedonic qualities of schemas play a significant part in the development of abiding preferences and aversions for environmental objects and events. Of course, the nature of these objects and events can have profound developmental consequences.

A fundamental developmental concept that I have not been able to address in this essay as fully as it deserves is *emergence*. Emergence refers to the appearance of new phenomena at a level of organization that requires new descriptive categories and new measures, as in the classic "whole that is greater than the sum of its parts." I believe that concepts such as *potentiation, functional autonomy, component schemas*, and *higher-order functional systems* refer to genuine emergent phenomena, as I have tried to illustrate with a few empirical examples. The precise sources and significance of such outcomes are imperfectly understood, however, and offer exciting prospects for future developmental research.

☐ Acknowledgment

Preparation of this chapter was supported by grants MH49033, MH57502, and RR00169 from the U.S. Public Health Service, National Institutes of Health. I thank John Capitanio and Sally Mendoza for their comments.

☐ References

Allport, G. W. (1937). *Personality: A psychological interpretation*. New York: Henry Holt.

Anderson, C. O., Kenney, A. M., & Mason, W. A. (1977). Effects of maternal mobility, partner, and endocrine state on social responsiveness of adolescent rhesus monkeys. *Developmental Psychobiology, 10,* 421–434.

Arling, G. L., & Harlow, H. F. (1967). Effects of social deprivation on maternal behavior of rhesus monkeys. *Journal of Comparative and Physiological Psychology, 64,* 371–377.

Beach, F. A. (1950). The snark was a boojum. *American Psychologist, 5,* 115–124.

Berkson, G. (1963). Stimuli affecting vocalizations and basal skin resistance of neonate chimpanzee. *Perceptual and Motor Skills, 17,* 871–874.

Berkson, G, (1967). Abnormal steretoped motor acts. In J. Zubin & H. F. Hunt (Eds.), *Comparative psychopathology* (pp. 76–94). New York: Grune & Stratton.

Berkson, G. (1968). Development of abnormal stereotyped behaviors. *Developmental Psychobiology, 1,* 118–132.

Berlyne, D. E. (1967). Arousal and reinforcement. In D. Levine (Ed.), *Nebraska Symposium on Motivation, 15* (pp. 1–110). Lincoln: University of Nebraska Press.

Berridge, K. C. (1996). Food reward: Brain substrates of wanting and liking. *Neuroscience and Biobehavioral Reviews, 20,* 1–25.

Bingham, H. C. (1928). Sex development in apes. *Comparative Psychology Monographs*, Serial No. 23, pp. 1–161.

Breuggeman, J. A. (1973). Parental care in a group of free-ranging rhesus monkeys (*Macaca mulatta*). *Folia Primatologica, 20,* 178–210.

Capitanio, J. P. (1984). Early experience and social processes in rhesus macaques (*Macaca mulatta*): I. Dyadic social interaction. *Journal of Comparative Psychology, 98,* 35–44.

Capitanio, J. P. (1985). Early experience and social processes in rhesus macaques (*Macaca mulatta*): II. Complex social interaction. *Journal of Comparative Psychology, 99,* 133–144.

Capitanio, J. P. (1999). Personality dimensions in adult male rhesus macaques: Prediction of behaviors across time and situation. *American Journal of Primatology, 47,* 299–320.

Capitanio, J. P., & Mason, W. A. (2000) Cognitive style: Problem solving by rhesus macaques (*Macaca mulatta*), reared with living or inanimate substitute mothers. *Journal of Comparative Psychology, 114,* 115–125.

Champoux, M., Byrne, E., DeLizio, R., & Suomi, S. J. (1992). Motherless mothers revisited: Rhesus maternal behavior and rearing history. *Primates, 33,* 251–255.

Clark, W. E. L. (1960). *The antecedents of man: Introduction to the evolution of the primates*, Chicago: Quadrangle Books.

Clarke, A. S., & Boinski, S. (1995). Temperament in nonhuman primates. *American Journal of Primatology, 37,* 103–125.

de Beer, G. (1958). *Embryos and ancestors*. Oxford, UK: Clarendon Press.

Deutsch, J., & Larsson, K. (1974). Model-oriented sexual behavior in surrogate-reared rhesus monkeys. *Brain, Behavior and Evolution, 9,* 157–164.

Dickinson, A., & Balleine, B. (1995). Motivational control of instrumental action. *Current Directions in Psychological Science, 4,* 162–167.

Eastman, R. F., & Mason, W. A. (1975). Looking behavior in monkeys raised with mobile and stationary artificial mothers. *Developmental Psychobiology, 8,* 213–221.

Elias, M. F. (1977). Relative maturity of cebus and squirrel monkeys at birth and during infancy. *Developmental Psychobiology, 10,* 519–528.

Fairbanks, L. A. (1996). Individual differences in maternal style: Causes and consequences for mothers and offspring. *Advances in the Study of Behavior, 25,* 579–611.

Fantz, R. L. (1958). Visual discrimination in a neonate chimpanzee. *Perceptual and Motor Skills, 8,* 59–66.

Flavell, J. H. (1963). *The developmental psychology of Jean Piaget*. New York: D. Van Nostrand.

Foley, J. P., Jr. (1934). First-year development of a rhesus monkey (*Macaca mulatta*) reared in isolation. *Journal of Genetic Psychology, 45,* 39–105.

Fragaszy, D. M., Baer, J., & Adams-Curtis, L. (1991). Behavioral development and maternal care in tufted capuchins *(Cebus apella)* and squirrel monkeys *(Saimiri sciureus)* from birth through seven months. *Developmental Psychobiology, 24,* 375–393.

Furth, H. G. (1969). *Piaget and knowledge: Theoretical foundations.* Englewood Cliffs, NJ: Prentice-Hall.

Gottlieb, G. (1987). The developmental basis of evolutionary change. *Journal of Comparative Psychology, 101,* 262–271.

Goy, R. W., & Goldfoot, D. A. (1974). Experimental and hormonal factors influencing development of sexual behavior in the male rhesus monkey. In: F. O. Schmitt & F. G. Worden (Rds.), *The neurosciences: Third study program* (pp. 571–581). Cambridge, MA: MIT Press.

Goy, R. W., & Wallen, K. (1979). Experimental variables influencing play, foot-clasp mounting and adult sexual competence in male rhesus monkeys. *Psychoneuroendocrinology, 4,* 1–12.

Goy, R. W., Wallen, K., & Goldfoot, D. A. (1974). Social factors affecting the development of mounting behavior in male rhesus monkeys. In W. Montagna & W. A. Sadler (Rds.), *Reproductive behavior* (pp. 223–247). New York: Plenum.

Hall, G. (1996). Learning about associatively activated stimulus representations: Implications for acquired equivalence and perceptual learning. *Animal Learning and Behavior, 24,* 233–255.

Hall, W. G., Arnold, H. M., & Myers, K. P. (2000). The acquisition of an appetite. *Psychological Science, 11,* 101–105.

Harlow, H. F. (1953). Mice, monkeys, men, and motives. *Psychological Review, 60,* 23–32.

Harlow, H. F. (1965). Sexual behavior in the rhesus monkey. In F. A. Beach (Ed.), *Sex and behavior* (pp. 234–265). New York: Wiley.

Harlow, H. F., Harlow, M. K., Dodsworth, R. O., & Arling, G. L. (1966). Maternal behavior of rhesus monkeys deprived of mothering and peer associations in infancy. *Proceedings of the American Philosophical Society, 110,* 58–66.

Harlow, H. F., Joslyn, W. D., Senko, M. G., & Dopp, A. (1966 Suppl.). Behavioral aspects of reproduction in primates. *Journal of Animal Science, 25,* 49–67.

Harlow, H. F., & Zimmerman, R. R. (1959). Affectional responses in the infant monkey. *Science, 130,* 421–432.

Hebb, D. O. (1949). *The organization of behavior.* New York: Wiley.

Hebb, D. O. (1953). Heredity and environment in mammalian behaviour. *British Journal of Animal Behaviour, 1,* 43–47.

Hill, S. D., McCormack, S. A., & Mason, W. A. (1973). Effects of artificial mothers and visual experience on adrenal responsiveness of infant monkeys. *Developmental Psychobiology, 6,* 421–429.

Hines, M. (1942). The development and regression of reflexes, postures, and progression in the young macaque. *Carnegie Institution of Washington Publication, 541,* 153–209.

Hoffman, K. A., Mendoza, S. P., Hennessy, M. B., & Mason, W. A. (1995). Responses of infant titi monkeys, *Callicebus moloch,* to removal of one or both parents: Evidence for paternal attachment. *Developmental Psychobiology, 28,* 399–407.

Holman, S. D., & Goy, R. W. (1980). Behavioral and mammary responses of adult female rhesus to strange infants. *Hormones and Behavior, 14,* 348–357.

Hunt, J. M. (1961). *Intelligence and experience.* New York: Ronald Press.

Jacobsen, C. F., Jacobsen, M. M., & Yoshioka, J. G. (1932). Development of an infant chimpanzee during her first year. *Comparative Psychology Monographs, 9*(1), Serial No. 41, pp. 1–94.

Kohda, M. (1985). Allomothering behaviour in new and old world monkeys. *Primates, 26,* 28–44.

Kraemer, G. W. (1992). A psychobiological theory of attachment. *Behavioral and Brain Sciences, 15,* 493–541.

Lancaster, J. B. (1971). Play-mothering: The relations between juvenile females and young infants among free-ranging vervet monkeys (*Cercopithecus aethiops*). *Folia Primatologica, 15,* 161–182.

Langer, J. (1969). *Theories of development.* New York: Holt, Rinehart and Winston.

Lashley, K. S. (1949). Persistent problems in the evolution of mind. *Quarterly Review of Biology, 24,* 28–42.

Lashley, K. S., & Watson, J. B. (1913). Notes on the development of a young monkey. *Journal of Animal Behavior, 3,* 114–139.

Lewis, M., & Goldberg, S. (1969). Perceptual-cognitive development in infancy: A generalized expectancy model as a function of the mother-infant interaction. *Merrill-Palmer Quarterly of Behavior and Development, 15,* 81–100.

Lorenz, K. Z. (1952). *King Solomon's ring.* New York: Thomas Y. Crowell Company.

Lorenz, K. Z. (1970). *Studies in animal and human behaviour, volume I* (Robert Martin, Trans.). Cambridge, MA: Harvard University Press.

Maestripieri, D., & Carroll, K. A. (1998a). Child abuse and neglect: Usefulness of the animal data. *Psychological Bulletin, 123,* 211–223.

Maestripieri, D., & Carroll, K. A. (1998b). Risk factors for infant abuse and neglect in group-living rhesus monkeys. *Psychological Science, 9,* 143–145.

Mason, W. A. (1960). The effects of social restriction on the behavior of rhesus monkeys: I. Free social behavior. *Journal of Comparative and Physiological Psychology, 53,* 582–589.

Mason, W. A. (1961a). Effects of age and stimulus characteristics on manipulatory responsiveness of monkeys raised in a restricted environment. *Journal of Genetic Psychology, 99,* 301–308.

Mason, W. A. (1961b). The effects of social restriction on the behavior of rhesus monkeys: II. Tests of gregariousness. *Journal of Comparative and Physiological Psychology, 54,* 287–290.

Mason, W. A. (1961c). The effects of social restriction on the behavior of rhesus monkeys: III. Dominance tests. *Journal of Comparative and Physiological Psychology, 54,* 694–699.

Mason, W. A. (1964). Sociability and social organization in monkeys and apes. In L. Berkowitz (Ed.), *Recent advances in experimental social psychology, vol. I* (pp. 277–305) New York: Academic Press.

Mason, W. A. (1965a). The social development of monkeys and apes. In I. DeVore (Ed.), *Primate behavior: Field studies of monkeys and apes* (pp. 514–543) New York: Holt.

Mason, W. A. (1965b). Determinants of social behavior in young chimpanzees. In A. M. Schrier, H. F. Harlow, & F. Stollnitz (Eds.), *Behavior of nonhuman primates, bol 2* (pp. 335–363) New York: Academic Press.

Mason, W. A. (1967). Motivational aspects of social responsiveness in young chimpanzees. In H. W. Stevenson, E. H. Hess, & H. Rheingold (Eds.), *Early behavior: Comparative and developmental approaches* (pp. 103–126). New York: Wiley.

Mason, W. A. (1968a). Scope and potential of primate research. *Science and Psychoanalysis, 12,* 101–118.

Mason, W. A. (1968b). Early social deprivation in the nonhuman primates: Implications for human behavior. In D. Glass (Ed.), *Environmental influences* (pp. 70–101) New York: Rockefeller University Press.

Mason, W. A. (1970a). Information processing and experiential deprivation: A biologic perspective. In F. A. Young & D. B. Lindsley (Eds.), *Early experience and visual information processing in perceptual and reading disorders* (pp. 302–323). Washington, DC: National Academy of Sciences.

Mason, W. A. (1970b). Early deprivation in biological perspective. In V. H. Denenberg (Ed.), *Education of the infant and young child* (pp. 25–50). New York: Academic Press.

Mason, W. A. (1971a). Motivational factors in psychosocial development. In W. J. Arnold & M. M. Page (Eds.), *Nebraska symposium on motivation* (pp. 35–67). Lincoln: University of Nebraska Press.

Mason, W. A. (1971b). Field and laboratory studies of social organization in Saimiri and Callicebus. In L. A. Rosenblum (Ed.), *Primate behavior: Developments in field and laboratory research, vol. 2* (pp. 107–137). New York and London: Academic Press.

Mason, W. A. (1973). Regulatory functions of arousal in primate psychosocial development. In C. R. Carpenter (Ed.), *Behavioral regulators of behavior in primates* (pp. 19–33). Lewisburg, PA: Bucknell University Press.

Mason, W. A. (1978). Social experience and primate cognitive development. In G. M. Burghardt & M. Bekoff (Eds.), *The development of behavior: Comparative and evolutionary aspects* (pp. 233–251). New York: Garland Press.

Mason, W. A. (1979). Ontogeny of social behavior. In P. Marler & J. G. Vandenbergh (Eds.), *Handbook of behavioral neurobiology, vol. 3: Social behavior and communication* (pp. 1–28). New York: Plenum.

Mason, W. A. (1985). Experiential influences on the development of expressive behaviors in rhesus monkeys. In G. Zivin (Ed.), *The development of expressive behavior: Biology–Environment Interactions* (pp. 117–152) New York: Academic Press.

Mason, W. A., & Berkson, G. (1975). Effects of maternal mobility on the development of rocking and other behaviors in rhesus monkeys: A study with artificial mothers. *Developmental Psychobiology, 8,* 197–211.

Mason, W. A., & Capitanio, J. P. (1988) Formation and expression of filial attachment in rhesus monkeys raised with living and inanimate mother substitutes. *Developmental Psychobiology, 21,* 401–430.

Mason, W. A., Davenport, R. K., Jr., & Menzel, E. W., Jr. (1968). Early experience and the social development of rhesus monkeys and chimpanzees. In G. Newton & S. Levine (Rds.), *Early experience and behavior* (pp. 440–480). IL: Charles C. Thomas Publisher.

Mason, W. A., & Green, P. C. (1962). The effects of social restriction on the behavior of rhesus monkeys: IV. Responses to a novel environment and to an alien species. *Journal of Comparative and Physiological Psychology, 55,* 363–368.

Mason, W. A., & Harlow, H. F. (1959). Initial responses of infant rhesus monkeys to solid foods. *Psychological Reports, 5,* 193–199.

Mason, W. A., Harlow, H. F., & Rueping, R. R. (1959). The development of manipulatory responsiveness in the infant rhesus monkey. *Journal of Comparative and Physiological Psychology, 52,* 555–558.

Mason, W. A., Hill, S. D., & Thomsen, C. E. (1971). Perceptual factors in the development of filial attachment. *Proceedings of the 3rd International Congress on Primatology*, Zurich, 1970, Vol. 3, pp. 125–133.

Mason, W. A., Hill, S. D., & Thomsen, C. E. (1974). Perceptual aspects of filial attachment in monkeys. In N. F. White (Ed.), *Ethology and Psychiatry* (pp. 84–93). Toronto: University of Toronto Press.

Mason, W. A., & Kenney, M. D. (1974). Redirection of filial attachments in rhesus monkeys: Dogs as mother surrogates. *Science, 183,* 1209–1211.

Mason, W. A., & Mendoza, S. P. (1998). Generic aspects of primate attachments: Parents, offspring and mates. *Psychoneuroendocrinology, 23,* 765–778.

Mason, W. A., Mendoza, S. P., & Moberg, G. P. (1991). Persistent effects of early social experience on physiological responsiveness. In A. Ehara, I. Kimura, O. Takenaka, & M. Iwamoto (Eds.), *Primatology today: Proceedings of the XIIIth Congress of the International Primatological Society, Nagoya and Kyoto, 18–24 July 1990,* pp. 469–471.

Mayeaux, D. J., & Mason, W. A. (1998). Development of responsiveness to novel objects in the titi monkey, *Callicebus moloch. Primates, 39,* 419–431.

Mendoza, S. P., & Mason, W. A. (1986). Parental division of labour and differentiation of attachments in a monogamous primate (*Callicebus moloch*). *Animal Behaviour, 34,* 1336–1347.

Menzel, E. W., Jr., Davenport, R. K., Jr., & Rogers, C. M. (1961). Some aspects of behavior toward novelty in young chimpanzees. *Journal of Comparative and Physiological Psychology, 54,* 16–19.

Mineka, S., Gunnar, M., 7 Champoux, M. (1986). Control and early socioemotional development: Infant rhesus monkeys reared in controllable versus uncontrollable environments. *Child Development, 57,* 1241–1256.

Mitchell, G. D. (1969). Paternalistic behavior in primates. *Psychological Bulletin, 71,* 399–417.

Mowbray, J. B., & Cadell, T. E. (1962). Early behavior patterns in rhesus monkeys. *Journal of Comparative and Physiological Psychology, 55,* 350–357.

Nissen, H. W. (1951). Phylogenetic comparison. In S. S. Stevens (Ed.), *Handbook of experimental psychology* (pp. 326–386) New York: John Wiley,.

Nissen, H. W. (1953). Instinct as seen by a psychologist. *Psychological Review, 60,* 291–294.

Nissen, H. W. (1954). Problems of mental evolution in the primates. *Human Biology, 26,* 277–287.

Piaget, J. (1970). *Structuralism,* New York: Harper and Row.

Piaget, J. (1971). *Biology and knowledge.* Chicago: The University of Chicago Press.

Rogers, C. M., & Davenport, R. K. (1969). Effects of restricted rearing on sexual behavior of chimpanzees. *Developmental Psychology, 1,* 200–204.

Rosenblum, L. A. (1968). Mother-Infant relations and early behavioral development in the squirrel monkey. In L. A. Rosenblum & R. W. Cooper (Rds.), *The squirrel monkey* (pp. 207–233) New York: Academic Press.

Rosenblum, L. A., & Cross, H. A. (1963). Performance of neonatal monkeys in the visual cliff-situation. *American Journal of Psychology, 76,* 318–320.

Rumbaugh, D. M., Savage-Rumbaugh, E. S., & Washburn, D. A. (1996). Toward a new outlook on primate learning and behavior: Complex learning and emergent processes in comparative perspective. *Japanese Psychological Research, 38,* 113–125.

Ruppenthal, G. C., Arling, G. L., Harlow, H. F., Sackett, G. P., & Suomi, S. J. (1976). A 10-year perspective of motherless-mother monkey behavior. *Journal of Abnormal Psychology, 85,* 341–349.

Sackett, G. P. (1965). Effects of rearing conditions upon the behavior of rhesus monkeys (*Macaca mulatta*). *Child Development, 36,* 855–868.

Schiller, P. H. (1952). Innate constituents of complex responses in primates. *Psychological Review, 59,* 177–191.

Schneirla, T. C. (1949). Levels in the psychological capacities of animals. In R. W. Sellars (Rd.), *Philosophy for the future* (pp. 243–286) New York: Macmillan.

Schneirla, T. C. (1952). A consideration of some conceptual trends in comparative psychology. *Psychological Bulletin, 49,* 559–597.

Schneirla, T. C. (1959). An evolutionary and developmental theory of biphasic processes underlying approach and withdrawal. In M. R. Jones (Ed.), *Nebraska symposium on motivation* (pp. 1–42) Lincoln: University of Nebraska Press.

Schneirla, T. C., & Rosenblatt, J. S. (1961). Behavioral organization and genesis of the social bond in insects and mammals. *American Journal of Orthopsychiatry, 31,* 223–253.

Schultz, A. H. (1956). Postembryonic age changes. In H. Hofer; A. H. Schultz, & D. Starck (Eds.), *Primatologia 1* (pp. 887–964) Basel: S. Karger.

Schusterman, R. J., Reichmuth, C. J., & Kastak, D. (2000). How animals classify friends and foes. *Current Directions in Psychological Science, 9,* 1–6.

Scott, J. P. (1954). The place of observation in biological and psychological science. *American Psychologist, 9,* 61–64.

Seay, B., Alexander, B. K., & Harlow, H. F. (1964). Maternal behavior of socially deprived rhesus monkeys. *Journal of Abnormal and Social Psychology, 69,* 345–354.

Senko, M. G. (1966). The effects of early, intermediate, and late experiences upon adult macaque sexual behavior. Unpublished master's thesis, University of Wisconsin.

Shea, B. T. (1983). Paedomorphosis and neoteny in the pygmy chimpanzee. *Science, 222,* 521–522.

Southwick, C. H., Beg, M. A., & Siddiqi, M. R. (1965). Rhesus monkeys in North India. In I. DeVore (Ed.), *Primate behavior: Field studies of monkeys and apes* (pp. 111–159). New York: Holt, Rinehart and Winston.

Terrace, H. S. (1984). Animal cognition. In H. L. Roitblat, T. G. Bever, & H. S. Terrace (Eds.), *Animal vognition* (pp. 7–28). Hillsdale, NJ: Lawrence Erlbaum Associates.

Troisi, A., & D'Amato, F. R. (1984). Ambivalence in monkey mothering: Infant abuse combined with maternal possessiveness. *Journal of Nervous and Mental Disease, 172,* 105–108.

Troisi, A,, D'Amato, F. R., Fuccillo, R., & Scucchi, S. (1982). Infant abuse, by a wild-born group-living Japanese macaque mother. *Journal of Abnormal Psychology, 91,* 451–456.

Wallen, K., Bielert, C., & Slimp, J. (1977). Foot clasp mounting in the prepubertal rhesus monkey: Social and hormonal influences. In S. Chevalier-Skolnikoff & F. E. Poirier (Eds.), *Primate bio-social development: Biological, social, and ecological determinants* (pp. 439–461). New York: Garland.

Wallen, K., Goldfoot, D. A., & Goy, R. W. (1981). Peer and maternal influences on the expression of foot-clasp mounting by juvenile male rhesus monkeys. *Developmental Psychobiology, 14,* 299–309.

Watson, J. S., & Ramey, C. T. (1972). Reactions to response-contingent stimulation in early infancy. *Merrill-Palmer Quarterly of Behavior and Development, 18,* 219–227.

Welker, W. I. (1961). An analysis of exploratory and play behavior in animals. In D. W. Fiske & S. R. Maddi (Eds.), *Functions of varied experience* (pp. 175–226). Homewood, IL: Dorsey Press.

Wood, B. S., Mason, W. A., & Kenney, M. D. (1979). Contrasts in visual responsiveness and emotional arousal between rhesus monkeys raised with living and those raised with inanimate substitute mothers. *Journal of Comparative and Physiological Psychology, 93,* 368–377.

Yerkes, R. M., & Tomlin, M. I. (1935). Mother-infant relations in chimpanzee. *Journal of Comparative Psychology, 20,* 321–359.

Rachel Keen Clifton

Learning about Infants

To begin with, one must have motivation. In my case the motivation to study the behavior of children can easily be traced to my own childhood. I was deeply influenced by my mother, Regina Simpson Keen, an elementary school teacher who conveyed her pleasure and fascination with children to me at an early age. Dinner-table conversations frequently entailed the recounting of events at the school, always with an emphasis on the child's personality, family background, or difficulties to be overcome. My mother first taught in a country school in rural Kentucky with several grades in one room, and she brought great understanding and empathy to this task. The children were poor, often walking barefoot for long distances and missing school to tend and harvest crops. Sometimes I accompanied her, and because I was not actually a student in the school, I became an observer at a very young age.

In addition to her depth of understanding for school-age children, my mother was also keenly sensitive to infant behavior. One incident stands out in particular. When I was around six years old a friend of my mother's had given birth to a child, and my mother had been to the hospital to see them. When she returned home she looked very depressed. She said that she could tell that the baby was "not right." I remember that others protested that she could not possibly tell from just looking at a newborn infant that something was wrong. But my mother said that the infant's movements of the head and limbs were abnormally jerky, that his cry was high-pitched and strange, and he had not been able to get his hand to his mouth. Of course she had said nothing to the parents, but sadly her diagnosis was absolutely correct. The child grew but never learned to talk and required round-the-clock care until his death many years later. The attending doctor had told the parents they had a normal, healthy newborn, but my mother's observations had indicated otherwise. For me as a child, the fact that newborn behavior could predict mental development years later made a deep impression on me.

Several events in graduate school conspired to bring me to the study of infants—an interest that has stayed with me throughout my career. Although no one at the Institute of Child Development at the University of Minnesota was doing research with infants at that time, Britten Ruebush, who had studied at Yale, offered a course on infant development in 1962, in which he assigned articles by Kessen, Lipsitt, Bronshtein, and others. I decided that I wanted to do my dissertation on newborn learning, and my adviser, Harold Stevenson, allowed me to do so, despite my having no experience working with infants. The literature that most influenced me was the Russian work reported by Bronshtein on newborn habituation. I modeled my dissertation plans after this work, presenting newborns with sounds differing in duration, frequency, and intertrial interval, using nonnutritive sucking as the response (Keen, 1964). The idea was that if a newborn were in the midst of a sucking burst and attended to a tone, there would be cessation of sucking. Here was a way to ask an immature organism if a stimulus had been detected and if it was discriminated from a previous one. The logic of the testing involved presenting a sound with certain characteristics repeatedly until response decrement occurred; if the response recovered when frequency or duration changed, one could conclude that the newborn had detected the change. In this way the sensory world of the newborn could be explored. In 1962 this was a novel, exciting idea, and history shows that the general paradigm of habituation and recovery to novelty was fully exploited over the next several decades by those investigating infant behavior.

In the early 1960s habituation and response recovery was being used to test newborn's response to odors (Lipsitt, Engen, & Kaye, 1963; Engen, Lipsitt, & Kaye, 1963), sound (Bartoshuk, 1962a, 1962b; Bridger, 1961), and visual stimuli (Fantz, 1964). This was the beginning of the explosion of infancy research that is still going on. What seems to have come together in the early 1960s is the combination of three things: new methodology, new technology, and new ideas. New methodologies were inspired by the Russian researchers such as Bronshtein and the Czech psychologist Hanus Papousek, so that researchers realized they could record and statistically analyze the newborn's responses to stimulation in the form of changes in respiration, heart rate, sucking, and head turning. In this country Robert Fantz introduced the idea of using newborn looking behavior to study their responses to visual patterns (Fantz, 1963). New technology, including computers, made it possible to handle large amounts of data generated by physiological measures such as heart rate and EEG. The introduction of videotape into the lab (Haith, 1969) made it easy to record behaviors like looking. The polygraph, although it had been around for decades and was used in adult psychophysiological research, had not been employed to record newborn sucking and heart rate responses until this period. But the most important sea change in newborn research was in the realm of ideas.

☐ The Orienting Reflex, Memory, and Motor Activity

My goal as a graduate student was to discover something exciting, something profound that would add significantly to our understanding of human behavior. Have I achieved this? Certainly not when I consider just my own work, but if I look beyond at the sum total of infancy research, what we have learned over the last four decades is truly astounding. One reason that it was so exciting to do research with newborns in the early 1960s was because we knew so little about their behavior or sensory capacities. How could we understand infants' reactions to the world and environmental events if we did not know the basic capabilities of their sensory systems and their ability to learn? Pediatric and child development textbooks as well as popular articles aimed at parents described the newborn as exceedingly immature, primarily responding reflexively to external stimulation. It was unclear how well (or even if) the newborn could hear or see or smell. Research on conditioning from the 1930s indicated newborns probably were not capable of simple association. A major drawback had been the lack of methods to explore these questions. Researchers such as Salapatek and Kessen (1966) who were interested in the newborn's visual system followed Fantz's lead and used looking behavior, but those interested in auditory perception had no easy solution. However, Bronshtein and colleagues (1958) had shown that nonnutritive sucking would work, while Bartoshuk (1962a, 1962b) and the team of Lipton, Richmond, and Steinschneider had shown heart rate to be a sensitive measure of response to sound (Steinschneider, Richmond, & Lipton, 1966). Lipsitt and colleagues had used respiration to study the newborn's sensitivity to odors (Lipsitt et al., 19663) and had again tackled the question of whether newborns could be conditioned (Lipsitt, 1963). This flurry of work with newborns excited a whole generation of graduate students between 1960 and 1965, including Leslie Cohen, Marshall Haith, Herb Kaye, Michael Lewis, Philip Salapatek, and Arnold Sameroff, as well as myself. Most of us continued to work with infants for many years or even for our entire careers.

In addition to exploring the sensory capacities of the newborn, psycho-physiological responses allowed one to study a fascinating phenomenon called the orienting reflex, described by Sokolov (1960, 1963) as a response to novel stimuli that would undergo habituation with repetition but return with the introduction of a new stimulus. My interest in the orienting reflex stemmed from a belief that brain-behavior relations in the infant could be discovered by researching this phenomenon. Sokolov's model (1960) placed the orienting reflex in the cortex, which made it attractive to study. Because the infant brain grows rapidly during the early months of life, one might be able to observe developmental changes in the orienting reflex that paralleled cortical growth. This was an idea that continued to intrigue me for years, and resurfaced in the 1980s with my research on an auditory phenomenon known as the precedence effect.

Although nonnutritive sucking had yielded interesting and reliable data in my dissertation, I still believed that heart rate might be a more sensitive measure than sucking to study learning and habituation. I took a three-year postdoctoral fellowship with Frances K. Graham at the University of Wisconsin to get training in the use of psychophysiological measures. The basic premise that we explored was that heart rate change could be used to study habituation and orienting in the infant. Habituation was viewed as the simplest form of learning, that is, learning to ignore a repetitive, nonsignal stimulus. Thorpe (1963) and others had described habituation as a very basic, ubiquitous phenomenon that could be shown in all manner of species. One of the important issues was how long habituation might last. If habituation was retained over a long time span—for several hours—one could be sure that the response decrement was not due to sensory adaptation or fatigue, but was a true ignoring of the impinging stimulus. To that end, we tested one group of newborns on day 1 and again 24 hours later on day 2, pairing them with a control group who received the same auditory stimulus for the first time on day 2. Habituation of heart rate acceleration to the tone was shown by infants on day 1, while on day 2 the initial large acceleration seen on early trials of day 1 was gone, although a lesser response remained throughout trials. The control group showed a large acceleration to the initial tones, heard for the first time on day 2. We concluded that newborns could retain habituation for at least 24 hours (Keen, Chase, & Graham, 1965). It is interesting to note that this study has been largely ignored in the literature. As recently as the 1980s chapters and books reviewing infant memory and learning claim there is no evidence of newborn learning retained longer than a few seconds (Slater, 1989; Bremner, 1988). Almost thirty years later a student of mine, Irina Swain, did a master's thesis replicating and extending our earlier conclusion (Swain, Zelazo, & Clifton, 1993). We found that not only did newborns retain habituation over a 24-hour period, but the habituation was *specific* to a particular sound. In this instance we used a female voice as the stimulus, repeating the same word throughout trials on day 1. If a newborn heard a particular word on day 1, they remained habituated on day 2 to the same word but responded anew if the word was changed. In light of DeCasper and Fifer (1980) and their subsequent work, this finding is not surprising because it appears that infants around the time of birth retain information about auditory stimuli heard while in the womb until after they are born. Perhaps our theories of infant memory are more ready to incorporate such data now, but in 1965 newborns were still regarded as virtually incapable of learning, and were certainly not expected to retain memory of what they had learned hours earlier.

The most significant publication completed during my postdoctoral fellowship was the *Psychological Bulletin* article "Heart rate change as a component of the orienting response" (Graham & Clifton, 1966). The work involved in the writing of this article was extremely satisfying. We posed a definite set of questions and then set about answering them by a critical and fairly exhaustive review of the literature. How could Sokolov's concepts of orienting and defense mechanisms be mapped onto cardiac responses? Could direction of heart rate change indicate the subject's cognitive processing? Although Sokolov (1963) described a variety of psychophysiological responses that indexed the orienting reflex, the form and direction of heart rate was not spelled out. Sokolov used the vasomotor response extensively, and it was one of the few measures whose directionality seemed to differentiate between orienting and the defense response, with vasodilation in the head indicative of the former and vasoconstriction indicative of the latter. However, the vasomotor response proved difficult to reproduce, and we reasoned that if a more easily recorded response like heart rate would also differentiate orienting and defense, this would be a boon. Since the 1950s and perhaps before, heart rate had been used to study reactions of human adults and animals to a wide variety of stimuli. We hoped that by organizing this massive literature concerning which response system the stimuli would be likely to evoke, patterns of directionality would emerge. Indeed, they did. John and Beatrice Lacey's research proved critical here. They noted that attention to external events evoked cardiac deceleration, whereas tasks requiring motivated inattention or ignoring the environment (for example, doing mental arithmetic) produced acceleration (Lacey, 1959; Lacey, Kagan, Lacey, & Moss, 1963). They hypothesized that direction of heart rate (HR) change reflected different interactions with the environment, which fit extremely well into the orienting/defense system division. Graham & Clifton (1966) concluded that HR deceleration was the cardiac component of the orienting response, while acceleration was probably a component of the defense response. This hypothesis was immediately put to the test by numerous investigators, and the article was so heavily cited during the next decade that it achieved the status of a "Citation Classic" in *Current Contents* in 1978.

An interesting developmental story emerged in connection with the orienting response. In the 1960s and early 1970s the newborn's response to auditory stimuli was unfailingly reported to be cardiac acceleration. Jackson, Kantowitz, & Graham (1971) posed the question, "Can the newborn show cardiac orienting?" and answered, "Probably not." This tentative answer fit with the general view of the newborn as an organism who responded to stimuli subcortically and defensively, but several researchers were challenged to tackle the problem. The answer turned out to be yes, the newborn does show cardiac orienting to auditory (Adkinson & Berg, 1976; Kearsley, 1973; Pomerleau-Malcuit & Clifton, 1973), visual (Sameroff, Cashmore, & Dykes, 1973; Gregg, Clifton, & Haith, 1976), and vestibular stimuli (Pomerleau-Malcuit & Clifton, 1973), but only provided certain conditions are met. These conditions include the use of stimuli that are not too intense, testing the infants in an alert state, and control over the infant's motor activity. My contribution to this literature is summarized in two chapters, one in a book devoted to research on habituation (Clifton & Nelson, 1976), and one in the 1978 *Minnesota Symposium on Child Psychology* (Clifton, 1978). My research made two points: (1) motor activity such as nonnutritive sucking or head turning causes the heart rate to accelerate, masking stimulus effects; (2) the importance of newborn state cannot be overemphasized, as the direction and amplitude of cardiac responses are greatly affected by arousal state.

The effect of motor activity turned out to be quite straightforward, but the way we came to investigate it makes an interesting story. In an effort to find cardiac orienting in the newborn in the early 1970s, Claudette Gregg, Marshall Haith, and I presented a black vertical bar moving horizontally on a white background, a stimulus known to elicit visual attention in the newborn. We expected that heart rate deceleration would be associated with visual fixation, and we photographed eye movements in conjunction with heart rate recording in order to measure this. Imagine our disappointment when heart rate *acceleration* appeared during visual fixation. At first I refused to believe our data, partly because theory strongly predicted that cardiac orienting should accompany visual orienting, and partly because in the meantime Sameroff et al. (1973) had published a study reporting HR deceleration to visual stimuli. In addition, Keith Berg had presented a paper at a meeting (later published as Adkinson & Berg, 1976) also reporting deceleration to visual stimuli. How did one explain our heart rate acceleration? I chose not to publish it until I understood better what was happening. I puzzled off and on for over a year, reading numerous method sections very carefully and making phone calls to ask authors for unreported details. Finally I determined that pacifiers were a common element among studies reporting HR acceleration, whereas no one who reported deceleration had used a pacifier. A post hoc analysis of our data separating "sucking" from "nonsucking" trials was possible because fortunately the polygraph recording heart rate had also recorded sucking, although it was not a response we had planned to analyze. This analysis showed that, given visual fixation to be in progress, HR accelerated on trials when babies were actively sucking, but the same babies showed deceleration on trials when there was little or no sucking (Gregg, Clifton, & Haith, 1976).

This observation led us to manipulate sucking in a subsequent study (Nelson, Clifton, Dowd, & Field, 1978) by varying the point at which an auditory stimulus was superimposed on the sucking burst-pause cycle. Auditory stimuli were more suited to this manipulation than visual stimuli because the infant did not have to be looking directly at the stimulus at onset; besides, with sucking controlled, one should be able to show HR deceleration in the auditory as well as the visual modality. We found a close synchronization between sucking and heart rate. Sucking was found to override stimulus effects so strongly that we concluded that pacifiers should be avoided altogether if HR was the dependent measure. Pacifiers were used routinely in many laboratories in the 1960s and 1970s in order to keep the infants in a more stable state with fewer limb movements. Very often sucking was not recorded or even noted in the method section because it was not regarded as a "response," or important in the situation. I concluded the 1978 chapter with the following reminder: "the heart is influenced by a multitude of neural commands from many different sources. Those of us who would infer psychological meaning from HR changes must be ever aware that we are dealing with a major life-sustaining organ in the body, subject to many controls" (Clifton, 1978). Although these words were directed at cardiac change, the warning can be generalized to many other situations in which complex psychological processes in infants are inferred by single behaviors such as looking, reaching, or head turning, all of which have multiple determinants.

The second issue that had an important influence on studies of cardiac orienting in unexpected ways was arousal state. An alert newborn could show large HR deceleration of 8 to 10 beats per minute to tones or visual stimuli. However, if the infant were drowsy, sleeping, or even near the end of an alert period, she/he would not show HR deceleration, but rather acceleration, which is indicative of a defense or startle response. This statement may seem straightforward now, but it took quite a few years to realize that state was so complex. In one study (Clifton & Nelson, 1976), infants who were judged awake at the beginning of the session were divided on the basis of how their state changed subsequently during the session. The state change that came later predicted their response early in the session better than the current state. Infants who remained awake responded with heart rate deceleration to the first presentation of a tone, but the group who fell asleep within 5 minutes responded with acceleration on the first trial. Campos & Brackbill (1973) also tested infants for a long period through several state transitions, and generally found deceleration during alertness and acceleration during sleep, the same directionality difference found for human adults in similar states (Berg, Jackson, & Graham, 1975; Johnson & Lubin, 1967; Johnson, Townsend, & Wilson, 1975). Because alert states are infrequent and brief in newborns, special efforts must be made to capture newborns in this receptive state. Otherwise the majority of infants will be tested in a state of decreased arousal, either throughout the session or for a good portion of it. Following this line of reasoning, one would predict that if state were ignored, heart rate acceleration would be the typical response of the newborn to stimulation, and indeed most of the studies recording newborn heart rate in the 1960s reported acceleration. By the time the infant is 4 to 5 months old, not only is an alert state more common, but the range of stimuli eliciting orienting has broadened considerably so that HR deceleration is the most typical response reported at older ages.

While it is clear that arousal state can affect the HR response, it can have a pervasive effect on other response systems as well. Changes in state occurring within an experimental session can bias responding for or against the hypotheses being tested, depending on the phenomenon being investigated and the response being measured. For example, increased responding is expected during a conditioning procedure, so if infants are becoming more alert over the session, some behavioral increases could come from this state change. As previously noted, a more typical state change for infants, especially newborns, is toward decreased arousal, which would lead to decreased responding, mimicking habituation. The effect of state changes on various response systems was the theme of a chapter written in collaboration with Michael Nelson, a postdoctoral fellow in my lab (Clifton & Nelson, 1976). We prepared a table showing how particular responses might be affected by changes in state over trials. Some reflexes get stronger in sleep, whereas others wane. We tried to alert researchers to the not-so-subtle effects of arousal state on phenomena that were being investigated. Certainly we were not the first to call attention to state. European researchers such as Prechtl (1958, 1974), as well as Wolff (1966) and Korner (1972) in the U.S., had made a point about the importance of arousal state, but most American researchers tended to regard state as a nuisance, something to be gotten around rather than something that was integral to the whole of the infant's responding. Certainly it was only when things did not work out as expected that I began to regard state as a variable to be investigated along with orienting and conditioning. In Clifton & Nelson (1976) we aimed our review of the literature at habituation/dishabituation because that paradigm was very popular in the 1960–1975 period. Habituation procedures are particularly susceptible to state changes because the necessity for repeated trials makes the sessions lengthy.

☐ Conditioning and the Role of Arousal

At the same time that state emerged as an important variable in affecting the HR response, it also claimed a central role in some work I was doing on conditioned head turning. During the 1960s researchers questioned whether newborns could be conditioned. True, there had been some early work in the 1930s by Dorothy Marquis and others, but when Lipsitt failed to get classical conditioning in the newborn after many attempts (Lipsitt, 1963), it appeared that while habituation was easy to obtain, classical conditioning was either difficult or impossible to achieve. The newborn was regarded as too immature to show this more advanced form of learning. As late as 1971 Sameroff concluded the newborn could not be classically conditioned.

In the mid-sixties Papousek, then in Prague, published work showing that a combination of classical and operant conditioning was possible, using head turning toward the side where a bottle was offered (Papousek, 1967). A tone (CS) signaled that the bottle was available, but no reinforcement was delivered unless the infant turned to the side of the tone (operant). Einar Siqueland and Lewis Lipsitt used this procedure, and reported success (Siqueland & Lipsitt, 1966). I was intrigued and decided to apply the same procedure to explore how medication given to mothers during labor and delivery might affect newborn behavior in this learning paradigm. I expected that infants born of mothers who received little or no medication would show better or quicker conditioning compared to infants born of mothers who had received heavier medication, even though pediatric examinations might detect few differences in their behavior. Subtle effects might be shown in a learning paradigm. In the 1950s and 1960s obstetricians often sought to relieve mothers' pain during labor and delivery, without realizing the detrimental consequences to the infant. Depending on hospital practices, infants might be born to tranquilized and heavily medicated mothers, but there was growing evidence that this could be harmful to the infant.

Our study (Clifton, Meyers, & Solomons, 1972) was partially successful, partially disappointing. We found no difference in newborns' behavior that was related to medication given to mothers during labor and delivery. There was abundant evidence from other studies that heavy medication could affect newborn behavior in terms of lack of vigor in sucking, general sluggishness, depressed state, and so on. The failure to find a difference in our groups may have been due to the obstetrical practices in the University Hospital in Iowa City, which followed a philosophy of medicating mothers as little as possible. Our No-Drug group received no medication whatsoever in the 4 hours before birth, although they did receive a local anesthetic during the birth. The Drug group received 30 to 60 mg of Nisentil, considered a light dose, during labor, as well as the local anesthetic during birth. We had no mothers who would be considered heavily medicated, whereas studies reporting differences in newborn behavior did include such groups. A second disappointment in our results was that evidence for conditioning was not strong. Although the Experimental group who received tones and stroking of the cheek (to elicit a head turn) paired with reinforcement (opportunity to suck on a bottle of formula) did show significantly more head turning than a Control group who received the same stimulation but unpaired, the effect occurred early in trials and disappeared later in the session. This did not fit our expectation of a learning curve. In fact, the most compelling difference we saw in the data was that infants who were judged as awake before the session began responded well to the paired stimuli, but infants who were judged as asleep and had to be awakened before the session responded poorly. This difference was statistically significant. Going back to Siqueland & Lipsitt (1966), we read that only newborns who were spontaneously alert were selected to be in their study. In addition, their criterion head turn was 5–10 degrees, whereas we had demanded 15 degrees.

I decided that our data should not be published until we understood a bit better what they meant. It was a partial replication of Siqueland & Lipsitt (1966) but not very satisfying. The issue of arousal state needed to be explored further. I had met both Siqueland and Lipsitt at meetings of the Society for Research in Child Development, but did not know either of them well. I decided to write Lipsitt about the problem. His answer came quickly and surprised me. He proposed that I come to Brown University and do a follow-up study with him and Siqueland. He would make his lab available and pay my salary during the stay. I have always considered Lipsitt's response to my query as the model of how scientists should behave when their work has been questioned. His attitude was "Let's work together to get to the bottom of the problem," and then he did everything possible to make it happen.

In our follow-up study (Clifton, Siqueland, & Lipsitt, 1972) we obtained trial-by-trial ratings of newborns' wakefulness on a 5-point behavioral scale, and all infants were spontaneously alert at the start of the session. Two effects of state were observed: (1) higher levels of arousal were associated with increased head turning regardless of whether the infant was in the Experimental or the Control group; and (2) Experimental subjects responded significantly more than Control subjects, but only when they were rated primarily as alert; the groups did not differ when they were rated primarily as drowsy or asleep. For example, on trials when infants were classified as "deeply asleep" or "light sleep," only a few scattered head turns were observed in either treatment group. When rated "alert," infants in the Experimental group were twice as likely to turn as Control infants. State acted to depress the baseline probability of responding, and consequently affected the exposure to reinforcement contingencies. Perhaps it should have come as no surprise that arousal state would interact with treatment, but in fact many published studies at that time did not ever allude to state or describe the arousal level of the participating infants. Serendipitously we also found out that temperature and humidity played a role in the results of Clifton, Siqueland, and Lipsitt (1972). The original Siqueland and Lipsitt (1966) study had been run in the fall and winter, whereas our follow-up study was run in July and August. Although the lab had air-conditioning, the nursery did not. We found that infants had to be tested before the 9:00 A.M. feeding; otherwise they would not meet our criterion of being spontaneously alert at the beginning of the session. Attempts to test later in the day were met with infants too drowsy to even begin testing; the contrast between the hot nursery (over 90 degrees many days) and the cool lab changed the awake but irritable infants into quietly sleeping ones! Marvin Simner, a postdoctoral fellow working with Lipsitt in the same lab that year, further documented this seasonal effect in an experiment on infant crying (Simner, 1971).

A study that brought together my interest in conditioning and my expertise with the HR response explored whether this autonomic response could be conditioned in newborns (Clifton, 1974). In part I was responding to Sameroff's (1971) challenge that newborns could not be classically conditioned although they could be operantly conditioned. It seemed to me that many of the failures to classically condition newborns had used motor responses to noxious stimuli (eyeblink to a bright light, foot withdrawal to electrotactual stimulation), which might not be the optimal situation for early learning. A decade of research had shown that HR change was a sensitive measure of habituation, and by combining it with an appetitive stimulus, one might show a classically conditioned HR change. The situation I devised shows the influence of my past work. Newborns were presented with an 8-second auditory stimulus CS (300 Hz square wave), a 6-second CS-UCS interval, and a 10-second presentation of glucose via nipple (UCS) that overlapped the last 2 seconds of the tone. The 6-second interval was thought to be long enough to observe a decelerative conditioned response to sound before the interference of sucking on the UCR to the glucose. In addition to the Conditioning Group, a Random Control Group and a Backward Conditioning Group checked on the effect of random CS-UCS pairings or explicit backward pairings. After 30 conditioning trials, all groups received 6 extinction trials of tone alone. It was a bit disappointing that no CR developed to the tone, so no evidence of anticipation was obtained. However, during extinction a large HR deceleration appeared to the absence of the UCS in the Conditioning Group only. I interpreted this to be a cardiac orienting response, a sort of "What happened?" response, when the UCS did not appear. Sokolov (1963, p. 41) described how the disruption of a temporal sequence of events could elicit an orienting reaction if the subject had learned the sequence. More recently Donahue & Berg (1991) have found that by 7 months infants also show the anticipatory "Get ready" response, that is, a conditioned HR response to the tone itself. The development of an anticipatory cardiac response may parallel the onset of other anticipatory behaviors, such as looking in the visual expectation paradigm (Haith, 1991). As such, it signals a distinct change in the way the infant interacts with the world, because anticipatory responses are prerequisite for planning and manipulating the environment to achieve one's ends. This hallmark of human behavior appears extremely early in ontogenetic development.

☐ An Intellectual Shift–Auditory Perception

We now come to a distinct break in the subject matter of my research efforts, although the change was not apparent for several years in published work. My interests shifted away from orienting, habituation, and conditioning toward auditory perception. The common thread between these lines of research is an abiding concern with brain-behavior relations in the infant. One of the attractions of Bronshtein and Sokolov's work was that orienting and habituation were related to "higher level" processes in the nervous system. In order for habituation of the OR to occur, a model in the brain must be formed; discrepancies between this neuronal model and a novel stimulus would elicit a return of the orienting response. By 1975 I felt that I had answered many questions originally posed concerning infants' detection and discrimination of sound, and their early learning abilities as displayed through habituation and conditioning. Many of the people who had worked on those projects had completed their Ph.D.s (Susan Goldberg, Tiffany Field) or postdoctoral fellowships (Andree Pomerleau, Gerard Malcuit, Michael Nelson, Arlene Little). A relaxed year of reading and thinking during a sabbatical at

Stanford University during 1975–1976 refocused my research on auditory perception.

My new interest centered on an illusion of spatial localization called the precedence effect. The precedence effect has to do with echo suppression, and it enables us to localize sound in the environment. Without it the original sound source would be heard along with numerous echoes reflected off surrounding objects and surfaces. The resulting confusion about directionality of sounds would make it impossible to determine the true direction of the source. Our nervous system, however, gives the greatest weight to the first-arriving, or preceding, sound, so that its direction dominates. The precedence effect results in the perception of a sound originating at its source location, with suppression of the echoes. What first caught my interest in the precedence effect was that animal research implicated the auditory cortex in its perception. Cats with auditory cortex lesions on one side were able to localize sounds from a single loudspeaker (SS) with no impairment. But when sound came from two loudspeakers (simulating a source with an echo) and one loudspeaker led the other by 7 ms, cats failed to localize this precedence effect (PE) sound when the leading sound was contralateral to the lesioned cortex. They continued to localize a PE sound when the lead was contralateral to the intact auditory cortex, as well as SS sounds from either side (Whitfield, Cranford, Ravizza, & Diamond, 1972).

I happened to be serving on the NIH Experimental Psychology Study Section with Irving Diamond about the time he published this work. I discussed with him the possibility that infants would show a developmental trend in perception of the precedence effect, such that localization of SS sound would appear before localization of PE sound. If perception of the precedence effect were cortically mediated, the newborn would not be expected to respond, even though the peripheral auditory system is quite well developed by 7 months gestation. Anatomical and neurophysiological work has documented the rapid postnatal growth and myelination of the cortex in the first year of life, but we have few functional behaviors that can be tied to this development. The comparison of localization to single source versus precedence effect sounds was appealing because the same behavior of head orienting could be used to assess perception of both types of sound. To adults, perception of a sound from two loud speakers, with the onset of one leading the other by a few milliseconds, is localized the same as if the sound came from only the leading loud speaker. If an infant perceived the precedence effect, he/she should turn toward the leading side of sound, the same response as when a single loud speaker was activated and the sound heard from that direction. Thus, response requirements could remain the same while perceptual processing changed. When I explained these ideas over lunch one day to Irving

Diamond, he was enthusiastic, and encouraged me by offering technical advice about stimulus presentation in my lab. Since then it has occurred to me that if Diamond had been uninterested or discouraging, I would probably have abandoned the ideas immediately because I felt I was on very uncertain ground in developing the hypotheses and taking on new technical areas of expertise. Even to produce the precedence effect in my lab required new equipment. This incident underlines the importance of senior investigators' interest and encouragement when they are approached by more junior colleagues and asked for help or advice.

The switch in emphasis to auditory localization also required measurement of a different response system. Heart rate change is a sensitive indicator of stimulus *detection,* but it is not a *directional* response. Muir and Field (1979) had shown that newborns reliably orient to a rattle sound presented through one loudspeaker. If newborns would not turn to a single source, they could not be tested for perception of the precedence effect, so the Muir and Field data assured me that head orienting toward sound was a feasible response in newborn infants.

From 1977 to 1984 my research was concentrated on understanding how and when the infant comes to respond to the precedence effect. Some highlights of our findings include the following facts. First, newborn heart rate change (an attentional response) is the same for SS and PE sounds, but head turning (a directional discrimination) differentiates between them (Clifton, Morrongiello, Kulig, & Dowd, 1981a; Morrongiello, Clifton, & Kulig, 1982). Second, there is a developmental trend in which SS localization appears earlier than PE localization in both humans (Clifton, 1985) and dogs (Ashmead, Clifton, & Reese, 1986). Third, the onset of PE localization in human infants is around 4–5 months (Clifton, Morrongiello, & Dowd, 1984), and co-occurs with other behavioral signs of spatial sensitivity such as reaching for sounding objects (Clifton, 1992). Fourth, head orienting toward single source sounds follows a U-shaped function; the response is observed in newborns, then disappears around 6–8 weeks of age, becoming much harder to elicit. When it reappears around 4–5 months, the infant also turns toward the leading side of PE sounds (Clifton et al., 1984; Muir, Clifton, & Clarkson, 1989). Finally, a comparison of 6-month-olds, 5-year-olds, and adults found that echo thresholds were higher in younger children than adults, so echo suppression mechanisms are still changing throughout at least the preschool period (Morrongiello, Kulig, & Clifton, 1984).

The picture of the infant that emerges from these findings is one of initial sensitivity to directional cues contained in sound coming from a single source. From birth the human infant is able to turn the head toward a sound (although not every sound is effective; see Clarkson & Clifton, 1991, for review of this issue). An alert state and upright, supported posture are critical to the expression of this response (Muir & Clifton, 1985). The disappearance and reappearance of head turning follows a course similar to reflexes like the neonatal grasping reflex, which disappears during the early months following birth and is replaced by voluntary reaching and grasping around 4 months. This similarity in time course led us to postulate that neonatal head turning toward single source sound was reflexive in nature (Muir & Clifton, 1985). Perception of the precedence effect, shown by consistent head orienting toward the leading side of sound, must await the maturation of brain areas responsible for recognizing and suppressing the echo or lagging sound. The coincidence of the reappearance of turning toward a single source sound with the onset of the precedence effect suggests that these are related events, and both events reflect the infant's growing knowledge of space, sounding objects in space, and the infant's position in relation to objects.

To begin an investigation of a new research area, auditory localization, meant that I needed new funding. My previous NIH grant had ended, and I wrote the new grant during the 1975–1976 sabbatical. Because I was then serving on the study section that had reviewed my previous grant, the new application was sent to a different panel. I was crushed when that panel disapproved my application—my only consolation being that it had a split vote, with a minority expressing approval. Basically the panel said that while I was highly qualified to do newborn research and had a good track record there, I did not have the expertise to conduct research on auditory localization. This was the first of three experiences that I was to have with funding agencies (both NSF and NIH) where a panel complimented past research and urged me to keep on doing what I was doing, and discouraged me (by not funding the grant) from going in a new direction. Each time I persisted, revised and resubmitted, and got funded the second time around. Sometimes this meant changing grant agencies, or requesting a different review panel within the same agency. The message here is that investigators should not take the blow personally, but be persistent, and if the ideas are good they should eventually be recognized. Over the years I have served four-year terms on three different NIH panels. I am well aware (and so is NIH) that there is a tendency to distrust and discourage investigators who submit an application that greatly diverges from their previous work. Sometimes this caution may be warranted, but science is not served if we try to keep investigators in the same mold. The innovative application must be rewarded, even if it is more risky. NIH has taken steps to explicitly encourage high-payoff/high-risk applications, and I applaud this. I will give an example later of research on long-term memory in infants that would not have had a chance of being funded because of the improbability of its outcome.

☐ Auditory Perception in Adults

By 1984 I felt again that I had answered the original questions posed, in this case questions about development of infants' perception of the precedence effect. It seemed unwise to continue research with infants until the phenomenon was better understood in adults. I was still fascinated by the precedence effect, but wanted to pursue it in fine detail with adults. The accidental discovery of a peculiar effect was the impetus in this research. One day in 1979 we were wiring the lab for an experiment in which a train of click pairs would switch suddenly so that what had been the leading loudspeaker would become the lagging, and vice versa. We planned to habituate 6-month-old infants to a sound that would be perceived as localized from one direction, then switch the direction to the opposite side and observe response recovery if infants discriminated the change in direction. We had a short delay between lead and lag loudspeakers of 7 ms, which gave adults (and presumably infants) a strong localization on the leading side. In this situation the adult listener has no conscious recognition of any sound coming from the lagging side, even though intensity is equal at both loudspeakers. Inside the sound proofed chamber, I expected to perceive a clean switch in localization of the click train from one side to the other when the leading side went from right to left. Instead I first heard clicks from the right (leading side), then clicks coming from *both* sides, followed by a fading out on the lagging side so that clicks seemed to be solely on the left (leading) side. I signaled my graduate student, John Dowd, in the equipment room that something had gone wrong, but he assured me that everything about the stimulus was fine. We tried the switch in lead and lag many times, always with the same result. What was peculiar about this effect was that it brought into question the explanation of the precedence effect as a hardwired mechanism in the brain that suppressed echoes purely on the basis of time delay. As noted earlier, the precedence effect is an auditory illusion that allows listeners to have the perception that they are hearing a single sound at its source, without competing echoes. The process by which the brain blocks the perception of echoes as competing stimuli is not understood, even today, but at that time it was generally assumed to be immutable. Yet the perception produced by the switch in locations gave the incongruous impression that the suppression of echoes could change back and forth within seconds. We puzzled about this interesting phenomenon and ran some naive adults to make sure that our perceptions could be reproduced. Because the research on precedence effect with infants was the lab's main focus, this adult research went no further at that time.

What happened next is one of the most striking chains of events in my scientific career. In 1986, inspired by reading Jens Blauert's book *Spatial*

Hearing (1983), which reported extensively on precedence effect research with adults, I wrote to him describing our peculiar finding and inquired whether it was a new finding and if he thought it was important. I received a prompt reply, with a positive answer to both questions. Using my description, he had reproduced the effect in his lab and had a student eager to pursue it. Blauert encouraged me to publish a report immediately. In an exchange of letters I demurred at first because I did not think our adult data were up to the standards of adult psychoacoustic research, but Blauert insisted because his lab wanted to work on the phenomenon but could not until I had published the first report. He suggested publication in the form of a letter to the editor of the *Journal of the Acoustical Society of America*, a form of brief report in this prestigious journal. The manuscript was warmly received for introducing a new phenomenon, but was rejected for publication because both reviewers wanted more data in a standard format. I had no more data and was ready to abandon the effort. I sent the reviews to Blauert, along with a letter encouraging him to go ahead. I was pleased that an internationally recognized leader in psychoacoustics and head of a major lab in Germany was interested in my finding and wanted to take it further. However, Blauert telephoned me and again insisted that I go ahead. He suggested that I send the manuscript back to the editor, explaining the situation, and that he would write a letter supporting its publication if necessary. I did this, and the manuscript was immediately accepted without further review (Clifton, 1987). The perceptual phenomenon of hearing the echo click after the switch in location has become known as the *Clifton effect,* and has now been studied in other labs (Blauert & Col, 1992; Grantham, 1996; Hartmann, 1997; Yost & Guzman, 1996) and figured prominently in Blauert's explication of the precedence effect in the revision of his classic 1983 book (Blauert, 1996).

I visited Blauert's lab in Bochum, Germany, in 1988. I was eager to meet a man who embodied my highest ideals for scientific conduct, in that he recognized another's ideas, offered support and advice, and refused to take advantage of another researcher's findings even when urged to do so. It is particularly significant that Blauert behaved this way toward an unknown person from another field, developmental psychology, who had never published in psychoacoustics.

The experience with Blauert piqued my interest in pursuing the precedence effect with adults. Fortunately, a colleague in communication disorders, Richard Freyman, also encouraged me and we formed a team to build a lab, obtain funding, and conduct studies in a collaboration that has continued ever since. Much of this work is summarized in Clifton and Freyman (1997). Because I am woefully lacking in both the technical and academic background for adult psychoacoustic research, this collaboration is an example of the symbiosis that cross-disciplinary research depends on. Freyman and I developed a theory for the precedence effect that emphasizes the role of cognitive factors in auditory perception. We found that listeners use ongoing acoustic information to set up an expectancy of what the next incoming sound, including the accompanying echoes, will be. If this expectancy is violated, the precedence effect breaks down and echoes are heard. As long as expectations are upheld, the perceptual experience of an echo identified as a separate sound is suppressed. Rather, information in the echo that informs the listener about room acoustics, such as its frequency content (McCall, Freyman, & Clifton, 1998), intensity (Freyman, McCall, & Clifton, 1998), time delay (Clifton, Freyman, Litovsky, & McCall, 1994), and location, is coded into and is perceived as part of the original sound. However, if that acoustic information is changed in a way that violates the listener's expectations, echo threshold drops and the echo is heard as a distinctly separate sound. For example, the Clifton effect is produced when a train of clicks sets up an expectation of the echo click in a certain location, and when the echo suddenly changes sides, the listener hears the echo as a separate sound, hence the perception of clicks coming from both the leading and lagging sides. We have proposed a new role for the precedence effect, that of informing the listener about room acoustics. This cognitive approach is a dramatic departure from the previous view that relegated the precedence effect to a suppression mechanism, probably located in the brain stem.

☐ From Auditory Perception to Reaching and Cognition

At the same time that I began to work on adult psychoacoustics, the research on infants' auditory development continued apace, though not on the precedence effect. Daniel Ashmead, a postdoctoral fellow, devised a way to test the fineness of discrimination of a sound's location, called minimal audible angle, in 6-month-old infants (Ashmead, Clifton, & Perris, 1987). The research with newborns became concentrated on the acoustical aspects of sound that elicit head orienting. This work was done in collaboration with Marsha Clarkson and is summarized in a chapter (Clarkson & Clifton, 1991). It turns out that not every sound is effective, but that the rattle sound, which Muir and Field and later our lab adopted from the Brazelton Neonatal Assessment Scale, is exceptionally good. Its broad bandwidth stimulates much of the cochlea, and the rhythmical shaking creates repeated onsets. We chopped this sound into small segments and analyzed the effects of duration and repetition rate. If the rattle sound is continuous, it must last for at least one second, or if chopped into 14-

millisecond segments, it remains effective if segments are repeated at a rate of 2/s, but not slower. It seems that rapid onsets must be repeated fast enough to let the immature, somewhat sluggish nervous system "add over" the silent intervals. When spread out more than 500 milliseconds apart, sound segments become ineffective, with each segment acting individually, so that even a long train remains below the threshold for eliciting head orienting.

Clarkson and I also investigated auditory development in older infants, 6 to 8 months, asking whether they could discriminate timbre (Clarkson, Clifton, & Perris, 1988) or the pitch of inharmonic sounds (Clarkson & Clifton, 1995), or tone complexes with the fundamental missing (Clarkson & Clifton, 1985), the latter also a problem for cats without an auditory cortex. Clarkson is continuing the work on auditory development, while my interest turned to questions of motor and cognitive development in the late 1980s.

How does a researcher get from one research area into another? The short answer is: gradually. A longer answer is that while the scientist is researching one set of questions, seemingly confined to one domain, he or she will notice some interesting behavior, some intriguing phenomenon that calls out to one's curiosity. Certainly, that is how I came to do adult psychoacoustic research on the precedence effect, and that is also how I slowly moved from the study of auditory development to motor and cognitive development. The shift came about because I began to use a different response—reaching—in my studies. Just as I had to go away from heart rate change and begin using head orienting as a response when I became interested in infants' discrimination of a directional phenomenon like the precedence effect, a similar push toward a new response came when my interest focused on auditory localization. To study auditory localization one needs a spatial response because sounds vary in distance as well as direction. Head orienting can indicate the infant's response to a sound's direction, but not distance. I was inspired to use reaching for objects as a test of auditory localization during a visit to Al Yonas's lab at the Institute of Child Development, University of Minnesota. Al had been using reaching for years to study infants' discrimination of visual cues used in depth perception (see Yonas & Granrud, 1985, for review). He found that infants would reach more often when presented with objects that appeared to be within reach than beyond reach. Similarly, why not use reaching for sounding objects in the dark to study infants' perception of auditory space? We proceeded to place toy rattles within and beyond reach (Clifton, Perris, & Bullinger, 1991; Litovsky & Clifton, 1992), and at various points in the azimuth (Perris & Clifton, 1988), and discovered that by 6 months of age, infants were quite accurate in reaching out and obtaining the toy in pitch-darkness from many different locations. Infants also appeared to have a sense of auditory space, and reached less when the toy was sounded beyond their reach.

Up to this point in my career I had studied individual aspects of infants' abilities. The auditory system had been explored by looking at infants' discrimination of location, pitch, timbre, and so on (for review, see Clifton, 1992). Association learning and habituation had been explored in the 1960s and 1970s. Like many other researchers working with infants at that time, I thought that by studying individual processes and abilities we could find out more about the world of infants—how they hear, see, feel, taste, smell, and learn. While this research posture was successful in that it led to a far better picture of how newborns and older infants experience the world through their sensory systems, it was ultimately limited. Piaget's theory of cognitive development emphasizes the transaction between infant and the environment. The concepts of assimilation and accommodation are somewhat opaque descriptions of the infant's commerce with the world. The Gibsonian concept of affordance has at its heart the idea of the organism's interaction with environmental objects and their properties (Gibson, 1979). Although these ideas had been around for many years, they began to have a heavy impact from the mid-1980s on. Eleanor Gibson persuasively presented the notion that perception and action are inseparable (Gibson, 1987). Her work on vision and locomotion beautifully exemplifies the concept of affordance applied to human infants (e.g., Gibson et al., 1987; Stoffregen, Schmuckler, & Gibson, 1987). Gibson's work pushed the field toward the study of the infant's perception of and interaction with the world, a trend that Bennett Bertenthal and I expanded on in our review of the literature (Bertenthal & Clifton, 1998). Perception and action are inextricably linked, but this had not been reflected in my early research, nor in most research in the two decades before the 1980s.

When I was in graduate school at the University of Minnesota (1959–1963), we were told quite explicitly that studying the "whole child" was no longer possible nor desirable. The old approach espoused by child psychology of an earlier era had emphasized the importance of considering all aspects of development when engaged in the scientific study of the child. (Indeed, a few faculty at the Institute still held this view at that time.) Instead, we graduate students of the early 1960s were advised to study individual aspects of development—vision, cognition, language, etc. The "whole child" was simply too complex; knowledge would be gained only through the study of specific aspects of development. For example, students of vision need not be concerned with cognition, and vice versa. Although at the time I assumed this stance was correct, I now regard this advice as specious and simply wrong. Close observation of infant behavior brought me to this conclusion, however, rather than an embracing of a particular theory.

The realization dawned gradually after I began to use reaching for objects as the primary dependent variable in my research. Although originally employed from a narrow point of view, as a means to study auditory localization, reaching turned out to literally open my eyes to the infant's interaction with the world. First we ventured into questions about motor control, especially the issue of whether infants used visually guided reaching. There was (and still is) a widespread belief, stemming from Piaget's observations (1952), that when infants first learn to reach for objects they guide movement by seeing their hand and the object, and use vision to bring them together. In a series of studies we have shown this to be wrong. Infants did not need to see their hand or the surround when reaching for objects, even at the onset of reaching at around 4 months of age (Clifton, Muir, Ashmead, & Clarkson, 1993). Even when more complex demands were made, such as matching the orientation of the hand to the orientation of the object (McCarty, Clifton, Ashmead, Lee, & Goubet, 2001) or catching a moving object (Robin, Berthier, & Clifton, 1996), infants did not need to see their hand at initiation of the reach or during transport and grasp. Finally, more fine-grained measures of reaching such as kinematic parameters did not differ for reaches in the dark and light (Clifton, Rochat, Robin, & Berthier, 1994). Our working hypothesis is that visual guidance of the reach is a late-developing ability, and is probably tied to maturation of fine motor control. In contrast, early in development reaching is controlled by coordinating proprioception from the arm and hand with sight (or sound) of the object.

In addition to issues of motor control and auditory perception, from the beginning we were struck by other aspects of infants' behavior in the dark that had deep implications for infant cognition. As the infant's hand approached the object in the dark, we observed the hand opening in anticipation of touch, and kinematic measures revealed deceleration prior to contact with the unseen object, the same as in light. These preparatory motor behaviors implied that infants "knew" an object was about to be grasped. We conducted a study (Clifton, Rochat, Litovsky, & Perris, 1991) in which 6½-month-old infants had to use memory for the size and shape of an object to guide their differential reaching for a large and a small object in the dark. We claimed that infants mentally represented the objects and based their reaching on this representation. However, because the objects made sound in the dark throughout the reach, one could argue that the continuous sound specified the continuous presence of the object, thus supporting memory for the object in the dark. In two recent studies we have shown that infants will reach differentially for objects in the dark when no sound is present (Goubet & Clifton, 1998; McCall & Clifton, 1999). In both cases infants heard sound in the dark that indicated the location and situation of a toy, but during the actual reach and search for the toy, sound was not present. Both experimental situations were fairly complex. Goubet and Clifton tested 6½-month-olds with an auditory event in the dark that indicated the direction in which a ball had moved, but not its resting location; in McCall and Clifton 8-month-olds were presented with a covered toy that had to be uncovered in the dark, requiring that a means/end action be executed, sight unseen. We concluded that infants can represent the movement, juxtaposition, and spatial location relative to their body of unseen objects and events. Furthermore, they can use this knowledge to guide their actions to achieve a goal.

One of the puzzles in infant data is the presumed discrepancy between reaching and looking data with regard to infants' representation of unseen objects. When infants as young as 3–4 months view objects and events, they appear to appreciate the solidity and position of unseen objects, yet they will not reliably search for a hidden toy until 8–9 months (see Haith, 1998, and Spelke, 1998, for opposing arguments on this topic). In presenting their model of development, Meltzoff and Moore (1998) say there is no discrepancy for 9-month-olds because by then infants will search for a hidden object, as well as show spatially directed visual search and preferential looking to impossible events. They say that the paradox of manual search versus looking only holds for young infants of 5–6 months. We disagree on both counts. First, we have found that when the demands of a reaching task are increased, even 9-month-olds appear not to understand the effect of a barrier that is partially hidden (Berthier, Bertenthal, Seaks, Sylvia, Johnson, & Clifton, 2001). So there is still a puzzle to be figured out at the older ages. Perhaps it will seem paradoxical, but we also disagree that reaching and looking data consistently conflict in younger infants. Our work using darkness to conceal the object rather than a cover in the light has *consistently* found that infants of 5–6 months and even younger (Clifton et al., 1993) will reach for unseen objects. In this regard our data are in agreement with claims made by those using the visual discrepancy paradigm (e.g., the work of Baillargeon, 1993, and Spelke et al., 1992). The real question is why infants readily reach for objects hidden by darkness at very young ages but do not uncover objects in the light until 8–9 months. There is not space here to reiterate our arguments, but see Goubet and Clifton (1998) and Clifton (2001). Our lab and other labs (Hood & Willatts, 1986; Stack, Muir, et al., 1989; Wishart, Dunkeld, & Bower, 1978) that have used reaching in the dark as a means of testing object representation find it present at the earliest ages that infants have been tested.

As must be obvious from the description above, I assume that an early system of representation exists in the infant, one that undoubtedly changes in form during development. I believe we are beyond asking the question: At what age does the infant have representation of occluded objects? We must get past proving or disproving Piaget's theory, and concentrate on developing a new theory of perception and action. Taking the existence of some form of representation as the starting point, my aim is to discover how this representation might serve the infant in functional ways, that is, in interactions with the world. By observing how infants look, reach, search, and interact with objects, both seen and unseen, we should be able to draw inferences about the nature of their representations, and, just as important, how those representations are used in action. The exploration of developmental changes in this representational system throughout the first two years of life is currently a major aim of my research.

In closing, I want to recount a final story of a foray into the study of long-term memory, because it is a prime example of high-risk, high-impact research. We had conducted a longitudinal study of infants' reaching for sounding objects in the dark, beginning when they were 8–10 weeks old and continuing until they were 20–22 weeks. Each week the babies came into the lab and were presented with objects in the light and in the dark, as we tried to capture the onset of reaching behavior in different lighting conditions (Clifton et al., 1991). About two years later, I proposed a somewhat preposterous idea to my colleague, Nancy Myers: that these children, now approaching 2 and 2½ years of age, might remember their lab experience. Somewhat to my surprise, Nancy, whose expertise is early memory, agreed, and suggested we test the idea by bringing them back in and repeating the early experience of the same-sounding objects in pitch-darkness in the same soundproofed chamber. We both agreed that this study was the longest of long shots (and would never be funded in an NIH proposal) but if it worked it would be the first experimental study to show long-term memory by toddlers for events that occurred under 6 months of age. The exciting results showed that indeed, children who had been in the lab two years before reached out, touched, and grabbed the toys significantly more often than a control group, matched for age and sex, who had not been in the lab before (Myers, Clifton, & Clarkson, 1987). In a subsequent study we showed that a lengthy, repeated lab experience in infancy was not necessary, that once was enough (Perris, Myers, & Clifton, 1990). Nancy Myers has continued this work, and has succeeded in demonstrating memory across even longer spans of time during the preschool period (Myers, Perris, & Speaker, 1994).

It has been an exciting ride since the early 1960s, as we have made discoveries of just how amazing the human infant is. I think the greatest legacy of this research is its impact on how the lay public regards infants. Research has influenced the press, popular books, and magazine articles so that infants are seen as responsive, intelligent, emotional, social, and sensitive beings from the beginning. They are still mysterious, but they have our profoundest respect.

☐ Acknowledgments

The writing of this manuscript was supported by a Research Scientist Award from the National Institute of Mental Health, MH 00332–20, and by Grant NIH RO1 HD27714. My deepest gratitude is extended to the wonderful colleagues, graduate students, undergraduate students, and postdoctoral fellows that I have had throughout my career.

☐ References

Adkinson, C., & Berg, W. K. (1976). Cardiac deceleration in newborns: Habituation, dishabituation, and offset responses. *Journal of Experimental Child Psychology, 21,* 46–60.

Ashmead, D. H., Clifton, R. K., & Reese, E. P. (1986). Development of auditory localization in dogs: Single source and precedence effect sounds. *Developmental Psychobiology, 19,* 91–104.

Ashmead, D. H., Clifton, R. K., & Perris, E. E. (1987). Precision of auditory localization in human infants. *Developmental Psychology, 23,* 641–647.

Baillargeon, R. (1993). The object concept revisited: New directions in the investigation of infants' physical knowledge. In C. E. Graurud (Ed.), *Visual perception and cognition in infancy* (pp. 265–315). Hillsdale, NJ: Lawrence Erlbaum Associates, Inc.

Bartoshuk, A. (1962a). Human neonatal cardiac acceleration to sound. *Perceptual Motor Skills, 15,* 15–27.

Bartoshuk, A. (1962b). Response decrement with repeated elicitation of human neonatal cardiac acceleration to sound. *Journal of Comparative and Physiological Psychology, 55,* 9–13.

Berg, W. K., Jackson, J. C., & Graham, F. K., (1975). Tone intensity and rise-decay time effects on cardiac responses during sleep. *Psychophysiology, 12,* 254–261.

Bertenthal, B. I., & Clifton, R. K. (1998). Perception and action. In D. Kuhn and R. Siegler (Eds.), *Cognition, perception, and language.* Vol. 2. of the *Handbook of child psychology* (5th ed., pp. 51–102), Gen. Ed., W. Damon. New York: Wiley.

Berthier, N. E., Bertenthal, B. I., Seaks, J. D., Sylvia, M. R., Johnson, R. L., & Clifton, R. K. (2001) Using object knowledge in visual tracking and reaching. *Infancy, 2,* 257–284.

Blauert, J. (1983). *Spatial hearing.* Cambridge, MA: MIT Press.

Blauert, J. (1996). *Spatial hearing: The psychophysics of human sound localization,* 2nd edition. Cambridge, MA: MIT Press.

Blauert, J., & Col, J. P. (1992). Irregularities in the precedence effect. In Y. Cazals, K. Horner, & L. Demany (Eds.), *Auditory physiology and perception* (pp. 531–538). Oxford: Pergamon Press.

Bremner, J. G. (1988). *Infancy.* Oxford, UK & New York: Basil Blackwell.

Bridger, W. H. (1961). Sensory habituation and discrimination in the human neonate. *American Journal of Psychiatry, 117,* 991–996.

Bronshtein, A. I., Antonova, T. G., Kamenetskaya, A. G., Luppova, N. N., & Sytova, V. A. (1958). On the development of the function of analyzers in infants and some animals at the early stages of ontogenesis. In *Problems of evolution of physiological functions*. OTS Report No. 60-51066. Translation available from U.S. Dept. of Commerce. Moscow: Academy of Science.

Campos, J. J., & Brackbill, Y. (1973). Infant state: Relationship to heart rate, behavioral response and response decrement. *Developmental Psychobiology, 6*, 9–19.

Clarkson, M. G., & Clifton, R. K. (1985). Infant pitch perception: Evidence for responding to pitch categories and the missing fundamental. *Journal of the Acoustical Society of America, 77*, 1521–1528.

Clarkson, M. G., & Clifton, R. K. (1995) Infants' pitch perception: Inharmonic tonal complexes. *Journal of Acoustical Society of America, 98*, 1372–1379.

Clarkson, M. G., & Clifton, R. K. (1991). Acoustic determinants of newborn orienting. In M. J. S. Weiss & P. R. Zelazo (Eds.), *Newborn attention: Biological constraints and the influence of experience* (pp. 99–119). Norwood, NJ: Ablex.

Clarkson, M. G., Clifton, R. K., & Perris, E. E. (1988). Infant timbre perception: Discrimination of frequency envelopes. *Perception and Psychophysics, 43*, 15–20.

Clarkson, M. G., & Clifton, R. K. (1991) Acoustic determinants of newborn orienting. In M. J. S. Weiss & P. R. Zelazo (Eds.), *Newborn attention: Biological constraints and the influence of experience* (pp. 99–119). Norwood, NJ: Ablex.

Clifton, R. K. (1974) Cardiac orienting and conditioning in infants. In P. A. Obrist, J. Brener, L. DiCara, & A. Black (Eds.), *Cardiovascular psychophysiology: Current issues in response to mechanisms, biofeedback, and methodology* (pp. 479–504). Chicago: Aldine Press.

Clifton, R. K. (1974). Heart rate conditioning in the newborn infant. *Journal of Experimental Child Psychology, 18*, 9–21.

Clifton, R. K. (1978). The effects of behavioral state and motor activity on infant heart rate. In A. Collins (Ed.), *Minnesota Symposium on Child Psychology, Volume 11* (pp. 64–97). Hillsdale, NJ: Lawrence Erlbaum Press.

Clifton, R. K. (1985). The precedence effect: Its implications for developmental questions. In S. Trehub & B. Schneider (Eds.), *Auditory development in infancy* (pp. 85-99). NY: Plenum.

Clifton, R. K. (1987). Breakdown of echo suppression in the precedence effect. *Journal of the Acoustical Society of America, 82*, 1834–1835.

Clifton, R. K. (1992) The development of spatial hearing in human infants. In L. A. Werner & E. W Rubel (Eds.), *Developmental psychoacoustics* (pp. 135–157). Washington, DC: American Psychological Association.

Clifton, R. K. (2001). Lessons from infants: 1960–2000. *Infancy, 2*, 285–309.

Clifton, R. K., Freyman, R. L., Litovsky, R. Y., & McCall, D. (1994). Listeners' expectations about echoes can raise or lower echo threshold. *Journal of Acoustical Society of America, 95*, 1525–1533.

Clifton, R. K., & Freyman, R. L. (1997). The precedence effect: Beyond echo suppression. In R. H. Gilkey & T. R. Anderson (Eds.), *Binaural and spatial hearing in real and virtual environments* (pp. 233–255) Mahwah, NJ: Lawrence Erlbaum Associates.

Clifton, R. K., Meyers, W. J., & Solomons, G. (1972). Methodological problems in conditioning the head turning response of newborn infants. *Journal of Experimental Child Psychology, 13*, 29–42.

Clifton, R. K., Morrongiello, B. A., & Dowd, J. M. (1984). A developmental look at an auditory illusion: The precedence effect. *Developmental Psychobiology, 17*, 519–536.

Clifton, R. K., Morrongiello, B. A., Kulig, J., & Dowd, J. (1981a). Newborns' orientation toward sound: Possible implications for cortical development. *Child Development, 52*, 833–838.

Clifton, R. K., Morrongiello, B. A., Kulig, J., & Dowd, J. M. (1981b). Developmental changes in auditory localization. In R. Aslin, J. Alberts, & M. Peterson (Eds.), *The development of perception: Psychobiological perspectives. Volume 1: Audition, somatic perception and the chemical senses* (pp. 141-160). New York: Academic Press.

Clifton, R. K., Muir, D. W., Ashmead, D. H., & Clarkson, M. G. (1993). Is visually guided reaching in early infancy a myth? *Child Development, 64,* 1099–1110.

Clifton, R. K., & Nelson, M. N., (1976). Developmental study of habituation in infants: The importance of paradigm, response system, and state of the organism. In T. J. Tighe & R. N. Leaton (Eds.), *Habituation: Neurological, comparitve, and developmental approaches* (pp. 159–205). Hillsdale, NJ: Erlbaum Press.

Clifton, R. K., Perris, E. E., & Bullinger, A. (1991). Infants' perception of auditory space. *Developmental Psychology, 27,* 187–197.

Clifton, R. K., Rochat, P., Litovsky, R. Y., & Perris, E. E. (1991). Object representation guides infants' reaching in the dark. *Journal of Experimental Psychology: Human Perception and Performance, 17,* 323–329.

Clifton, R. K., Rochat, P., Robin, D. J., & Berthier, N. E. (1994) Multimodal perception in human infants. *Journal of Experimental Psychology: Human Perception and Performance, 20,* 876–886.

Clifton, R. K., Siqueland, E., & Lipsitt, L. (1972). Conditioned head turning in human newborns as a function of conditioned response requirements and states of wakefulness. *Journal of Experimental Child Psychology, 13,* 43–57.

DeCasper, A. J., & Fifer, W. P. (1980). Of human bonding: Newborns prefer their mothers' voices. *Science, 208*(4448), 1174–1176.

Donohue, R. L., & Berg, W. K. (1991). Infant heart-rate responses to temporally predictable and unpredictable events. *Developmental Psychology, 27*(1), 59–66.

Engen, T., Lipsitt, L. P., Kaye, H. (1963). Olfactory responses and adaptation in the human neonate. *Journal of Comparative and Physiological Psychology, 56*(1), 73–77.

Fantz, R. (1963). Pattern vision in newborn infants. *Science, 140,* 296–297.

Fantz, R. (1964). Visual experience in infants: Decreased attention to familiar patterns relative to novel ones. *Science, 146,* 668–670.

Freyman, R. L., McCall, D. M., & Clifton, R. K. (1998). Intensity discrimination for precedence effect stimuli. *Journal of the Acoustical Society of America, 103,* 2031–2041.

Gibson, E. J. (1987). Exploratory behavior in the development of perceiving, acting, and the acquiring of knowledge. *Annual Review of Psychology, 39,* 1–41.

Gibson, E. J., Ricco, G., Schmuckler, M. A., Stoffregen, T. A., Rosenberg, D., & Taormina, J. (1987). Detection of the traversability of surfaces by crawling and walking infants. *Journal of Experimental Psychology: Human Perception and Performance, 13,* 533–544.

Gibson, J. J. (1979). *The ecological approach to visual perception.* Boston: Houghton Mifflin.

Goubet, N., & Clifton, R. K. (1998). Object and event representation in 6 2-month-old infants. *Developmental Psychology, 34,* 63–76.

Graham, F. K., & Clifton, R. K. (1966). Heart rate change as a component of the orienting response. *Psychological Bulletin, 65,* 305–320.

Grantham, D. W. (1996). Left-right asymmetry in the buildup of echo suppression in normal-hearing adults. *Journal of the Acoustical Society of America, 99,* 1118–1123.

Gregg, C., Clifton, R.K., & Haith, M. (1976). A possible explanation for the frequent failure to find cardiac orienting in the newborn infant. *Developmental Psychology, 12,* 75–76.

Haith, M. M. (1969). Infrared television recording and measurement of ocular behavior in the human infant. *American Psychologist, 24,* 279–283.

Haith, M. M. (1991). Gratuity, perception-action integration, and future orientation in infant vision. In F. S. Kessel, M. H. Bornstein, & A. J. Sameroff (Eds.), *Contemporary constructions of the child: Essays in honor of William Kessen* (pp. 23–43). Hillsdale, NJ: Erlbaum.

Haith, M. M. (1998). Who put the cog in infant cognition? Is rich interpretation too costly? *Infant Behavior and Development, 21,* 167–179.

Hartmann, W. M. (1997). Listening in a room and the precedence effect. In R. H. Gilkey & T. B. Anderson (Eds.), *Binaural and spatial hearing in real and virtual environments.* Hillsdale, NJ: Erlbaum.

Hood, B., & Willatts, P. (1986). Reaching in the dark to an object's remembered position: Evidence for object permanence in 5-month-old infants. *British Journal of Developmental Psychology, 4,* 57–65.

Jackson J. C., Kantowitz, S. R., & Graham, F. K. (1971). Can newborns show cardiac orienting? *Child Development, 42,* 107–121.

Johnson, L. C., & Lubin, A. (1967). The orienting reflex during waking and sleeping. *Electroencephalography and Clinical Neurophysiology, 22,* 11–21.

Johnson, L. C., Townsend, R. E., & Wilson, M. R. (1975). Habituation during sleeping and waking. *Psychophysiology, 12,* 574–584.

Kearsley, R. B. (1973). Neonatal response to auditory stimulation: A demonstration of orienting and defensive behavior. *Child Development, 44,* 582–590.

Keen, R. E. (1964). The effects of auditory stimuli on sucking behavior in the human neonate. *Journal of Experimental Child Psychology, 1,* 348–354.

Keen, R. E., Chase, H. H., & Graham, F. K. (1965) Twenty-four-hour retention by neonates of an habituated heart rate response. *Psychonomic Science, 2,* 265–266.

Korner, A. F. (1972). State as variable, as obstacle, and as mediator of stimulation in infant research. *Merrill-Palmer Quarterly, 18,* 77–94.

Lacey, J. I. (1959). Psychophysiological approaches to the evaluation of psychotherapeutic process and outcome. In E. A. Rubenstein & M. B. Parloff (Eds.), *Research in psychotherapy.* Washington, DC: APA.

Lacey, J. I., Kagan, J., Lacey, B. C., & Moss, H. A. (1963). The visceral level: Situational determinants and behavioral correlates of autonomic response patterns. In P. H. Knapp (Ed.), *Expression of the emotions in man.* New York: International Universities Press.

Lipsitt, L. P. (1963). Learning in the first year of life. In L. P. Lipsitt & C. C. Spiker (Eds.) *Advances in child development and behavior, vol. 1* (pp. 147–195). New York: Academic Press.

Lipsitt, L. P., Engen, T., & Kaye, H. (1963). Developmental changes in the olfactory threshold of the neonate. *Child Development, 34*(2), 371–376.

Litovsky, R. Y., & Clifton, R. K. (1992) Use of sound pressure level in auditory distance discrimination. *Journal of Acoustical Society of America, 92,* 794–802.

McCall, D. D., & Clifton, R. K. (1999) Infants' means-end search for hidden objects in the absence of visual feedback. *Infant Behavior & Development, 22,* 179–195.

McCall, D. D., Freyman, R. L., & Clifton, R. K. (1998). Sudden changes in spectrum of an echo cause a breakdown of the precedence effect. *Perception and Psychophysics, 60,* 593–601.

McCarty, M.E., Clifton, R. K., Ashmead, D. H., Lee, P., & Goubet, N. (2001). How infants use vision for grasping objects. *Child Development, 72,* 973–987.

Meltzoff, A. N., & Moore, M. K. (1998). Object representation, identity, and the paradox of early permanence: Steps toward a new framework. *Infant Behavior and Development, 21,* 201–235.

Morrongiello, B., Clifton, R., & Kulig, J. (1982). Newborn cardiac and behavioral orienting responses to sound under varying precedence-effect conditions. *Infant Behavior and Development, 5,* 249–259.

Morrongiello, B., Kulig, J., & Clifton, R. (1984). Developmental changes in auditory temporal perception. *Child Development, 55,* 461–471.

Muir, D., & Clifton, R. (1985). Infants' orientation to the location of sound sources. In G. Gottlieb & N. Krasnegor (Eds.), *Measurement of audition and vision in the first year of post-natal life: A methodological overview* (pp. 171–194). Norwood, NJ: Ablex.

Muir, D., & Field, J. (1979) Newborn infants orient to sounds. *Child Development, 50,* 431–436.

Muir, D. W., Clifton, R. K., & Clarkson, M. G. (1989). The development of a human auditory localization response: A U-shaped function. *Canadian Journal of Psychology, 43,* 199–216.

Myers, N. A., Clifton, R. K., & Clarkson, M. G. (1987). When they were very young: Almost-threes remember two years ago. *Infant Behavior and Development, 10,* 123–132.

Myers, N. A., Perris, E. E., & Speaker, C. J. (1994). Fifty months of memory: A longitudinal study in early childhood. *Memory, 2,* 383–415.

Nelson, M. N., Clifton, R. K., Dowd, J., & Field, T. (1978). Cardiac responding to auditory stimuli in newborn infants: Why pacifiers should not be used when heart rate is the major dependent variable. *Infant Behavior and Development, 1,* 277–290.

Papousek, H. (1967). Experimental studies of appetitional behavior in human newborns and infants. In H. W. Stevenson, E. H. Hess, & H. L. Rheingold (Eds.), *Early behavior: Comparative and developmental approaches* (pp. 249–278). New York: Wiley.

Perris, E. E., & Clifton, R. K. (1988). Reaching in the dark toward sound as a measure of auditory localization in infants. *Infant Behavior & Development, 11,* 473–492.

Perris, E. E., Myers, N. A., & Clifton, R. K. (1990). Long-term memory for a single infancy experience. *Child Development, 61,* 1796–1807.

Piaget, J. (1952). *The origins of intelligence in children.* New York: Norton.

Pomerleau-Malcuit, A., & Clifton, R. K. (1973). Neonatal heart rate response to tactile, auditory, and vestibular stimulation in different states. *Child Development, 44,* 485–496.

Prechtl, H. F. R. (1958). The directed head turning response and allied movements in the human baby. *Behavior, 13,* 212–242.

Prechtl, H. F. R. (1974). The behavioral states of the newborn infant (a review). *Brain Research, 76,* 185–212.

Robin, D. J., Berthier, N. E., & Clifton, R. K. (1996) Infants' predictive reaching for moving objects in the dark. *Developmental Psychology, 32,* 824–835.

Salapatek, P., & Kessen, W. (1966) Visual scanning of triangles by the human newborn. *Journal of Experimental Child Psychology, 3,* 155–167.

Sameroff, A. J. (1971). Can conditioned responses be established in the newborn infant? *Developmental Psychology, 5,* 1–12.

Sameroff, A., Cashmore T., & Dykes, A. (1973). Heart rate deceleration during visual fixation in human newborns, *Developmental Psychology, 8,* 117–119.

Simner, M. L. (1971). The newborn's response to the cry of another infant. *Developmental Psychology, 5,* 136–150.

Siqueland, E. R., & Lipsitt, L. P. (1966). Conditioned headturning in human newborns. *Journal of Experimental Psychology, 3,* 356–376.

Slater, A. (1989). Visual memory and perception in early infancy. In A. Slater & G. Brennan (Eds.), *Infant Development.* Hove U.K.: Lawrence Erlbaum Associates, pp. 43–71.

Sokolov, E. N. (1960). Neuronal models and the orienting reflex. In M. A. B. Brazier (Ed.), *The central nervous system and behavior* (pp. 187–276) Madison, NJ: Madison Printing Co.

Sokolov, E. N. (1963). *Perception and the conditioned reflex.* New York: Macmillan.

Spelke, E. (1998). Nativism, empiricism, and the origins of knowledge. *Infant Behavior & Development, 21,* 181–200.

Spelke, E., Breinlinger, K., Macomber, J., & Jacobson, K. (1992). Origins of knowledge. *Psychological Review, 99,* 605–632.

Stack, D., Muir, D., Sheriff, F., & Roman, J. (1989). Development of infant reaching in the dark to luminous objects and invisible sounds. *Perception, 18,* 69–82.

Steinschneider, A., Lipton, E. L., & Richmond, J. B. (1966). Auditory sensitivity in the infant: Effect of intensity on cardiac and motor responsivity. *Child Development, 37*(2), 233–252.

Stevenson, H. W., Keen, R. E., & Knights, R. (1963). Parents and strangers as reinforcing agents for children's performance. *Journal of Abnormal and Social Psychology, 67,* 183–186.

Stoffregen, T. A., Schmuckler, M. A., & Gibson, E. J. (1987). Use of central and peripheral optical flow in stance and locomotion in young walkers. *Perception, 16,* 113–119.

Swain, I. U., Zelazo, P. R., & Clifton, R. K. (1993). Newborn memory for speech sounds retained over 24 hours. *Developmental Psychology, 29,* 312–323.

Thorpe, W. H. (1963). *Learning and instinct in animals,* 2nd ed. Cambridge, MA: Harvard University Press.

Whitfield, I. C., Cranford, J., Ravizza, R., & Diamond, I. T. (1972). Effects of unilateral ablation of auditory cortex in cat on complex sound localization. *Journal of Neurophysiology, 35*(5), 718–731.

Wishart, J., Bower, T. G. R., & Dunkeld, J. (1978). Reaching in the dark. *Perception, 7,* 507–512.

Wolff, P. H. (1966). The causes, control, and organization of behavior in the neonate. *Psychological Issues, 5*(1, Whole No. 17).

Yonas, A., & Granrud, C. (1985). Reaching as a measure of visual development. In G. Gottlieb & N. Krasnegor (Eds.), *Measurement of audition and vision in the first year of postnatal life: A methodological overview* (pp. 301–322). Norwood, NJ: Ablex.

Yost, W. A., & Guzman, S. J. (1996). Auditory processing of sound sources: Is there an echo in here? *Current Directions in Psychological Science, 5,* 125–131.

CHAPTER
7

George F. Michel

Development of Infant Handedness

In 1975, I began my investigation of the development of handedness during infancy with the intention of identifying whether experiential factors contributed toward the predominance of right-handedness in all human populations. Although some investigators had argued that handedness developed from social learning and explicit training, such evidence could not account for why the right hand would have been the hand selected for specific training in all cultures. Clearly, the predominance of right-handedness was a universal feature of all human cultures, leading many to conclude that its development was controlled in detail by genetic factors perhaps operating on the development of those left-hemisphere structures involved in the control of right-hand actions. I thought that the investigation of the development of handedness during infancy would reveal patterns of self-generated experiences that would lead to the predominance of right-handedness.

Handedness is readily amenable to genealogical analysis (cf, Corballis, 1997). Annett (cf, 1970, 1972, 1974, 1975, 1978) proposed a genetic theory of handedness and laterality that seemed most suited to both the genealogy data and for developmental investigation. Annett's empirical work demonstrated that handedness was continuously distributed in the population. That is, the differences between hands in both skill and preference vary continuously among individuals. Also, the typical classes of handedness (e.g., left-handed, right-handed, ambidextrous) are somewhat arbitrarily imposed (like "short," "tall," and "average" are imposed on the continuous distribution of people's height). Annett argued that our handedness distribution is right-shifted, making humans unique among species. That is, only humans exhibit predominance, in the population, of one hand preference for use (the right). Thus, according to Annett, there are two aspects to handedness: the difference in skill or use between the two hands or forelimbs (this occurs in other species), and the predominance of right-handedness in the human population.

According to Annett, the first aspect of handedness reflects random events, whereas the second reflects the operation of a gene. Annett's single allele model for this right shift closely matched the genealogical data on the distribution of handedness among generations. For example, two left-handed parents would be lacking the allele that biases the development of right-handedness and hence their offspring would have only a 50/50 probability of being left-handed (as a consequence of the random aspect of handedness). Indeed, only about 44 percent of the offspring of two left-handed parents are themselves left-handed (Annett, 1974). Annett argued that the slight right-handed bias (56 percent) in these offspring reflected their development in a right-biased world, created by the dominance of right-handers in the population.

Annett (1975) proposed that the presence of the "right-shift" allele in an individual biased the development of left-hemisphere control of language abilities and that such specialization then indirectly contributed to the development of right-handedness. Consequently, handedness and hemispheric control of language would be associated, but not completely. In contrast, I speculated that the allele might provide a rightward bias in an early precursor for the development of infant handedness.

I planned to identify behavioral patterns in newborn infants that would promote both a bias in an individual's experience (that would affect the infant's hand-use preference) and a bias in the distribution of these behavioral patterns (so that most, but not all, infants would likely develop a right-hand-use preference). I wanted to show how experience could contribute to the development of handedness during infancy. Then I would investigate how the development of handedness could contribute to the development of other forms of hemispheric specialization of function.

However, I soon discovered that pursuing the relation of the development of handedness to the development of other forms of hemispheric specialization of functions had to await a solid understanding of the development of handedness. To achieve that understanding, I had to create a measure of infant hand-use preference that was reliable and valid across a wide age range (with its concomitant extensive changes in the infant's developing manual skill and cognitive abilities). Moreover, the assessment had to be insensitive to (1) the properties of the objects used to elicit manual actions, and (2) the mode of presentation of the objects. I had to identify a statistically defensible technique for classifying an infant's hand-use preference as "right," "left," or "no preference" so that I could track an infant's hand-use preference across assessments at different ages. I had to separately identify hand-use preferences for reaching for objects, from those manifested during the manipulation of objects, and I had to separately examine unimanual manipulation preferences from those involving role-differentiated bimanual manipulations. Finally, I had to examine how a hand-use preference relates to the development of the infant's other manual skills and cognitive abilities.

So what began as an intention to identify the experiential influences contributing to the development of the right-hand predominance in human handedness shifted to determining exactly what handedness is during infancy. Instead of identifying the role of handedness development in the development of other forms of hemispheric specialization of function, I am investigating the function of handedness during infancy. Handedness is an aspect of hemispheric specialization, and I will continue to conduct research designed to show how experience can contribute to the development of such specialization. However, at present, the study of the development of handedness during infancy can only be a model for the investigation of the development of other forms of hemispheric specialization.

☐ Why Study Infant Handedness?

As an undergraduate at Rutgers University–Newark, I administered a series of studies on perception designed by Dorothy Dinnerstein. Much psychophysical research requires numerous repetitions of a very limited set of stimuli yielding mathematically precise models of perception. However, ordinary perception does not occur in such an extensively repetitive manner. Dinnerstein (1971) argued that in the "real world," the perceptual evaluation of any particular stimulus is derived from the spatial and temporal contexts of stimulation within which the stimulus occurs. One set of our experiments examined how the perception of either the felt weight or size of an object in the judging hand was affected by the weight or size of a "context" object simultaneously felt in the nonjudging hand. The results yielded an interesting asymmetry to these intermanual contextual influences. The felt size of an object in the individual's preferred hand (the right hand for nearly every college student volunteer) was affected by the size of the "context" object that was felt simultaneously with the nonpreferred hand. In contrast, the felt weight of an object in the individual's nonpreferred hand was affected by simultaneously hefting a weight in the preferred hand. Thus, individual handedness seemed to affect contextual influences on two different kinds of haptic perception.

Reporting these studies in an application for an NIH predoctoral fellowship led to brief but intensive study (one week in February 1970) of callosectomized patients in Roger Sperry's laboratory at Caltech. A member of the committee reviewing fellowship applications, Colwyn Trevarthen (a postdoctoral associate of Sperry's) wondered whether the observed asymmetry in haptic perception of size and weight might reveal something about the differential functioning of the left and right hemispheres. Size, but not weight, perception may be a spatial function requiring right-hemisphere processing. Hence right-hand size information entering the left hemisphere must be sent via the corpus callosum to the right hemisphere for processing where the left-hand contextual effects have already had their effect. When the size judgments are made with the left hand, the information is already processed by the time the right-hand context information gets to the right hemisphere. Hence, the right hand contexts have no influence on size judgments of the left hand. The reverse may occur for weight perception. In reply to Trevarthen's invitation to collaborate at Caltech, Dinnerstein sent me. Although no publication ensued, the experience prompted my interest in hemispheric specialization of function.

Although Trevarthen and I failed to find any intermanual contextual effect on small (but perceptible) differences in haptic perception of size and weight, we discussed the origins of hemispheric specialization. We agreed that the hemispheric differences in function are likely to be adaptive, but we disagreed about how such adaptive species-typical characteristics might develop. Without evidence, I argued for a developmental pattern of experience-individual interactions over time that was consistent with Lehrman's (1953, 1970) notions about the development of species-typical (instinctive) behavior of animals. Trevarthen argued for a more internal model in which epigenetic processes of neural development ensured emergence of the neural circuitry responsible for the differences in function. Experience might disrupt this process, but development within the environment of evolutionary adaptedness permitted but did not construct the development of hemispheric specialization. In this sense, the differences between the hemispheres were innate.

My doctoral dissertation identified the specific experiences, associated with a ring dove reproductive cycle (from courting to fledging young) that enable progesterone to "induce" the dove's expression of incubation behavior (cf, Michel, 1985). Previous experience with establishing a nest site, and not with incubation itself or exposure to its own progesterone secretion, provided the dove's nervous system with the sensitivity that would allow progesterone injections to rapidly (within 2 hours) facilitate the expression of incubation behavior. Moreover, the expression of incubation required the presence of a noncourting mate and a nest filled with eggs. Thus, the dove's previous experience, current hormonal condition, and current stimulus situation together were responsible for the emergence of incubation behavior, a species-typical behavior pattern.

Therefore, I left Rutgers with three dominant notions:

1. That individual experience (often not involving either learning or even those experiences that intuitively might seem to be relevant) could form an integral component of the developmental expression of species-typical behavior;
2. That the role of hormonal and neural states in the emergence and organization of species-typical behaviors requires attending to specific patterns of spatial and temporal contextual processes. That is, the individual's current hormonal and neural states reflect the consequences of the individual's previous and concurrent experience with social and physical environmental factors. Such experience has short-term and long-term effects on the individual's hormonal and neural condition and functioning;
3. That although I respected and valued the role played by knowledge of biological functioning in understanding the organization and expression of behavior, I also respected and valued the role played by knowledge of the psychological (social and experiential) conditions.

I began my first academic position (1971) at Boston University wanting to study the development of hemispheric specialization for language abilities. However, the literature on developmental psycholinguistics convinced me that an infant's and young child's language abilities were inferred from tasks that I considered too ephemeral for investigations of the development of hemispheric specialization. Worse still were the techniques used to assess infant hemispheric specialization for language function. Some research sought lateral asymmetries in gross neuroanatomy that were similar to those adult asymmetries presumed to underlie hemispheric specialization for language. Other research sought reliable differences in the lateral asymmetries evoked in averaged EEG patterns by multiple presentations of specific linguistic versus nonlinguistic stimuli. Some research used the habituation/dishabituation of nonnutritive sucking paradigm to investigate ear (hemisphere) differences in the detection of changes in linguistic versus nonlinguistic auditory stimuli. Each of these research techniques had serious deficiencies for reliable investigation of the development of hemispheric specialization of function (cf, Michel, 1983, 1987, 1988).

In contrast, handedness appeared to be a behavior that could be readily measured and seemed to be an aspect of hemispheric specialization of function that could be reliably and validly examined during infant development. Moreover, some evidence from adults linked a right-hand preference to the manifestation of hemispheric specialization for language. Therefore, investigation of the development of infant handedness seemed to be a good prerequisite for investigating the development of hemispheric specialization for language.

☐ Finding the Precursors of Infant Handedness

For over three decades (e.g., Kinsbourne, 1997), "progressive lateraliza-tion" and "unchanging lateralization" have been the only "theories" about the development of hemispheric specialization of function, and both are supported by studies of language. In 1967, Lenneberg proposed the pro-gressive lateralization theory, with hemispheric specialization first appear-ing around 2 years of age and continuing to increase until adolescence. Maturational processes somehow assured left-hemisphere dominance for language functions. In contrast, other researchers (e.g., Kinsbourne, 1975, 1981, and Witelson, 1980) proposed that the differences in the way the right and left hemispheres process information does not change during development. Instead, as each psychological function develops, it may reach a level of complexity that requires utilization of the specialized pro-cesses of one of the hemispheres. At that stage in development (and there-after) the function has become lateralized. Thus, the hemispheres do not change with development, only the tasks that they execute change, yield-ing the impression of progressive lateralization. Each function eventually settles into the hemisphere whose processing character is most efficient and effective for that ability. The expression of lateralized asymmetries for languagelike functions at very early ages of infancy is considered strong evidence against progressive lateralization and for unchanging lateraliza-tion.

From my perspective, early forms of lateralization are not the same as later forms of lateralization. Thus, lateralization develops, but not in the manner described by progressive lateralization. Earlier forms of lateral-ized processing can contribute to the development of later forms of later-alized processing. In contrast to the progressive lateralization notion, the hemispheres need not be equipotential at birth. However, the processing asymmetry at birth need not be the same processing asymmetry exhib-ited later in development as proposed by the unchanging lateralization theory. I presumed that the study of the development of handedness would demonstrate this argument. That is, the earliest forms of handedness would both differ from later forms and contribute to the development of those later forms.

According to Annett (1975), the "right-shift" allele in an individual biased the development of right-handedness by creating left-hemispheric specialization for language. However, there were other potential precursors for handedness development that seemed more relevant than specializing the hemispheres for language. Gerry Turkewitz (cf. 1977) had reported that most neonates prefer to lie with their heads turned to the right when supine. Much earlier, Gesell (cf. Gesell & Ames, 1947) had reported a similar result and suggested that the head orientation would induce an asymmetric tonic neck reflex (ATNR) throughout the infant's first 3–4 months. Also, Gesell reported that the direction (right or left) of the ATNR was predictive of handedness at 10 years of age.

I speculated that the visual regard of one hand during the ATNR might lead to its preferred use in reaching, which in turn would develop into a hand-use preference for obtaining, exploring, and manipulating objects. I also speculated that the development of the neural processes underlying these hand-use preferences might be relevant to the development of the neural processes underlying speech (cf. Arbib & Rizzolatti, 1997; Armstrong, 1999; Petitto, 2000). Thus, hemispheric specialization for handedness could concatenate during infancy into hemispheric specialization for speech control and then to language.

My graduate student Jane Coryell suggested that we examine some of these speculations by observing whether the direction of the ATNR results in asymmetry of hand regard and whether that contributes to asymmetry of reaching for objects. Thus, we (Coryell & Michel, 1978) videotaped the head orientation preference, ATNR, and the "reaching" to a visual stimulus of 16 infants at 1, 2, 4, 6, 8, 10, and 12 weeks of age. Since several studies seemingly demonstrated early reaching behavior, even in neonates (Bower, 1974), we expected to observe how the head orientation preference and ATNR gradually shaped an asymmetrical reaching preference. We discovered that the influence of the head orientation preference on hand regard did not require an ATNR (frequency of self-induced ATNR increased slowly to 6 weeks of age and then rapidly declined). Nevertheless, the much more prevalent and distinctive head orientation preference, a rightward direction for 12 infants and a leftward for 2 (2 infants exhibited no clear preference), created striking differences between the hands in hand regard. Although reaching for an object had not yet begun by 12 weeks of age, only at 12 weeks did the visual presentation of the object increase hand movements (prereaching behavior?), and the hand that had received the most regard (the right for most infants) was the more active hand. The left hand was more active for the two infants with a leftward head orientation preference.

This study raised the following questions: What was the origin of the infant's head orientation preference? Does the head orientation preference lead to a hand-use preference for reaching? Why did we not find early reaching? Would a leftward head orientation preference reliably lead to a left-hand preference for reaching? The last question is important because the association between a predominant rightward head orientation and a predominant right-hand-use preference would be high simply by chance. This chance association is the origin of many of the observed associations between right-handedness and left-hemisphere functions.

☐ What Is the Origin of the Neonate's Head Orientation Preference?

Previous research had reported that the newborn's general postural preference or "position of comfort" approximates its prenatal posture (Chapple & Davidson, 1941; Dunn, 1975). In part, the infant's postural preference is a consequence of the properties of segmental reflexes, muscles and their afferents that are calibrated prenatally and may reflect or create intrauterine positional preferences (cf. Michel, 1983). Therefore, since most neonates exhibited a postural preference in which their heads were oriented toward the right, I predicted that they likely manifested a rightward head orientation prenatally.

Descriptions of neonatal plagiocephaly indicated that frequently the right side of the infant's jaw had been pressed prenatally against the right shoulder (Parmelee, 1931). Steele and Javert (1942) observed that 53 percent of 763 fetuses were in a left occiput anterior (LOA) or transverse (LOT) position before their heads began to descend through the birth canal. In contrast, only 34 percent were in a ROA/ROT position. Therefore, I speculated that the fetuses in an LOA/LOT position were also likely to have their heads oriented to their right, and vice versa for fetuses in the ROA/ROT position.

Position of the infant's head during delivery has been reported to be a reliable indicator of the orientation that the fetus (Hughey, 1985) achieves some 3–4 weeks before delivery (Vartan, 1945). Therefore, with the help of a graduate student, Rhoda Goodwin, I examined the relation between birth position, as recorded by the obstetricians at the Boston Beth Israel Hospital, and neonatal head orientation preference (NHOP). We predicted that LOA/LOT position would be associated with a rightward NHOP (R-NHOP), and the less frequent ROA/ROT birth position would be associated with a leftward NHOP (L-NHOP). Examination of 109 neonates (over sampling to obtain 51 with a ROA/ROT position) revealed a significant association between birth position and direction of NHOP (Michel & Goodwin, 1979). Over 60 percent of the LOA/LOT infants had significant R-NHOPs, as compared to 23 percent of ROA/ROT infants. In contrast, 16 percent of ROA/ROT infants had significant L-NHOPs, as compared to only 3 percent of LOA/LOT infants. However, 61 percent of the ROA/

ROT infants had "weak" NHOPs, as compared to 37 percent of LOA/LOT infants. Therefore, although LOA/LOT seemed associated with R-NHOP, ROA/ROT seemed associated primarily with a weak NHOP.

These results are interpretable within Annett's theory that a single allele is associated with a right-shift in the population (handedness and NHOP), and when it is not present, handedness and NHOP distribute more or less randomly in the population. Thus, LOA/LOT could be an indicator that the allele was present in an individual. However, this interpretation is suspect, because the obstetricians had grown impatient with the need to record the birth position data for us. Toward the end of our sampling, they discovered that we were seeking a large sample of rare ROA/ROT infants. Thereafter, the proportion of babies delivered in the ROA/ROT position greatly increased. It is likely that many of our "ROA/ROT" infants were not.

Work by Brian Hopkins and colleagues (cf. Hopkins & Ronnqvist, 1998) using ultrasonography may eventually reveal whether prenatal conditions are related to postnatal NHOP. They reported that the heads of ten fetuses were predominantly turned to the right, but only after 32 weeks of gestation. Unfortunately, the relation between fetal position and neonatal head orientation preference was not examined. They did find that the appearance of the fetal rightward head orientation coincides with the emergence of behavioral states. Thus, fetal, like neonatal, head orientation preference may be neurally generated and not passively imposed by the uterine conditions.

Since fetal behavior is not controlled by cortical mechanisms, the rightward head turn likely reflects the operation of brain-stem mechanisms. Thus, Annett's allele may affect subcortical mechanisms that affect the behavior of the fetus and neonate. These behavioral asymmetries and their subcortical mechanisms, in turn, likely affect the development of cortical mechanisms involved in hemispheric specialization for handedness and perhaps language.

☐ Is Neonatal Head Orientation Preference Related to Infant Hand-Use Preference?

To examine this relation I first had to describe the distribution of head orientation preferences in neonates. I twice assessed, during the 16–48-hour postpartum period, the supine head orientation of 150 normal infants. Each assessment consisted of two 2-minute observations. Each observation began with the infant's head being held in a midline position for one minute by the observer. Thereafter, the orientation of the infant's head was recorded at 6-second intervals for 1 minute. The head orientation was rightward if the infant's chin passed the right nipple and left-ward if it passed the left nipple. No orientation was recorded if the chin remained between the two nipples. Frequency of right and left head orientation was recorded for all assessment periods and transformed into a z-score. The data revealed that the infant's head orientation was continuously distributed across infants but that the distribution was highly skewed toward the right (Michel, 1981). The distribution of NHOP is similar to the distribution reported for children and adult handedness (Annett, 1972). Therefore, Annett's right-shift factor could be associated with a lateral asymmetry of neonatal or fetal posture.

From this population of neonates, I selected 10 with a distinctive rightward preference (R-NHOP = z-score > 2.0) and 10 with an equally distinctive leftward preference (L-NHOP = z-score < −2.0). These 20 infants had their head orientation preference, hand regard, and hand use video-taped (Michel & Harkins, 1986) during 12 visits from birth to 18 months of age. The L-NHOP infants would help determine whether a leftward NHOP is a precursor of left-handedness or is only associated with a random distribution of handedness (as predicted by Annett's model).

The data showed that NHOP predicted supine head orientation preference (SHOP), as measured at 3, 6, and 8 weeks of age, for only 75 percent of the infants. Of the 10 infants assessed as having a rightward NHOP, 2 subsequently exhibited a relatively weak leftward SHOP (L-SHOP). Also, 3 infants with assessed leftward NHOP exhibited a strong rightward SHOP (R-SHOP). Does the NHOP differ from the SHOP? It is more likely that the longer (each visit provided 10 minutes of data), more sophisticated assessment (there were four separate assessments at each of the three ages) of SHOP captured the infant's head orientation preference better than the brief neonatal assessment.

The data also showed that SHOP influenced both hand regard and hand activities. The hand on the "face-side" was more active (in arm, wrist, and finger movements) than the "skull-side" hand. Also, SHOP was associated highly with the infant's HOP when seated in an infant seat inclined to 35 or 60 degrees. Therefore, we used SHOP as a predictor of hand-use preference for reaching. However, this time we assessed reaching while the infant was seated and presented with a yellow ball stimulus mounted on a blue backboard. For two presentations, a single yellow ball was presented in midline and the ball differed in size between presentations (Ping-Pong–sized 4 cm diameter, or 8 cm diameter). For two presentations, two yellow balls were presented simultaneously, each in line with each of the infant's shoulders. Again, the two balls were either 4 cm or 8 cm in diameter. Each presentation lasted 120 seconds. Beginning at 32 weeks of age, reaching was assessed by presenting 20 different infant toys. We did not get reliable reaching (contacting the balls) until 4 months of age. However, the direction of SHOP predicted the hand typically used for reaching and grasping for each of the seven assessment periods from 4 to 18 months of age.

Since the leftward SHOP was strongly associated with left-hand-use preference and not a random distribution of hand-use preference, I proposed that the infant's SHOP directly influences the development of handedness. Annett's allele could create a right-shift in handedness distribution by affecting a right-shift in SHOP. However, it is the direction of SHOP that influences the early development of a hand-use preference for reaching. Unfortunately, no other study has examined the relation between an L-SHOP and the later manifestation of a left-hand-use preference for reaching for objects. Nor has the relation between an L-SHOP and/or left-hand-use preference for reaching during infancy and subsequent handedness as a child or adult been examined.

If hand regard were the crucial link between SHOP and handedness, then the development of handedness in blind infants ought to be different. In apparent contradiction, studies of congenitally blind adults showed a typical right-handed bias (Fertsch, 1947), and the handedness of blind children between the ages of 6 and 14 years does not differ from that of sighted children across a range of tasks (Ittyeral, 1993). I discovered that congenital blindness comes in many forms, with the overwhelming majority involving vision with poor acuity. Therefore, most congenitally blind infants can see the movements of the face-side hand during their SHOP. Also, programs for the blind emphasize early training of right-handedness when teaching blind infants to use their hands. The only prediction I would make about congenitally blind infants is that their handedness would not be as strongly related to maternal handedness. Of course, the data show that SHOP creates more asymmetries between the hands than just hand regard. SHOP-associated brain-stem-generated hand movements (and the nonvisual sensory feedback that these movements engender) create another bias in the input to the two hemispheres during their early postnatal development that can play a role in the development of hand-use preferences.

☐ Are There Any More Obvious Influences on Handedness Development?

Studies of parent and offspring adult handedness find a stronger mother-offspring than father-offspring association (Annett, 1978; Ashton, 1982). Left-handed mothers are more likely than left-handed fathers to have left-handed offspring (McGee & Cozad, 1980). Even among right-handed parents, there is a stronger mother-offspring than father-offspring association.

We (Harkins & Michel, 1988) assessed the hand-use preferences for reaching for objects of 42 infants, ranging in age from 6 to 13 months (36 were older than 8 months), using a valid and reliable procedure (Michel, Ovrut, & Harkins, 1985). There were three groups of 14 infants each: (1) those with left-handed mothers and right-handed fathers; (2) those with right-handed mothers and left-handed fathers; (3) those with two right-handed parents. Nine of the 14 infants with left-handed mothers exhibited strong left-hand-use preferences for reaching and manipulation, whereas only two had strong right-hand-use preferences. None of the infants born to left-handed fathers or two right-handed parents had left-hand-use preferences. Seven infants born to left-handed fathers and 10 infants born to two right-handed parents had strong right-hand-use preferences. Since these results accord with those reported in the genealogical studies, the mechanism influencing this relationship must operate early in the development of the individual.

Mother-infant handedness concordance may be one mechanism for the relationship between maternal and offspring handedness. I (Michel, 1992) found that infants (of right-handed mothers) who exhibited a left-hand-use preference at 7 months showed a weaker preference at 9 and 11 months. In contrast, infants of right-handed mothers who exhibited a right-hand-use preference at 7 months showed an increase in the strength of that preference. Analysis of mother-infant play patterns revealed that the mother's handedness greatly affected her hand use with the toys and that her infant tended to match the mother's hand use when playing with that toy. Although the mothers were unaware of the hand-use preferences of their infants, they seemed to be affecting their infants' handedness during routine play with objects.

Could left-handed mothers influence the hand-use preferences of their infants by the infant's matching the mother's hand use? My graduate student, Christopher Mundale (1992), recorded the maternal hand-use actions that would bias infant hand use for 12 left-handed mothers as compared to 12 right-handed mothers and 10 mothers without distinct handedness (as measured by questionnaire). The infants ranged in age from 7 to 13 months, and only three had strong left-hand-use preferences. Although left-handed mothers used their left hand when playing with their infants more often than mothers in the other two groups, left-handed mothers used their right hand when playing much more frequently than right-handed mothers used their left hand. Thus, a right-handed infant's matching of a right-handed mother's hand use would strengthen the infant's preference, but such matching by a left-handed infant would weaken that preference. In contrast, left-handed mothers might affect the preference of right-handed infants only moderately.

☐ How Should Infant Handedness be Assessed?

Hand-use preference is particularly difficult to assess in infants because its manifestation can be influenced greatly by the level of the infant's manual ability. The extensive changes in manual skill that occur during infancy require that a hand-use preference be identified in different skills (e.g., reaching, manipulation) and with different object properties. Therefore, we (Michel, Ovrut, & Harkins, 1985) used objects that varied in complexity and which enticed infants from 4 to 16 months to reach for and manipulate them. Thus, hand-use preferences for both reaching with apprehension of the object and manipulation skill could be assessed independently.

The presentation of the objects was varied among single objects presented in midline (some either on a table and others suspended in midair via a string) and identical twin objects with each presented in line with one of the infant's shoulders. Again, some of the twin objects were presented on a table and some suspended in midair via a string. Neither the type of object (whether or not it had movable parts) nor its mode of presentation (as singletons or twins or placed on a table or suspended in air) had any effect on the infant's hand use (Michel & Baker, in prep). Therefore, preferences of hand use reflect aspects about the infant and not biases in the assessment task.

By recording manual actions with 21–28 items, this assessment permitted identification of two types of infants: those with hand-use preference scores that were unlikely to occur by chance, and those with scores that could have occurred by chance. Moreover, the assessment preferences were validated by comparison with the infant's performance in a semistructured block play situation. I have used this procedure in all subsequent studies of infant handedness. I know of no other studies of infant handedness that have used my assessment procedure or that have provided reliability and validity information for the assessment procedure that was used. In studies of the relation between adult handedness and other factors, poor assessment procedures for handedness can generate spurious results (Bryden & Steenhuis, 1991; Steenhuis & Bryden, 1989). I do not see why such caution would not apply equally, if not more so, to infants.

☐ Is There Any Value to a Distinct Asymmetry in Population Handedness Distribution?

The right bias in handedness appears to be an ancient characteristic in the hominid lineage (Spennemann, 1984) associated with tool-working skills

(Falk, 1980; Frost, 1980; Toth, 1985). Effective tool-working action requires extensive role-differentiated bimanual skill in which handedness is important (Vauclaire, 1993). Since tool manufacture evolved before language, the social transmission of tool-working skills likely occurred without verbal mediation. Thus the facilitation of the observational learning of manual skills was likely an important factor favoring a population bias in human handedness. An undergraduate assistant and I (Michel & Harkins, 1985) tested the influence of concordance of adult handedness between "teacher" and "student" on the student's ability to acquire a manual skill (i.e., how to tie a set of knots). Either a left-handed or right-handed teacher repeatedly demonstrated, without verbal instruction or cues, how to tie a knot and the students (who were either left- or right-handed) tried to tie the knot after each demonstration. Discordant handedness between teacher and student (irrespective of who was left-handed) significantly delayed acquisition of the skills when compared to individuals concordant for handedness. With the exception of our study, no one has demonstrated any advantage to an individual if his/her handedness is the same as that of the majority of people.

Annett (1975) proposed that the right bias in handedness is an incidental consequence of a left-hemisphere dominance in the control of speech. However, our study suggests that a bias in handedness evolved as a means of facilitating the social transmission of tool-working skills before the evolution of speech skills. This raises two questions: Why is right- and not left-handedness predominant, and why are any individuals in the population left-handed? The maintenance of distinctly different behavioral types (polyethism), like the maintenance of polymorphism in a population, usually means that the minority type is associated with characteristics that are relatively more advantageous for certain aspects of the population's ecology. Left-handers may have characteristics that are more functional than right-handers for certain conditions (cf. Hardyck & Petrinovich, 1977; Mebert & Michel, 1980). In contrast, Annett (1995) proposed that the heterozygous individual has several intellectual advantages over either type of homozygous individual. We need more research evidence to resolve this difference.

That the bias is right rather than left is likely a consequence of the bias in SHOP and its influence on the development of handedness. The evolution of an upright posture altered the pelvic girdle such that infants are born at a less developed state. This, coupled with the infant's inability to hold on to the mother, increased the likelihood of prolonged periods in supine or semi-reclined positions in which asymmetrical biases of posture could induce an asymmetrical bias in the development of manual skills. Speech then would have evolved within a neurobehavioral context that already encouraged a left-hemisphere advantage for coordinating the precise timing and order of motor actions.

☐ Is There Any Value to Manifesting a Hand-Use Preference during Infancy?

Eugene Goldfield and I used a cross-sectional design to identify age-related changes in the pattern of coordinating the movements of the two hands during bimanual reaching and the consequences of asymmetrical perturbations (a minor barrier to the trajectory of one of the hands) on that coordination (Goldfield & Michel, 1986a). Until 10 to 12 months of age, the coordination of the two hands during bimanual reaching seems to reflect bilateral activation of homotopic muscles resulting in temporally and spatially synchronous movement patterns between the hands (Goldfield & Michel, 1986b). Subsequently, bimanual reaching exhibits a role-differentiated pattern of temporally sequenced complementary actions, likely involving functional development of the corpus callosum.

Subsequent investigation of bimanual reaching involved a longitudinal study of 20 infants with stable right-hand-use preferences at 7, 9, 11, and 13 months of age. Each infant reached for a "Nerf" soccer ball under three conditions: both wrists wore 350 g wrist weights, or only the left or only the right wrist wore the weight. To maintain a bimanual reach the weights required differential adjustment of the force of muscle contraction for each arm (in order to compensate for the added weight), rather than activating a different order of muscles in order to change trajectory in the barrier condition. When both wrists were weighted, the number of bimanual reaches increased until 13 months, when nearly all reaches were bimanual. Weighting the left wrist disrupted bimanual reaching more than weighting the right wrist, especially at 9 and 11 months. Thus, bimanual coordination is more easily maintained when the preferred hand, rather than the nonpreferred hand, is perturbed.

In 1973, Bruner reported that at 5–7 months, after an object is grasped, presentations of additional objects will be ignored or the grasped object will be dropped when retrieving additional objects. Later in development, an additional object will be acquired by storing the first object by transferring it to the other hand or placing it nearby. Bruner argued that the development of these multiple object management skills contributes to cognitive development. Storing objects implies an ability to delay behavior and to maintain an internal representation of the location of the stored object. Managing more than one object at a time permits the discovery and practice of using one object as a tool on another object. Also, when two or more objects are available for holding, differences in their physical properties become salient. Thus, developmental advances in multiple object management skills encourage developmental advances in cognition. Kathleen Kotwica and I (Kotwica & Michel, in press) demonstrated that infants with stable hand-use preferences from 7 to 13 months of age are more advanced in this pattern of sensorimotor intelligence than infants without a stable hand-use preference.

Kotwica assessed the ability of 38 infants to acquire and manage multiple objects during the period from 7 to 13 months of age. She presented four attractive objects one after another and videotaped (for detail coding) the manual actions employed. The occurrence of intermanual transfer was recorded, as were the strategies used when a third or fourth attractive object was presented after both hands were full. Infants without a stable hand-use preference were delayed in the development of storage skills, especially those involving intermanual transfer.

An important aspect of Kotwica's study was the identification of the storage strategy. We proposed that a manual strategy would be identified by a strong contingent relationship among the manual acts that preceded "storage." Without a contingent sequence, storage could have occurred fortuitously (unintentionally). Detailed coding of the manual actions revealed that the infants with stable handedness not only accomplished the acquisition and storage of multiple objects before those infants without stable handedness, but that they also exhibited an orderly pattern (skill) in the acts comprising that accomplishment. The occasional multiple object acquisitions and storage accomplishments of infants without stable handedness appeared to be unintended. Thus, Kotwica found that a hand-use preference during infancy facilitates the development of multiple object management skills and hence, perhaps, cognitive development as well.

Role-differentiated bimanual action is an important skill for the manufacture of tools (Vauclaire, 1993) and may depend upon efficient interhemispheric communication (Michel, 1998). Marliese Kimmerle and I (Kimmerle, et al., in press) videotaped the manual actions of 24 infants from 7 to 13 months of age during play with toys in order to identify the relations of role-differentiated bimanual skill to other bimanual and unimanual skills. Bimanual role-differentiated actions were observed in 67 percent of the 7-month-old infants. However, at this age such actions were both extremely brief in duration and represented a very small percentage of the infant's total manual repertoire (4 percent). By 11 months, role-differentiated bimanual actions occur with greater frequency and they are influenced by the characteristics of the toys (Kimmerle, Mick, & Michel, 1995). Also by 11 months, the infant begins to exhibit a hand-use preference for role-differentiated bimanual manipulation of objects. By 13 months, role-differentiated bimanual manipulation represents about 20 percent of every infant's manual repertoire, and most infants display a hand-use preference in the action.

Interestingly, detailed coding of the actions preceding an instance of role-differentiated bimanual manipulation revealed that none of the instances at 7 and 9 months was preceded by an orderly sequence of acts. We proposed that the earlier instances were unintended consequences of manipulating objects that could afford role-differentiated bimanual manipulation. Thus, only by one year of age do infants begin to intentionally engage in role-differentiated bimanual manipulation with a distinct hand-use preference.

☐ The Development of Infant Handedness

So, what has my research revealed about the development of handedness? Neonates exhibit a set of laterally asymmetric postures when supine or seated that likely represent a continuation of patterns of behavior manifested *in utero*. These postures provide asymmetries of visual and proprioceptive experiences for the manual actions of the young infant. Most neonates exhibit a right bias in their SHOP that is maintained for two months after birth and results in more right- than left-hand regard, activity, and hand-to-mouth actions. The minority of infants with a left-biased SHOP show greater left- than right-hand regard, activity, and hand-to-mouth actions. Because of the SHOP, the face-side hand has better proprioceptive, motor-program, and visuospatial map systems than the skull-side hand and should be more successful in prehension. Thus, direction of SHOP biases a hand preference for prehension.

Because a hand-use preference for prehension precedes both bimanual object manipulation and intermanual object transfer, the preferred hand obtains more objects and can engage in more unimanual object manipulation and manually coordinated oral and visual examination of the properties of objects than the nonpreferred hand. This difference in experience can promote skill differences in unimanual manipulation and subsequently the development of hand-use preferences in role-differentiated bimanual manipulation. Thus, by the end of their first year, infants have acquired the fundamental manual skills that have uniquely specified the hominid branch of primates (Bradshaw & Rogers, 1993). Child and adult handedness develop from these fundamentals of infancy.

Although no step in the sequence of infant handedness development is obligatory, the sequence is highly probable in most human cultures. If SHOP influenced the development of hand-use preference, then handedness ought to develop randomly in those cultures that practice infant binding, since binding would interfere with SHOP. However, examination of the Human Resource Area Files, an extensively cross-indexed compilation of anthropological information about human cultures, revealed that cultures that practiced infant binding did not exhibit more left-handedness than cultures that did not. Indeed, some exhibited far fewer left-handers. The HRAF did reveal that many cultures only bind the infant for short periods (2–6 hours/day) as a "baby-sitting" technique. Such short periods of binding might not seriously disrupt SHOP.

Those cultures that bind for longer periods (e.g., certain cultures bind the infant's head to a board to create a flat occipital region) have a very small percentage of left-handers (about 1 percent) and very strict cultural proscriptions against left-handedness. Perhaps long-term binding is a recent attribute of the culture. If the asymmetry of SHOP contributed to the asymmetry of handedness, then interfering with SHOP would permit handedness to develop more randomly and raise the proportion of left-handers to levels equivalent to that of right-handers. The proscriptions against left-handedness were likely instituted because binding interfered with SHOP and consequently left-handedness greatly increased. The cultural proscriptions reestablished the right-hand predominance.

HRAF also revealed that cultures that keep infants in relatively unfettered conditions have the greatest proportion of left-handers in the population. Thus, cultures with a high incidence of left-handedness (about 15–18 percent) in subarctic regions (Inuit and Eskimo) kept their infants unclothed and reclined on slightly concave sealskin hammocks for several months after birth. Cultures in equatorial regions that also used slightly concave infant "beds" had similar proportions of left-handers. These proportions of left-handers were equivalent to the proportion of neonates with L-NHOPs. Unlike the long-term binding condition, the proportion of left-handers in the population of unfettered infant cultures would never approximate the proportion of right-handers. Therefore, the cultural data may be interpreted to support the notion that SHOP contributes to the development of handedness. Thus, Annett's right-biasing factor likely operates by producing a bias in SHOP.

Can the normal spontaneous posture and movements of the neonate contribute to the development of neuromotor asymmetries with potential long-term consequences for the neuropsychological character of the individual? Most infants maintain stable hand-use preferences throughout the 6- to 14-month age range and right-handedness predominates. All of the differences that are a consequence of the infant's hand-use preference will result in hemispheric differences in the structural and functional organization of the primary and secondary sensory and motor cortices, supplementary motor areas, several prefrontal areas, basal ganglia, thalamic nuclei, cerebellar nuclei, and so forth. Infants without stable hand-use preferences exhibit delays in the development of several sensorimotor skills that may contribute to cognitive development. Since certain information is poorly shared between hemispheres before 10 to 12 months of age, the effects of the hand-use preference on the organization of each hemisphere can occur in relative isolation from each other. Thus, the evolution of language skills may have occurred within an early developmental context of a lateralized asymmetry of hemisphere organization prompted by the infant's predominant right-hand-use preference.

☐ Acknowledgment

Some of my research was supported by grants from the National Institute of Mental Health (1R01 MH 35528), the National Institute of Child Health and Human Development (1 R01 HD 16107 & HD 22399), and the DePaul University Research Council.

☐ References

Annett, M. (1970). The growth of manual preference and speed. *British Journal of Psychology, 61*, 303–321.

Annett, M. (1972). The distribution of manual asymmetry. *British Journal of Psychology, 63*, 343–358.

Annett, M. (1974). Handedness in the children of two left-handed parents. *British Journal of Psychology, 65*, 129–131.

Annett, M. (1975). Hand preference and the laterality of cerebral speech. *Cortex, 11*, 305–328.

Annett, M. (1978). Genetic and nongenetic influences on handedness. *Behavior Genetics, 8*, 227–249.

Annett, M. (1995). The right shift theory of a genetic balanced polymorphism for cerebral dominance and cognitive processing. *Current Psychology of Cognition, 14*(5), 427–480.

Arbib, M., & Rizzolatti, G. (1997). Neural expectations: A possible evolutionary path from manual skills to language. *Communication and Cognition, 29*, 393–424.

Armstron, D. (1999). *Original signs: Gesture, sign and the sources of language.* Washington, DC: Gallauder University Press.

Ashton, G. C. (1982). Handedness: An alternative hypothesis. *Behavior Genetics, 12*, 125–147.

Bower, T. G. R. (1974). *Development in infancy.* San Francisco: Freeman.

Bradshaw, J., & Rogers, L. (1993). *The evolution of lateral asymmetries, language, tool use, and intellect.* New York: Academic Press.

Bryden, M., & Steenhuis, R. E. (1991). Issues in the assessment of handedness. In F. L. Kitterle (Ed.), *Cerebral laterality: Theory and research* (pp. 35–51). Hillsdale, NJ: Erlbaum.

Chapple, C. & Davidson, D. (1941). A study of the relationship between fetal position and certain congenital deformities. *Journal of Pediatrics, 18*, 483-493.

Corballis, M. C. (1997). The genetics and evolution of handedness. *Psychological Review, 104*(4), 714–727.

Coryell, J. F., & Michel, G. F. (1978). How supine postural preferences of infants can contribute toward the development of handedness. *Infant Behavior and Development, 1*, 245–257.

Dinnerstein, D. (1971). Adaptation level and structural interaction: Alternative or complementary concepts. In M. H. Appley (Ed.), *Adaptation level theory* (pp. 81–93). New York: Academic Press.

Dunn, P. M. (1975). Congenital postural deformities. *British Medical Bulletin, 32,* 71–72.

Falk, D. (1980). Language, handedness and primate brains: Did Australopithecines sign? *American Anthropologist, 82,* 72-79.

Fertsch, P. (1947). Hand dominance in reading braille. *American Journal of Psychology, 60,* 335–349.

Frost, G. T. (1980). Tool behavior and the origins of laterality. *Journal of Human Evolution, 9,* 447–459.

Gesell, A., & Ames, L. B. (1947). The development of handedness. *Journal of Genetic Psychology, 70,* 155–175.

Goldfield, E. C., & Michel, G. F. (1986a). Ontogeny of infant bimanual reaching during the first year. *Infant Behavior and Development, 9,* 81–89.

Goldfield E. C., & Michel, G. F. (1986b). Spatiotemporal linkage in infant interlimb coordination. *Developmental Psychobiology, 19,* 97–102.

Goodwin, R., & Michel, G. F. (1981). Head orientation position during birth, in neonatal period, and hand preference at 19 weeks. *Child Development, 52,* 819–826.

Hardyck, C., & Petrinovich, L. F. (1977). Left-handedness. *Psychological Bulletin, 84,* 385–404.

Harkins, D. A., & Michel, G. F. (1988). Evidence for a maternal effect on infant handedness preferences. *Developmental Psychobiology, 21,* 535–541.

Hopkins, B., & Ronnqvist, L. (1998). Human handedness: Developmental and evolutionary perspectives. In F. Simion & G. Butterworth (Eds.), *The development of sensory, motor and cognitive capacities in early infancy: From perception to cognition* (pp. 191–236). East Sussex, UK: Psychology Press.

Hughey, M. J. (1985). Fetal position during pregnancy. *American Journal of Obstetrics and Gynecology, 153,* 885–886.

Ittyeral, M. (1993). Hand preference and hand ability in congenitally blind children. *Quarterly Journal of Experimental Psychology, 46A,* 35–50.

Kimmerle, M., Kotwica, K. A., & Michel, G. F. (in press). Precursors for the emergence of role differentiated manual actions of infants.

Kimmerle, M., Mick, L.A., & Michel, G.F. (1995). Bimanual role-differentiated toy play during infancy. *Infant Behavior and Development, 18,* 299-308.

Kinsbourne, M. (1975). The ontogeny of cerebral dominance. *Annals of the New York Academy of Sciences, 263,* 244–250.

Kinsbourne, M. (1981). The development of cerebral dominance. In S. B. Filskov & T. J. Boll (Eds.), *Handbook of clinical neuropsychology* (pp. 399–417). New York: Wiley.

Kinsbourne, M. (1997). The development of lateralization. In H. W. Reese & M. D. Franzen (Eds.), *Biological and neuropsychological mechanisms: Life-span developmental psychology* (pp. 181–197). Mahwah, NJ: Erlbaum.

Kotwica, K. A., & Michel, G. F. (In press). Stable hand-use preferences and the development of multiple object management skills in 7- to 13-month-old infants.

Lehrman, D. S. (1953). A critique of Konrad Lorenz's theory of instinctive behavior. *Quarterly Review of Biology, 28,* 337–363.

Lehrman, D. S. (1970). Semantic and conceptual issues in the nature-nurture problem. In L. A. Aronson, E. Tobach, D. S. Lehrman, & J. S. Rosenblatt (Eds.) *Development and evolution of behavior: Essays in Memory of P. T. Schneirla* (pp. 17–52). San Francisco: Freeman.

Lenneberg, E. (1967). *Biological foundations of language.* New York: Wiley.

McGee, M. G., & Cozad, T. (1980). Population genetic analysis of human hand preference: Evidence for generation differences, familial resemblance, and maternal effects. *Behavior Genetics, 10,* 263–275.

Mebert, C. J., & Michel, G. F. (1980). Handedness in artists. In J. Herron (Ed.), *Neuropsychology of left-handedness* (pp. 273–280). New York: Academic Press.

Michel, G. F. (1981). Right-handedness: A consequence of infant supine head-orientation preference? *Science, 212,* 685–687.

Michel, G. F. (1983). Development of hand-use preference during infancy. In G. Young, S. Segalowitz, C. Cortea, & S. Trehub (Eds.), *Manual specialization and the developing brain* (pp. 33–70). New York: Academic Press.

Michel, G. F. (1985). Experiential influences on hormonally dependent ring dove parental care. *Annals of the New York Academy of Sciences, 474,* 158–169.

Michel, G. F. (1987). Self-generated experience and the development of lateralized neurobehavioral organization in infants. In J. S. Rosenblatt, C. G. Beer, M.-C. Busnel, & P. J. B. Slater (Eds.), *Advances in the study of behavior, vol. 17* (pp. 61–84). New York: Academic Press.

Michel, G. F. (1988). A neuropsychological perspective on infant sensorimotor development. In C. Rovee-Collier & L. P. Lipsitt (Eds.), *Advances in infancy research, vol. 5* (pp. 1–38). Norwood, NJ: Ablex.

Michel, G. F. (1991). Development of infant manual skills: Motor programs, schemata, or dynamic systems? In J. Fagard & P. H. Wolff (Eds.), *The development of timing and temporal organization in coordination of action* (pp. 175–199). New York: Elsevier.

Michel, G. F. (1992). Maternal influences on infant hand-use during play with toys. *Behavior Genetics, 22,* 163–176.

Michel, G. F. (1998). A lateral bias in the neuropsychological functioning of human infants. *Developmental Neuropsychology, 14,* 445–469.

Michel, G. F., & Goodwin, R. (1979). Intrauterine birth position predicts newborn supine head position preferences. *Infant Behavior and Development, 2,* 29–38.

Michel G. F., & Harkins, D. A. (1985). Concordance of handedness between teacher and student facilitates learning manual skills. *Journal of Human Evolution, 14,* 597–601.

Michel G. F., & Harkins, D. A. (1986). Postural and lateral asymmetries in the ontogeny of handedness during infancy. *Developmental Psychobiology, 19,* 247–258.

Michel, G. F., Harkins, D. A., & Meserve, A. (1990). Sex differences in neonatal state and lateralized head orientation. *Infant Behavior and Development, 13,* 461–467.

Michel, G. F. & Moore, C. L. (1978). *Biological perspectives in developmental psychology.* Monterey, CA: Brooks/Cole.

Michel, G. F., Ovrut, M. R., & Harkins, D. A. (1985). Hand-use preference for reaching and object manipulation in 6- through 13-month-old infants. *Genetic, Social, and General Psychology Monographs, 111,* 409–427.

Mundale, C. J. (1992). Influences of maternal handedness and behavior on infant hand-use preferences. Unpublished Master's thesis, Psychology Department, DePaul University.

Parmelee, A. M. (1931). Molding due to intra-uterine posture. *American Journal of Diseases of Children, 42,* 1155–1159.

Petitto, L. A. (2000). On the biological foundations of language. In H. Lane & K. Emmorey (Eds.), *The signs of language revisited.* Mahwah, NJ: Erlbaum

Previc, F. H. (1991). A general theory concerning the prenatal origins of cerebral lateralization in humans. *Psychological Review, 98,* 299–334.

Spennemann, D. R. (1984). Handedness data on the human neolithic. *Neuropsychologia, 22,* 613–615.

Steele, K. B., & Javert, C. T. (1942). Mechanisms of labor for transverse positions of the vertex. *Surgical Gynecology and Obstetrics, 75,* 477–480.

Steenhuis, R. E., & Bryden, M. P. (1989). Different dimensions of hand preference that relate to skilled and unskilled activities. *Cortex, 25,* 289–304.

Toth, N. (1985). Archeological evidence for preferential right-handedness in lower and middle Pleistocene and its possible implications. *Journal of Human Evolution, 14,* 35–40.

Turkewitz, G. (1977). The development of lateral differences in the human infant. In S. Harnad, R. W. Doty, L. Goldstein, J. Jaynes, & G. Krauthammer (Eds.), *Lateralization in the nervous system* (pp. 251–260). New York: Academic Press.

Turkewitz, G., Moreau, T., & Birch, H.G. (1966). Head position and receptor organization in the human neonate. *Journal of Experimental Psychology, 4,* 169-177.

Vartan, C. K. (1945). Behavior of the fetus in utero with special reference to the incidence on breech presentation at term. *Journal of Obstetrics and Gynecology (British), 52,* 417–434.

Vauclair, J. (1993). Tool use, hand cooperation and the development of object manipulation in human and nonhuman primates. In A. F. Kalverboer, B. Hopkins, & R. Geuze (Eds.), *Motor development in early and late childhood: Longitudinal approaches* (pp. 205–216). New York: Cambridge University Press.

Witelson, S. F. (1980). Neuroanatomical asymmetry in left-handers: A review and implications for functional asymmetry. In J. Herron (Ed.), *Neuropsychology of left-handedness* (pp. 79–114). New York: Academic Press.

Gerald Turkewitz

Wasn't I Stupid: Or, Once You Know, It's So Obvious

In this essay I intend to examine the creative tension that exists between theory and experimentation and to provide a case study of the way in which mismatches between the two provide the impetus for dynamic changes in our understanding of psychological processes. I will also advance the thesis that being wrong is frequently more productive than being right. In fact, it is my contention that the primary value of experimentation is to produce mismatches between extant explanations for a phenomenon and new data. Absent such mismatches, explanation or theory remains static, with no reason for radical change.

Although being wrong has not been a unique event during my career, I will present only a single case history to document my contention that having an expectation based on theory not turn out to be empirically valid can be valuable. Before presenting this illustration of my thesis I want to point out that when I say there is an advantage to be derived from finding a mismatch between theory and data, I am not speaking of a total discrepancy between the two but rather of the case where there is substantial agreement between theory and data but with a peculiarity in the data—to use the more technical term, a glitch.

In attempting to make my point I must at least in part abandon the standard procedure for scientific presentation. According to François Jacob, "writing a paper is to substitute order for the disorder and agitation that animate life in the laboratory . . . to replace the real order of events and discoveries by what appears as the logical order, the one that should have been followed if the conclusions were known from the start" (1988, p. 318). Although this style may be suitable for the communication of substantive scientific information, it is not appropriate to developing an understanding of the scientific process, and that is what this communication is concerned with. Therefore, I will attempt to be historically more accurate, and hence probably more confusing, than is the case with a more standard scientific presentation.

Although the case study I will present stems from developmental-cognitive neuropsychology, I believe the point I wish to derive from it is applicable in all domains of science. Its applicability to physics is rather poignantly marked in a recent news article in *Science* (Taubes, 1996) discussing a recent study in particle physics: "There's a powerful incentive to take anomalies like the CDF event seriously. If real, they would go a long way to relieving the field's current frustration, which is a frustration born of success: the remarkable agreement between the Standard Model and all the experimental data ever gathered. It has been 20 years, for instance, since a particle physics experiment has turned up anything that was both surprising and real. "It's a bit sad," says Ting, "that everything agrees with the Standard Model" (p. 474).

☐ Face Recognition: Shifting Hemispheres and Shifting Conceptions

The case study which I will present indicates how findings in a study of adult face perception that did not quite match conceptual expectations led to a series of revisions in the model, with each new study yielding results that did not quite suit the model. This led through a series of rather minor changes to a radically different view of the process involved in the perception of faces and of the nature of the relationships between the cerebral hemispheres in the recognition of faces. The way in which this data-driven theory was then applied to infant facial recognition and its implications for the development of cognitive functioning will be presented, together with a consideration of how to bring the revised conceptual framework back into the laboratory.

Phillis Ross-Kossak and I carried out the work on face perception over a period of four or five years. During this time we went from a rather conventional view of the way in which the brain functions in the processing of facial information to a considerably more complex view that has implications for understanding human development, and most particularly the shaping of modes of cognition.

We began our study of facial recognition in adults with the expectation that we would use these as a basis from which to explore hemispheric specialization for facial recognition in infants. Our initial study (Ross & Turkewitz, 1981) was designed to produce descriptive data for utilization as a baseline in subsequent investigation. It entailed presenting subjects with four faces, one at a time. The faces were black-and-white slides that were presented on a screen in a manner that resulted in their being projected to the left or right hemisphere. Based on previous data, we expected to find a right-hemisphere advantage on this task, and we did. However, we also found that a substantial number of subjects showed a left-hemisphere advantage on the task. Armed with our own data, we examined the literature more closely and found that our results were, in fact, in agreement with those of others who had explored facial recognition, that is, a general right-hemisphere advantage with a fairly substantial proportion of subjects showing a left hemisphere advantage (Springer & Deutsch, 1981).

Previous investigators had not commented on the number of subjects showing the anomalous pattern of advantage, and we assumed that it was because they ascribed it to measurement error. Although this was certainly a possibility, it was a rather mundane and boring one, therefore we set about trying to come up with a more interesting explanation to account for two types of hemispheric advantage.

In trying to understand the difference between the two types of subjects we quickly decided that it was unlikely that those with a left-hemisphere advantage for facial recognition had a generally different pattern of brain organization than did the more typical subjects. This seemed particularly evident as we, along with others who had investigated the phenomenon, had tested for handedness and excluded left-handers from the sample. It seemed extremely unlikely that the 30 to 40 percent of right-handed subjects with a left-hemisphere advantage in our study had atypical overall patterns of brain organization. This is because the best estimates available for the incidence of right- as opposed to left-hemisphere specialization for speech in familial right-handed individuals does not exceed 5 percent (Harris & Carlson, 1988).

At that time there were a few studies that had found different directions of advantage in recognizing different categories of faces, for instance, famous faces and unfamiliar faces (Marzi & Berlucchi, 1977); or faces of colleagues and of strangers or friends (Leehey & Cahn, 1979; Young & Bion, 1981). In addition, there was the well-known Bever and Chiarello (1974) study in which it had been found that trained musicians showed a left-hemisphere advantage on a chord-recognition task on which less musically sophisticated people showed a right-hemisphere advantage. These findings suggested that the same task (e.g., recognizing a chord) could be accomplished utilizing different hemispheric specializations and achieving the recognition in different ways. Although this had been proffered as an explanation by a number of investigators, it had never been subjected to experimental scrutiny. It seemed to us that it would be relatively simple to determine if subjects showing a left-hemisphere advantage on our task were recognizing the faces on a different basis from those showing a right-hemisphere advantage. There are two basically different ways of recognizing any complex stimulus pattern, and these have been ascribed to opposite hemispheres (Bogen, 1969). So, for example, it is possible to recognize a face in terms of its overall configuration, that is, in terms of the relationships that exist between its components. This type of gestalt or holistic recognition is a function that is generally better subserved in the right than in the left hemisphere. Alternatively, it is possible to recognize a face in terms of its distinctive features, such as a pointy nose or thick lips. This type of analytic recognition is viewed as better served by the left than the right hemisphere. If those individuals showing different hemispheric advantages were indeed recognizing the faces on the two different bases ascribed to the different hemispheres, then modifying the configuration of the faces should have a more disruptive effect on those subjects showing a right-hemisphere advantage. In contrast, modifying or eliminating some of the distinctive features of the faces should impair the performance of the subjects with a left-hemisphere advantage more than that of those with a right-hemisphere advantage. That is precisely what happened when we inverted the faces with one group of subjects and blocked out specific features (e.g., covered the nose or eyes) with a different group of subjects (Ross & Turkewitz, 1981). Under these conditions, subjects identified as having a right hemisphere advantage in recognizing the upright, full-featured faces showed a bigger disruption of performance following inversion and a smaller disruption following feature deletion than did subjects with a left-hemisphere advantage.

We interpreted these findings to mean that individuals differed in terms of their processing strategy and that the difference reflected either facial recognition with left-hemisphere processing (i.e., analytic mode) or with right-hemisphere processing (i.e., holistic mode). That is, we believed that the differences we found represented relatively stable differences between individuals with regard to the manner in which they accomplished facial recognition. In fact, we titled our paper "Individual differences in cerebral asymmetries for facial recognition." We then set about checking the reliability of our typology by testing subjects on the same unmodified upright faces on two separate occasions (Turkewitz and Ross, unpublished). We were surprised and not a little dismayed to find that our task yielded nonreliable results. Some subjects who showed a relatively large visual field advantage on the initial presentation of the faces showed a relatively small advantage on subsequent testing, and, even worse, some subjects who showed a right visual field advantage on initial testing showed a left visual field advantage on subsequent testing, and vice versa.

Because our previous studies had yielded robust effects and because they seemed to make good sense we were reluctant to concede that the results we had obtained were simply due to the vagaries of unreliable data. Instead we reformulated our position and changed the way we thought about the meaning of our reliability check. The concept of test-retest reliability is based on the notion that you are examining an essentially static phenomenon. That is, it is fairly obvious that if the same test yields different results when given at two different times, it is due to the fact that something about the organism has changed during the interval between the two tests. When this happens in tests of reliability the assumption is generally that the changes are nonsystematic and that the test is not appropriate for measuring the function being examined. This certainly makes sense when we are trying to measure something that is supposed to be more or less stable over at least relatively brief periods of time (e.g., intelligence or aptitude). However, when changes from tests to retests are not random but instead are systematic in some fashion it suggests not error in measurement but rather that we are dealing with a dynamically changing process. This is evident when we consider some dynamic process such as learning where we don't even speak of test-retest but rather of trials. Here the expectation is that change in the results from one trial to another is an accurate reflection of a process leading to change. When viewed in this light, it suggests that "unreliable" test-retest results, far from being a source for dismay, may in fact serve as an indicator that something developmentally more interesting than stasis is in operation. Based on this sort of post hoc reasoning we decided that we had been stupid to expect consistency from our subjects and that we did not yet have to scrap our interesting finding that some people used a left-hemisphere mode of processing faces and others a right-hemisphere mode. Instead we set about trying to determine what dynamic process could be at work to produce our "unreliable" results.

The first reasonable alternative to a stable left-hemisphere or right-hemisphere type that this empirically driven change in stance resulted in was the possibility that people utilize both left-hemisphere and right-hemisphere approaches for the identification of faces and that they utilize these serially. That is, rather than some people using a right- and others using a left-hemisphere mode of face processing, we postulated that the same individual uses both a right- and a left-hemisphere mode of face processing but changes the mode utilized over time. We couldn't use data previously reported by others to examine this possibility because standard practice in presenting results of facial recognition studies is to present data aggregated across trials. Although we could go back and examine our

own data sequentially, we realized that this would not be maximally useful because we had given our subjects a period during which we familiar-
ized them with the faces that they would later be asked to identify. Consequently, if we were dealing with a dynamic process in which there were
shifts in the mode of processing with accompanying shifts in hemispheric
advantage, it would be best to examine the process before subjects were
exposed to the faces.

In our next studies (Ross & Turkewitz, 1982) we attempted to do precisely that by presenting a set of four previously unfamiliar faces for recognition and examining hemispheric advantage in their recognition across
sequential blocks of trials rather than as an overall measure. We expected
we would find a relatively steady progression with an initial left-hemisphere advantage gradually waning until it shifted to an advantage for
the right hemisphere. That is, we believed that the reason we and others
had found such a relatively high proportion of individuals with a left-
hemisphere advantage on this presumably right-hemisphere task was
because the rate of shifts in processing strategy and advantage are not
uniform across individuals. Therefore, we believed that all subjects began
with a left-hemisphere advantage and that those subjects showing the
right-hemisphere advantage had simply made the transition to a right-
hemisphere advantage more rapidly than those showing a left-hemisphere
advantage.

When we (Ross & Turkewitz, 1982) examined the data from a study in
which we presented subjects with a set of four initially unfamiliar faces,
we found that there were indeed systematic shifts in hemispheric advantage with increasing familiarization. However, these shifts were not quite
what we had anticipated. First of all, even at the beginning of the task,
that is, during the first block of 24 trials, some subjects exhibited a right-
hemisphere and others a left-hemisphere advantage in identifying the
faces. It was still possible that we were correct and that all subjects started
with a left-hemisphere advantage early during the initial 24-trial block
but rapidly shifted to a right-hemisphere advantage. This possibility was
largely ruled out by the finding that subjects beginning testing with a left-
hemisphere advantage (i.e., those with a left-hemisphere advantage on
block 1) showed the hypothesized linear shift from a left- to a right-hemisphere advantage, whereas those starting with a right-hemisphere advantage showed a more complex pattern. That is, a trend analysis showed
that subjects who began testing with a right-hemisphere advantage exhibited a significant quadratic trend in their index of hemispheric advantage. This significant quadratic trend represented a shift from an initial
right-hemisphere advantage to a left-hemisphere advantage, with an ultimate return to a right-hemisphere advantage. This was a finding that
could not be incorporated into our initial formulation of a more or less

uniform shift from a left- to a right-hemisphere advantage, even when the possibility of only a brief initial left-hemisphere advantage, was considered. This violation of expectation led us to reconsider the nature of processing strategies, and the implications of two temporally separate periods when there was a right-hemisphere advantage.

Our first thought was that the two separate periods with a right-hemisphere advantage might represent periods when different strategies were being utilized. If that were the case, then the usual breakdown into analytic or holistic processing could not be right. What could the requisite third mode of processing be? One appealing possibility was that the third mode of processing suggested by the obtained quadratic, that is, right-left-right sequence of hemisphere advantage, was an integrated analytic and holistic mode of processing. According to this scheme, some subjects would begin processing faces on a configurational basis in terms of the relationship between the parts and show a right-hemisphere advantage. At some later point, they would shift to identifying the faces in an analytic mode and utilize distinctive features as the basis for identification and show a left-hemisphere advantage. We postulated (Ross-Kossak & Turkewitz, 1986) that subsequent to this some individuals would advance to a processing mode that integrated information concerning both configuration and distinctive elements. This merger of holistic and analytic processes would result in the ability to see a forest that was composed of individual trees and should therefore result in superior performance.

Largely because of its position in the obtained right-left-right progression, we assigned this integrative ability to the right hemisphere, although in retrospect there were also other data suggesting that the right hemisphere would have an advantage in integrating information from the two hemispheres. Thus it has been found that the left prefrontal area has a much higher gray/white matter ratio than has the right prefrontal area (Gur, Packer, Hungerbuhler, Reivich, Obrist, Amarnex, & Sackheim, 1980), suggesting that the left prefrontal cotex is characterized by dense unmyelinated neurons designed for intraregional connectivity, with the right prefrontal cortex having relatively more long, myelinated fibers better suited for interregional connectivity (Goldberg & Costa, 1981; Gur et al., 1980). Indeed, when the performance of individuals who showed the canonical right-left-right sequence of hemispheric advantage was compared to that of subjects showing other patterns, it was found that they did make more correct facial identifications. We also obtained indirect evidence suggesting that there were two modes of right-hemisphere advantage and that they constituted a relatively primitive and an advanced mode of function. Thus, in a study of children of different ages we (Turkewitz & Ross-Kossak, 1984) found a bimodal distribution of error scores for girls with a right-hemisphere advantage, with some of them doing more poorly than a comparably aged group of girls with a left-hemisphere advantage and some doing distinctly better. There was only a single mode for younger girls. This suggests that younger girls and some older girls employ only the relatively primitive right-hemisphere mode and hence perform relatively poorly, whereas some of the older girls were able to advance to the integrated right-hemisphere mode and exhibited superior performance.

Having conceptualized three different processing strategies, we explored their implications for an understanding of efficacy in facial identification. I will return to this later. At this point, I am going to leave that part of the story and briefly discuss how the changes in our thinking, brought about by our need to make sense out of data that didn't conform to our expectations, influenced my views about the development of cognition. To do this I have to digress a bit into what might appear to be tangential material but which will ultimately become integrated into the overall story.

☐ Origins of Hemispheric Specialization

Newborn infants are differentially responsive to speech and nonspeech signals, with a left-hemisphere advantage for speech. This is based on the finding that at birth infants exhibit a right-ear, left-hemisphere advantage for the processing of speech (see Previc, 1991, and Turkewitz, 1993, for reviews). I have proposed a model for how prenatal experience could give rise to this neonatal hemispheric specialization (Turkewitz, 1989, 1991, 1993) but I won't go into it now. The model calls attention to the fact that on more than 50 percent of the occasions when a caregiver approaches an infant he or she begins speaking before becoming visible (Gustafson, Green, & Kalinowski, 1993). Therefore, it is likely that when an infant sees an adult's face the left hemisphere is already occupied with processing speech. This leaves the right hemisphere available for processing facial information. What makes this significant is the fact that the infant brain probably functions differently from that of older children or adults. For example, because of its relatively unmyelinated state there there is greater likelihood of nonsynaptic or ephaptic transmission between contiguous areas of the brain. As a result, this makes activation of an entire hemisphere or at least larger areas of a hemisphere more likely in a newborn than in older individuals, where adjacent areas of a hemisphere would, by virtue of myelination, be more insulated from each other. At the same time, because the corpus callosum is very late in becoming myelinated, the two hemispheres would be relatively isolated from each other, with reduced interhemispheric facilitation and inhibition (Wittleson & Kigar, 1988; Yakovlev & Lecours, 1967).

In addition to the postulated separate and concurrent processing of face and voice, at this stage of development the infant has poor high and middle spatial frequency resolving ability (Aslin, 1987). This means that only low-frequency spatial information would be available. It is possible to recognize faces using only low-frequency spatial information; however, such recognition would of necessity be based on configurational information, because when only low-frequency spatial information is available, what you have is essentially a fuzzy face with little featural definition. Although with such a fuzzy face it is not possible to identify specific features, the face is clearly a face and the individual is recognizable from the location of the features in relation to each other (Sergent, 1986). But such faces are more similar to each other than are faces containing more high-frequency spatial information. Because of the aforementioned constraints imposed by the neonatal visual system, face processing is likely to be based on configurational information. As the visual system matures, changes in the infant's visual acuity make more of the middle- and high-frequency spatial information available, thereby enabling identification of specific features. However, at the time that this featural information becomes newly available the face still contains configurational information that is most likely still processed in the right hemisphere. Because the corpus callosum is still poorly myelinated, there would be only limited communication and interference between the hemispheres, so that both types of processing could be carried out concurrently, although without integration. In other words, face and speech processing could occur in parallel. It should be noted that this type of parallel processing would be unlikely in adults because of inhibitory effects across the callosum. However, in adults one could expect serial switching between right- and left-hemisphere processing.

It is precisely the notion of serial switching that prompted me to come up with the developmental model. In addition to the evidence indicating switching in hemispheric advantage over the course of increasing familiarization with faces, there is also evidence suggesting that at least during early stages of complex information processing there are advantages to the serial development of processing modes. Thus data from adults indicate a relatively strong association between magnitude of visual field advantage during early stages of familiarization and proficiency. Those subjects having bigger differences between the number of correct identifications in the two visual fields make more correct identifications than do individuals with smaller initial visual field advantages (Ross-Kossak & Turkewitz, 1984). This suggests an advantage to an information-processing strategy in which attention is focused on one aspect of a stimulus array until it has been mastered and then shifts to processing another aspect of the array. This advantage would accrue from the reduction of concurrent competing demands for processing while allowing for the kind of comprehensive knowledge of an object provided by an integrated holistic and analytic appreciation for the characteristics of the object.

This conceptualization, based upon our findings with adults, fed back upon my view of the developmental process. It became apparent that the same object could be processed in multiple ways, and that while adaptive behavior could result from any single mode of information processing, the use of multiple modes would represent an enhanced level of functioning. Furthermore, the achievement of an integrated holistic and analytic processing could better be achieved by independent attainment of some proficiency with each mode of processing prior to their integration. This suggests that the sequencing of information-processing modes may be influential in determining eventual proficiency. When viewed in terms of ontogenetic processes, it becomes apparent that limitations characteristic of various stages of development provide for an orderly sequence in the characteristic modes of information processing. This is a point that, together with Pat Kenny (Turkewitz & Kenny, 1982), I had previously made with reference to sensory functioning. We had previously argued that the sequential development of the sensory systems—tactile, vestibular, chemical, auditory, and visual—provided structure and organization to the perceptual functioning of the developing organism. According to this view the limited input at early stages of development prevented overload and allowed later-developing systems to utilize modes of functioning originating within the earlier-developing systems. The current expansion of this position views cognitive functioning as also being strongly influenced by constraints of available information that become relaxed during the course of development.

To recapitulate, I already held the view that the timing of developmental events helped to shape intersensory relationships and the nature of perceptual functioning. Please note that my use of the concept of timing refers to "the temporal relationships between the components of an integrated system" (Turkewitz & Devenny, 1993, p. 1), whereas sequential timing refers to hemispheric interactions and thus is by no means synonymous with the original concept of timing. In other words, sequential timing is concerned with the state of organization of a system when it is perturbed. The findings in adults of a complex sequence of change in the hemispheric advantage in facial recognition led to a consideration of the manner in which characteristics of infants could give rise to this type of switching of hemispheric advantage. This has led to the view that limitations on the type of visual spatial information available to the infant constrain him/her to process facial information in terms of configuration. Because of a previously developed left-hemisphere specialization for processing speech and a characteristic of mothers to begin speaking to their infants prior to their becoming available within the infant's visual field, it was postulated that the infant's initial configurational processing of facial information was performed with a right-hemisphere advantage. It was further postulated that relaxation of the visual constraints leading to the availability of information concerning specific features led to the development of analytic processing that by default was carried out in the left hemisphere. It is, therefore, my contention that the characteristic left-hemisphere analytic and right-hemisphere holistic modes of processing have their origins in the developmental history of the infant. I have extended this view by suggesting that characteristics of the infant, including certain sensory limitations, can facilitate concept formation. That is, the unavailability of middle- and high-frequency spatial information simplifies the formation of the concept of faces by reducing the differences between faces, thereby emphasizing their similarities.

Although all of these implications stem from information obtained in the laboratory, they obviously go well beyond anything that we have data to sustain. The task is then to go back into the laboratory and correct the misinterpretations stemming from my attempts to make sense of previous unanticipated results. Fortunately there are myriad ways in which to expand the position advanced. For example, it would be predicted that infants from cultures in which mothers don't begin speaking before approaching their infants would show a different pattern of hemispheric specialization than do infants from Western cultures. It would also be predicted that at a certain stage infants could more readily form concepts with degraded rather than highly defined stimuli. I have no doubt that I will be wrong with regard to at least some of the particulars that stem from the suggestions I have advanced. In fact, I greatly look forward to the challenges that will be presented when I once again have to say, "wasn't I stupid."

☐ References

Aslin, R. N. (1987). Visual and auditory development in infancy. In J. Osofsky (Ed.), *Handbook of Infant Development*, 2nd ed. (pp. 5–97). New York: Wiley.

Bever, T. G., & Chiarello, R. (1974). Cerebral dominance in musicians and nonmusicians. *Science, 185,* 537–539.

Bogen, J. E. (1969). The other side of the brain II: An appositional mind. *Bulletin of the Los Angeles Neurological Society, 34,* 191–220.

Goldberg, E., & Costa, L. (1981). Hemisphere differences in the acquisition and use of descriptive systems. *Brain and Language, 14,* 144–173.

Gur, R. C., Packer, I. K., Hungerbuhler, J. P., Reivich, M., Obrist, W. D., Amarnek, W. S., & Sackhein, H. A. (1980). Differences in the distribution of gray and white matter in human cerebral hemispheres. *Science, 207,* 1226–1228.

198 Conceptions of Development

Gustafson, G. E., Green, J. A., & Kalinowski, L. L. (1993). *The development of communicative skills: Infants' cries and vocalizations in social context.* Paper presented at the Biennial Meeting of the Society for Research in Child Development, New Orleans, LA.

Harris, L. J., & Carlson, D. F. (1988). Pathological left-handedness: An analysis of theories: Developmental implications and evidence. In D. L. Molfese & S. J. Segalowitz (Eds.), *Brain lateralization in children* (pp. 289–372). New York: Guilford.

Jacob, F. (1988). *The statue within: An autobiography* (F. Philip, Trans.). New York: Basic Books.

Leehey, S. C., & Cahn, A. (1979). Lateral asymmetries in the recognition of words, familiar faces, and unfamiliar faces. *Neuropsychologia, 17,* 619–365.

Marzi, C. A., & Berlucchi, G. (1977). Right visual field superiority for accuracy of recognition of famous faces in normals. *Neuropsychologia, 15,* 751–756.

Previc, F. H. (1991). A general theory concerning the prenatal origins of cerebral lateralization in humans. *Psychological Review, 98,* 299–334.

Ross, P., & Turkewitz, G. (1981). Individual differences in cerebral asymmetries for facial recognition. *Cortex, 17,* 199–214.

Ross, P., & Turkewitz, G. (1982). Changes in hemispheric advantages in processing facial information with increasing stimulus familiarization. *Cortex, 18,* 489–499.

Ross-Kossak, P., & Turkewitz, G. (1984). Relationship between changes in hemispheric advantage during familiarization to faces and proficiency in facial recognition. *Neuropsychologia, 22,* 471–477.

Ross-Kossak, P., & Turkewitz, G. (1986). A micro and macrodevelopmental view of the nature of changes in complex information processing: A consideration of changes in hemispheric advantage during familiarization. In R. Bruyer (Ed.), *The neuropsychology of face perception and facial expression* (pp.125–145). Hillsdale NJ: Erlbaum.

Sergent, J. (1986). Methodological constraints on neuropsychological studies of face perception in normals. In R. Bruyer (Ed.), *The neuropsychology of face perception and facial expression* (pp.91–124). Hillsdale NJ: Erlbaum.

Springer, S. P., & Deutsch, G. (1981). *Left brain, right brain.* San Francisco: Freeman.

Taubes, G. (1996). Rare sightings beguile physicists. *Science, 272,* 474–476.

Turkewitz, G. (1989). A prenatal source for the development of hemispheric specialization. In D. L. Molfese & S. J. Segalowitz (Eds.), *Brain lateralization in children developmental implications* (pp. 73–82). New York, Guilford.

Turkewitz, G. (1991). Perinatal influences on the development of hemispheric specialization and complex information processing. In M. J. S. Weiss & P. R. Zelazo (Eds.) *Newborn attention biological constraints and the influence of experience* (pp. 443–465). Norwood, NJ: Ablex.

Turkewitz, G. (1993). The influence of timing on the nature of cognition. In G. Turkewitz & D. A. Devenny (Eds.), *Developmental time and timing* (pp. 125–142). Hillsdale, NJ:Erlbaum.

Turkewitz, G., & Devenny, D. A. (1993). Timing and the shape of development. In G. Turkewitz & D. A. Devenny (Eds.), *Developmental time and timing* (pp. 1–11). Hillsdale, NJ: Erlbaum.

Turkewitz, G., & Kenny, P. A. (1982). Limitations on input as a basis for neural organization and perceptual development: A preliminary theoretical statement. *Developmental Psychobiology, 15,* 357–368.

Turkewitz, G., & Ross-Kossak, P. (1984). Multiple modes of right hemisphere information processing: Age and sex differences in facial recognition. *Developmental Psychobiology, 20,* 95–103.

Wittleson, S. F., & Kigar, D. L. (1988). Anatomical development of the corpus callosum in humans: A review with reference to sex and cognition. In D. L. Molfese & S. V. J. Segalowitz (Eds.), *Developmental implications of brain lateralization* (pp. 35–58). New York, Guilford.

Yakovlev, P. I., & Lecours, A. R. (1967). The myelogenetic cycles of regional maturation of the brain. In A. Minkowski (Ed.), *Regional eevelopment of the brain in early life*. Oxford, Blackwell Scientific Publications.

Young, A. W., & Bion, P. J. (1981). Accuracy of naming laterally presented known faces by children and adults. *Cortex, 17*, 97–106.

CHAPTER

David F. Bjorklund

Memory, Strategies, Knowledge, and Evolution: The Evolution of a Developmentalist

I started graduate school in 1971 at the University of Dayton, working with Eliot Butter on topics of children's haptic perception and individual differences in cognitive styles. Although individual differences would always interest me, a remnant of my days in Dayton, the focus of my research in my first two decades in developmental psychology would be on children's memory.

I began my career as a memory development researcher in 1973, my first year in the graduate program at the University of North Carolina at Chapel Hill. The field of memory development was new and hot just then. It had only been two years earlier that John Flavell's (1971) discipline-organizing paper "What is memory development the development of?" had been published, and I was fortunate enough to fall under the tutelage of Peter Ornstein, who had just published a groundbreaking study of children's organization in memory (Liberty & Ornstein, 1973), and had embarked on an ambitious research program investigating the development of children's rehearsal during memory tasks. The cognitive-developmental perspective of memory that people such as Flavell and Ornstein were advocating was quite different from the associationistic, verbal-learning perspective that I had learned about and been bored by as an undergraduate. This seemed like new territory and an area that promised to ask important questions, not just about memory, but about the nature of cognitive development. The dominant perspective at the time was that memory development could best be explained in terms of strategy development. With age, children are more likely to use memory strategies and to use them with increasing effectiveness. Strategies were viewed as a form of complex intentional behavior, and by studying the development of memory strategies, one was learning about the development of intentional control, a central issue of cognitive development.

Although my focus in graduate school was clearly on cognitive development under the influence of Peter Ornstein, during my first semester at North Carolina I had the great fortune to partake in a Developmental Proseminar taught by Gilbert Gottlieb, Robert Cairns, and Harriet Rheingold. There I learned about developmental psychobiology, the bidirectionality of structure and function, the importance of developmental timing, the concept of probabilistic epigenesis, and behavioral neophenotypes. Although I did not pursue these ideas in my memory research, the basic concepts and "big picture" view of development stayed with me and prepared me for my much later "second career" in developmental psychology.

In this chapter, I first outline my research on memory strategy development, focusing on the role of knowledge base on children's memory behavior. This has been the main line of my research since leaving graduate school, and, I believe, tells a reasonably coherent story. However, few lives, including research lives, are ever as coherent as they appear in retrospect, and there are often secondary paths that cross, influence, and are influenced by the mainline path (a true bidirectionality of structure and function). Following the description of my "main" cognitive-developmental research program, I take a few steps backward and describe the route I was simultaneously traveling that led me to become an evolutionary developmental psychologist.

☐ The Development of Strategic Memory

Through the 1970s and well into the 1980s, research and theory on strategic-memory development blossomed, and a canonical view emerged. Preschool children were viewed as being essentially astrategic. However, by kindergarten age, or so, children would use simple strategies, which would be replaced over time with increasingly effective and complicated strategies. Strategies were viewed as *the cause* of memory development. Older children remember more than younger children because they are more strategic. This cause-effect relation was illustrated by the findings of training experiments, in which astrategic children are instructed to use a memory strategy and realize corresponding improvements in recall as a result. This phenomenon, of young children failing to produce a strategy spontaneously but then benefiting from strategic training, was termed a *production deficiency* (Flavell, 1970). The training experiment became the principal tool of memory development researchers, and most experiments focused on the factors that were thought to be responsible for children's production deficiencies and their remediation (see Harnishfeger & Bjorklund, 1990, for an historical review).

My own career started very much as a disciple of this canonical view (e.g., Bjorklund, Ornstein, & Haig, 1977), and I selected as my "best guess" candidate for the "explanation" for production deficiencies developmental differences in *knowledge base*, children's long-term memory representations of facts and information. Very early on, our findings led us to question some of the primary tenets of the "memory development as strategy development" perspective, and future research indicated an increasingly complicated picture of strategy development.

Knowledge and Memory Development

While conducting a series of failed experiments on encoding specificity in children's memory (a program that Brian Ackerman [1987] managed to conduct successfully), Barbara Zeman, a graduate student in a seminar I was teaching, observed how her son was able to remember nearly perfectly all of the members of his current school class in preparation for addressing Valentine's Day cards. Was this a trivial observation, or might it reflect an exception to the typical memory abilities of 8-year-olds?

We immediately set out to perform a series of *class-recall* experiments, in which children, usually late in the school year, were asked to recall, in any order they wished, their current school classmates (e.g., Bjorklund & Zeman, 1982, 1983). First-, third-, and fifth-grade children performed very well on this task (although usually not perfectly), recalling at much higher rates than when given lists of categorizable words (e.g., different examples of FRUITS, TOOLS, FURNITURE). More critically, they rarely went about remembering their classmates' names randomly. When examining their recall, children usually remembered the names according to some structure—seating arrangement, sex of child, reading groups, alphabetically, or friendship patterns, for example. However, children rarely displayed ceiling levels of *clustering* (the statistical measure of the extent to which children remember related items together, relative to chance). They had significantly higher levels of clustering than when they remembered lists of categorized words, but they frequently switched between modes of organization (e.g., by seating arrangement for the first half of their recall, to sex of child for the second half).

Of substantial interest was the fact that many children were often unaware of using any strategy (e.g., recalling by seating arrangement) on this task. When asked, after recall, how they had remembered so many names and did they remember them in any special order, many children professed that they did nothing special or did not remember them in any special order. Others claimed, quite confidently, that they had used a particular strategy (e.g., "Mrs. Anderson calls roll every morning, and I remembered them the way she calls the names, alphabetically"), but inspection of their recall indicated no evidence of using the strategy they had professed. But perhaps more critically, children who were aware of the strategy they had been using (i.e., showing good *metamemory*, knowledge of their own memory functioning) recalled only slightly more names than children who were unaware of using any strategy (i.e., showing poor metamemory).

This finding distressed us a bit initially. Metamemory had been proposed to be the key to good strategic memory. Older children have better metamnemonic awareness than younger children (e.g., Kreutzer, Leonard, & Flavell, 1975), and it was this enhanced metamemory that was "responsible" for the more strategic approach, and thus higher levels of memory performance, of older relative to younger children (e.g., Brown, 1978; Flavell & Wellman, 1977). At one level, our results supported this interpretation. Consistent children (those whose professed strategy was consistent with their observed strategy) did have higher levels of recall and clustering than Not Consistent children, but the differences were small. It seemed clear to us that the high levels of recall on this task were not attributed to metamnemonic competence, and they may not even be attributed to enhanced strategy use. This latter interpretation was supported by a subsequent experiment, in which children were instructed to recall all the members of their current classmates either by seating arrangements or by sex of child (Bjorklund & Bjorklund, 1985). Children were able to do this nearly perfectly. Yet their level of recall was no greater than that of children who recalled the names in any order they wished (with much lower levels of clustering).

These findings suggested to us that the rules for memory development were different when children had detailed knowledge of the to-be-remembered information, such as the members of their current school class. Although children recalled their classmates' names according to well-ordered schemes, their verbal reports suggested that they were not doing so deliberately. Rather, once getting started, the well-established relations among the names in this knowledge base were easily activated, resulting in the recall of other related names *without the need of an intentional strategy*. Sometimes, while recalling the names of all the children in a particular reading group, for example, one name (e.g., Jason M.) would trigger the recall of a name outside of the reading group (e.g., Jason T.), and, as a result, a child would switch from organizing his or her recall according to one scheme (reading groups) to another (sex of child). What looked like strategic behavior was actually the product of the relatively automatic activation of well-established semantic-memory relations. In other words, having a detailed knowledge base produced strategiclike behavior in the absence of "real" (i.e., intentional and effortful) strategies. Yet, we proposed, in the process of recalling names "automatically" by some organizational scheme, children may recognize that they are doing something smart. ("Hey, all those kids sit together. Maybe I'll try to remember the rest of the kids by where they sit.") That is, children may discover strategies by examining the products of their recall, which will lead to intentional strategy use. Thus, in this case, good memory performance, afforded by a well-developed knowledge base, results in good metamemory awareness, which may, in turn, produce subsequent enhancements of recall.

But is such a pattern limited to special (and some may say trivial) situations, such as children's recall of their classmates, or may something similar be occurring for memory strategy development in general? To find out, we began a research program to assess the degree to which children of different ages display organization in their recall as a function of their underlying knowledge base and the relation such knowledge and organization has with memory performance.

A first step in the process involved collecting age-norms for sets of categorically related words. Research at the time had indicated that natural-language categories (e.g., BIRDS, FURNITURE, FRUIT) could be described in terms of a *prototype*, or best example of a category, and that individual items could be rated in terms of how typical each one was to its prototype (e.g., Rosch, 1975). Adults showed high levels of agreement concerning how "typical" various exemplars were of their categories and processed typical category information faster and more efficiently than atypical category information (e.g., Keller & Kellas, 1978; Rosch, 1975). We wondered whether category structure, as measured by typicality ratings, varied with age (Bjorklund, Thompson, & Ornstein, 1983).

To test this, we presented college students and children in kindergarten, grade 3, and grade 6 with sets of items from familiar natural-language categories and asked them, separately for each category tested, (1) to determine whether or not pictured items were members of the designated category (several foil items were included in each category set), and (2) for those items selected, to rate each one in terms of how typical it was of its category on a 3-point scale. We found age differences in the percentage of items children included in their categories, with children of all ages including almost all adult-defined highly typical items as category exemplars, but denying that the less-typical adult-defined exemplars were indeed category members. Also, when looking at the rank orders of the typicality judgments within each category, the ratings became more adultlike with increasing age (mean correlations between the ratings of the college students and the three child groups = .72, .78, and .90 for kindergarten, grade 3, and grade 6 children, respectively). These findings indicated significant age-related differences in category knowledge. However, when, in a different study (Bjorklund & Jacobs, 1984), we asked children in grades 3, 4, 6, and 8, and college students to rate items in terms of *associative strength* (e.g., *dog-cat; salt-pepper* versus *dog-lion; salt-mustard*), we found no significant age differences in ratings. Thus, we concluded that associative relations develop earlier than categorical relations, and, if so, these differences should be manifest in children's memory performance.

We confirmed this in one study, in which children in grades 1, 4, and 7 were asked to sort sets of pictures into groups for later recall (Bjorklund & de Marchena, 1984). The items could be grouped according to categorical relations (e.g., *head-feet; hat-shoes*) or, simultaneously, by associative relations (e.g., *head-hat; feet-shoes*). In two experiments, the youngest children showed a strong preference for associative sorting, whereas the older children sorted primarily in terms of categorical relations. (Figure 9.1 presents the sorting results of one of these experiments.) Also, levels of clustering were high, even for the young children when measured in terms of associative "categories." In other experiments, children's memory performance with adult-defined lists of items (i.e., lists based on adult norms) was contrasted with lists of items categorized based on age-appropriate norms (Bjorklund & Thompson, 1983) or children's self-generated lists (i.e., lists based on typicality ratings made by the children in a previous session) (Bjorklund, 1988). The results of these experiments were also clear. Children performed better, especially on atypical items, when age-appropriate norms were used. In later research, we demonstrated that children are more likely to show strategic behavior, and more likely to transfer a trained strategy, when recalling typical as opposed to atypical sets of items (Bjorklund & Buchanan, 1989).

I think that one nondevelopmental study using self-generated versus adult-generated typicality norms was particularly telling of the role of background knowledge on children's memory performance. Several researchers had demonstrated that poor readers were less likely to use memory strategies, and had lower levels of memory performance accordingly, than comparable groups of good readers (e.g., Bauer, 1979; Worden, 1983). One possibility for the lower memory performance of the poor readers, we speculated, was not their ineffective use of strategies, but a deficient knowledge base. To investigate this, Jean Bernholtz and I

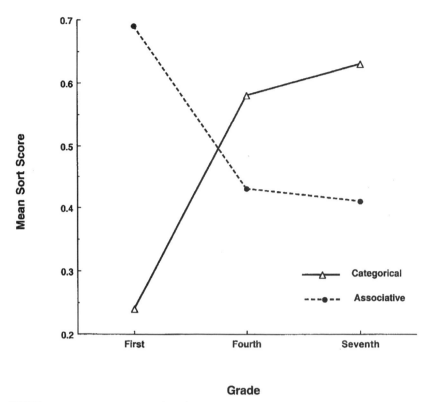

FIGURE 9.1. Mean categorical and associate sort scores for children in grades 1, 4, and 7. From Bjorklund & de Marchena, 1984, Experiment 1.

(Bjorklund & Bernholtz, 1986) selected groups of good and poor readers from junior high schools and asked them to rate sets of items in terms of category typicality, much as children did in the normative study by Bjorklund, Thompson, and Ornstein (1983) discussed earlier. The ratings of the poor readers were similar to those of third-grade children from the normative sample, and much less like those of adults (mean correlation of ratings with adults = .77) than those of the good readers (mean correlation of ratings with adults = .86). In subsequent experiments, good and poor readers were given sets of categorically related words for a memory test. Children received either sets of typical and atypical words based on self-generated norms or adult-generated norms. When using adult-generated norms, the good readers recalled more items and showed higher levels of clustering than the poor readers. These group differences were nonsignificant, however, when self-generated norms were used. In other words, it appears that the primary problem on memory tasks of poor readers, just as for young children, is their impoverished knowledge base.

When group differences in knowledge base are eliminated by using self-generated norms, so are differences in strategic memory. We arrived at a similar conclusion for the differences that are typically found between learning-disabled and nondisabled children on memory span tasks (Krupski, Gaultney, Malcolm, & Bjorklund, 1993).

In one study, we investigated the connection between (a) early-developing, and apparently automatically activated, associative relations, (b) later-developing, and presumably more deliberately implemented, categorical relations, and (c) memory (Bjorklund & Jacobs, 1985). We gave children in grades 3, 5, 7, and 9 and college students sets of categorically *organized* words that included pairs of high associates within each category. For example, the category MAMMALS consisted of the words: *dog, cat, cow, lion, tiger*. In addition to all being related by virtue of their being mammals, two pairs (*dog, cat; lion, tiger*) were also highly associated. We found that when we presented the list items blocked by categories (but not by associates), recall was high for all groups of participants and the relation between recall and clustering was significant at each age. Levels of recall and clustering were also high when items were blocked by associates; however, the correlation between recall and clustering was nonsignificant for the third-, fifth-, and seventh-grade children in this condition, suggesting to us that when recall is mediated by associative relations, children's memory is not being guided by explicit and deliberate strategy use, but rather by the relatively automatic activation of associative relations. But, although we believed that such associative recall was not strategic, we believed that it could lead to strategic, categorical recall, at least in some children. To assess this, we examined the recall of participants who had been presented items randomly for evidence that the recall of associative pairs (e.g., *dog, cat*) would lead to the subsequent recall of other categorically related items (e.g., *dog, cat, cow, lion*). We computed all intracategory strings of three words or more that were led by the recall of an associative pair (see Figure 9.2). As can be seen, the seventh- and ninth-grade children showed a high incidence of category clusters following the recall of an associative pair, suggesting that these older children used the associative pair to prompt the recall of nonassociated, category items. The proportion of category clusters led by associative pairs was less for the college students, presumably because they did not require high associativity to prompt categorical recall. In contrast, nonassociated category relations were not easily activated by the third and fifth graders, making the associative prompts relatively ineffective in eliciting subsequent clustering.

We conducted one additional line of knowledge-based research, examining the strategic memory performance of children who were "expert" in some specific domain such as baseball or soccer. This work was all con-

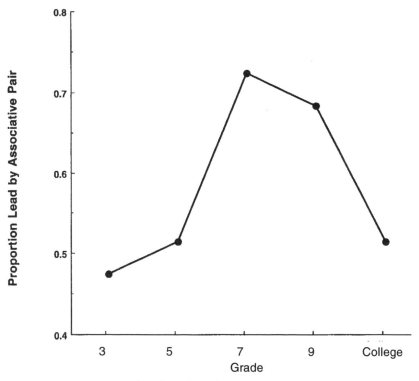

FIGURE 9.2. Proportion of total number of intracategory word strings of length three, four, and five to those leading with a high-associative word pair by grade. From Bjorklund & Jacobs, 1985. Copyright © 1985 by Academic Press.

ducted in association with my good friend and brilliant colleague Wolfgang Schneider, who is quite an expert on expertise himself (e.g., Schneider, Körkel, & Weinert, 1989; Schneider, Gruber, Gold, & Opwis, 1993). We believed that by studying expert children we could make broader statements about the role of knowledge than we could by studying children's memory for sets of familiar words or members of their current classmates. In class recall, all children can be considered "experts" for the target information. But this expertise is acquired relatively automatically, without any apparent effort or special motivation, and is restricted to a small range of exemplars. Children who develop an expert's knowledge of baseball or soccer, however, must usually put a good deal of effort into gaining their expertise, and the organization of their knowledge base may differ accordingly, as may the relation between knowledge, strategy use, and memory.

In several experiments, school-age children expert in their knowledge of baseball or soccer were given sets of sort-recall or free-recall tasks, both using categorizable items from their domain of expertise and items from "neutral" categories. These children were also contrasted with groups of novice children. (In most of these studies, we also examined the effects of individual differences in psychometrically measured intelligence on memory performance, but that's another story. See Bjorklund & Schneider, 1996.) Expert children consistently remembered more in their domain of expertise than for the neutral lists, and outperformed the novice children on the specialized sets of items but not on the neutral sets, all clear indications of the strong role of knowledge base on children's memory performance. However, just as in research with young children, the benefits of detailed knowledge for expert children was not always expressed via enhanced strategy use. Rather, the substantial differences in memory performance were accompanied by only marginally greater strategy use, at best (Gaultney, Bjorklund, & Schneider, 1992; Schneider & Bjorklund, 1992; Schneider, Bjorklund, & Maier-Brückner, 1996). These findings suggest that the enhanced performance on strategic tasks for expert children is primarily mediated by item-specific effects associated with their more elaborated knowledge base rather than through more effective use of strategies (see Bjorklund & Schneider, 1996).

My colleagues and I interpreted our findings, and those of others (e.g., Ackerman, 1986; Rabinowitz, 1984; Schneider, 1986), as reflecting a central role of knowledge base on children's strategic memory (Bjorklund, 1985, 1987a; Bjorklund, Muir-Broaddus, & Schneider, 1990). At one point, I argued that, for the strategy of memory organization, "most of the age changes in the organization of children's recall are not strategic, but rather can be attributed to developmental changes in the structure and content of children's conceptual representation" and that "the regular improvements observed in memory organization over the course of the preschool and elementary school years can most parsimoniously be attributed to developmental differences in the structure of semantic memory and the ease with which certain types of semantic relationships can be activated" (1985, p. 103). This position was regarded as being extreme (see Schneider & Pressley, 1989), and I have tempered, somewhat, my "strong" position on the role of knowledge base on children's memory performance over the years as I have mellowed with age (e.g., Bjorklund et al., 1990). Nonetheless, I believe that the findings from our laboratory clearly indicated that age-related differences in children's world knowledge were responsible, in large part, for the corresponding differences that were observed in memory performance, and that much of these differences were not mediated by strategies. Subsequent research has generally supported our interpretation (see Alexander & Schwanenflugel, 1994; Hasselhorn, 1995).

Utilization Deficiencies

In many of our knowledge-base studies, we found a pattern that did not fit with the mainline thinking about the relation between strategy use and memory performance. In many cases, differences in strategy use did not predict differences in memory performance (e.g., Bjorklund & Bernholtz, 1986; Bjorklund & Jacobs, 1985; Bjorklund & Zeman, 1982; Gaultney et al., 1992; Schneider & Bjorklund, 1992). We weren't the only people to notice this. Patricia Miller (1990) observed a similar pattern in her research with simple selective-attention strategies, and called the phenomenon a *utilization deficiency*. Unlike the seemingly ubiquitous production deficiency, here children use the strategy but it does not improve their performance, or improves it substantially less than when older children use the same strategy. In later research, we demonstrated that elementary school–age children frequently used an organization strategy on a multitrial free-recall task without gaining any benefit from the strategy (Bjorklund, Coyle, & Gaultney, 1992; Coyle & Bjorklund, 1996). Children would show a significant increase in clustering on consecutive trials, but no corresponding increase in recall. However, some of these children displayed enhanced recall on later trials, suggesting that the utilization deficiency was short lived. Children even displayed utilization deficiencies when *instructed* to use a strategy. For example, we trained fourth-grade children to sort and recall items by categories, and, as a result, their levels of both recall and clustering increased (Bjorklund, Schneider, Cassel, & Ashley, 1994). On subsequent transfer trials (administered immediately and one week after training), however, children's levels of recall decreased, despite the fact that levels of categorical sorting and clustering remained high (see Figure 9.3). That is, these children displayed a utilization deficiency after training. Meta-analyses of over thirty years of memory development research indicated that utilization deficiencies were found in over 90 percent of studies examining children's spontaneous strategy use (Miller & Seier, 1994) and in over 50 percent of memory training studies (Bjorklund, Miller, Coyle, & Slawinski, 1997).

How can one explain utilization deficiencies? We interpreted the pattern of results as reflecting the operation of several different factors, but most importantly the fact that strategies are effortful operations and that young children may not always have the available resources to benefit from using them (Bjorklund & Coyle, 1995; Bjorklund et al., 1997). Strategies are expensive in terms of mental effort, and younger children must use more of their limited resources to execute a strategy than older children (e.g., Bjorklund & Harnishfeger, 1987; Guttentag, 1984; Kee & Davies, 1990). As a result, the advantage they provide the older or more prac-

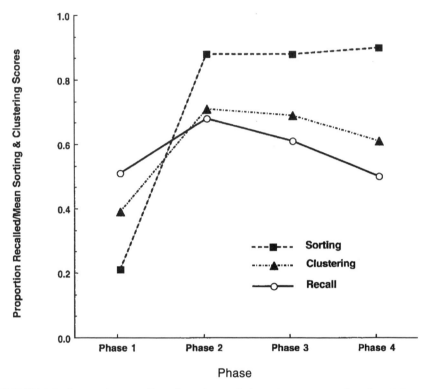

FIGURE 9.3. Proportion recall, and sorting and clustering scores at baseline (Phase 1), training (Phase 2), immediate transfer (Phase 3), and one-week transfer (Phase 4) for third- and fourth-grade children. Data from Bjorklund, Schneider, Cassel, & Ashley, 1994.

ticed child in terms of cognitive efficiency is not yet realized for the novice. This is because too much of a child's limited mental resources are used in executing the strategy, leaving too few resources to allocate to actual task performance (see Kee, 1994). With practice, aspects of the strategy become more automated and performance improves.

My interest in memory development shifted away from the role of knowledge on memory performance and utilization deficiencies to issues of children's eyewitness memory and suggestibility (see Bjorklund, Brown, & Bjorklund, in press, for a review of this work) and to children's use of multiple and variable strategies (e.g., Bjorklund & Roseblum, 2001, in press; Coyle & Bjorklund, 1997; Hock, Park, & Bjorklund, 1998). My involvement with the former issue reflected a change in emphasis in the field of memory development away from deliberate, strategic memorizing toward more "natural" event memory; it also reflected cognitive developmental science addressing a critical social issue relating to the increasing numbers of children testifying in legal matters, either as victims or witnesses of crimes (see Bjorklund, 2000). The latter issue of children's multiple and variable strategy use acknowledged the substantial intraindividual variability in children's cognitive performance following a model based on Darwin's idea of natural selection. Basically, children are proposed to have many strategies available to them to solve a set of problems that compete with one another for use (see Siegler, 1996). These topics continue to hold my interest, and the selectionist account I was advocating for strategy development was consistent with other interests that I had been developing over the years. It is to these interests that I now turn.

☐ The Role of Inhibition Mechanisms in Memory Development and a Segue to Evolutionary Psychology

My preferred interpretation of the effects of knowledge on strategy development revolved around the concept of limited resources. Children's strategic memory (and other aspects of their cognition) was limited by the availability of mental resources (often expressed in terms of mental space, mental effort, or processing time). With increasing age and experience, children have available to them greater resources, making strategy use more likely and more effective. When children had detailed knowledge for a domain, they could process that information more efficiently, reducing the processing demands and increasing their level of performance (Bjorklund, 1985, 1987a; Bjorklund et al., 1990).

In 1990, Valerie Reyna, Charles Brainerd, and I edited a special edition of *Developmental Review* dealing with "limited resource models of cognitive development." In preparing an article for this issue, Charles Brainerd alerted me to a recent paper by Lynn Hasher and Rose Zacks (1988) that dealt with the role of inhibition in older adults' cognition. Katherine Harnishfeger (now Katherine Kipp) and I extended Hasher and Zack's ideas and developed a model that proposed that, with age, children are increasingly able to keep irrelevant information out of working memory, and as a result have greater functional capacity (Bjorklund & Harnishfeger, 1990; Harnishfeger & Bjorklund, 1993, 1994). Subsequent research from a variety of labs has generally supported our interpretation of young children's inefficient inhibition (e.g., Kipp & Pope, 1997; Lorsbach, Katz, & Cupak, 1998), but I raise the issue here not so much to illustrate how my thinking and research changed with respect to memory development, but how I inadvertently became involved in evolutionary psychology.

I had been reading popular and not-so-popular works dealing with evolution for some time, and, as a developmentalist, I believed that there is surely some important connection between ontogeny and phylogeny. Some of my readings led me to primate research (e.g., Byrne & Whiten, 1988) and the observation of deception in monkeys and apes. Deception involves inhibition (e.g., not looking at the source of hidden food when a dominant animal is around and liable to take it for himself). We proposed that the ability to inhibit prepotent social and sexual responses was critical for the effective running of a hominid social group, and that this ability was later co-opted for other, more cognitive tasks, including reasoning, theory of mind, and possibly language (Bjorklund & Harnishfeger, 1995; Bjorklund & Kipp, 2002). We also speculated that ancient women were more likely to develop heightened inhibition skills than ancient men. We based our hypothesis on parental investment theory (Bjorklund & Shackelford, 1999; Trivers, 1972), which proposes that, because of the potential consequence of any act of copulation, women need to be more cautious in choosing a sex partner than men, and thus may have developed better inhibitory skills in the social arena. Greater inhibitory skills would also be beneficial for dealing with the demands presented by infants and young children, responsibilities traditionally handled by women. Thus, we reasoned, women may have evolved greater inhibitory skills than men, at least in some domains. We provided preliminary confirmation of our hypothesis in a review of the literature, illustrating greater female inhibitory abilities in the behavioral, social, and sexual domains, but not on cognitive tasks (Bjorklund & Kipp, 1996). As a result of my theorizing about evolutionary issues, I began to view development differently and realized that an evolutionary perspective on development might have great benefit for the field.

☐ The Making of An Evolutionary Developmental Psychologist

My entry into evolutionary psychology was not as abrupt as it might appear from the story I've told so far. As I mentioned earlier in this chapter, my graduate training in developmental psychology extended beyond cognitive development and left me thinking much like a developmental psychobiologist. Although the lessons I learned from Gilbert Gottlieb, Robert Cairns, and Harriet Rheingold, and the intellectual atmosphere emphasizing the developmental systems perspective that surrounded me during my graduate school days at Chapel Hill, did not noticeably affect my empirical research, it did affect my thinking. My lectures in both my undergraduate and graduate classes at Florida Atlantic University reflected these views, which held implicitly the fact that complicated developmental adaptations were the product of natural selection.

Neonatal Imitation as an Ontogenetic Adaptation

I first put some of this training to good use while working on the first edition of my textbook *Children's Thinking* (1989). In reviewing research on infant cognition, I became fascinated with the topic of neonatal imitation, a phenomenon that Andrew Meltzoff and M. Keith Moore had first clearly demonstrated in 1977. The phenomenon seemed real, even though not all researchers observed it (e.g., McKenzie & Over, 1983), but several alternative interpretations existed. Most researchers rejected the possibility that infants were learning, via operant or classical conditioning, to match the gestures of the model. Meltzoff and Moore's (1977) preferred interpretation held that neonatal imitation reflected true selective imitation, guided by the integration of information from one sensory modality (vision) with information from another (proprioception derived from self-initiated movements). A third alternative was that the matching behaviors were a form of an innate-releasing mechanism. Support for this latter interpretation was provided by evidence that imitation decreases to chance levels by two months of age (e.g., Fontaine, 1984) and by the demonstration that a variety of stimuli will elicit the target behaviors (e.g., tongue protrusion) (e.g., Jacobson, 1979).

If neonatal imitation is a form of innate-releasing mechanism, what sort of function might it have? Thinking of the functional value of this early behavior brought to mind R. W. Oppenheim's (1981) description of *transient ontogenetic adaptations*, characteristics of young organisms that serve to adapt them to the environment they currently find themselves inhabiting and not to one they will inhabit as an adult. I proposed that neonatal imitation was an ontogenetic adaptation, with its primary function being to facilitate infant-mother social interaction at a time when infants cannot easily control their own behavior (Bjorklund, 1987b). Tentative support for this position was later provided by a study in which a significant relationship between imitation in newborns and later mother-infant social interactions at three months of age was reported; infants who showed high levels of neonatal imitation had more social interactions with their mothers three months later (Heimann, 1989).

The Adaptive Value of Developmental Immaturity

The idea that some aspects of infancy might be adaptive only to that time in development should not be surprising, but it raised the issue that perhaps some aspects of early development that we consider to be immature are actually adaptations. I began to think seriously about this issue when a graduate student of mine, Brandi Green, insisted that I should read some of the papers she was reading in her graduate seminar in developmental psychobiology taught by Ingrid Johanson. Among the papers she thought I'd be particularly interested in was one by Gerald Turkewitz and Patricia Kenny (1982), who proposed that some of the sensory and motor limitations of infants may have an adaptive function, protecting their developing brain, for example, from overstimulation. Might there be some immature aspects of older children's cognitions that play an adaptive function and are not simply examples of "poor thinking" that they need to out grow?

One possibility of immature cognition that may have some adaptive value, we believed, concerned young children's tendency to overestimate their abilities. Perhaps by overestimating their competence, young children attempt more activities and persist in the face of what a more metacognitively competent child would perceive as failure.

In a series of studies, we examined preschool children's knowledge of their own imitative abilities, or *meta-imitation* (Bjorklund, Gaultney, & Green, 1993). When asked to evaluate their own imitative skills, preschoolers overestimated how well they thought they would be able to imitate a task (prediction) on 56.9 percent of all attempts. Underestimation was infrequent (5.1 percent). Children were a bit better at evaluating their own behavior following an attempt at imitating a model (postdiction), but still overestimated on 39.6 percent of the attempts. Again, underestimations were rare (2.5 percent). Younger preschoolers (mean age = 3 years, 7 months) were somewhat more likely to overestimate their imitative abilities than older preschoolers (mean age = 5 years, 2 months).

In a follow-up study, we related the meta-imitation accuracy of 3-, 4-, and 5-year-old children to a verbal IQ measure. We hypothesized that, for the oldest group, brighter children should have better meta-imitative accuracy, a pattern that is typically found between cognition and metacognition in older children (e.g., Schneider, Körkel, & Weinert, 1987). This relation may be reversed, however, for the younger preschoolers, for whom being out of touch with their generally poor imitation abilities may be a blessing. The pattern of correlations between children's accuracy of their imitative abilities and verbal IQ scores is presented in Figure 9.4. (Because almost all children overestimated their abilities, lower scores represent less overestimation, and thus greater accuracy, and higher scores represent more overestimation, and thus greater inaccuracy.) Five-year-old children who were more accurate in predicting and postdicting their imitative abilities (i.e., who overestimated less) had higher IQs than did less accurate children. In contrast, 3-, and especially 4-year-old children with higher IQs were those who most overestimated their imitative abilities. We interpreted these findings as reflecting a benefit of poor meta-imitation for young children. Young children's immature metacognitive

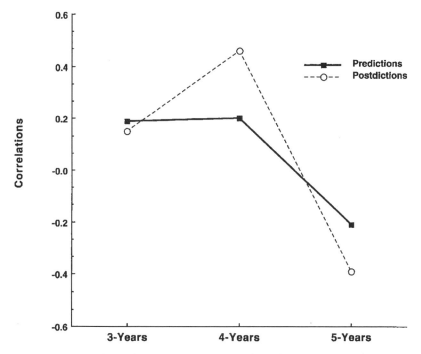

FIGURE 9.4. Correlation between IQ scores and prediction and postdiction scores for 3-, 4-, and 5-year old children. (Note that negative correlations imply that children with higher IQs overestimated less, i.e., were more accurate, than did children with lower IQs). Figure from Bjorklund, 1997a; data from Bjorklund, Gaultney, & Green, 1993.

knowledge permits them to imitate a broad range of behaviors without the knowledge that their attempts are inadequate. As a result, bright young children continue to experiment with new behaviors and practice old ones, improving their skills at a time when trial-and-error learning is so important. As children's motor skills improve, so do their metacognitive abilities, which later in development are associated with more advanced cognition.

We thought that the adaptive value of immature meta-imitation for young children may not be an isolated phenomenon. Following the lead of Turkewitz and Kenny (1982), we proposed that certain aspects of immature cognition may have adaptive value for children at that time in development and are not only limitations that must be overcome (Bjorklund & Green, 1992). For example, young children's egocentricity may bias them to relate information to themselves, resulting in enhanced learning (e.g., Mood, 1979; Foley & Ratner, 1998), and their poor metamemory abilities may result in children persisting to use memory strategies that are not currently effective (utilization deficiencies) but will be with practice (e.g., Bjorklund, 1997a). Even language acquisition may benefit from immature cognition. For example, both Newport (1991) and Elman (1994) proposed that young children's limited working-memory capacity constrains the amount of information they can process at a single time, but the result is a simplified corpus that makes easier the task of discovering the rules of language. This reduced capacity is accompanied by the simplified language adults speak to infants and young children, further reducing the information-processing demands and enhancing the process of language acquisition (e.g., Bjorklund & Schwartz, 1996).

I extended my ideas about the adaptive value of immaturity beyond cognitive development to human development in general (Bjorklund, 1997a). Most contemporary child developmental psychologists, understandably, view early accomplishments as preparations for later development. I argued, however, that some aspects of infancy and childhood are not specific preparations for adulthood but are designed by evolution to adapt the child to its present environment and not necessarily to a future one. For example, retardation of development (neoteny) has played a role in the evolution of *Homo sapiens*, prolonging childhood and extending to postnatal life the rapid brain growth characteristic of prenatal mammals, among other things (see, e.g., Gould, 1977). I applied the concept of ontogenetic adaptations (Oppenheim, 1981) to various aspects of behavioral and cognitive development (e.g., play, early perceptual experience, early learning), and argued that developmental theorists should ask what function a characteristic may play in the life of a child at that particular time in development, rather than always looking for how it may serve as a preparation for later development. This is a perspective taken by contemporary developmental psychobiologists, whose subjects are mainly infrahuman mammals and birds (e.g., Oppenheim, 1981; Spear, 1984; Turkewitz & Kenny, 1982), but one that is rarely considered by developmental psychologists whose main focus is children.

I found a like-minded colleague during a sabbatical stay at the University of Georgia in Anthony Pellegrini. (Our initial contacts were at adjoining lockers in the university gym, with Tony being an avid swimmer and I a persistent basketball player.) Tony was interested in the role of recess in education, believing that it benefited children's development, and he was lamenting the disappearance of recess from American children's school days. He saw my arguments for the adaptive value of immaturity as a theoretical (or metatheoretical) justification for the positive effects of recess he believed existed, and we wrote two papers on the topic (Pellegrini & Bjorklund, 1996, 1997). But perhaps more important than these two papers, Tony and I shared an interest in the broader application of evolutionary psychology to human development, with his expertise and interests being more in social development and ethology and mine in cognitive development and developmental psychobiology. Over the next several years, we developed our ideas.

Evolutionary Developmental Psychology

My theorizing about the adaptive value of developmental immaturity was explicitly couched in Darwinian principles. By the early 1990s, I was convinced that the field of cognitive development could benefit from an evolutionary perspective, and presented a paper stating this at the 1991 meeting of the Society for Research in Child Development ("In search of a metatheory for cognitive development {or Piaget is dead and I don't feel so good myself}," later published as an essay in *Child Development*, 1997b). I was reading much about the new field of evolutionary psychology (e.g., Barkow, Cosmides, & Tooby, 1992; Buss, 1995), which I found intriguing, but which I thought failed to treat ontogenetic development seriously in its theorizing. There was much that had been written about developmental issues from an evolutionary psychological perspective (e.g., Belsky, Steinberg, & Draper, 1991; Fernald, 1992), but I found no overarching developmental perspective in the new evolutionary psychology. David Geary's (1995) ideas about biologically primary abilities (those selected over the course in evolution, such as language) and biologically secondary abilities (those built upon primary abilities and nurtured by culture, such as reading), and the origin of many human sex differences (Geary, 1996, 1998), dealt explicitly with broader developmental issues, and caused me to think more deeply about development within the field of evolutionary psychology.

Thinking leads to writing,* and Tony Pellegrini and I wrote, but never published, a paper dealing with the application of evolutionary theory to contemporary education. I was invited to present the Psy Chi Keynote Address at the 1997 meeting of the Southwestern Psychological Association and chose as my topic "An evolutionary perspective on human development." With my graduate student Rhonda Douglas Brown, I argued for the application of evolutionary theory to contemporary education in a commentary to a paper written by James Byrnes and Nathan Fox (1998) on the application of developmental cognitive neuroscience to education (Brown & Bjorklund, 1998). Then, in late 1998, after completing the writing for the third edition of my textbook *Children's Thinking*, I decided it was time to organize my thoughts about evolution and development. With colleagues, I published two articles describing the new field of evolution-

---

*I identify with Jerome Bruner's (1990) statement to the effect "I write to see what I think."

ary developmental psychology (Bjorklund & Pellegrini, 2000; Geary & Bjorklund, 2000), and in 2002 Tony Pellegrini and I completed the first book-length treatment of the topic (*The Origins of Human Nature: Evolutionary Developmental Psychology*). In the interim, colleagues and I wrote articles applying evolutionary psychology to social development (Bjorklund & Pellegrini, 2002), parenting (Bjorklund & Yunger, 2001; Bjorklund, Yunger, & Pelligrini, 2002), schooling (Bjorklund & Bering, in press), and play (Pellegrini & Bjorklund, in press), all in an effort to bring evolutionary thinking to mainstream developmental psychology. Below, I outline briefly what I see as the basic premises of this emerging field.

1. There is need for an extended childhood to learn the complexities of human social communities. *Homo sapiens* have a life history in which they spend a disproportionate amount of time as prereproductives. From an evolutionary perspective, the benefits associated with an extended period of immaturity must have outweighed the costs. Those benefits can be seen in mastering the complexities of a human social community. The increasing social complexity of hominid groups required a greater awareness of ourselves and the needs and motivations of others so that we could better understand, and perhaps manipulate, others. This required not only a large brain, but also a long time to accomplishment. It was the confluence of a large brain, social complexity, and an extended juvenile period that set the stage for the modern human mind.

2. Evolutionary developmental psychology involves the expression of evolved, epigenetic programs, as described by the developmental systems approach (e.g., Gottlieb, 1991, 1998; Gottlieb, Wahlsten, & Lickliter, 1998), from conception through old age. New structures do not arise fully formed, but are the result of the bidirectional relationship between all levels of biological and experiential factors, from the genetic through the cultural. "Experience," from this perspective, involves not only events exogenous to the individual but also self-produced activity, such as the firing of a nerve cell. Functioning at one level influences functioning at adjacent levels, with constant feedback between levels. Evolved psychological mechanisms can be thought of as genetically coded "messages" that, following epigenetic rules, interact with the environment over time to produce behavior. Because the experiences of each individual are unique, this suggests that there should be substantial plasticity in development and seems at odds with evolutionary psychology's contention for universal, "innate" features (as in the claims of neonativists such as Pinker [1994]). In fact, there is much that is universal about the form and function of members of a species, despite this plasticity. The reason for this is that individuals inherit not only a species-typical genome, but also a species-typical environment, beginning with the prenatal environment. To

the extent that individuals grow up in environments similar to those of their ancestors, development should follow a species-typical pattern. From the developmental systems perspective, there are no simple cases of either genetic or environmental determinism. Infants are not born as blank slates; evolution has prepared them to "expect" certain types of environments and to process some information more readily than others. Yet it is the constant and bidirectional interaction between various levels of organization, which changes over the course of development, that produces behavior. For example, differences in the quality and quantity of parental investment affect children's development and influence their subsequent reproductive and childcare strategies (e.g., Belsky et al., 1991; Surbey, 1998).

3. There have been different selection pressures on organisms at different times in ontogeny, and some characteristics of infants and children were selected in evolution to serve an adaptive function at that time in development and not to prepare them for later adulthood.

4. Most, but not all, evolved psychological mechanisms are proposed to be domain-specific in nature, such as those involved with language acquisition (see, e.g., Pinker, 1994) and theory of mind (see e.g., Baron-Cohen, 1995).

5. Although many adaptive characteristics of infancy and childhood are selected for that time in development only and are not preparations for later life, other aspects of childhood *do* serve to prepare the way for adulthood and were also selected over the course of evolution. Many sex differences in social and cognitive abilities are good examples (see, e.g., Geary, 1998).

6. Because evolved mechanisms were adaptive to ancestral environments, they are not always adaptive for contemporary people, and this is seen in children's maladjustment to some aspects of formal schooling (e.g., Bjorklund & Bering, in press; Geary, 1995; Pellegrini & Bjorklund, 1996).

Our argument is that an evolutionary perspective can be valuable for developing a better understanding of human ontogeny, and also that a developmental perspective is important for a better understanding of evolutionary psychology.

Deferred Imitation in Enculturated Juvenile Great Apes

Before completing this section on my still-emerging life as an evolutionary developmental psychologist, I believe it is worth mentioning a new line of empirical research I have pursued, consistent with my "official" new view of development. Much can be learned about human development, I believe, by studying other species, and for my primary area of interest, human cognitive development, our phylogenetically close cousins, the great apes, are the most appropriate, but rarely available, species of choice. In the fall of 1996, Jesse Bering, an undergraduate student in the Anthropology Department at Florida Atlantic University, made me an offer I could not refuse. He was a volunteer at the Orangutan and Chimpanzee Conservation Center, temporarily housed at Parrot Jungle in Miami. Jesse told me that the director, Patricia Ragan, would be receptive to a small research project with the six apes housed at the Center, and asked if I would be interested in developing a project with him. Having no experience working with great apes, I immediately said yes.

The apes, three chimpanzees (*Pan troglodytes*) and three orangutans (*Pongo pygmaeus*), all juveniles, were special in that each had been reared by humans, much as human children are, from shortly after birth. There is a debate in the primatology literature about the role of *enculturation* in the cognitive development of great apes (e.g., Call & Tomasello, 1996; Tomasello, 1994). Enculturated (i.e., human-reared) apes (mainly chimpanzees) are proposed to develop more humanlike cognitive functions than mother-reared apes. Despite the lack of formal laboratory facilities, I believed that we could ask some interesting questions about the role of enculturation on the cognitive development of this small group of chimpanzees and orangutans.

In a first study (Bering, Bjorklund, & Ragan, 2000), we modified a procedure developed by Tomasello, Savage-Rumbaugh, and Kruger (1993), who demonstrated greater deferred (delayed) imitation of tool use in human-reared than mother-reared common chimpanzees (*P. troglodytes*) and bonobos (pygmy chimpanzees, *Pan paniscus*) of varying age. (In fact, there is little evidence from controlled experiments that mother-reared chimpanzees display deferred imitation of tool use.) We extended the findings of Tomasello and his colleagues, demonstrating deferred imitation of tool use in juvenile common chimpanzees (most of the subjects in the study by Tomasello et al. were bonobos) and, for the first time, orangutans under controlled situations. We extended these findings in a 2-year longitudinal study of the youngest chimpanzee and orangutan (Bjorklund, Bering, & Ragan, 2000), and in a study that demonstrated that chimpanzees are able to generalize what they learned via imitation to similar, but not identical, sets of objects (Bjorklund, Yunger, Bering, & Ragan, 2002), which, we argued, was some of the strongest evidence to date of "true" deferred imitation of tool use in chimpanzees.

These studies illustrated the acquisition of species-atypical cognitive abilities as a result of a species-atypical rearing environment. Such a demonstration, of course, is nothing new. Z.-Y. Kuo (1967) long ago demonstrated that raising many species of birds and mammals in species-atypical environments can produce species-atypical behavior. What is compelling here is that the species-atypical behavior displayed by the enculturated juvenile great apes is a reflection of symbolic representation, the keystone of human cognition. Although it is speculative, data such as these suggest that early rearing conditions can modify the course of cognitive development in a species-atypical way, possibly leading to changes that, over many generations and constant environmental (i.e., rearing) conditions, can result in changes in what constitutes species-typical behavior (i.e., cognitive evolution) (cf. Gottlieb, 1992).

☐ Concluding Remarks

I have heard it said that a generalist is someone who learns less and less about more and more, whereas a specialist is someone who learns more and more about less and less. Although these are, of course, only caricatures, I believe that my disposition has always been more of that of the generalist, although my intellectual limitations have constrained the topics to which my thoughts have generalized. My generalist leanings have also caused me to look for broad, general explanations for development, or at least for some aspects of development. For example, I believe that age-related differences in knowledge base account for a substantial portion of children's cognition, and that knowledge "works" through the relatively domain-general mechanisms relating to efficiency of processing and working-memory capacity (perhaps via inhibitory mechanisms). My adoption of the developmental systems perspective and evolutionary psychology as models for development reflects, I believe, my attempt to find general metatheories that can explain development, at least at one level of analysis.

However, despite my affinity for general explanatory mechanisms and overarching theories, I have come to realize that development is not that easily explained. In pursuing different topics in developmental psychology as a researcher, textbook author, journal reviewer, and editor, or simply as an interested reader, I have come to realize that there is no single answer to "how does development proceed?" Development has many causes, and different aspects of development show different patterns of change. Some aspects of development are more under the influence of strong biologic/genetic factors, whereas others are more amenable to exogenous environmental influence. Some aspects of ontogeny can be explained by the development of domain-general mechanisms that display substantial stability over time, whereas others are more under the influence of domain-specific mechanisms that may show little cross-age stability. There is much variability in children's abilities at any point in time, both between different children and within a single child, and there are different developmental pathways to the same outcome. But none of these statements should mask the fact that all development proceeds as the result of the dynamical and reciprocal transaction of a child's biological constitution (including genetics) and his or her physical and social environment (including culture), or that children's cognitive and social abilities and development are the product of hundreds of thousands of years of evolution. There are some general truths about development, I believe, and these are worth pursuing so long as one does not forget that one of the truths is that development, particularly human development, is variable both between and within individuals, and across different physical, behavioral, and cognitive systems.

☐ Acknowledgments

I would like to thank Barbara Bjorklund for comments on an earlier draft of this chapter, and would like to express my thanks and appreciation to my teachers, colleagues, and students who have influenced me and collaborated with me over the years.

☐ References

Ackerman, B. P. (1986). Retrieval search for category and thematic information in memory by children and adults. *Journal of Experimental Child Psychology, 42,* 355–377.

Ackerman, B. P. (1987). Descriptions: A model of nonstrategic memory development. In H. W Reese (Ed.), *Advances in child development and behavior* (vol. 20., pp. 143–183). Orlando, FL: Academic Press.

Alexander, J. M., & Schwanenflugel, P. J. (1994). Strategy regulation: The role of intelligence, metacognitive attributes, and knowledge base. *Developmental Psychology, 30,* 709–723.

Barkow, J. H., Cosmides, L., & Tooby, J. (Eds.) (1992). *The adapted mind: Evolutionary psychology and the generation of culture.* New York: Oxford University Press.

Baron-Cohen, S. (1995). *Mindblindness: An essay on autism and theory of mind.* Cambridge, MA: MIT Press.

Bauer, R. H. (1979). Memory, acquisition, and category clustering in learning-disabled children. *Journal of Experimental Child Psychology, 27,* 365–383.

Bering, J. M., Bjorklund, D. F., & Ragan, P. (2000). Deferred imitation of object-related actions in human-reared juvenile chimpanzees and orangutans. *Developmental Psychobiology, 36,* 218–232.

Belsky, J., Steinberg, L., & Draper, P. (1991). Childhood experience, interpersonal development, and reproductive strategy: An evolutionary theory of socialization. *Child Development, 62,* 647–670.

Bjorklund, D. F. (1985). The role of conceptual knowledge in the development of organization in children's memory. In C. J. Brainerd & M. Pressley (Eds.), *Basic processes in memory development: Progress in cognitive development research* (pp. 103–142). New York: Springer-Verlag.

Bjorklund, D. F. (1987a). How age changes in knowledge base contribute to the development of children's memory: An interpretive review. *Developmental Review, 7,* 93–130.

Bjorklund, D. F. (1987b). A note on neonatal imitation. *Developmental Review, 7,* 86–92.

Bjorklund, D. F., (1988). Acquiring a mnemonic: Age and category knowledge effects. *Journal of Experimental Child Psychology, 45,* 71–82.

Bjorklund, D. F. (1989). *Children's thinking: Developmental function and individual differences* (1st edition). Pacific Grove, CA: Brooks/Cole.

Bjorklund, D. F. (1997a). The role of immaturity in human development. *Psychological Bulletin, 122,* 153–169.

Bjorklund, D. F. (1997b). In search of a metatheory for cognitive development (or, Piaget is dead and I don't feel so good myself). *Child Development, 68,* 142–146.

Bjorklund, D. F. (April, 1997c). *An evolutionary perspective on human development.* Psi Chi Keynote Address presented at the Southwestern Psychological Association, Fort Worth, TX.

Bjorklund, D. F. (Ed.) (2000). *False-memory creation in children and adults: Theory, research, and implications.* Mahwah, NJ: Erlbaum.

Bjorklund, D. F., & Bering, J. M. (in press). The evolved child: Applying evolutionary developmental psychology to modern schooling. *Learning and Individual Differences.*

Bjorklund, D. F., Bering, J., & Ragan, P. (2000). A two-year longitudinal study of deferred imitation of object manipulation in a juvenile chimpanzee (*Pan troglodytes*) and orangutan (*Pongo pygmaeus*). *Developmental Psychobiology, 37,* 229–237.

Bjorklund, D. F., & Bernholtz, J. E. (1986). The role of knowledge base in the memory performance of good and poor readers. *Journal of Experimental Child Psychology, 41,* 367–393.

Bjorklund, D. F., & Bjorklund, B. R. (1985). Organization versus item effects of an elaborated knowledge base on children's memory. *Developmental Psychology, 21,* 1120–1131.

Bjorklund, D. F., Brown, R. D., & Bjorklund, B. R. (in press). Children's eyewitness memory: Changing reports and changing representations. To appear in P. Graf & N. Ohta (Eds.), *Lifespan memory development.* Cambridge, MA: MIT Press.

Bjorklund, D. F., & Buchanan, J. J. (1989). Developmental and knowledge base differences in the acquisition and extension of a memory strategy. *Journal of Experimental Child Psychology, 48,* 451–471.

Bjorklund, D. F., & Coyle, T. R. (1995). Utilization deficiencies in the development of memory strategies. In F. E. Weinert & W. Schneider (Eds.), *Memory performance and competencies: Issues in growth and development* (pp. 161–180). Hillsdale, NJ: Erlbaum.

Bjorklund, D. F., Coyle, T. R., & Gaultney, J. F. (1992). Developmental differences in the acquisition of an organizational strategy: Evidence for the utilization deficiency hypothesis. *Journal of Experimental Child Psychology, 54,* 434–448.

Bjorklund, D. F., & de Marchena, M. R. (1984). Developmental shifts in the basis of organization in memory: The role of associative versus categorical relatedness in children's free-recall. *Child Development, 55,* 952–962.

Bjorklund, D. F., Gaultney, J. F., & Green, B. L. (1993). "I watch therefore I can do": The development of meta-imitation over the preschool years and the advantage of optimism in one's imitative skills. In R. Pasnak & M. L. Howe (Eds.), *Emerging themes in cognitive development, Vol. II: Competencies* (pp. 79–102). New York: Springer-Verlag.

Bjorklund, D. F., & Green, B. L. (1992). The adaptive nature of cognitive immaturity. *American Psychologist, 47,* 46–54.

Bjorklund, D. F., & Harnishfeger, K. K. (1990). The resources construct in cognitive development: Diverse sources of evidence and a model of inefficient inhibition. *Developmental Review, 10,* 48–71.

Bjorklund, D. F., & Harnishfeger, K. K. (1987). Developmental differences in the mental effort requirements for the use of an organizational strategy in free recall. *Journal of Experimental Child Psychology, 44,* 109–125.

Bjorklund, D. F., & Harnishfeger, K. K. (1995). The role of inhibition mechanisms in the evolution of human cognition and behavior. In F. N. Dempster & C. J. Brainerd (Eds.), *New perspectives on interference and inhibition in cognition* (pp. 141–173). New York: Academic Press.

Bjorklund, D. F., & Jacobs, J. W. (1984). A developmental examination of ratings of associative strength. *Behavior Research Methods, Instruments & Computers, 16,* 568–569.

Bjorklund, D. F., & Jacobs, J. W. (1985). Associative and categorical processes in children's memory: The role of automaticity in the development of organization in free recall. *Journal of Experimental Child Psychology, 39,* 599–617.

Bjorklund, D. F., & Kipp, K. (1996). Parental investment theory and gender differences in the evolution of inhibition mechanisms. *Psychological Bulletin, 120,* 163–188.

Bjorklund, D. F., & Kipp, K. (2002). Social cognition, inhibition, and theory of mind: The evolution of human intelligence. In R. J. Sternberg & J. C. Kaufman (Eds.), *The evolution of intelligence* (pp. 27–53). Mahwah, NJ: Erlbaum.

Bjorklund, D. F., Miller, P. H., Coyle, T. R., & Slawinski, J. L. (1997). Instructing children to use memory strategies: Evidence of utilization deficiencies in memory training studies. *Developmental Review, 17,* 411–442.

Bjorklund, D. F., Muir-Broaddus, J. E., & Schneider, W. (1990). The role of knowledge in the development of children's strategies. In D. F. Bjorklund (Ed.), *Children's strategies: Contemporary views of cognitive development* (pp. 93–128). Hillsdale, NJ: Erlbaum.

Bjorklund, D. F., Ornstein, P. A., & Haig, J. R. (1977). Developmental differences in organization and recall: Training in the use of organizational techniques. *Developmental Psychology, 13,* 175–183.

Bjorklund, D. F., & Pellegrini, A. P. (2000). Child development and evolutionary psychology. *Child Development, 71,* 1687–1708.

Bjorklund, D. F., & Pellegrini, A. P. (2002). Evolutionary perspectives on social development. In P. K. Smith & C. Hart (Eds.) *Handbook of social development* (pp. 44–59). London: Blackwell.

Bjorklund, D. F., & Pellegrini, A. P. (2002). *The origins of human nature: Evolutionary developmental psychology.* Washington, DC: American Psychological Association.

Bjorklund, D. F., & Rosenblum, K. E. (2001). Children's use of multiple and variable addition strategies in a game context. *Developmental Science, 4,* 183–193.

Bjorklund, D. F., & Rosenblum, K. E. (in press). Context effects in children's selection and use of simple arithmetic strategies. *Journal of Cognition and Development.*

Bjorklund, D. F., & Schneider, W. (1996). The interaction of knowledge, aptitudes, and strategies in children's memory performance. In H. W. Reese (Ed.), *Advances in child development and behavior* (vol. 26, pp. 59–89). San Diego: Academic Press.

Bjorklund, D. F., Schneider, W., Cassel, W. S., & Ashley, E. (1994). Training and extension of a memory strategy: Evidence for utilization deficiencies in the acquisition of an organizational strategy in high- and low-IQ children. *Child Development, 65,* 951–965.

Bjorklund, D. F., & Schwartz, R. (1996). The adaptive nature of developmental immaturity: Implications for language acquisition and language disabilities. In M. Smith & J. Damico (Eds.), *Childhood language disorders* (pp. 17–40). New York: Thieme Medical Publishers.

Bjorklund, D. F., & Shackelford, T. K. (1999). Differences in parental investment contribute to important differences between men and women. *Current Directions in Psychological Science, 8,* 86–89.

Bjorklund, D. F., & Thompson, B. E. (1983). Category typicality effects in children's memory performance: Qualitative and quantitative differences in the processing of category information. *Journal of Experimental Child Psychology, 35,* 329–344.

Bjorklund, D. F., Thompson, B. E., & Ornstein, P. A. (1983). Developmental trends in children's typicality judgments. *Behavior Research Methods and Instrumentation, 15,* 350–356.

Bjorklund, D. F., & Yunger, J. L. (2001). Evolutionary developmental psychology: A useful framework for evaluating the evolution of parenting. *Parenting: Science and Practice, 1,* 63–66.

Bjorklund, D. F., & Yunger, J. L., Bering, J. M., & Ragan, P. (2002). The generalization of deferred imitation in enculturated chimpanzees *(Pan trogledytes). Animal Cognition.*

Bjorklund, D. F., Yunger, J. L., & Pellegrini, A. D. (2002). The evolution of parenting and evolutionary approaches to childrearing. In M. Bornstein (Ed.), *Handbook of parenting* (2nd ed.), *Vol. 1, The biology of parenting* (pp. 3–30). Mahwah, NJ: Erlbaum.

Bjorklund, D. F., & Zeman, B. R. (1982). Children's organization and metamemory awareness in the recall of familiar information. *Child Development, 53,* 799–810.

Bjorklund, D. F., & Zeman, B. R. (1983). The development of organizational strategies in children's recall of familiar information: Using social organization to recall the names of classmates. *International Journal of Behavioral Development, 6,* 341–353.

Brown, A. L. (1978). Knowing when, where, and how to remember: A problem of metacognition. In R. Glasser (Ed.), *Advances in instructional psychology* (pp. 77–165). New York: Halstead Press.

Brown, R. D., & Bjorklund, D. F. (1998). The biologizing of cognition, development, and education: Approach with cautious enthusiasm. *Educational Psychology Review, 10,* 355–373.

Bruner, J. S. (1990). *Acts of meaning.* Cambridge, MA: Harvard University Press.

Buss, D. M. (1995). Evolutionary psychology. *Psychological Inquiry, 6,* 1–30.

Byrne, R., & Whiten, A. (Eds.) (1988). *Machiavellian intelligence: Social expertise and the evolution of intellect in monkeys, apes, and humans.* Oxford: Clarendon Press.

Byrnes, J. P., & Fox, N. A. (1998). The educational relevance of research in cognitive neuroscience. *Educational Psychology Review, 10,* 297–342

Call, J. & Tomasello, M. (1996). The effects of humans on the cognitive development of apes. In A. E. Russon, K. A. Bard, & S. T. Parker (Eds.), *Reaching into thought: The minds of the great apes* (pp. 371–403). New York: Cambridge University Press.

Coyle, T. R., & Bjorklund, D. F. (1996). The development of strategic memory: A modified microgenetic assessment of utilization deficiencies. *Cognitive Development, 11,* 295–314.

Coyle, T. R., & Bjorklund, D. F. (1997). Age differences in, and consequences of, multiple-and variable strategy use on a multitrial sort-recall task. *Developmental Psychology, 33,* 372–380.

Elman, J. (1994). Implicit learning in neural networks: The importance of starting small. In C. Umilta & M. Moscovitch (Eds.), *Attention and performance XV: Conscious and nonconscious information processing* (pp. 861–888). Cambridge, MA: MIT Press.

Fernald, A. (1992). Human maternal vocalizations to infants as biologically relevant signals: An evolutionary perspective. In J. H. Barkow, L. Cosmides, & J. Tooby (Eds.), *The adapted mind: Evolutionary psychology and the generation of culture* (pp. 391–428). New York: Oxford University Press.

Flavell, J. H. (1970). Developmental studies of mediated memory. In H. W. Reese & L. P. Lipsitt (Eds.), *Advances in child development and child behavior* (vol. 5, pp. 181–211). New York: Academic Press.

Flavell, J. H. (1971). First discussant's comments: What is memory development the development of? *Human Development, 14,* 272–278.

Flavell, J. H., & Wellman, H. M. (1977). Metamemory. In R. V. Kail & J.W. Hagen (Eds.),

Perspectives on the development of memory and cognition (pp. 3–33). Hillsdale, NJ: Erlbaum.

Foley, M. A., & Ratner, H. H. (1998). Children's recoding in memory for collaboration: A way of learning from others. *Cognitive Development, 13,* 91–108.

Fontaine, R. (1984). Imitative skill between birth and six months. *Infant Behavior and Development, 7,* 323–333.

Gaultney, J. F., Bjorklund, D. F., & Schneider, W. (1992). The role of children's expertise in a strategic memory task. *Contemporary Educational Psychology, 17,* 244–257.

Geary, D. C. (1995). Reflections of evolution and culture in children's cognition: Implications for mathematical development and instruction. *American Psychologist, 50,* 24–37.

Geary, D. C. (1996). Sexual selection and sex differences in mathematical abilities. *Behavioral and Brain Sciences, 19,* 229–284.

Geary, D. C. (1998). *Male, female: The evolution of human sex differences.* Washington, DC: APA.

Geary, D. C., & Bjorklund, D. F. (2000). Evolutionary developmental psychology. *Child Development, 71,* 57–65

Gottlieb, G. (1991). Experiential canalization of behavioral development: Theory. *Developmental Psychology, 27,* 4–13.

Gottlieb, G. (1992). *Individual development and evolution: The genesis of novel behavior.* New York: Oxford University Press.

Gottlieb, G. (1998). Normally occurring environmental and behavioral influences on gene activity: From central dogma to probabilistic epigenesis. *Psychological Review, 105,* 792–802.

Gottlieb, G., Wahlsten, D., & Lickliter, R. (1998). The significance of biology for human development: A developmental psychobiological systems view. In R. M. Lerner (Ed.), *Theoretical models of human development. The handbook of child psychology* (5th ed., pp. 233–273), Vol. 1 of Gen. Ed. W. Damon. New York: Wiley.

Gould, S. J. (1977). *Ontogeny and phylogeny.* Cambridge, MA: Harvard University Press.

Guttentag, R. E. (1984). The mental effort requirement of cumulative rehearsal: A developmental study. *Journal of Experimental Child Psychology, 37,* 92–106.

Harnishfeger, K. K., & Bjorklund, D. F. (1990). Children's strategies: A brief history. In D. F. Bjorklund (Ed.), *Children's strategies: Contemporary views of cognitive development* (pp. 1–22). Hillsdale, NJ: Erlbaum.

Harnishfeger, K. K., & Bjorklund, D. F. (1993). The ontogeny of inhibition mechanisms: A renewed approach to cognitive development. In M. L. Howe & R. Pasnak (Eds.), *Emerging themes in cognitive development, Vol. I: Foundations* (pp. 28–49). New York: Springer-Verlag.

Harnishfeger, K. K., & Bjorklund, D. F. (1994). The development of inhibition mechanisms and their relation to individual differences in children's cognitions. *Learning and Individual Differences, 6,* 331–355.

Hasher, L., & Zacks, R. T. (1988). Working memory, comprehension, and aging: A review and a new view. In G. H. Bower (Ed.), *The psychology of learning and motivation: Advances in research and theory* (vol. 22, pp. 193–224). San Diego: Academic Press.

Hasselhorn, M. (1995). Beyond production deficiency and utilization inefficiency: Mechanisms of the emergence of strategic categorization in episodic memory tasks. In F. E. Weinert & W. Schneider (Eds.), *Memory performance and competencies: Issues in growth and development* (pp. 141–159). Hillsdale, NJ: Erlbaum.

Heimann, M. (1989). Neonatal imitation gaze aversion and mother-infant interaction. *Infant Behavior and Development, 12,* 495–505.

Hock, H. S., Park, C. L., & Bjorklund, D. F. (1998). Temporal organization in children's strategy formation. *Journal of Experimental Child Psychology, 70,* 187–206.

Jacobson, S. W. (1979). Matching behavior in the young infant. *Child Development, 50,* 425–430.

Kee, D. W. (1994). Developmental differences in associative memory: Strategy use, mental effort, and knowledge-access interactions. In H. W. Reese (Ed.), *Advances in child development and behavior* (vol. 25, pp. 7–32). New York: Academic Press.

Kee, D. W., & Davies, L. (1990). Mental effort and elaboration: Effects of accessibility and instruction. *Journal of Experimental Child Psychology, 49,* 264–274.

Keller, D., & Kellas, G. (1978). Typicality as a dimension of encoding. *Journal of Experimental Psychology: Human Learning and Memory, 4,* 78–85.

Kipp, K., & Pope, S. (1997). The development of cognitive inhibition in stream-of-consciousness and directed speech. *Cognitive Development, 12,* 239–260.

Kreutzer, M. A., Leonard, C., & Flavell, J. H. (1975). An interview study of children's knowledge about memory. *Monographs of the Society for Research in Child Development, 40* (Serial No. 159).

Krupski, A., Gaultney, J. F., Malcolm, G., & Bjorklund, D. F. (1993). Learning disabled and nondisabled children's performance on a serial recall task: The facilitating effect of knowledge. *Learning and Individual Differences, 5,* 199–210.

Kuo, Z.-Y. (1967). *The dynamics of behavior development: An epigenetic view.* New York: Random House.

Liberty, C., & Ornstein, P. A. (1973). Age differences in organization and recall: The effects of training in categorization. *Journal of Experimental Child Psychology, 15,* 169–186.

Lorsbach, T. C., Katz, G. A., & Cupak, A. J. (1998). Developmental differences in the ability to inhibit the initial misinterpretation of garden path passages. *Journal of Experimental Child Psychology, 71,* 275–296.

McKenzie, B., & Over, R. (1983). Young infants fail to imitate facial and manual gestures. *Infant Behavior and Development, 6,* 85–96.

Meltzoff, A. N., & Moore, M. K. (1977). Imitation of facial and manual gestures by human neonates. *Science, 198,* 75–78.

Miller, P. H. (1990). The development of strategies of selective attention. In D. F. Bjorklund (Ed.), *Children's strategies: Contemporary views of cognitive development* (pp. 157–184). Hillsdale, NJ: Erlbaum.

Miller, P. H., & Seier, W. L. (1994). Strategy utilization deficiencies in children: When, where, and why. In H. W. Reese (Ed.), *Advances in child development and behavior* (vol. 25, pp. 107–156). New York: Academic Press.

Mood, D. W. (1979). Sentence comprehension in preschool children: Testing an adaptive egocentrism hypothesis. *Child Development, 50,* 247–250.

Newport, E. L. (1991). Contrasting concepts of the critical period for language. In S. Carey & R. Gelman (Eds.), *Epigenesis of mind: Essays in biology and knowledge* (pp. 111–130). Hillsdale, NJ: Erlbaum.

Oppenheim, R. W. (1981). Ontogenetic adaptations and retrogressive processes in the development of the nervous system and behavior. In K. J. Connolly & H. F. R. Prechtl (Eds.), *Maturation and development: Biological and psychological perspectives* (pp. 73–108). Philadelphia: International Medical Publications.

Pellegrini, A. D., & Bjorklund, D. F. (1996). The place of recess in school: Issues in the role of recess in children's education and development: An introduction to the theme. *Journal of Research in Childhood Education, 11,* 5–13.

Pellegrini, A. D., & Bjorklund, D. F. (1997). The role of recess in children's cognitive performance. *Educational Psychologist, 32,* 35–40.

Pellegrini, A. D., & Bjorklund, D. F. (in press). The ontogeny and phylogeny of children's object and fantasy play. *Human Nature.*

Pinker, S. (1994). *The language instinct: How the mind creates language.* New York: Morrow.

Rabinowitz, M. (1984). The use of categorical organization: Not an all-or-none situation. *Journal of Experimental Child Psychology, 38,* 338–351.

Reyna, V. F., Brainerd, C. J., & Bjorklund, D. F. (Eds.) (1990). Limited resource models of cognitive development [Special issue]. *Developmental Review, 10.*

Rosch, E. (1975). Cognitive representations of semantic categories. *Journal of Experimental Psychology: General, 7,* 192–233.

Schneider, W. (1986). The role of conceptual knowledge and metamemory in the development of organizational processes in memory. *Journal of Experimental Child Psychology, 42,* 218–236.

Schneider, W., & Bjorklund, D. F. (1992). Expertise, aptitude, and strategic remembering. *Child Development, 63,* 461–473.

Schneider, W., Bjorklund, D. F., & Maier-Brückner, W. (1996). The effects of expertise and IQ on children's memory: When knowledge is, and when it is not enough. *International Journal of Behavioral Development, 19,* 773–796.

Schneider, W., Gruber, H., Gold, A., & Opwis, K. (1993). Chess expertise and memory for chess positions in children and adults. *Journal of Experimental Child Psychology, 56,* 328–349.

Schneider, W., Körkel, J., & Weinert, F. E. (1987). The effects of intelligence, self-concept, and attributional style on metamemory and memory behaviour. *International Journal of Behavioral Development, 10,* 281–299.

Schneider, W., Körkel, J., & Weinert, F. E. (1989). Domain-specific knowledge and memory performance: A comparison of high- and low-aptitude children. *Journal of Educational Psychology, 81,* 306–312.

Schneider, W., & Pressley, M. (1989). *Memory development between 2 and 20.* New York: Springer-Verlag.

Siegler, R. S. (1996). *Emerging minds: The process of change in children's thinking.* New York: Oxford University Press.

Spear, N. E. (1984). Ecologically determined dispositions control the ontogeny of learning and memory. In R. Kail & N. E. Spear (Eds.), *Memory development: Comparative perspectives* (pp. 325–358). Hillsdale, NJ: Erlbaum.

Surbey, M. K. (1998). Parent and offspring strategies in the transition at adolescence. *Human Nature, 9,* 67–94.

Tomasello, M. (1994). The question of chimpanzee culture. In R. W. Wrangham, W. C. McGrew, F. B. B. de Waal, & P. G. Heltne (Eds.), *Chimpanzee cultures* (pp. 301–317). Cambridge: Harvard University Press.

Tomasello, M., Savage-Rumbaugh, S., & Kruger, A. C. (1993). Imitative learning of actions and objects by children, chimpanzees, and enculturated chimpanzees. *Child Development, 64,* 1688–1705.

Trivers, R. (1972). Parental investment and sexual selection. In B. Campbell (Ed.), *Sexual selection and the descent of man* (pp. 136–179). New York: Aldine de Gruyter.

Turkewitz, G., & Kenny, P. (1982). Limitations on input as a basis for neural organization and perceptual development: A preliminary theoretical statement. *Developmental Psychobiology, 15,* 357–368.

Worden, P. E. (1983). Memory strategy instruction with the learning disabled. In M. Pressley & J. R. Levin (Eds.), *Cognitive strategy research: Psychological foundations* (pp. 129–153). New York: Springer-Verlag.

CHAPTER

Sandra E. Trehub

The Musical Infant

☐ First Step: Creating the Scientist

The long intellectual journey toward my conception of infants as "musical" began with graduate training (1969–1973) in a program that awarded degrees in theoretical and experimental psychology. The one-size-fits-all program at McGill University required students to select one of two broad domains of investigation—one involving human, the other involving nonhuman participants. The choice (human participants for me) had consequences for office and laboratory assignments but not for course selection. Content courses were considered unnecessary for intelligent adults, who were expected to acquire the requisite knowledge and skills by independent reading, observing, thinking, rethinking, and productive interchange with others. Progress along this path of self-directed learning was assessed periodically by means of comprehensive examinations. And *comprehensive* they were, covering *all* areas of psychology. The lucky students—and I was fortunate to be among them—received no feedback about their performance. The unlucky few received discreet invitations to leave the program.

The thinking behind such a minimally structured program was that students—budding scholars, no doubt—required chunks of unencumbered time in which to read, reflect, and submit their ideas (half-baked or otherwise) to empirical evaluation. The notion of simply extending the research program of others (supervisors, particularly), if not unthinkable, was frowned upon. Instead, students were expected to address novel questions, preferably by novel means. Practicalities such as the availability of suitable equipment were to be ignored. Equipment could be borrowed, if necessary, and technicians would be at our disposal to help set up new laboratories, as required, for innovative research.

Lessons from Donald Hebb

With the exception of statistics and a memorable seminar course, there were no courses to speak of. That memorable seminar, which occurred in our first year of graduate study, was led by Donald Hebb, who is best known for his theoretical account of perceptual learning (Hebb, 1949). Meetings of "Hebb's seminar" consisted of five- or ten-minute student presentations on a variety of topics, with discussion following each presentation. Hebb considered the brevity of talks and strict time limits as critical components of training for a life of scholarship. As he noted, psychologists often encroached upon the time allotted to other presenters at professional meetings. In addition, wordy communications invariably raised the specter of muddled thinking.

My first assignment, of which I have singularly vivid memories, was on "purposive behavior." In the five minutes allotted, I was expected to provide a synthesis and critique of *all* relevant ideas from philosophy, psychology, and other sciences, and from all relevant historical periods. Moreover, the talk was to be delivered in "suitable style," which precluded memorization and anything beyond a few cue cards.

The day of reckoning brought additional sources of anxiety, not the least of which was Hebb's stopwatch. At the conclusion of five or ten minutes, Hebb abruptly terminated the presentation in progress, even if that left the speaker in midsentence. Equally exasperating was his propensity to interrupt student orations (halting the stopwatch, first) to inquire about some fine point of English usage, and to share Fowler's views on the issue. Moreover, presenters who were unusually polished in their style prompted accusations of memorization. Hebb reserved his most intimidating tactics, however, for the question period following each presentation: "Are you *sure* you want to retain that position on *X*?" The typical response was for students to retract the positions painstakingly constructed during the past several weeks. Finally, there were the indecipherable symbols scribbled in Hebb's notebook after each presentation. According to popular lore, Hebb was not evaluating students' performance. Rather, he was estimating their promise as experimental psychologists.

I would not want to suggest that the seminar was a source of unrelenting stress. At times, Hebb regaled us with fascinating tales of his experiences and experiments in virtually every area of psychology (and involving several species). He was surprisingly modest in describing his interactions and collaborations with the major players in psychology (now key figures in the history of psychology, along with Hebb). It was especially comforting to learn that Hebb's notable achievements did not result from a meticulous master plan. Rather, the twists and turns in his career arose as frequently from lack of opportunities as from opportunities. Suspecting that Hebb's goals were loftier than our own, we inquired about the factors underlying his career choice (an especially unusual one in his era). Without hesitation or embarrassment, he indicated that his principal reason for pursuing graduate studies in psychology was failure to secure employment in his first occupational choice—schoolteaching. It was clear that, throughout his career, serendipity played as great a role as did diligence. In his own way, then, Hebb provided subtle or not-so-subtle encouragement for intellectual risk-taking.

Initiating Research with Infants: Speech Perception

Were it not for the cult of autonomy and novelty that reigned at McGill (and the legendary success of a failed schoolteacher), it is unclear whether I would have selected infant speech perception as the focus of my research. No faculty member had worked with infants, nor had any studied speech perception. What seems like a foolhardy decision, in retrospect, seemed perfectly reasonable at the time (to me, at least). Moreover, I was aided and abetted in this enterprise by the methodological revolution that had begun in the 1960s and was still under way.

Indeed, findings obtained with the new methods challenged traditional empiricist portrayals of infants as helpless and perceptually incompetent. For example, Fantz (1963), with his simple but ingenious preferential-looking technique, paved the way for a new era of research in early vision (see Kessen, Haith, & Salapatek, 1970). Similarly, the creative combination of reinforcement with infants' propensity to suck nonnutritively (Siqueland & DeLucia, 1969; for a review, see Jusczyk, 1985) propelled the study of speech perception in infancy (e.g., Eimas, Siqueland, Jusczyk, & Vigorito, 1971). Subsequently, conditioned head turning toward a sound source (Eilers, Wilson, & Moore, 1977; for a review, see Kuhl, 1985) provided further impetus to the study of infant audition. These methodological advances occurred at a time of theoretical flux, which involved increasing receptivity to biological influences on behavior (see Gordon & Slater, 1998).

Buoyed by my enthusiasm for the study of infant speech perception, I consulted with Peter Eimas, an innovator in this domain. Eimas was studying categorical perception (Eimas et al., 1971) with the high-amplitude sucking procedure—a technique that I proposed to use. He graciously demonstrated the procedure while I took copious notes about the requisite equipment and supplies (e.g., polygraph, pressure transducer, blind nipples). On my return, I made the rounds of various laboratories at McGill (especially the well-funded medical science laboratories) and borrowed whatever equipment I needed. Next, I prevailed upon a phonetics technician for assistance in stimulus preparation and an electronics technician to convert the borrowed components into a functional apparatus. The major obstacle, as I saw it, was telephone solicitation of parents who had placed birth announcements in local newspapers. Parents astonished me, however, with their cooperation, as did the researchers and technicians whom I approached.

A typical workday at the time involved calibrating equipment, driving a succession of parents and infants to and from the laboratory, and conducting the test sessions. My schedule was undeniably hectic, but I was prepared to do whatever was necessary (within ethical limits, of course) to attract families with infants. Within a few months, I had a steady stream of infants 3 weeks to 4 months of age, each infant contributing, in one way or another, to the unfolding story of consonant, vowel, and tone perception (Trehub, 1973, 1975, 1976; Trehub & Rabinovitch, 1972). Years later I learned that one of my earliest infant participants was renamed *Sandra* after her visit to the lab. That gesture by the mother—a recent Asian immigrant—was aimed at enhancing the girl's scholarly potential. My namesake ultimately fulfilled her mother's dreams by obtaining a prestigious graduate degree.

Transition to Faculty Status

The laissez-faire spirit at McGill did not lead to survival of the fittest students but of the most independent. Ultimately, independence had its benefits, especially when my status changed from graduate student to faculty member (University of Toronto, 1973). Setting up an infant perception laboratory was relatively easy the second time around (e.g., no begging or borrowing required). One carryover from graduate student days was my commitment to parents—providing them with considerable attention and information in exchange for their contribution to the research enterprise. Thus, a ten-minute test session usually translated to a forty-five-minute visit. Gone forever (and not missed at all) was my dual role as taxi driver and telephone solicitor.

During my early years at the University of Toronto, I continued to study speech perception in infancy (e.g., Trehub, 1979; Trehub & Chang, 1977;

Trehub & Curran, 1979), gradually extending my reach into other domains of auditory development. My interest in basic auditory processes was piqued by the "blank wall" that I faced, at times, when attempting to interpret findings in infant speech perception. The sparse research on early audition stood in sharp contrast to the burgeoning literature on infant vision (see Schneider & Trehub, 1985a, 1985b). Bruce Schneider and I, assisted by graduate and postdoctoral trainees, began to explore hitherto neglected questions about the limits of hearing in infancy and early childhood (e.g., Schneider, Trehub, & Bull, 1980; Trehub, Schneider, & Endman, 1980)—a line of research that has continued over the years (e.g., Schneider, Bull, & Trehub, 1988; Schneider, Trehub, Morrongiello, & Thorpe, 1986; Trehub & Henderson, 1996; Trehub, Schneider, & Henderson, 1995; Trehub, Schneider, Morrongiello, & Thorpe, 1988, 1989). Marianne Fallon, a graduate student with incomparable energy, recently injected new vigor into this program with her research on children's perception of speech in degraded listening environments (e.g., Fallon, Trehub, & Schneider, 2000, in press).

Launching Infant Music Perception

Another talented graduate student, Hsing-Wu Chang, rekindled the adventurous spirit of my graduate student days by suggesting an improbable line of research—infants' perception of musical patterns. From the perspective of what we know now, it was an astute choice, but not when viewed in the context of the 1970s (see Trehub, 1998). Research on infant auditory perception had been restricted primarily to single sounds, whether speech syllables (e.g., Eimas et al., 1971; Morse, 1972; Trehub, 1973; Trehub & Rabinovitch, 1972; Werker, Gilbert, Humphrey, & Tees, 1981) or tones (e.g., Trehub, 1973; Wormith, Pankhurst, & Moffitt, 1975). The assumption was that multisyllabic or multitone patterns would be beyond the processing capabilities of infants. The potentially intriguing part of this endeavor was ascertaining how infants would handle a novel auditory sequence that exceeded their immediate memory span. Would they generate an incomplete yet veridical representation of the pattern (e.g., the initial few pitches)? Alternatively, would they generate a summary representation, or gloss, of the entire pattern (e.g., its pitch contour), omitting specific details—the typical adult strategy in comparable circumstances? Or would they simply tune out when presented with such complex material?

Undeterred by the prospect of considerable effort (including a new procedure—habituation-dishabituation of heart rate deceleration) for uncertain gain, we forged ahead. The high-risk venture yielded ample compensation (Chang & Trehub, 1977a, 1977b), most especially the encouragement it provided for long-term study in this domain. Since that time, other gifted graduate students (Leigh Thorpe, Laurel Trainor, Glenn Schellenberg, Tonya Bergeson, Tali Shenfield), postdoctoral scholars (Annabel Cohen, Barbara Morrongiello, Anna Unyk, David Hill, Takayuki Nakata), and research assistants (Marilyn Barras, Donna Laxdal, Stuart Kamenetsky) have made significant contributions to this research thrust. In the following pages, I present details of infants' remarkable precocity in the perception of musical patterns.

☐ Infants' Precocity in Music Perception

An appreciation of infants' ability to perceive musical features is not possible without a cursory understanding of adult abilities in this domain. After hearing a brief, novel melody, adults forget numerous details such as the exact pitch level (e.g., whether the melody began on middle C or some other pitch), the exact tempo (i.e., how fast or slow), and the exact tune (e.g., whether it ended with *mi-do* or *re-do*) (Bartlett & Dowling, 1980; Dowling, 1994). What they remember, instead, is global information about pitch contour (i.e., whether successive pitches rise, fall, or stay the same) and timing (e.g., the location of major accents). As a result, they confuse distortions of the tune with the original version, provided the contour remains unchanged. Such confusion is especially likely when the comparison pattern is presented at a different pitch level from the original (i.e., transposed).

For familiar melodies (e.g., "The Star-Spangled Banner"), adults recognize and can often reproduce the tune (i.e., the relations between pitches) and rhythm (i.e., relative note durations, pattern of accents). Nevertheless, they generally forget the exact pitch level (Attneave & Olson, 1971) and tempo (Gabrielsson, 1993). In other words, they retain the essence of a familiar melody, which transcends specific pitches and durations. Adults perform at intermediate levels of proficiency with unfamiliar melodies that follow culture-specific conventions (Cuddy, Cohen, & Mewhort, 1981; Schellenberg & Trehub, 1999). These skills are usually attributed to long-term exposure to music, whether that exposure is formal (e.g., music lessons) or incidental (Bharucha, 1987; Krumhansl, 1990). Nevertheless, mounting evidence about infants' perception of musical patterns suggests otherwise (for reviews, see Trehub, 2000, 2001; Trehub, Schellenberg, & Hill, 1997).

In general, music perception skills in infancy are assessed by having infants listen to a repeating pattern (i.e., the standard pattern) presented from a laterally displaced loudspeaker. Infants are rewarded for turning to the loudspeaker if they do so within 3–4 seconds of the target change. Turns at other times have no consequences. Thus, more frequent turns following a changed pattern rather than an unchanged pattern indicate that infants can detect the target change (see Trehub, Thorpe, & Morrongiello, 1987). Moreover, detection of the change implies that infants have encoded the relevant feature of the standard pattern. Otherwise, they would be unable to notice changes in that feature. When the standard and comparison patterns are presented at the same pitch level (e.g., Trehub, Bull, & Thorpe, 1984), infants can use absolute cues (e.g., change in one or more specific pitches or durations) to solve the discrimination task. When the standard and comparison patterns are presented at different pitch levels, as in typical adult studies, infants must use relational cues to solve this more challenging task. The latter version of the task has been used in much of the infant research to be reported.

Contour and Rhythm

Like adults, infants perceive the invariance of melodies across transpositions, or pitch levels (Chang & Trehub, 1977a; Trehub et al., 1987). They are particularly adept at detecting changes in pitch contour whether the comparison pattern is presented at the same pitch level as the original pattern (Trehub et al., 1984; Trehub, Thorpe, & Morrongiello, 1985) or at different pitch levels (Trehub et al., 1987). Similarly, infants perceive the invariance of rhythm across changes in tempo (Trehub & Thorpe, 1989). They also perceive the invariance of timbre (i.e., tone quality) across changes in pitch, loudness, and duration (Trehub, Endman, & Thorpe, 1990). In other words, they engage in relational processing, which is essential for the perception and appreciation of music.

Nevertheless, the aforementioned skills are relevant to speech as well as musical contexts. For example, differential responses to ID and AD speech (Cooper & Aslin, 1990, 1994; Fernald, 1985; Fernald & Kuhl, 1987; Pegg, Werker, & McLeod, 1992; Werker, Pegg, & McLeod, 1994) and to ID messages of approval and disapproval (Fernald, 1993; Papousek, Bornstein, Nuzzo, Papousek, & Symmes, 1990) depend, among other things, on infants' ability to detect differences in contour, pitch level, tempo, rhythm, and timbre. Contour, tempo, and rhythm also distinguish caregivers' playful speech from her soothing speech (Fernald, 1989, 1991; Trehub, Trainor, & Unyk, 1993). Moreover, very young infants distinguish their mother's vocal timbre from that of a stranger (DeCasper & Fifer, 1980; Mehler, Bertoncini, Barrière, & Jassik-Gerschenfeld, 1978) and their native language-to-be from a language with contrasting rhythm (Mehler et al., 1988; Nazzi, Jusczyk, & Johnson, 2000).

Intervals

What is more surprising is the ever-increasing list of infant skills that are music-specific. In some circumstances, infants detect relative pitch, or interval, changes in the absence of contour cues (e.g., Cohen, Thorpe, & Trehub, 1987; Trainor & Trehub, 1992, 1993a, 1993b; Trehub, Thorpe, & Trainor, 1990), as would be necessary for distinguishing patterns such as *do-so-fa-mi-do* from *do-so-fa-re-do* presented at different pitch levels. What has become clear is that infants, children, and adults perform substantially better on such within-contour discriminations when the component tones of the standard tone sequence are related by small-integer frequency ratios (e.g., 3:2 and 4:3) rather than large-integer ratios (Schellenberg & Trehub, 1994, 1996a, 1996b).

Tones an octave (12 semitones) apart exemplify a 2:1 ratio; tones 7 semitones apart (*perfect fifth* interval) exemplify a 3:2 ratio; and tones 5 semitones apart (*perfect fourth* interval) exemplify a 4:3 ratio. By contrast, the interval defined by 6 semitones, the tritone, exemplifies the ratio of 45:32. Intervals with small-integer frequency ratios play a prominent role in Western music. They also figure prominently in music across cultures (Meyer, 1956; Sachs, 1943; Trehub, Schellenberg, & Hill, 1997). Moreover, there are numerous historical references to these intervals (octaves, perfects fifths, and perfect fourths) as *perfect consonances* (the origin of *perfect* in their labels), indicating their particularly pleasant sound (see Bower, 1980; Dostrovsky, 1980; Hill, 1986). By contrast, the interval known as the tritone (45:32 ratio) has had a rather different history, including its designation, in medieval times, as *diabolus in musica* (Piston, 1969, p. 27) or "the devil in music" (Kennedy, 1994, p. 901).

Infants' aesthetic preferences reveal further adult-infant parallels. For example, infants respond with greater attention and more positive affect to musical pieces dominated by consonant intervals than to those with many dissonant intervals (Trainor & Heinmiller, 1998; Zentner & Kagan, 1996, 1998). It is unlikely that this preference for consonance arises from infants' experience, despite the richness of their musical environment. Newborns whose parents are deaf sign-language users show comparable preferences for consonant over dissonant music (Masataka, personal communication, 1999). Overall, these findings are consistent with the view that some intervals are *natural* or inherently easy to perceive, which runs counter to prevailing views about the arbitrariness of musical intervals (Burns, 1999).

Scales

In contrast to intervals, which specify the relations between two tones, scales indicate the intermediate pitches between the two tones that bound an octave. One similarity (among many differences) in scales across cultures is variation in step size (Sloboda, 1985). For example, the Western major scale has two-semitone steps, as in *do-re*, and one-semitone steps, as in *ti-do*. This unequal-step feature of scales is presumed to be perceptually advantageous for adult listeners (e.g., Butler, 1989; Shepard, 1982). If this advantage has an inherent basis, it should be evident in infancy.

We presented 9-month-old infants and adults with three types of ascending-descending scales: (1) the major scale, an unequal-step scale that would be highly familiar to adults; (2) an artificial, unequal step scale that was obviously unfamiliar; and (3) an artificial equal-step scale (Trehub, Schellenberg, & Kamenetsky, 1999). Listeners' task was to detect mistunings (i.e., changes less than a semitone) in the context of each scale type. Infants performed significantly more poorly on the equal-step scale than on the two unequal-step scales (major and artificial), which did not differ from one another. Comparable accuracy on the major scale and the artificial, unequal-step scale rules out familiarity as a factor in infants' performance. By contrast, familiarity played a critical role in adults' detection of mistunings. Specifically, adults performed substantially better on the major scale than on the two unfamiliar scales (unequal- and equal-step), which did not differ from one another. Presumably, adults' knowledge of the major scale interfered with their processing of the other scales, just as their knowledge of native-language phonology can interfere with their perception of nonnative sounds (Best, 1994; Polka, 1995). In any case, infants' performance offers support for the view that unequal-step scales facilitate perceptual processing.

Culture-Specific and Culture-General Factors

We also documented the relative contribution of culture-general and culture-specific factors to melody discrimination in 9-month-old infants, 5-year-old children, and musically trained adults (Schellenberg & Trehub, 1999). One focus of interest was on pattern simplicity, or the number of repeated tones—a culture-general factor. In general, one would expect pattern simplicity to enhance performance. With increasing exposure to music, however, culture-specific conventions might dominate perceptual processing, attenuating the advantages of pattern simplicity. The culture-specific factor involved melodies based on the highly conventional major chord (*do-me-sol*) or on the less conventional diminished chord (*ti-re-fa*).

As expected, infants performed better on melodies with more repeated tones, an effect that was unrelated to pattern conventionality. Although 5-year-olds showed comparable effects of pattern simplicity, these effects were greater in conventional than in unconventional contexts. Finally, pattern simplicity influenced adults' performance only in the context of conventional melodies. In short, increasing age and musical exposure result in progressively greater culture-specific contributions and corresponding reductions in culture-general contributions.

Summing Up: Infant Music Perception

Collectively, studies of music perception in infancy reveal numerous biases or predispositions for the processing of music or musiclike input. These include a focus on global features such as contour (Trehub et al., 1984, 1987) and rhythm (Trehub & Thorpe, 1989), enhanced processing of intervals with small-integer frequency ratios (Schellenberg & Trehub, 1996b) and of melodies that include such intervals (Cohen et al., 1987; Trainor & Trehub, 1993a, 1993b; Trehub et al., 1990), and enhanced processing of unequal-step scales (Trehub et al., 1999). These striking similarities in music processing on the part of infants with limited exposure to music and adults with long-term exposure point in one direction—to biological contributions.

There is little indication that exposure to music or speech contributes to these biases in particular. In fact, there is evidence to the contrary, specifically, that exposure may reduce the impact of the initial biases, as was the case for unequal-step scales (Trehub et al., 1999) and pattern simplicity (e.g., Schellenberg & Trehub, 1999; Trainor & Trehub, 1994). In some instances, greater implicit knowledge of music leads adults to perform more poorly than naive infants (e.g., Trainor & Trehub, 1992), much like adults' poor performance (and infants' good performance) on some foreign speech sounds (e.g., Werker & Tees, 1984). Although developmental changes in the processing of musical structure have been documented (e.g., Andrews & Dowling, 1991; Krumhansl & Keil, 1982; Lynch & Eilers, 1991; Morrongiello & Roes, 1990; Schellenberg & Trehub, 1999; Trainor & Trehub, 1994), these changes unfold over years rather than months.

☐ Infants' Musical World

Infants' unexpected precocity in music processing raised questions about the utility of such skills in early life. For example, to what extent do infants encounter music in their environment? Intensely curious about this issue, Anna Unyk and I scoured anthropological and ethnomusicological reports for evidence of music in the lives of infants. The search proved to be more difficult than anticipated. The greatest barrier was the all-too-common devaluation of women's activities, which meant that informants in many cultures saw no need to share "inferior" examples of music (e.g., lullabies) with visiting scholars (usually men). Instead, they showed the "best" or most highly valued examples, which included war songs, work songs, epic songs, and other material typically performed by men. Only when women began to traverse the same scholarly route did musical material emerge from the context of maternal interactions with infants (e.g., Koskoff, 1987; Sakata, 1987).

In view of psychologists' keen interest in vocal interactions between mothers and infants (e.g., Fernald, 1991; Papoušek, 1992), it is difficult to understand why something as ubiquitous as maternal singing had escaped their attention. Accordingly, I asked Anne Fernald whether she had encountered maternal singing while collecting her maternal speech samples. She elaborated at length on the problems posed by maternal singing, especially its interference with the collection of speech materials. When apprised of my attempts to study maternal singing, Fernald mused, "Now, why didn't *I* think of that?" In any case, I embarked on a program of research aimed at uncovering musical features in the infant's environment.

Musical Speech

Several investigators have drawn attention to musical features in speech directed to infants. Such speech, in English as in most other languages, is notable for its rhythmicity, repetitiveness, slow tempo, high pitch, pitch variability, and distinctive pitch contours (e.g., Cooper, 1993, 1997; Fernald, 1991; Grieser & Kuhl, 1988; Papoušek, Papoušek, & Symmes, 1991; Stern, Spieker, & MacKain, 1982). These features, in combination, yield a kind of singsong that straddles the boundaries of speech and music. In fact, the term "melodies" is often applied to caregivers' infant-directed (ID) utterances (e.g., Fernald, 1989, 1991, 1992a; Papoušek, 1992).

The prosody of ID speech is thought to be intrinsically meaningful (e.g., Fernald, 1992a) by virtue of acoustic features that are universal signals of particular emotions (Frick, 1985; Murray & Arnott, 1993; Scherer, 1986). Beyond such intrinsic meanings, however, are possibilities for acquiring extramusical meanings from the co-occurrence of specific speech melodies and nonmusical contexts. For example, caregivers in different societies use rising or rise/fall ID pitch contours to attract or maintain infants' attention, falling contours to soothe infants, and low, flat contours to prevent or stop behaviors that are dangerous or undesirable (Fernald, 1989, 1991; Papoušek et al., 1991).

What happens when the vocal channel is unavailable, as with deaf, manually communicating mothers and their deaf or hearing infants? The ID signing of such mothers involves greater rhythmicity and repetitiveness, slower tempo, and larger, more contrastive movements than does their signed communication with adults (Erting, Prezioso, & O'Grandy Hynes, 1990; Masataka, 1992). Just as ID speech imports elements from music, ID signing seems to import elements from dance. The result, in both cases, is a style of communication that is more expressive and dramatic than the usual adult-directed (AD) style.

According to Trainor, Austin, and Desjardins (2000), the characteristic distinctions between ID and AD speech do not arise from infant-directedness per se, but rather from differences in emotional expressiveness. When Trainor et al. (2000) compared samples of mothers' ID and AD speech that expressed comparable emotions, they found surprisingly few acoustic differences. Although pitch contours, often considered the hallmark of ID speech, differed across the three emotions considered—love/comfort, surprise, and fear—they did not differ across ID and AD contexts (Trainor et al., 2000). By contrast, mean fundamental frequency, or pitch, was higher in ID than in AD samples.

Was elevated pitch level a genuine by-product of infant-directedness, or did it stem from the artificiality of the AD situation? The ID and AD contexts used by Trainor et al. (2000) involved scripted utterances (e.g., "Hey honey, come over here."). In contrast to mothers' ID versions, which were addressed to their own infants, AD versions were addressed to an unfamiliar, emotionally disengaged adult (the experimenter). It is possible, then, that the discrepancy in pitch level across contexts reflected differences in the speaker's emotionality or engagement. Nevertheless, the elimination of pitch-contour and pitch-range differences across ID and AD contexts highlights the acoustic consequences of emotional intentions. Perhaps the marked distinctions between deaf mothers' signed ID and AD messages (Erting et al., 1990; Masataka, 1992) would diminish or disappear in situations that have comparable emotive intent.

Caregivers' Singing

The widespread interest in ID speech is attributable, in part, to its potential role in language acquisition (Fernald, 1992b; Jusczyk & Kemler Nelson, 1996) and its obvious links to socioemotional development. By contrast, the relation between ID singing and other domains of development is less clear. Thus, despite the apparent universality of singing to infants (Brakeley,

1950; Trehub & Schellenberg, 1995; Tucker, 1984), there has been remarkably little study of this behavior (see Trehub & Trainor, 1998), even in other disciplines. We know, however, that North American mothers sing a great deal while caring for their infants (Trehub, Unyk, et al., 1997), as do mothers and other caregivers throughout the world (Tucker, 1984). Moreover, all cultures have a special genre of music for children, which consists of lullabies and play songs (Trehub & Schellenberg, 1995; Trehub & Trainor, 1998).

With the exception of North America and Europe, where play songs dominate, lullabies are more commonly sung to infants (Trehub & Schellenberg, 1995; Trehub & Trainor, 1998). The greater relative importance of lullabies in much of the world may be attributable to the prevalence of co-sleeping (i.e., mothers sleeping with infants) in many societies (Morelli, Rogoff, Oppenheim, & Goldsmith, 1992; Super & Harkness, 1986) and the preference for soothing over arousing interactions with infants (Toda, Fogel, & Kawai, 1990).

Lullabies differ from play songs and other song types in their words and melodies. Whereas lullaby lyrics typically praise infants or present soothing images from nature (with occasional threats for those who resist sleep), play song lyrics are more variable (Trehub & Schellenberg, 1995; Trehub & Trainor, 1998). Moreover, lullaby tunes are perceptually distinct from other song tunes. In one study, (Trehub, Unyk, & Trainor, 1993a), adults were presented with pairs of unfamiliar foreign lullabies and nonlullabies that were matched on culture, tempo, and musical style. Listeners identified the lullabies at better than chance levels, even when the materials were electronically filtered to remove potential verbal cues (e.g., onomatopoeia, alliteration, syllable repetition). In another study (Unyk, Trehub, Trainor, & Schellenberg, 1992), listeners were asked to judge which member of each song pair was simpler or more repetitive. Listeners' choices on the latter task paralleled their lullaby identification judgments, indicating that simplicity of form is a cue to the identity of lullabies.

The distinctiveness of ID singing is not merely a matter of song repertoire, or *what* the mother sings, but rather *how* she sings. Instrumental measurements reveal that mothers' ID song performances are characterized by higher pitch, greater fundamental frequency perturbations (i.e., jitter), and slower tempo compared to the same songs sung by the same singer in the infant's absence (Trainor, 1996; Trainor, Clark, Huntley, & Adams, 1997; Trehub, Unyk, & Trainor, 1993b; Trehub, Unyk, et al., 1997). Interestingly, these features of maternal singing have been linked to emotionality. For example, elevated pitch and pitch perturbations are associated with greater emotionality, joy in particular (Bachorowski & Owren, 1995; Murray & Arnott, 1993). By contrast, slower tempo is associated with affection and tenderness (Davitz, 1964; Fonagy & Magdics, 1963).

Thus, the principal acoustic differences between ID and non-ID performances of the same song by the same singer are consistent with greater emotionality of the ID versions. Unlike non-ID speech, however, non-ID singing is not usually directed toward a single individual. Thus, it is unclear whether the acoustic differences between ID and non-ID singing would be reduced or eliminated in contexts with comparable emotional intentions (e.g., love songs), as is the case for emotional ID and AD speech (Trainor et al., 2000).

Singing in the course of caregiving is not restricted to infancy. Indeed, such singing generally continues through the preschool period, at least. In principle, then, one could establish which vocal adjustments stem from an infant audience as opposed to no audience (e.g., Trainor et al., 1997; Trehub et al., 1993; Trehub, Unyk, et al., 1997) and which stem from the presence of infant versus preschool listeners. To this end, Bergeson and Trehub (1999) had mothers sing the same song separately to their infant and preschooler. Although the two song versions were much more similar than were the infant-present and infant-absent versions of previous studies (e.g., Trainor et al., 1997; Trehub, Unyk, & Trainor, 1993b), some differences remained. On average, mothers' pitch was one semitone higher for infants than for preschoolers. This pitch elevation is consistent with findings from infant-present and infant-absent contexts, which is not to suggest that mothers were unengaged when singing to their preschoolers. In fact, naive adults' ratings of the "loving" quality of the performances did not differ across contexts. Another performance difference concerned the articulation of lyrics. Specifically, mothers pronounced the words of their songs more clearly for their preschooler than for their infant—an appropriate adjustment to the linguistic status of the listener.

The acoustic differences between ID and non-ID singing have perceptual consequences, at least for adults. Naive adults readily distinguish ID from non-ID songs of English- and Hindi-speaking mothers (Trehub et al., 1993b). They also distinguish parents' simulations of ID performances (no infant present) from their genuine ID versions (Trehub, Unyk, et al., 1997). If singers' emotionality, real or simulated, is a critical contributor to ID performances, then credible simulations may require acting skill that goes beyond the capabilities of most parents. As noted, mothers' performances of the same song for infants and preschoolers differ in subtle ways, but these differences are discernible to naive adult listeners (Bergeson & Trehub, 1999).

Stereotyped ID singing is not limited to mothers or to primary caregivers. Preschool children alter their singing style in the presence of their infant sibling (Trehub, Unyk, & Henderson, 1994), which may reflect heightened arousal or arousing intentions. Fathers raise their pitch and sing more slowly in ID than in non-ID contexts (Trehub, Unyk, et al., 1997), which parallels the performance adjustments of mothers and preschoolers. In some respects, however, fathers' ID singing differs from that of mothers. For example, fathers produce playful performances for their infant sons and soothing performances for their infant daughters (Trehub, Hill, & Kamenetsky, 1997), in contrast to mothers, whose performances are more closely tied to infant state than to gender.

Differences between ID Speech and Singing

Despite the global parallels between ID speech and singing, there are notable differences that are often obscured by confusing or overlapping terminology. One such example is the contrasting usage of *melody* in speech and musical domains. Bolinger (1986) and other linguists use *melody* and *speech melody* as alternate designations of intonation. Thus, melody in speech refers to global pitch contour, or the pattern of rising and falling pitch in an utterance. The corresponding feature in music is *melodic contour*, or simply, *contour*, which is defined without regard to exact distances between successive pitches. By contrast, musical melodies have specifiable rhythms and precisely defined pitch distances between adjacent notes. Thus, it is meaningful to consider specific renditions of songs, but not utterances, as being *in tune*.

Unlike the speech/song comparisons to date, which have involved different participants and procedures, Bergeson and Trehub (2002) evaluated speech and song productions from the same mothers. Mothers were recorded while they interacted with their infants—speaking and singing a song—on two occasions separated by a week or more. On the second visit, mothers were asked to sing the same song; they were also asked to include some of the verbal phrases that they had used previously. For the latter purpose, they were given a short list of stereotyped phrases transcribed from the earlier session. All sessions were videotaped to ensure that that any changes in maternal behavior were not attributable to differences in infant state.

With respect to song repetitions, certain similarities across sessions would be expected, specifically those pertaining to defining features of songs such as tunes, rhythms, and lyrics. Beyond these features, however, there is considerable scope for flexibility. For example, songs maintain their identity despite changes in pitch level (i.e., higher or lower), provided the relations between pitches are retained. Thus, "Twinkle, Twinkle, Little Star" or any other song has no correct starting pitch except when performances are coordinated with other singers or instrumentalists. Similarly, there is no correct tempo for songs; what must remain invariant is the relative duration of component notes, or the rhythm.

In principle, then, mothers were free to vary their pitch level and tempo across repetitions over the one-week period. They were simply asked to sing the same song and to use some of the same verbal phrases, with no further guidance provided. As it turned out, mothers' song reproductions revealed remarkable similarity in pitch level, the mean difference being less than a semitone. Indeed, several mothers sang at the identical pitch level on both occasions. By contrast, repetitions of the same verbal phrase differed by about five semitones. Tempo, measured in beats per minutes, differed by a mere 3 percent for song repetitions but by 20 percent for speech repetitions. Despite the absence of an obvious model (beyond long-term memory of tunes and words), the pitch and tempo of mothers' repeated songs were more accurate than college students' repeated renditions of folk songs (Halpern, 1989) or their favorite pop recordings (Levitin, 1994; Levitin & Cook, 1996). It is fair to say, then, that mothers provide signature versions of songs for their infants.

To what extent were the defining features of songs—tunes and rhythms—retained in mothers' speech to infants? If mothers used the same tunes when repeating their stereotyped utterances (e.g., "What are you doing?" "Hi, Sweetie"; "Are you going to tell me a story?") from one week to the next, that would render the utterances songlike. If they retained the pitch contours but not the tunes of repeated verbal phrases across weeks, that would indicate the fusion of content and expressive form. Finally, phrase repetitions might not be tied to specific tunes or pitch contours, in contrast to the phrases of songs. In fact, Bergeson and Trehub (2002) found little stability in the tunes or pitch contours that accompanied specific verbal phrases. Although repetitions of pitch contours were evident across the one-week period, they were typically accompanied by different verbal content. By contrast, the rhythmic form of mothers' utterances was relatively stable by poetic standards, but somewhat less stable if measured with conventional means for notating musical rhythms.

Thus, maternal speech is not truly songlike (i.e., fixed words and tunes), nor does it involve signature phrase-contour pairings or musical rhythms. These findings do not speak to the oft-repeated claim that melodic form has primacy over verbal content in maternal utterances to preverbal infants (e.g., Fernald, 1989; Papoušek et al., 1991). Moreover, it remains to be determined whether mothers have *signature* contours or tunes coupled with diverse verbal content.

The ubiquity of caregivers' singing and quasi-musical speech means that infants are surrounded by musical elements for much of their waking time. Unlike adult members of their community, whose musical input is largely prerecorded or "frozen," infants experience "live" improvised performances that are finely tuned to their age level and mood. In this sense, infants' musical experiences are similar to those of their preindustrial forebears.

☐ Infants' Interest in ID Speech and Song

ID Speech

There are numerous demonstrations of infants' enhanced responsiveness to ID over AD speech. For example, infants are more attentive and show more positive affect to audio or audiovisual recordings of ID speech than to comparable recordings of AD speech (Cooper & Aslin, 1990; Fernald, 1985; Kaplan, Goldstein, Huckeby, Owren, & Cooper, 1995; Pegg et al., 1992; Werker & McLeod, 1989; Werker et al., 1994). Moreover, the emotional valence of ID speech has differential consequences for infant listeners, who exhibit more positive affect to the prosody of approving than to disapproving utterances (Fernald, 1993; Papoušek et al., 1990). Obviously, exposure cannot be ruled out as the factor responsible for the preferences of 4- and 5-month-old infants. If fetal exposure to the mother's voice (DeCasper, Lecanuet, Busnel, Granier-Deferre, & Maugeais, 1994; Richards, Frentzen, Gerhardt, McCann, & Abrahms, 1992) contributes to postnatal preferences, one would expect preferential responding to AD over ID speech. There is no evidence to this effect, however. Instead, newborns prefer ID over AD speech (Cooper & Aslin, 1990).

ID speech may be intrinsically interesting to infants because of high signal variability, for example, its greater pitch range (Cooper, 1997; Fernald et al., 1989) and dynamic range (whisper to loud voice) relative to AD speech. Perhaps it is not surprising, then, that deaf infants show greater attention and more positive affect to videotaped ID than to AD messages in Japanese sign language (Masataka, 1996). Comparable preferences by hearing infants from hearing families (Masataka, 1998) rule out exposure as an explanatory factor. Nevertheless, emotionally expressive elements and signal variability may make independent contributions to infants' responsiveness to ID communications in speech and sign.

ID Singing: Unfamiliar Singers

One way of assessing infants' differential responsiveness to contrasting musical selections is to monitor their looking time to one of two sound sources (loudspeakers) while they listen to each sample (Trainor, 1996). Affective responsiveness to contrasting musical samples can be evaluated by video-recording infants as they listen to each sound type. Adults can subsequently judge infants' affect or enjoyment from the soundless videotapes (Trehub & Henderson, 1994). Such procedures have revealed greater attention and heightened affect to ID songs than to non-ID songs (Trainor, 1996; Trehub & Henderson, 1994). The higher pitch level of ID relative to non-ID singing may play a critical role in infant preferences. In fact, infants exhibit greater attention to higher-pitched than to lower-pitched versions of the same song by the same singer (O'Neill, Trainor, & Trehub, 2001; Trainor & Zacharias, 1998). They also exhibit differential responsiveness to soothing and playful renditions of the same song (Rock, Trainor, & Addison, 1999).

Although the 6-month-old participants in these studies might have had considerable experience with their caregivers' songs, they were tested with unfamiliar singers (i.e., recordings from mothers of other 6-month-olds). Nevertheless, there are numerous similarities in singing style and repertoire across mothers (Bergeson & Trehub, 1999; Trehub, Unyk, et al., 1997). Thus, an unfamiliar voice may not detract from infants' preference for the familiar ID style. Masataka (1999) demonstrated, however, that newborn infants prefer ID to non-ID singing even when they have deaf parents who communicate by means of sign language (precluding prenatal exposure). These findings are consistent with inherent preferences for the ID style and inconsistent with experiential interpretations. In short, infants may be attracted to various acoustic features that index emotionality in human speech and singing.

ID Singing: Familiar Singers

Studies of ID singing have focused on the acoustic features of caregivers' songs and their consequences for infant listeners. Moreover, the evaluation of such consequences involved unfamiliar singers and highly impoverished stimuli. For example, infants had no access to the expressive facial and body movements that typically accompany caregivers' performances for infants. Thus, it is likely that the findings to date underestimate the impact of ID singing. In one study that featured videotaped maternal performances of speech and song (Nakata & Trehub, 2000; Trehub & Nakata, 2000), infants exhibited significantly more visual regard of mothers during singing compared to speaking episodes.

The difficulty of evaluating the impact of ID singing is exacerbated by infants' tendency to reduce their activity level and emotional expressiveness during periods of intense engagement. Physiological measures might provide a suitable alternative or supplement to measures of overt behavior. The widespread use of singing to soothe or amuse infants (Trehub &

Schellenberg, 1995; Trehub & Trainor, 1998) and the increasing use of music in therapeutic contexts with infants (Cassidy & Standley, 1995; Lorch, Lorch, Diefendorf, & Earl, 1994) may reflect the arousal-regulating potential of music. No doubt, there are physiological consequences of maternal singing, but the challenge lies in identifying a suitable, noninvasive measure.

Salivary cortisol levels, which can be measured noninvasively and reliably index autonomic arousal (Kirschbaum & Helhammer, 1994), emerged as a possibility. Although the measure is typically used to detect elevations (e.g., Stansbury & Gunnar, 1994) or reductions in stress (e.g., Gunnar, Larson, Hertsgaard, Harris, & Brodersen, 1992) in moderately stressful situations, we thought it might be sensitive to the consequences of maternal singing, even for contented (i.e., nonfussy) infants.

We had mothers sing to their infants for a period of 10 minutes (Shenfield, Trehub, & Nakata, 2000). Immediately prior to the onset of singing, infant saliva samples were obtained for subsequent assay; a second saliva sample was obtained 10 minutes after the end of singing (i.e., 20 minutes from the onset of singing). Videotapes of the test session were coded for instances of infant loss of interest or distress and for contingent changes in mothers' performance. The proportion of infant loss-of-interest instances that resulted in maternal performance changes (e.g., tempo change, onset of clapping) yielded an index of maternal responsiveness.

For the group as a whole, maternal performances did not produce reliable changes in salivary cortisol level from pre- to postsinging periods. Consideration of individual infants, however, revealed a striking pattern of change, specifically, very high negative correlations of initial cortisol levels with cortisol changes. This pattern reflected modest increases in cortisol for infants with low initial levels and modest decreases for infants with higher initial levels. In other words, maternal singing had clear arousal-modulating effects. In addition, maternal responsiveness had consequences for infant attention. Infants of highly responsive performers sustained their attention from early to later phases of the singing episode. Infants of less sensitive performers showed attentional decrements over the same period. These effects were not attributable to playful versus soothing styles of performance, because all mothers sang in a moderately playful style. Moreover, the effects on infant attention did not result from performance changes in general but rather from performance maneuvers that were contingent on infant behavior. As in other types of maternal interactions, the outcome depends on fine-tuning to the affective or attentional needs of infants. Overall, infants' enhanced responsiveness to quasi-musical speech and ID singing from the early days of life confirms their interest in musical aspects of their environment.

☐ Are Infants Musical?

When we speak of adults as musical, we generally have in mind special performance skills or more than the usual interest in music. Obviously, infants cannot be musical in that sense. They *can* be musical in other ways, however. As we have seen, infants are unusually precocious at perceiving musical features, given their limited exposure to music (mere months) and the informality of that exposure (via caregivers' singing). We have also learned that the everyday world of infants is musically dense or enriched. Despite caregivers' lack of awareness of infants' perceptual precocity with respect to music, they surround infants with musical elements in the form of singing and quasi-musical speech. Finally, infants exhibit keen interest in these musical aspects of their environment, which entices caregivers to provide encore after encore. On the basis of these factors, I would argue that infants are uniquely prepared to become musical in the full sense of the word. So, are infants musical? Yes, indeed.

☐ Acknowledgments

Preparation of this chapter was assisted by grants from the Natural Sciences and Engineering Research Council and the Social Sciences and Humanities Research Council of Canada.

☐ References

Andrews, M. W., & Dowling, W. J. (1991). The development of perception of interleaved melodies and control of auditory attention. *Music Perception, 8,* 349–368.

Attneave, F., & Olson, R. K. (1971). Pitch as a medium: A new approach to psychophysical scaling. *American Journal of Psychology, 84,* 147–166.

Bachorowski, J. A., & Owren, M. J. (1995). Vocal expression of emotion: Acoustical properties of speech are associated with emotional intensity and context. *Psychological Science, 6,* 219–224.

Bartlett, J. C., & Dowling, W. J. (1980). Recognition of transposed melodies: A key-distance effect in developmental perspective. *Journal of Experimental Psychology: Human Perception and Performance, 6,* 501–515.

Bergeson, T. R., & Trehub, S. E. (1999). Mothers' singing to infants and preschool children. *Infant Behavior & Development, 22,* 51–64.

Bergeson, T.R., & Trehub, S. E. (2002). Pitch, tempo, and rhythm in mothers' speech and song to infants. *Psychological Science, 13,* 71–74.

Best, C. T. (1994). The emergence of native-language phonological influences in infants: A perceptual assimilation model. In H. Nussbaum & J. Goodman (Eds.), *The development of speech perception: The transition from speech sounds to spoken words* (pp. 167–224). Cambridge, MA: MIT Press.

Bharucha, J. J. (1987). Music cognition and perceptual facilitation: A connectionist framework. *Music Perception, 5,* 1–30.

Bolinger, D. L. (1986). *Intonation and its parts.* Stanford, CA: Stanford University Press.

Bower, C. (1980). Boethius, Anicius, Manlius Severinus. In S. Sadie (Ed.), *The new Grove dictionary of music and musicians* (vol. 2, p. 844). London: Macmillan.

Brakeley, T. C. (1950). Lullaby. In M. Leach & J. Fried (Eds.), *Standard dictionary of folklore, mythology, and legend* (pp. 653–654). New York: Funk & Wagnalls.

Burns, E. M. (1999). Intervals, scales, and tuning. In D. Deutsch (Ed.), *The psychology of music, 2nd ed.* (pp. 215–264). San Diego: Academic Press.

Butler, D. (1989). Describing the perception of tonality in music: A critique of the tonal hierarchy theory and proposal for a theory of intervallic rivalry. *Music Perception, 6,* 219–242.

Cassidy, J. W., & Standley, J. M. (1995). The effect of music listening on physiological responses of premature infants in the NICU. *Journal of Music Therapy, 32,* 208–227.

Chang, H. W., & Trehub, S. E. (1977a). Auditory processing of relational information by young infants. *Journal of Experimental Child Psychology, 24,* 324–331.

Chang, H. W., & Trehub, S. E. (1977b). Infants' perception of temporal grouping in auditory patterns. Child Development, 48, 1666–1670.

Cohen, A. J., Thorpe, L. A., & Trehub, S. E. (1987). Infants' perception of musical relations in short transposed tone sequences. *Canadian Journal of Psychology, 41,* 33–47.

Cooper, R. P. (1993). The effect of prosody on young infants' speech perception. In C. Rovee-Collier & L. P. Lipsitt (Eds.), *Advances in infancy research, vol. 8* (pp. 137–167). Norwood, NJ: Ablex.

Cooper, R. P. (1997). An ecological approach to infants' perception of intonation contours as meaningful aspects of speech. In C. Dent-Read & P. Zukow-Goldring (Eds.), *Evolving explanations of development: Ecological approaches to organism-environment systems* (pp. 55–85). Washington, DC: APA.

Cooper, R. P., & Aslin, R. N. (1990). Preference for infant-directed speech in the first month after birth. *Child Development, 61,* 1584–1595.

Cooper, R. P., & Aslin, R. N. (1994). Developmental differences in infant attention to the spectral properties of infant-directed speech, *Child Development, 65,* 1663–1677.

Cuddy, L. L., Cohen, A. J., & Mewhort, D. J. K. (1981). Perception of structure in short melodic sequences. *Journal of Experimental Psychology: Human Perception and Performance, 7,* 869–883.

Davitz, J. R. (1964). Personality, perception, and cognitive correlates of emotional sensitivity. In J. R. Davitz (Ed.), *The communication of emotional meaning* (pp. 57–68). New York: McGraw-Hill.

DeCasper, A. J., & Fifer, W. P. (1980). Of human bonding: Newborns prefer their mothers' voices. *Science, 208,* 1174–1176.

DeCasper, A. J., Lecanuet, J.-P., Busnel, M-C., Granier-Deferre, C., & Maugeais, R. (1994). Fetal reactions to recurrent maternal speech. *Infant Behavior and Development, 17,* 159–164.

Dostrovsky, S. (1980). Physics of music, 1: to Mersenne. In S. Sadie (Ed.), *The new Grove dictionary of music and musicians* (vol. 14, pp. 664–665). London: Macmillan.

Dowling, W. J. (1994). Melodic contour in hearing and remembering melodies. In R. Aiello & J. A. Sloboda (Eds.), *Musical perceptions* (pp. 173–190). New York: Oxford University.

Eilers, R. E., Wilson, W. R., & Moore, J. M. (1977). Developmental changes in speech discrimination in infants. *Journal of Speech and Hearing Research, 20,* 766–780.

Eimas, P. D., Siqueland, E. R., Jusczyk, P., & Vigorito, J. (1971). Speech perception in infants. *Science, 171,* 303–306.

Erting, C. J., Prezioso, C., & O'Grandy Hynes, M. (1990). The interactional context of deaf mother-infant communication. In V. Volterra & C. J. Erting (Eds.), *From gesture to language in hearing and deaf children* (pp. 97–106). Berlin: Springer.

Fallon, M., Trehub, S. E., & Schneider, B. A. (2000). Children's perception of speech in multitalker babble. *Journal of the Acoustical Society of America, 108,* 3023–3029.

Fallon, M., Trehub, S. E., & Schneider, B. A. (in press). Children's use of semantic cues in degraded listening environments. *Journal of the Acoustical Society of America.*

Fantz, R. L. (1963). Pattern vision in newborn infants. *Science, 140,* 296–297.

Fernald, A. (1985). Four-month-old infants prefer to listen to motherese. *Infant Behavior and Development, 8,* 181–195.

Fernald, A. (1989). Intonation and communicative intent in mothers' speech to infants: Is the melody the message? *Child Development, 60,* 1497–1510.

Fernald, A. (1991). Prosody in speech to children: Prelinguistic and linguistic functions. *Annals of Child Development, 8,* 43–80.

Fernald, A. (1992a). Human maternal vocalizations to infants as biologically relevant signals: An evolutionary perspective. In J. H. Barkow, L. Cosmides, & J. Tooby (Eds.), *The adapted mind: Evolutionary psychology and the generation of culture.* Oxford: Oxford University Press.

Fernald, A. (1992b). Meaningful melodies in mothers' speech to infants. In H. Papoušek, V. Jürgens, & M. Papoušek (Eds.), *Nonverbal vocal communication: Comparative and developmental aspects* (pp. 262–282). Cambridge, UK: Cambridge University Press.

Fernald, A. (1993). Approval and disapproval: Infant responsiveness to vocal affect in familiar and unfamiliar languages. *Child Development, 64,* 657–674.

Fernald, A., & Kuhl, P. K. (1987). Acoustic determinants of infant preference for motherese. *Infant Behavior and Development, 10,* 279–293.

Fernald, A., Taeschner, T., Dunn, J., Papousek, M., de Boysson-Bardies, B., & Fukui, I. (1989). A cross-language study of prosodic modifications in mothers' and fathers' speech to preverbal infants. *Journal of Child Language, 16,* 477–501.

Fonagy, I., & Magdics, K. (1963). Emotional patterns in intonation and music. *Zeitschrift für Phonetik, 16,* 293–326.

Frick, R. W. (1985). Communicating emotion: The role of prosodic features. *Psychological Bulletin, 97,* 412–429.

Gabrielsson, A. (1993). The complexities of rhythm. In T. J. Tighe & W. J. Dowling (Eds.), *Psychology and music: The understanding of melody and rhythm* (pp. 93–120). Hillsdale, NJ: Erlbaum.

Gordon, I., & Slater, A. (1998). Nativism and empiricism: The history of two ideas. In A. Slater (Ed.), *Perceptual development: Visual, auditory, and speech perception in infancy* (pp. 73–103). Hove, UK: Psychology Press.

Grieser, D. L., & Kuhl, P. K. (1988). Maternal speech to infants in a tonal language: Support for universal prosodic features in motherese. *Developmental Psychology, 24,* 14–20.

Gunnar, M., Larson, M., Hertsgaard, L., Harris, M., & Brodersen, L. (1992). The stressfulness of separation among 9-month-old infants: Effects of social context variables and infant temperament. *Child Development, 63,* 290–303.

Halpern, A. R. (1989). Memory for the absolute pitch of familiar songs. *Memory and Cognition, 17,* 572–581.

Hebb, D. O. (1949). *The organization of behavior.* New York: Wiley.

Hill, C. C. (1986). Consonance and dissonance. In D. M. Randel (Ed.), *The new Harvard dictionary of music* (pp. 197–199). Cambridge, MA: Belknap Press.

Jusczyk, P. W. (1985). On characterizing the development of speech perception. In J. Mehler & R. Fox (Eds.), *Neonate cognition: Beyond the blooming, buzzing confusion* (pp. 199–229). Hillsdale, NJ: Erlbaum.

Jusczyk, P. W., & Kemler Nelson, D. G. (1996). Syntactic units, prosody, and psychological reality during infancy. In J. L. Morgan, K. Demuth (Eds.), *Signal to syntax: Bootstrapping from speech to grammar in early acquisition* (pp. 389–409). Mahwah, NJ: Erlbaum.

Kaplan, P. S., Goldstein, M. H., Huckeby, E. R., Owren, M. J., & Cooper, R. P. (1995). Dishabituation of visual attention by infant- versus adult-directed speech: Effects of frequency modulation and spectral composition. *Infant Behavior and Development, 18,* 209–223.

Kennedy, M. (1994). Song. *The Oxford dictionary of music* (2nd ed.). Oxford: Oxford University Press.

Kessen, W., Haith, M. M., & Salapatek, P. H. (1970). Human infancy: A bibliography and guide. In P. H. Mussen (Ed.), *Carmichael's manual of child psychology* (3rd ed., vol. 1) (pp. 287–445). New York: Wiley.

Kirschbaum, C., & Helhammer, D. H. (1994). Salivary cortisol in psychoneuroendocrine research: Recent developments and applications. *Psychoneuroendocrinology, 19,* 313–333.

Koskoff, E. (1987). An introduction to women, music, and culture. In E. Koskoff (Ed.), *Women and music in cross-cultural perspective* (pp. 1–23). Westport, CT: Greenwood Press.

Krumhansl, C. L. (1990). *Cognitive foundations of musical pitch.* New York: Oxford University Press.

Krumhansl, C. L., & Keil, F. C. (1982). Acquisition of the hierarchy of tonal functions in music. *Memory and Cognition, 10,* 243–-251.

Kuhl, P. K. (1985). Methods in the study of infant speech perception. In G. Gottlieb & N. A. Krasnegor (Eds.), *Measurement of audition and vision in the first year of postnatal life: A methodological overview* (pp. 223–251). Norwood, NJ: Ablex.

Levitin, D. J. (1994). Absolute memory for musical pitch: Evidence from the production of learned melodies. *Perception & Psychophysics, 56,* 414–423.

Levitin, D. J., & Cook, P. R. (1996). Memory for musical tempo: Additional evidence that auditory memory is absolute. *Perception & Psychophysics, 58,* 927–935.

Lorch, C. A., Lorch, V., Diefendorf, A. O., & Earl, P. W. (1994). Effect of stimulative and sedative music on systolic blood pressure, heart rate, and respiratory rate in premature infants. *Journal of Music Therapy, 31,* 105–118.

Lynch, M. P., & Eilers, R. E. (1991). Children's perception of native and non-native musical scales. *Music Perception, 9,* 121–132.

Masataka, N. (1992). Motherese in a signed language. *Infant Behavior and Development, 15,* 453–460.

Masataka, N. (1996). Perception of motherese in a signed language by 6-month-old deaf infants. *Developmental Psychology, 32,* 874–879.

Masataka, N. (1998). Perception of motherese in Japanese Sign Language by 6-month-old hearing infants. *Developmental Psychology, 34,* 241–246.

Masataka, N. (1999). Preference for infant-directed singing in 2-day-old hearing infants of deaf parents. *Developmental Psychology, 35,* 1001–1005.

Mehler, J., Bertoncini, J., Barrière, M., & Jassik-Gerschenfeld, D. (1978). Infant recognition of mother's voice. *Perception, 7,* 491–497.

Mehler, J., Jusczyk, P. W., Lambertz, G., Halsted, N., Bertoncini, J., & Amiel-Tison, C. (1988). A precursor of language acquisition in young infants. *Cognition, 29,* 143–178.

Meyer, L. B. (1956). *Emotion and meaning in music.* Chicago: University of Chicago Press.

Morelli, G., Rogoff, B., Oppenheim, D., & Goldsmith, D. (1992). Cultural variation in infants' sleeping arrangements: Questions of independence. *Developmental Psychology, 28,* 604–613.

Morrongiello, B. A., & Roes, C. (1990). Developmental changes in children's perception of musical sequences: Effects of musical training. *Developmental Psychology, 26,* 814–820.

Morse, P. A. (1972). The discrimination of speech and nonspeech stimuli in early infancy. *Journal of Experimental Child Psychology, 13,* 477–492.

Murray, I. R., & Arnott, J. L. (1993). Toward the simulation of emotion in synthetic speech: A review of the literature on human vocal emotion. *Journal of the Acoustical Society of America, 93,* 1097–1108.

Nakata, T., & Trehub, S. E. (2000, November). *Maternal speech and singing to infants.* Presented at the Society for Music Perception and Cognition, Toronto, ON.

Nazzi, T., Jusczyk, P. W., & Johnson, E. K. (2000). Language discrimination by English-learning 5-month-olds: Effects of rhythm and familiarity. *Journal of Memory and Language, 43,* 1–19.

O'Neill, C., Trainor, L. J., & Trehub, S. E. (2001). Infants' responsiveness to fathers' singing. *Music Perception, 18,* 409–425.

Papoušek, M. (1992). Early ontogeny of vocal communication in parent-infant interactions. In H. Papoušek, V. Jürgens, & M. Papousek (Eds.), *Nonverbal vocal communication: Comparative and developmental approaches* (pp. 230–261). Cambridge, UK: Cambridge University Press.

Papoušek, M., Bornstein, H., Nuzzo, C., Papoušek, H., & Symmes, D. (1990). Infant responses to prototypical melodic contours in parental speech. *Infant Behavior and Development, 13,* 539–545.

Papoušek, M., Papoušek, H., & Symmes, D. (1991). The meanings of melodies in motherese in tone and stress languages. *Infant Behavior and Development, 14,* 415–440.

Pegg, J. E., Werker, J. F., & McLeod, P. J. (1992). Preference for infant-directed over adult-directed speech: Evidence from 7-week-old infants. *Infant Behavior and Development, 15,* 325–345.

Piston, W. (1969). *Harmony.* New York: Norton.

Polka, L. (1995). Linguistic influences in adult perception of non-native vowel contrasts. *Journal of the Acoustical Society of America, 97,* 1286–1296.

Richards, D. S., Frentzen, B., Gerhardt, K. J., McCann, M. E., & Abrahms, R. M. (1992). Sound levels in the human uterus. *Obstetrics & Gynecology, 80,* 186–190.

Rock, A., Trainor, L., & Addison, T. (1999). Distinctive messages in infant-directed playsongs and lullabies. *Developmental Psychology, 35,* 527–534.

Sachs, C. (1943). *The rise of music in the ancient world: East and West.* New York: Norton.

Sakata, H. L. (1987). Hazara women in Afghanistan: Innovators and preservers of a musical tradition. In E. Koskoff (Ed.), *Women and music in cross-cultural perspective* (pp. 85–95). Westport, CT: Greenwood Press.

Schellenberg, E. G., & Trehub, S. E. (1994). Frequency ratios and the discrimination of pure tone sequences. *Perception & Psychophysics, 56,* 472–478.

Schellenberg, E. G., & Trehub, S. E. (1996a). Children's discrimination of melodic intervals. *Developmental Psychology, 32,* 1039–1050.

Schellenberg, E. G., & Trehub, S. E. (1996b). Natural musical intervals: Evidence from infant listeners. *Psychological Science, 7,* 272–277.

Schellenberg, E. G., & Trehub, S. E. (1999). Culture-general and culture-specific factors in the discrimination of melodies. *Journal of Experimental Child Psychology, 74,* 107–127.

Scherer, K. R. (1986). Vocal affect expression: A review and a model for future research. *Psychological Bulletin, 99,* 143–165.

Schneider, B. A., Bull, D., & Trehub, S. E. (1988). Binaural unmasking in infants. *Journal of the Acoustical Society of America, 83,* 1124–1132.

Schneider, B. A., & Trehub, S. E. (1985a). Behavioral assessment of basic auditory abilities. In S. E. Trehub & B. A. Schneider (Eds.), *Auditory development in infancy* (pp. 104–114). New York: Plenum.

Schneider, B. A., & Trehub, S. E. (1985b). Infant auditory psychophysics: An overview. In G. Gottlieb & N. A. Krasnegor (Eds.), *Measurement of audition and vision during the first year of postnatal life: A methodological overview* (pp. 113–126). Norwood, NJ: Ablex.

Schneider, B. A., Trehub, S. E., & Bull, D. (1980). High-frequency sensitivity in infants. *Science, 207,* 1003–1004.

Schneider, B. A., Trehub, S. E., Morrongiello, B. A., & Thorpe, L. A. (1986). *Auditory sensitivity in preschool children. Journal of the Acoustical Society of America, 79,* 447–452.

Shenfield, T., Trehub, S. E., & Nakata, T. (2000, July). *Infants' response to maternal singing.* Poster presented at the International Conference on Infant Studies, Brighton, UK.

Shepard, R. N. (1982). Geometrical approximations to the structure of musical pitch. *Psychological Review, 89,* 305–333.

Siqueland, E. R., & DeLucia, C. A. (1969). Visual reinforcement of non-nutritive sucking in human infants. *Science, 165,* 1144–1146.

Sloboda, J. A. (1985). *The musical mind: The cognitive psychology of music.* Oxford: Clarendon Press.

Stansbury, K., & Gunnar, M. R., (1994). Adrenocortical activity and emotion regulation. *Monographs of the Society for Research in Child Development, 59,* 108–134.

Stern, D. N., Spieker, S., & MacKain, K. (1982). Intonation contours as signals in maternal speech to prelinguistic infants. *Developmental Psychology, 18,* 727–735.

Super, C. M., & Harkness, S. (1986). Temperament, development, and culture. In R. Plomin & J. Dunn (Eds.), *The study of temperament: Continuities, change and challenge.* Hillsdale, NJ: Erlbaum.

Toda, S., Fogel, A., & Kawai, M. (1990). Maternal speech to three-month-old infants in the United States and Japan. *Journal of Child Language, 17,* 279–294.

Trainor, L. J. (1996). Infant preferences for infant-directed versus non-infant-directed play songs and lullabies. *Infant Behavior and Development, 19,* 83–92.

Trainor, L. J., Austin, C. M., & Desjardins, R. N. (2000). Is infant-directed speech prosody a result of the vocal expression of emotion? *Psychological Science, 11,* 188–195.

Trainor, L. J., Clark, E. D., Huntley, A., & Adams, B. (1997). The acoustic basis of infant preferences for infant-directed singing. *Infant Behavior and Development, 20,* 383–396.

Trainor, L. J., & Heinmiller, B. M. (1998). Infants prefer to listen to consonance over dissonance. *Infant Behavior and Development, 21,* 77–88.

Trainor, L. J., & Trehub, S. E. (1992). A comparison of infants' and adults' sensitivity to Western musical structure. *Journal of Experimental Psychology: Human Perception and Performance, 18,* 394–402.

Trainor, L. J., & Trehub, S. E. (1993a). Musical context effects in infants and adults: Key distance. *Journal of Experimental Psychology: Human Perception and Performance, 19,* 615–626.

Trainor, L. J., & Trehub, S. E. (1993b). What mediates infants' and adults' superior processing of the major over the augmented triad? *Music Perception, 11,* 185–196.

Trainor, L. J., & Trehub, S. E. (1994). Key membership and implied harmony in Western tonal music: Developmental perspectives. *Perception & Psychophysics, 56,* 125–132.

Trainor, L. J., & Zacharias, C. A. (1998). Infants prefer higher-pitched singing. *Infant Behavior and Development, 21,* 799–805.

Trehub, S. E. (1973). Infants' sensitivity to vowel and tonal contrasts. *Developmental Psychology, 9,* 91–96.

Trehub, S. E. (1975). The problem of state in infant speech discrimination studies. *Developmental Psychology, 11,* 116.

Trehub, S. E. (1976). The discrimination of foreign speech contrasts by infants and adults. *Child Development, 47,* 466–472.

Trehub, S. E. (1979). Reflections on the development of speech perception. *Canadian Journal of Psychology, 33,* 369–381.

Trehub, S. E. (1998). Music as a window on infant audition. *Current Topics in Acoustical Research, 2,* 105–118.

Trehub, S. E. (2000). Human processing predispositions and musical universals. In N. L. Wallin, B. Merker, & S. Brown (Eds.), *The origins of music* (pp. 427–448). Cambridge, MA: MIT Press.

Trehub, S. E. (2001). Musical predispositions in infancy. *Annals of the New York Academy of Sciences, 930,* 1–16.

Trehub, S. E., Bull, D., & Thorpe, L. A. (1984). Infants' perception of melodies: The role of melodic contour. *Child Development, 55,* 821–830.

Trehub, S. E., & Chang, H. W. (1977). Speech as reinforcing stimulation for infants. *Developmental Psychology, 13,* 170–171.

Trehub, S. E., & Curran, S. (1979). Habituation of infants' cardiac response to speech stimuli. *Child Development, 50,* 1247–1250.

Trehub, S. E., Endman, M., & Thorpe, L. A. (1990). Infants' perception of timbre: Classification of complex tones by spectral structure. *Journal of Experimental Child Psychology, 49,* 300–313.

Trehub, S. E., & Henderson, J. L. (1994). Caregivers' songs and their effect on infant listeners. In I. Deliège (Ed.), *Proceedings of the 3rd International Conference for Music Perception and Cognition* (pp. 47–48). Liège, Belgium: ESCOM.

Trehub, S. E., & Henderson, J. L., (1996). Temporal resolution in infancy and subsequent language development. *Journal of Speech and Hearing Research, 39,* 1315–1320.

Trehub, S. E., Hill, D. S, & Kamenetsky, S. B. (1997). Parents' sung performances for infants. *Canadian Journal of Experimental Psychology, 51,* 385–396.

Trehub, S. E., & Nakata, T. (2000, August). *Musical emotions: A perspective from development.* Symposium presentation, International Society of Music Perception and Cognition, Keele, UK.

Trehub, S. E., & Rabinovitch, M. S. (1972). Auditory-linguistic sensitivity in early infancy. *Developmental Psychology, 6,* 74–77.

Trehub, S. E., & Schellenberg, E. G. (1995). Music: Its relevance to infants. *Annals of child development, 11,* 1–24.

Trehub, S., Schellenberg, E., & Hill, D. (1997). The origins of music perception and cognition: A developmental perspective. In I. Deliege & J. Sloboda (Eds.), *Perception and cognition of music* (pp. 103–128). East Sussex, UK: Psychology Press.

Trehub, S. E., Schellenberg, E. G., & Kamenetsky, S. B. (1999). Infants' and adults' perception of scale structure. *Journal of Experimental Psychology: Human Perception and Performance, 25,* 965–975.

Trehub, S. E., Schneider, B. A., & Endman, M. (1980). Developmental changes in infants' sensitivity to octave-band noises. *Journal of Experimental Child Psychology, 29,* 282–293.

Trehub, S. E., Schneider, B. A., & Henderson, J. L. (1995). Gap detection in infants, children, and adults. *Journal of the Acoustical Society of America, 98,* 2532–2541.

Trehub, S. E., Schneider, B. A., Morrongiello, B. A., & Thorpe, L. A. (1988). Auditory sensitivity in school-age children. *Journal of Experimental Child Psychology, 46,* 273–285.

Trehub, S. E., Schneider, B. A., Morrongiello, B. A., & Thorpe, L. A. (1989). Developmental changes in high-frequency sensitivity. *Audiology, 28,* 241–249.

Trehub, S. E., & Thorpe, L. A. (1989). Infants' perception of rhythm. Categorization of auditory sequences by temporal structure. *Canadian Journal of Psychology, 43,* 217–229.

Trehub, S. E., Thorpe, L. A., & Morrongiello, B. A. (1985). Infants' perception of melodies: Changes in a single tone. *Infant Behavior and Development, 8,* 213–223.

Trehub, S. E., Thorpe, L. A., & Morrongiello, B. A. (1987). Organizational processes in infants' perception of auditory patterns. *Child Development, 58,* 741–749.

Trehub, S. E., Thorpe, L. A., & Trainor, L. J. (1990). Infants' perception of *good* and *bad* melodies. *Psychomusicology, 9,* 5–15.

Trehub, S. E., & Trainor, L. J. (1998). Singing to infants: Lullabies and play songs. *Advances in Infancy Research, 12,* 43–77.

Trehub, S. E., Trainor, L. J., & Unyk, A. M. (1993). Music and speech processing in the first year of life. In H. W. Reese (Ed.), *Advances in Child Development and Behavior* (vol. 24, pp. 1–35). New York: Academic Press.

Trehub, S. E., Unyk, A. M., & Henderson, J. L. (1994). Children's songs to infant siblings: Parallels with speech. *Journal of Child Language, 21,* 735–744.

Trehub, S. E., Unyk, A. M., Kamenetsky, S. B., Hill, D. S., Trainor, L. J., Henderson, J. L., & Saraza, M. (1997). Mothers' and fathers' singing to infants. *Developmental Psychology, 33,* 500–507.

Trehub, S. E., Unyk, A. M., & Trainor, L. J. (1993a). Adults identify infant-directed music across cultures. *Infant Behavior and Development, 16,* 193–211.

Trehub, S. E., Unyk, A. M., & Trainor, L. J. (1993b). Maternal singing in cross-cultural perspective. *Infant Behavior and Development, 16,* 285–295.

Tucker, N. (1984). Lullabies. *History Today, 34,* 40–46.

Unyk, A. M., Trehub, S. E., Trainor, L. J., & Schellenberg, E. G. (1992). Lullabies and simplicity: A cross-cultural perspective. *Psychology of Music, 20,* 15–28.

Werker, J. F., Gilbert, J. H., Humphrey, K., & Tees, R. C. (1981). Developmental aspects of cross-language speech perception. *Child Development, 52,* 349–355.

Werker, J. F., & McLeod, P. J. (1989). Infant preference for both male and female infant-directed talk: A developmental study of attentional and affective responsiveness. *Canadian Journal of Psychology, 43,* 230–246.

Werker, J. F., Pegg, J. E., & McLeod, P. J. (1994). A cross-language investigation of infant preference for infant-directed communication. *Infant Behavior and Development, 17,* 321–331.

Werker, J. F., & Tees, R. C. (1984). Cross-language speech perception: Evidence for perceptual reorganization during the first year of life. *Infant Behavior and Development, 7,* 49–63.

Wormith, S. J., Pankhurst, D., & Moffitt, A. R. (1975). Frequency discrimination by young infants. *Child Development, 46,* 272–-275.

Zentner, M. R., & Kagan, J. (1996). Perception of music by infants. *Nature, 383,* 29.

Zentner, M. R., & Kagan, J. (1998). Infants' perception of consonance and dissonance in music. *Infant Behavior and Development, 21,* 483–492.

Linda B. Smith

How to Be Smart:
Lessons from Word Learning

I began my undergraduate studies in engineering because I wanted to know how things work. I still want to know "how things work," but the "thing" I study now is cognition. My shift from machines to living minds was fostered by a part-time undergraduate job at the University of Wisconsin–Madison. In this job, I tested moderately retarded children in a simple task. It worked like this: I showed the child a red triangle and a green triangle. I let the child lift the objects—one at a time—until the child found a candy under the red triangle. Then I showed the child a red square and a green square and let the child find the candy—under the red square. I continued this way until the child learned to always search under the red triangle and red square without error. Then I showed the child two new objects—a red cross and a green cross. Would the child search under the red cross? The children I tested all failed. They could not seem to see the commonality in red triangles, red squares, and red crosses. I was perplexed; what could be causing these children not to see the solution—red— that was in plain view?

The children's failures bothered me even more when I took courses in psychology and found out that this task was not peculiarly difficult for children with low IQs. It is peculiarly difficult for all young children. A 3-year-old destined to be a rocket scientist does not know that if candies are found under red triangles and red squares, they will be found under red crosses (Tighe, Glick, & Cole, 1971; Kendler, 1974). This puzzling fact took me from machines to mind, from majoring in engineering to majoring in psychology.

More recently, my work on attentional learning has brought me from minds back to thinking about machines. In 1992, I was asked to give the keynote address at the Canadian Symposium in Artificial Intelligence; in 1996, I was asked to present a workshop to scientists working in artificial intelligence for the Central Intelligence Agency; and in 1999, along with Esther Thelen, I went to Japan to talk to a group of robotocists. I do not work in artificial intelligence and do not really know very much about it. So why would these kind of people, as my mother bluntly asked about the CIA, want to talk to me, a nice lady who studies children?

Why indeed? Human cognitive development is a demonstration proof of how to create flexible, adaptive, inventive intelligence. I know of no smart human thinkers—experts in any domain—who did not start out as babies. What we know about how human cognition is *made* is very powerful information for creating artificial intelligence (for further reading, see Brooks, 1991; Pfeiffer & Scheier, 1999). Accordingly, with my engineering origins in mind, I offer three lessons from the developmental laboratory, maxims for building powerful intelligences: start stupid, be contextually sensitive, and be open to multiple influences.

☐ Start Stupid

How can we build a device that acts intelligently in the way that we do: that talks about the world, that reasons scientifically, invents new machines and medicines, and creates novels, plays, poetry, and films? The answer from both classic artificial intelligence and nativist theories of human cognition is to build it all in. The idea that we are born smart was the favored theoretical view when I was a graduate student (1973–1977) at the University of Pennsylvania. The arguments for innate ideas went something like this:

1. There are many unique domains of knowledge. What children learn about language, about space, about causality, about number, about other minds, are all specific to those specific domains. Nothing beyond the most superficial metaphors exist across domains. Clearly, then, different learning mechanisms—mechanisms specific to learning in such specific domains as language, number, and space—must exist.

2. One cannot get something from nothing. In cognitive development, this idea is often presented in terms of the problem of induction. Briefly, there are an infinite number of objectively correct generalizations from any data set, that is, from any set of experiences. In order for children to

arrive at the *right* generalizations from their experiences, they must come equipped with content-specific constraints on the generalizations that can be formed.

3. The empirical evidence on children's learning strongly implicates domain-specific constraints on what is learned. Children learn differently about syntax, for example, than they do about number or space. In brief, the data on development itself suggest that children have content-specific expectations about the categories that comprise different domains.

4. The smartness of children's domain-specific learning—their learning about language, about space, about number, about other minds—stands in marked contrast to their general problem-solving skills. How can young children who cannot even seem to learn that the candy is hidden under the red one, rapidly learn the complex and abstract structures that make up their language? The general cognitive processes of infants and very young children just do not seem smart enough on their own to yield the competence children exhibit in specialized domains.

These arguments were new and felt *avant-garde* in the 1970s when I was at Penn. They were certainly compelling to many people there (see, e.g., Baillargeon, Spelke, & Wasserman, 1985; Gelman, 1978; Gleitman & Wanner, 1982 ; Goldin-Meadow & Feldman, 1977; Keil, 1981; Osherson, 1981). But I found them troubling and I was unable to join the fold. There were two problems from my point of view. First, "innate ideas" did not explain the fact of development. Two-year olds do not think like 4-year-olds, who do not think like 8-year-olds, and so on. Second, "innate ideas" were offered as static, inert, knowledge representations; how they actually worked in real time and real tasks was unspecified. My engineer's desire for an implementable mechanism—for a specification of how it actually worked—was not satisfied.

For builders of artificial intelligence, the nativist stance on the origins of intelligence also did not prove helpful in the end. It is simply too hard to pre-think and pre-solve all possible situations that an intelligent device might encounter. This approach works only in narrowly constrained domains, like playing chess, but not in solving problems in the more variable and more complex real world. The classic AI approach of built-in intelligence led to what are called "brittle" intelligences, intelligences that break down whenever anything just slightly out of the ordinary is encountered (see Pfeiffer & Scheier, 1999). People are not "brittle" in this way; they gracefully adapt and improvise when confronted with something new.

Children's attentional learning suggests a way to build "nonbrittle" intelligence: let the device discover—by interacting in the world—what kinds of specialized learning mechanisms it needs. That is, instead of starting smart, the device *becomes* smart.

The Shape Bias in Early Noun Learning

Consider this example drawn from a real observation of word learning by my son when he was 20 months old. We were driving in the country and we saw a huge tractor working in a field. We stopped to watch and we talked about it. It was a a big green John Deere with bright yellow wheels. It was all very interesting as it rumbled by and Gordon was quite taken with it and with the clouds of dust flying in its wake. A week later, we saw another tractor, but this one was not at all like the original John Deere. It was an old small red one parked as a lawn ornament in front of a landscape company. Gordon saw it before I did and he spontaneously called it "tractor." How did he do this?

Gordon's generalization of the name "tractor" from the big John Deere to the small antique tractor is both remarkable and abolutely ordinary. It is remarkable because it is not at all clear how Gordon could know that this antique tractor and the original John Deere are both to be called "tractor." How did Gordon know when I used the word "tractor" for that big John Deere that I was talking about tractors and not specifically John Deeres or not big green things with yellow wheels or not things that create dust clouds in fields? In brief, Gordon's calling that antique tractor "tractor" is remarkable because he apparently knew, from *a single instance of naming*, the whole category of things to which the name referred. Gordon's generalization of the word "tractor" to a new instance is ordinary in the sense that ordinary two-year-olds do it all the time. Smart one-trial learning of whole categories defies ordinary psychological mechanisms of trial-and-error learning. Thus it is not surprising that some have attempted to explain children's nearly error-free noun generalizations in terms of specialized innate mechanisms, and more specifically in terms of preknowledge about the possible meanings of nouns (see Markman, 1989).

In 1988, Barbara Landau, Susan Jones, and I began a long-term program of research on this remarkable and ordinary word learning. In our first experiment, we attempted a laboratory analog of Gordon's one-trial learning of "tractor." We showed children a novel object, named it, and then we presented them with other objects. And we asked: After learning the name of one thing, what other things would these children call by the same name? More specifically, we showed 2- and 3-year-old children the novel wooden object illustrated in Figure 11.1. The object was named with a novel count noun, "This is a dax." The children were then presented with the test objects also depicted in Figure 11.1 and asked about each, "Is this a dax?" What we found is this: children generalized "dax" to test objects that were the same shape as the exemplar but not to test objects that were different in shape. The degree of children's selective attention to shape was remarkable. Children extended the name "dax" to

Exemplar

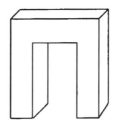

Test objects

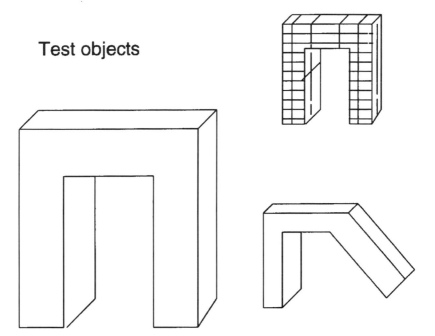

FIGURE 11.1. Sample stimuli used in the novel noun generalization task of Landau, Smith, and Jones, 1988.

same-shaped test objects that were 100 times the exemplar in size and also to those made of sponge or chicken wire.

Think about what this highly selective attention to shape does for young word learners. They do not need to figure out by trial and error what "dax" refers to; instead they can immediately know that the word refers to the shape of the thing—not its color, texture, size, or location. Just as young Gordon knew that "tractor" named tractor-shaped things, these children knew that "dax" named dax-shaped things. This bias to attend to shape should help children learn object names if most objects are named by shape. Critically, basic-level object categories and the noun categories commonly learned early appear to be shape-based (Rosch, 1973; Biederman, 1987; Samuelson & Smith, 1999).

Thus children's systematic attention to shape may explain how Gordon and other children infer the just right category from hearing one instance named. Apparently, Gordon knew to call the antique tractor "tractor" because it was the same global shape as the John Deere. But how do we explain Gordon's attention to shape? How does it work? A good engineer who is looking for a mechanism to solve some problem would look first at tried-and-true approaches that have worked to solve a lot of problems in the past. And, that is where I looked, among the tried-and-true learning mechanisms.

An Associative Learning Account

Associative learning is the most fundamental and universal mechanism of psychological change (for discussion, see A. Clark, 1993). Whenever one perceptual cue is regularly associated with another, the presence of the first will come to automatically increase attention to the second. The automatic control of selective attention by associative learning is a widespread mechanism and well-documented in babies, young children, adults, and nonhuman animals. Two facts suggest that it is also a process that could create the shape bias in children's object-name learning.

First, although children become smart learners of object names, they are not smart at the start. Children first begin to comprehend words around nine months, and they say their first words a little later. And for the first six months of word learning, they aquire words slowly and errorfully, not at all like Gordon's immediate mapping of the word "tractor" to the just right category. At first, young children often have quite wrong ideas about what a word means, calling all vehicles from bikes to planes *car*, or calling oranges, fingernails, and plates *moon*, or calling swans and robins *duck* (for further examples see E. Clark, 1973; Macnamara, 1982; Mervis, 1987). In the beginning, children apparently need multiple repeated examples to figure out just what the class of things is that gets called *car* or *moon* or *duck*. It is not until children are close to their second birthday, and know as many as 50 to 150 words (Gershkoff-Stowe & Smith, 1997; Samuelson & Smith, 1999) that they are fast learners of object names. These facts fit the idea that children learn to attend to shape by learning object names. During the initial slow phase, as they learn object names one by one, they may also learn to attend to shape.

Second, the kinds of nouns children acquire early set the right circumstances for attentional learning. That is, there is a perceptible cue that is regularly associated with naming objects by shape. The perceptible cue is the set of syntactic frames asociated with count nouns. Table 11.1 provides a description of the first 100 nouns in the productive vocabulary of 8 children as reported in parental diaries (Gershkoff-Stowe & Smith, 2001; see also Samuelson & Smith, 1999). By syntactic criteria, two-thirds of these nouns are count nouns. This is important because not only are names for common objects typically count nouns (chair, cup, dog, and so on), but these nouns are defined by syntactic properties that present clear and potentially usable cues to children: the determiner *a*, numerals, and the plural. And, most critically, we found in a comprehensive analysis of these early noun categories that over 90 percent consisted of things of similar shape (by adult judgment of category structure; see Samuelson & Smith, 1999). Here then is the idea: as children slowly learn early nouns, they must hear count-noun syntactic frames, "This is a _____," "See the two _____s," used to present names of objects, names for things of similar shape. The syntactic cues associated with naming thus could become cues that automatically shift attention to shape, to just the right property for learning object names.

A Training Study

We have conducted many studies of this idea that are correlational in nature (See Smith, 1995, 1999, for reviews). In these studies, we show in various ways that the nouns particular children know determine how

TABLE 11.1. Proportions of kinds of nouns among the first 25, 50, and 100 nouns and the proportion of count nouns judged by adults to refer to things in shape-based categories. Nouns classified as both count and mass (e.g., muffin) or character names (e.g., Ernie, as in "I have two Ernies") are not included.

Nouns in productive vocabulary	Kind of noun (proportion total)			Proportion count nouns naming objects in shape-based categories
	Count	Proper	Mass	
0–25	.73	.18	.06	.98
26–50	.70	.14	.06	.94
51–100	.68	.08	.14	.93

those children generalize novel names for novel objects. But if one really understands the mechanism behind some phenomenon, then one ought to be able to go beyond correlation. One ought to be able to experimentally make the phenomenon happen. Thus, if we are right about how the shape bias gets made through associative learning, then we ought be able to make a shape bias in children who do not yet have one—by associating names with objects in shape-based categories. Accordingly, we tried to experimentally make a shape bias in 17-month-old infants; at this age, children are still slow noun learners and do not typically show a shape bias in novel noun-learning experiments (Smith, Jones, Landau, Samuelson, & Gershkoff-Stowe, 2002).

The children in the Training condition came to the laboratory once a week for nine weeks and were given extensive training on novel categories. These were all made-up categories containing just two objects that matched only in shape, as shown in Figure 11.2. In the course of the

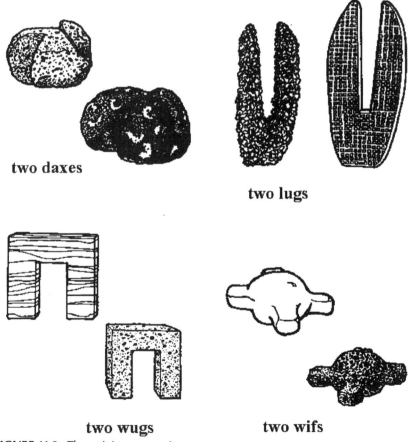

FIGURE 11.2. The training categories.

weekly play sessions, we named the objects repeatedly, using clear-cut markers of count nouns, potential cues to be linked to attention to shape: "Where's the wif? Oh, that wif is down the hole. Here's a lug; here's the other lug. Two lugs in the wagon." Other children, age- and vocabulary-matched to the children in the Training condition, were assigned to a variety of control conditions—No training, Categorization training without naming, Naming categories not organized by shape.

At the end of the experiment, we gave all the children brand-new objects and named them with brand-new names, and asked them what other objects could be called by that name, the typical novel noun generalization task. The children in the Training condition, but not those in the Control conditions, generalized these new names systematically to new instances by shape. The finding that the children who were trained with count-noun syntax to name objects in shape-based categories transferred that learning to the learning of new categories is the important one. It shows that attentional learning of the kind posited by the associative learning account can create a *learning bias*.

And this laboratory-created shape bias *is* a learning bias that drives subsequent development. Specifically, this laboratory-induced shape bias enabled the children in the Training condition to learn more object names, real English words, in their everyday lives outside the lab. We measured the number of words, real English words, in the children's productive vocabularies at the start and end of training. Figure 11.3 shows the change in vocabulary from the beginning to the end of the experiment. The children in the Training condition showed on average a 166 percent increase in number of count nouns in their vocabularies over the course of training. In contrast, children in the No training Control condition showed only a 73 percent increase in average number of count nouns. Not only did we create a shape bias, we created one that altered the course of learning outside the lab.

These results provide an example of how general-purpose learning mechanisms like associative learning can make themselves smart, how they can create an attentional bias that then facilitates and drives future learning.

Why Start Stupid?

The training results show that we can teach children to be smarter learners, with real-life consequences for those children. We believe the training procedure mimics (and speeds up) the learning that goes on naturally as children learn early nouns, nouns that are overwhelmingly count nouns and overwhelmingly name objects by shape. But does it have to be this

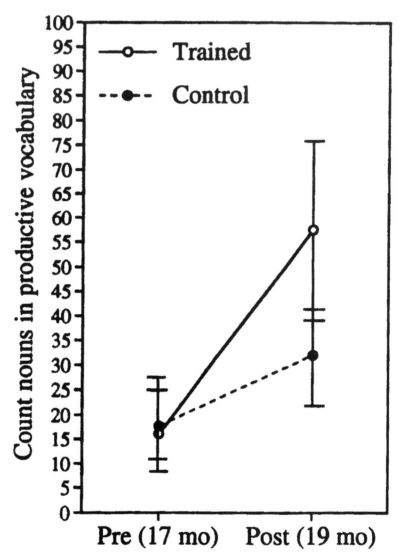

FIGURE 11.3. Number of count nouns in children's vocabularies pre- and post-training.

way? Is starting with dumb general processes really the better way to build intelligence? If children need to attend to shape to learn object categories, why didn't evolution just build in that bias? Wouldn't that be better engineering? Wouldn't it be easier?

I don't know if building a shape bias in would be easier in terms of the needed biological and psychological mechanisms, but I do know it would not be as smart. The value of starting stupid and letting the child *learn* what learning mechanisms it needs is that the same general learning processes can develop whatever learning mechanisms *are* needed. That brings us to the next lesson.

☐ Be Contextually Sensitive

Traditional theories of cognition, both of the artificial and the biologically real, concentrated on the stability of cognition. In psychological terms, the question is how people manage to have stable ideas about kinds given all the messy and idiosyncratic variability in the world. How, for example, do we manage to think about the same thing, dog, both when the input is the sentence *That is an odd dog* and some mutt we pass on the street? We do this, according to the traditional view, because we possess an underlying knowledge structure, a concept, of what it means to be a dog. This concept of dog sits in our head until it is needed, until it is activated by some perceptual event. We *know* that the speaker is talking about a dog, we *know* that we have seen a dog, when this concept is activated. The reason, in this view, that we understand the same thing each time we think about dogs is because we activate the very same concept. Taking the traditional view as self evident, Frank Keil (1994) put it this way:

> Shared mental structures are assumed to be constant across repeated categorizations of the same set of instances and different from other categorizations. When I think about the category of dogs, a specific mental representation is assumed to be responsible for that category and roughly the same representation for a later categorization of dogs by myself or by another (p. 169).

When I was in graduate school at Penn this was the clearly dominant view. Everyone who was au courant studied knowledge representations because it was assumed that the highest, most advanced, most mature forms of intelligence are the ones that are the most stable and context-free. Consequently, there was little interest in process—in perceiving, remembering, attending, and learning. Knowledge representations, not process, were definitely the important stuff. Again, the accepted wisdom did not sit well with me. It seemed to me that knowledge only matters in the here and now, when it is brought to bear in some real and idiosyncratic moment of knowing, and attending must be part of that.

Attention is naturally and inherently variable. Thus, young children, even those who know many names for things in shape-based categories, do *not* always attend to shape. We saw this context sensitivity in our very first study of the shape bias. We included a control condition in which children were simply asked to pick an object "like" the exemplar. In this kind of control task, children do not attend to shape or to any other dimension in a systematic way (Landau, Smith, & Jones, 1988). This makes sense if naming, if count-noun syntactic frames, are the learned context cues that shift attention to shape. Without these cues in the here and now, there is nothing, mechanistically speaking, to push attention to shape. Our subsequent studies found that there are other contexts in which children do not attend to shape even when naming objects. In fact, we found that these contexts *increase* with development. This developmental trend is summarized in Figure 11.4 (see Smith, 1995; 1999, for reviews of the specific experiments).

Consider first the developmental function labeled "count noun." This function summarizes a variety of experiments using the task in which children are shown a novel object, it is labeled by a count noun, and the children are asked what objects are instances of the lexical category. The shape bias grows in this context, emerging between 18 and 24 months. Now consider the function in the figure labeled "similarity." This function summarizes findings in studies in which the child is shown a novel object, it is not named, and the child is asked which other objects are like the exemplar. In this control task, children older than 30 months do not selectively attend to shape, but younger children sometimes do. There is a brief developmental period after the emergence of the shape bias in

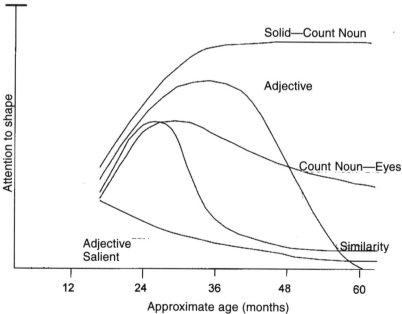

FIGURE 11.4. Summary curves of how attention to shape in different task contexts changes with development.

which it is overgeneralized to nonnaming tasks. Thus, it seems that in the early course of learning object names, attention to shape increases generally, but then becomes specific to naming.

With development, the shape bias also becomes specific to specific kinds of novel words. In two series of experiments (Smith, Jones, & Landau, 1992; Landau, Jones, & Smith, 1992), we examined children's interpretations of novel words presented in syntactic frames that specify the word as an adjective (e.g., "This is a dax one," and "See how dax that is."). Young children interpreted the novel word as referring to objects of the same shape; older children did not. Instead, the adjective frame pushed older children's attention away from shape. I represent these results in the figure with the function labeled "adjective."

Words are not the only factors that matter in these tasks. The power of words to organize attention also depends on the stimuli. This fact is illustrated by comparing the function labeled "adjective" with the one labeled "adjective + salient color." In one series of experiments (Smith, Jones, & Landau, 1992), we showed that whether an adjective frame pushed attention to or away from shape depended on how salient the other dimensions were for younger children. Finally, consider the function labeled "count-noun eyes." During the period of vocabulary increase from 2 to 3 years, young children increasingly interpret novel names for things with animacy features (eyes or feet) differently from names for things without those features. As children know more and more names for both animals and man-made objects, they generalize names for animals by multiple properties and names for artifacts by specifically and only shape (see Jones, Smith, & Landau, 1991; Jones & Smith, 1998; Yoshida & Smith, 2000).

What we see, all told, is a marvelous emergence of context specificity in which children seem to bring everything they know—whatever they know—to bear on their interpretation of a novel word. Different contexts—linguistic, task, and stimulus—work together to organize children's attention to objects in different ways that exquisitely fit the different contexts. This is intelligence at work, much much smarter than always attending to shape.

☐ Be Open to Multiple Influences

The evidence suggests that attention becomes smart in the service of word learning because it is an open process, a process altered by experience. Attention is also a process open to the idiosyncrasies of the here and now. Everyday experience, confirmed by over a century of research in experimental psychology, shows attention to be attracted by intensity, movement, change, and novelty—stimulus properties that universally engage.

Naturally, attention-grabbing stimulus properties also affect children's interpretations of novel words (Smith, Jones, & Landau, 1992; Smith, Jones, & Landau, 1996; Samuelson & Smith, 1998). For example, in one of our experiments on novel adjective learning, we found that young children's interpretation of adjectives (but not their interpretation of nouns) depended on the illumination in the room! In one condition, we used normal room illumination and the young children interpreted the novel adjective as referring to shape, just like they interpreted a novel noun. In another condition, we shined a spotlight on the object and the children interpreted the novel adjective not as referring to shape but to color. Why? Because we had put glitter in the paint. Under the spotlight the colors glowed and sparkled. Sparkle attracts attention, and children interpreted the novel adjective as referring to that sparkly color. Importantly, however, sparkles grabbed the children's attention when the novel word was presented in an adjectival frame, "This is a dax one," but not when it was presented in a count-noun frame, "This is a dax." Sparkling colors in the context of count-noun syntax and its strong link to shape, lead to attention to shape. But sparkling colors in the context of adjectival syntax lead attention to the sparkling colors.

This seemingly simple result contains a lesson of profound importance. The syntactic frame of an adjective leads sometimes to shape, sometimes to color; sparkling colors sometimes pull attention away from shape, sometimes not. What the child attends to and links to the novel word depends on the precise combination of forces on attention, forces that reflect both past learning and the details of the here and now. This means, as William James put it over a hundred years ago, "no two ideas are ever exactly the same, which is the proposition we started to prove. The proposition is more important theoretically than it at first sight appears" (1890, pp. 234–235).

The theoretical importance is that attending and knowing, and thus learning and knowledge, are always changing. Figure 11.5 helps in thinking about how this is so. At any moment there are multiple forces on attention—linguistic, learned contextual cues, idiosyncratic immediate forces like sparkling glitter. What one attends to and what one learns at any moment in time depends on all of these. And what one attends to at any moment will lead to learning, changing what will be attended to in the next moment. This, then, is a continually adapting *living* system, that builds its own developmental trajectory through time. There is no end product here, no developmental outcome, but a system continually being tuned by and staying in tune with the world. At every moment, learned associations cause attention weights to shift to reflect the utility of particular dimensions in similar contexts. And thus attention always brings past experiences to bear on the present. At every moment, direct stimu-

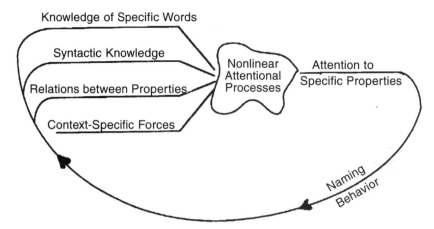

FIGURE 11.5. Multiple forces influence attention.

lus effects, like sparkling glitter, keep attention fresh and timely so that it incorporates the singularities of the here and now. Because the focus of attention emerges in the moment from the mix of these multiple forces, it is creative. Such a system does not need to know ahead of time anything specific about what adjectives mean in the context of glitter. A novel learning bias can emerge from the novel combination of the local peculiarities with past learning. It is the openness of attention, its susceptibility to continuous change, that makes attention able to continuously adjust itself and thus smartly adapt. This is not a "brittle" system; it does not break when presented with the unusual or the unknown; instead, it improvises.

This improvisation, this in-the-moment melding of past learning and current input, is essential if development is to happen. Consider again, the evidence on children's interpretations of novel adjectives—with and without spotlighted objects. In the context of a spotlight (but not in the context of ordinary illumination), children interpret novel words presented in count-noun frames differently than they do novel words presented in adjectival frames. This means that they know something about the different meanings of nouns and adjectives. But what exactly? And what do we mean by knowing? And how does it lead to the next developmental step?

Children's different interpretations of novel nouns and novel adjectives given spotlighted sparkling objects can be explained without positing any specific knowledge about the semantics of nouns and adjectives. To see this, assume that young children, say 2-year-olds, have learned only that the syntactic frame of a count noun, "That's a _____," is associated with attending to shape. From all that is known about associative learning, one would expect a generalization gradient around this original learning: children's attention to shape should decrease in word learning situations as those situations become increasingly dissimilar to the context of original learning. More specifically, the pull of shape should be less if we make the syntactic frame less similar to that of a count noun. Thus, the simple idea of a generalization gradient predicts that the strength of the pull to shape will be weaker in the context of a novel adjective because "This is a dax one" is only partially similar to that of a count noun, "This is a dax." In this way, "knowing" only about nouns could account for the differential effect of a spotlight on interpreting novel words in noun-versus-adjective frames. My purpose in raising this possibility, however, is not to "explain away" children's apparent knowledge about adjectives. They do "know" something, but this is knowledge that resides in the perceptible differences between count noun and adjective frames and in generalization gradients.

The key idea is this: generalization gradients over original learning make children's attention variable and thus *open* to new learning. Because children are less likely to attend to shape in the context of an adjective than a noun, then they are likely to learn differently about adjectives than nouns. Attention will be more easily captured by the idiosyncratic forces of the moment. And in this way, new relevant cues pertinent to the task will be added to the mix. It is this variability of attention in the moment that enables children to keep on learning and not to get stuck in the one first solution found, a solution that might be right in only some contexts. If attention were not perturbable by the idiosyncratic, if generalization was not graded, if children just always attended to shape, their word-learning mechanism would be "brittle"—breaking down and useless beyond the domain of common nouns for common objects.

Rochel Gelman (1990) once asked, "How is it that our young attend to inputs that will support the development of concepts they share with their elders?" The complex self-organizing system pictured in Figure 11.5 is an answer to this question. The very nature of attentional processes—their openness to learning, to the immediate input—create self-adjusting learning biases. Children know what inputs to attend to because they have an attentional system that is always in motion, always learning, always adapting.

☐ An Indiana Perspective

This view of attention and development as a self-organizing system is profoundly different from the arguments for domain-specific innate ideas that dominated discussions when I was a graduate student at Penn. Those old arguments pointed to the specificity, fastness, smartness of development and came to the conclusion that in order for development to happen as it does, we must come with specific knowledge about specific content—about number, about space, about other minds, about noun categories—that directs development. The evidence on the shape bias presents an example of another possibility. Development is specific, fast, and smart, but *it makes itself*; there is no driver.

Larissa Samuelson and I (Samuelson & Smith, 2000) attempted to summarize these developmental ideas using Figure 11.6. The figure is a schematic depiction of how a developmental trajectory might emerge from the operating on the attentional system pictured in Figure 11.5. The focus of attention at any given moment is given by ***t**. The forces that determine attention at that moment are the immediate input, the just-previous activity of the system, and attentional learning. The immediate input to the system at a particular moment in time is represented by **It**. The multiple processes of perceiving, remembering, and attending are indicated by arrows between the input and the individual moment of knowing, and between one moment of knowing and the next. Importantly, since the activity at ***t** is in part determined by the activity at $\mathbf{*t}_{-1}$, it is also partly determined by the activity at $\mathbf{*t}_{-2}, \mathbf{*t}_{-3}, \ldots \mathbf{*t}_{-n}$. Each moment of knowing thus brings with it the history of its own past activity. Further, since each act of knowing permanently changes attention and the contexts to which it is sensitive, the attentional system itself changes. It will not be the same at time **n** as it was at time **n-1**. We see in this picture the unification of real time and developmental time, the same processes that push attention around in the here and now also create the developmental trajectory, potentiating attention to some properties and thus shaping learning. Developmentalists should recognize the larger ideas about developmental process in this picture; they are similar to Piaget's early theory in which cognitive change emerges progressively out of the child's interactions with the world. In Figure 11.6, as for Piaget, each interaction is the product of past interactions and a causal agent of change potentiating future interactions.

This idea of development creating itself has support in many domains beyond the shape bias; indeed, it has become the thrust of developmental research at Indiana—evident in Alberts's studies of nipple-seeking in newborn rats (Abel, Ronca, & Alberts, 1998), in West's study of how cowbirds learn songs (West, King, & Duff, 1990), in Thelen's studies of the development of walking (Thelen & Ulrich, 1991), in Jones's studies of the mechanistic bases of infant facial imitation (Jones, 1996), and in Mix's studies of the perceptual bases of infants' knowledge of numbers (Clearfield & Mix, 1999). In all these domains, evidence is emerging showing how general processes create new opportunities for learning that build seamlessly on

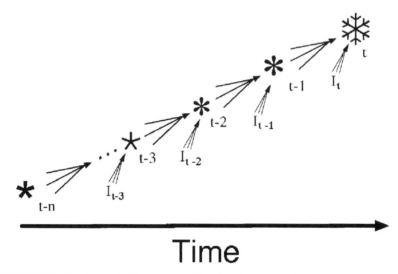

Time

FIGURE 11.6. A schematic illustration of the development of attentional learning. See text for clarification.

each other. In each domain, the behavior, the developmental trajectory as a whole, seems predestined. But the directedness of development is made one open, variable, contingent step at a time.

Let us return, then, to my starting point. Why can't young children who know that candy is to be found under red squares and triangles not automatically know that they are also to be found under red crosses? The answer is in Figure 11.5. There are no forces to move attention in this task because dimensions are all (by the experimenter's design) of equal salience and because children have no contextually relevant experiences. Attention has to be moved, and there is nothing in this task to move it. Now, why is attentional learning relevant to building androids, why should those devoted to creating artificial intelligences want to know what we know about babies and children? The answer lies in understanding how attention through its own operation becomes smart.

☐ References

Abel, R. , Ronca, A., & Alberts, J. (1998). Perinatal stimulation facilitates suckling onset in newborn rats. *Developmental Psychobiology, 32,* 91–99.

Baillargeon, R., Spelke, E. & Wasserman, S. (1985). Object permanence in five-month-old infants. *Cognition, 20,* 191–208.

Biederman, I. (1987). Recognition by components: A theory of human image understanding, *Psychological Review, 94,* 115–147.

Brooks, R.A. (1991). Intelligence without representation. *Artificial Intelligence, 47,* 139–160.

Clark, A. (1993). *Associative engines: Connectionism, concepts, and representational change*. Cambridge, MA: MIT Press.

Clark, E. V. (1973). What's in a word: On the child's acquisition of semantics in his first language. In T. E. Moore (Ed.), *Cognitive development and the acquisition of language*. New York: Academic Press.

Clearfield, M. W., & Mix, K. S. (1999) Number versus contour length in infants' discrimination of small visual sets. *Psychological Science, 10*, 408–411.

Gelman, R. (1978). Cognitive development. *Annual Review of Psychology, 29*, 297–332.

Gelman, R. (1990). First principles organize attention to and learning about relevant data: Number and the animate-inanimate distinction as examples. *Cognitive Science, 79*, 79–106.

Gershkoff-Stowe, L., & Smith, L. B. (1997). A curvilinear trend in naming errors as a function of early vocabulary growth. *Cognitive Psychology*, 34, 37–51.

Gershkoff-Stowe, L., & Smith, L. B. (2001). The first hundred nouns. Manuscript submitted for publication.

Gleitman, L. R., & Wanner, E. (1982). Language acquisition: the state of the state of the art. In E. Wanner & Gleitman, L. R. (Eds), *Language acquisition: The state of the art*, Cambridge, UK: Cambridge University Press.

Goldin-Meadow, S., & Feldman, H. (1997). The development of language-like communication without a language model. *Science, 197*, 401–403.

James, W. (1890). *Principles of psychology*. New York: Henry Holt & Co.

Jones, S. (1996). Imitation or exploration? Young infants' matching of adults' oral gestures. *Child Development, 67*, 1952–1969.

Jones, S., & Smith, L. B. (1998). How children name objects with shoes. *Cognitive Development, 13*, 323–334.

Jones, S., Smith, L., & Landau, B. (1991). Object properties and knowledge in early lexical learning. *Child Development, 62*, 499–516.

Keil, F. (1981). Children's thinking: What never develops? *Cognition, 10*, 159–166.

Keil, F. C. (1994). Explanation, association, and the acquisition of word meaning. In L. R. Gleitman & B. Landau (Eds.), *Lexical acquisition*, Cambridge, MA: MIT Press.

Kendler, T. S. (1974) The effect of training and stimulus variables on the reversal-shift ontogeny. *Journal of Experimental Child Psychology, 17*, 87–106.

Landau, B., Smith, L. B., & Jones, S. S. (1988). The importance of shape in early lexical learning. *Cognitive Development, 59*, 299–321.

Landau, B., Jones, S. S., & Smith, L. B. (1992). Syntactic context and the shape bias in children's and adult's lexical learning. *Journal of Memory and Language, 31*, 807–825.

Macnamara, J. (1982). *Names for things: A study of human learning*. Cambridge, MA: MIT Press.

Markman, E. M. (1989). *Categorization and naming: in children: Problems of induction*. Cambridge, MA: MIT Press.

Mervis, C. B. (1987). Child-basic object categories and lexical development. In U. Neisser (Ed.), *Concepts and conceptual development: Ecological and intellectual factors in categorization*. Cambridge, UK: Cambridge University Press.

Osherson, D. (1981) Modularity as an issue for cognitive science. *Cognition, 10*, 241–242.

Pfeifer, R. & Scheier, C. (1999) *Understanding intelligence*. Cambridge, MA: MIT Press.

Rosch, E. (1973). On the internal structure of perceptual and semantic categories. In T. E. Moore (Ed.), *Cognitive development and the acquisition of language* (pp. 111–144). San Diego, CA: Academic Press.

Samuelson, L., & Smith, L. B. (1998). Memory and attention make smart word learning: An alternative account of Akhtar, Carpenter and Tomasello. *Child Development, 69*, 94–104.

Samuelson, L., & Smith, L. B. (1999). Ontology, category structure and syntax. *Cognition, 71*, 1–33.

Samuelson, L., & Smith, L. B. (2000). Grounding development in cognitive processes. *Child Development, 71*, 98–106.

Smith L. B. (1995). Self-organizing processes in learning to learn words: Development is not induction. In C. A. Nelson (Ed.), *New perspectives on learning and development: Minnesota Symposium for Child Development* (pp. 1–32). New York: Academic Press.

Smith, L. B. (1999). Children's noun learning: How general processes make specialized learning mechanisms. In B. MacWhinney (Ed.), *The emergence of language* (pp. 277–304). Mahwah, NJ: LEA.

Smith, L. B., Jones, S. S., & Landau, B. (1992). Count nouns, adjectives, and perceptual properties in children's novel word interpretations. *Developmental Psychology, 28*, 273–289.

Smith, L.B., Jones, S., & Landau, B. (1996). Naming in young children: A dumb attentional mechanism? *Cognition, 60*, 143–171.

Smith, L. B., Jones, S., Landau, B. Samuelson, L., & Gershkoff-Stowe, L. (2002). Object name learning provides on-the-job training for attention. *Psychological Science, 13*, 13–18.

Thelen, E., & Ulrich, B. (1991). Hidden skills: A dynamic systems analysis of treadmill stepping during the first year. *Monographs of the Society for Research in Child Development, 56*(1) [Serial No. 223], 104.

Tighe, T., Glick, J., & Cole, M. (1971). Subproblem analysis of discrimination-shift learning. *Psychonomic Science, 24* ,159-160.

West, M., King, A., & Duff, M. (1990) Communicating about communicating: When innate is not enough. *Developmental Psychobiology, 23*, 585–598.

Yoshida, H., & Smith, L. B. (in press). Shifting ontological boundaries: How Japanese- and English-speaking children generalize names for animals and artifacts. *Developmental Sciences.*

Kurt Fischer
Zheng Yan

The Development
of Dynamic Skill Theory

In this age of focus on mind and brain, the complexity of the human mind is clear, as in this common bit of wisdom:

> The earth is very complex, but the sky is more complex. The sky is very complex, but the universe is even more complex. The universe is very complex, but the human mind is by far the most complex.

How can we understand development of human beings' minds in all their complexity, richness, and diversity? The conventional wisdom is to *dissect* a living system so that people are able to study the system one motionless piece at a time. Can we understand, for example, children's interactions, understandings, and feelings in their family by dividing memory, social roles, norms, and learning contingencies and analyzing them separately? This paradigm has so long dominated most of the behavioral, developmental, and educational sciences that people are accustomed to viewing many human characteristics such as children's intelligence or adults' emotion as fixed, clear-cut, and unconnected entities.

With dynamic skill theory (Fischer, 1980b; Fischer & Bidell, 1998), we*

---

*The first person plural will be used throughout the chapter to represent over thirty years of collaboration between the first author and his mentors, colleagues, and students in developing dynamic skill theory, including the writing of this chapter. The first person singular will be used to refer to Kurt Fischer. The major collaborators include Catherine Ayoub, Bennett Bertenthal, Thomas Bidell, Daniel Bullock, Rosemary Calverley, Joseph Campos, Ching Ling Cheng, Roberta Corrigan, Edmund Fantino, Nira Granott, Marshall Haith, Jane have tried to take a different perspective. Like examining a car that is moving on the road or studying a river that is running on the riverbed, skill theory is designed to *unpack* but not dissect human development in order best to understand the development of human mind and action in all their complexity, richness, and diversity. This theory offers a *dynamic* framework for describing, assessing, analyzing, and explaining how person and world function together in human development, building on the tools of dynamic systems theory, like some other contemporary viewpoints (Damon, 1998; Fogel, 1993; Lewis, 2000; Parke, Ornstein, Rieser, & Zahn-Waxler, 1994; Thelen & Smith, 1994; van Geert, 1998). As examples in the chapter, we will focus on skill analyses of children's social interactions, especially in their families, unpacking the activities, understandings, and feelings within a common framework that helps us interpret them all in place together.

☐ A Thirty-Year Intellectual Journey

Like most complex theories, dynamic skill theory has undergone a long course of development within the sociohistorical context of its time. Starting from the late 1960s, it has been a 30-year-long intellectual journey in which we have actively explored human action and thought, constructively synthesized diverse perspectives and methods, and persistently linked theory to method and data in research, all in collaboration with a number of colleagues. Our broad goal is to understand what, how, and why human beings develop and learn.

In this chapter, we will first present *how* dynamic skill theory has evolved by describing three major phases in its development:

1. Birth of the theory (roughly from the early 1970s to the early 1980s). The central theme in this phase was analyzing systematic change in the *organization* of action and thought.
2. Early growth of the theory (roughly from the early 1980s to the early

Haltiwanger, Helen Hand, Susan Harter, Rebecca Hencke, Jin Li, Bruce Kennedy, Karen Kitchener, Catherine Knight, Susie Lamborn, Michael Mascolo, Gil Noam, James Parziale, Sandra Pipp, Pamela Raya, Samuel Rose, Phillip Shaver, Paul van Geert, Lianquin Wang, Malcolm Watson, Michael Westerman, and many others. The theorizing process has been significantly influenced by the classic work of Piaget, Erikson, J. M. Baldwin, Hebb, Kohlberg, C. S. Peirce, Skinner, H. S. Sullivan, Vygotsky, H. Werner, and Wittgenstein, as well as more contemporary work by Mary Ainsworth, John Bowlby, Roger Brown, Jerome Bruner, Robbie Case, Noam Chomsky, Howard Gardner, J. J. Gibson, Jerome Kagan, Robert LeVine, Peter Molenaar, Robert Thatcher, Esther Thelen, Han van der Maas, Sheldon White, Beatrice and John Whiting, and David Wood.

1990s). The central theme moved to examining complex *variations* in the organization of action and thought, including systematic change.

3. Later growth of the theory (roughly from the later 1980s to 2000). The central theme became explaining the constructive *dynamics* underlying complex variations in learning, development, and emotional state.

At the end of the chapter, we will analyze *why* the theory has evolved by discussing four major factors that contributed significantly to the dynamic development of the theory:

A. Following our noses: pursuing persistently a general question about development or learning while letting our observations shape our direction.
B. Opening our eyes: consistently integrating new insights and tools to further build the framework.
C. Moving our legs: actively intertwining conceptual improvements and methodological advances in empirical research to develop the theory.
D. Holding each other's hands: working closely with students, colleagues, and mentors to construct the theory in a supportive social context.

For readers who are interested in studying more about the theory, Fischer and Bidell (1998) provide a broad introduction to the framework, placing skill theory in a wider context of dynamic approaches to development and variation.

☐ Birth of the Theory: Analyzing Change in Organization of Action and Thought

In the late 1960s and the early 1970s, the intellectual environment in the behavioral sciences in American universities was mixed: Piaget's (1970b) structuralism (constructivism) was starting to become a mainstream theoretical school, while classical behaviorism remained strong in the training of new developmental psychologists. Both behaviorism and constructivism had fundamental influence on the initial construction of dynamic skill theory. Also, in Harvard University's interdisciplinary Social Relations Department, many renowned scholars, such as Roger Brown, Jerome Bruner, Erik Erikson, Jerome Kagan, Lawrence Kohlberg, B. F. Skinner, Harrison White, Sheldon White, John and Beatrice Whiting, and Peter Wolff, were teaching a variety of theories of psychology, anthropology, sociology, child development, and pedagogy. This interdisciplinary training in theory and research made deep marks on development of the theory.

A reasonable place to mark as the starting point for dynamic skill theory is Kurt Fischer's (1970) doctoral dissertation entitled *The Structure and Development of Sensory-Motor Actions*. This research followed the behavioral tradition of conducting a series of strictly defined empirical studies of animal learning in a laboratory. At the same time, it took a new structural perspective in analyzing changes in the organization of activities as rats learned to run an S-shaped maze or pigeons learned to peck in a two-link variable-interval reinforcement schedule. In these experiments we found four distinct phases of learning (microdevelopment) in sensorimotor behaviors that were similar for both rats and pigeons—phases defined empirically by a microdevelopmental sequence of four clear patterns of activity (Fischer, 1975, 1980a). For example, in the second phase animals began the task slowly, but once they started, they performed quickly and intensely and had difficulty interrupting their actions to learn or attend to something new in the situation. In the final phase animals performed the entire task relatively quickly and could easily interrupt their actions and learn something new about the situation.

Although this discovery of change in organization with learning was exciting, it raised a major question: How could these changes be described and analyzed? There was no theoretically sound, empirically feasible analytical system for analyzing and assessing the structures that animals and people learn in such tasks. Classical behaviorist psychology had primarily examined response rates of specific behaviors in context, providing few tools for analyzing their organization. Structural developmental psychology, including Piaget (1936/1952, 1957, 1983), Vygotsky (1962), Werner (1957), and Kohlberg (1969), had focused mainly on general developmental structures, providing few tools for analyzing change and variation in organization of specific activities. We needed a set of tools and concepts for analyzing changes in the organization of action and thought. To build a useful analytic system, we would need to bring together many components into what is now called a dynamic systems perspective. The systems theory of that time (for example, von Bertalanffy, 1968) provided promising concepts but few tools for analyzing organization and variation in specific activities. Dynamic systems theory had not yet been built in the biological and behavioral sciences. We were like an infant "groping" to find a means to our goal (Piaget, 1936/1952)—following our nose to find a way.

In the ten years after the 1970 dissertation research, we worked to devise an analytic system of new methods closely tied to theory for analyzing change and variation in development and learning (e.g., Fischer, 1972, 1975, 1980a, 1980b). The first breakthrough came with our close interpretation of specific examples of behaviors that developed in individual infants and children. At first, we used them to try to understand Piaget's explanations of stages and equilibration processes (Inhelder &

Piaget, 1955/1958, 1959/1964; Piaget, 1936/1952, 1937/1954, 1946/ 1951). The series of advances in concepts and methods led to the formulation of skill theory, as published in the 1980 *Psychological Review* paper entitled "A theory of cognitive development: The control and construction of hierarchies of skills" (Fischer, 1980b). This paper marks the birth of skill theory, the initial form of what has developed into dynamic skill theory.

In this paper, we synthesized a decade of thinking and research to produce a new theoretical framework for analyzing cognitive development and learning. Its central theme was concepts and methods for assessing and analyzing changes in the organization of individual human activities (actions and thoughts). This framework included key interconnected concepts, including skill, cognitive control, set, skill hierarchy (levels, tiers, and transformation rules), collaboration of person and environment, developmental sequence and synchrony, recurring growth cycles, task analysis, unevenness (*décalage*), task domain, skill domain, and microdevelopment. For all these, the starting point is the concept of *skill*, which is why we chose the name "skill theory."

Skill

Different from competence, ability, or capacity, *skill* is a concept that is context-based and task-specific. I (KF) had extensive knowledge of behaviorist concepts such as context, task, and stimulus control (Skinner, 1938, 1969), and I worked with Jerome Bruner as a postdoctoral fellow while he was elaborating the concept of skill (Bruner, 1970, 1973). In seminars and coffee shops, a group of us debated how organism and environment could work together. Focusing on analyzing specific activities of individual people or animals, we always ended up including the context as key, along with the organism's actions. We could find only one concept that directly included both person and environment in the same entity— skill. A person can have a skill for building with a particular set of toy blocks, telling a story about one's family, cooperating with Mother and Father at the dinner table, fighting with Sister at the dinner table, operating Grandmother's sewing machine, playing tennis on a grass court, or doing analysis of variance with a computer statistics program. Concepts of ability, competence, capacity, concept, intelligence, and even scheme (Piaget, 1936/1952) did not have that meaning. Interestingly, many languages, including French, do not seem to have a word like "skill" for designating activities in a specific task or context. The term "skill" is thus the best choice.

Levels and Tiers

A related concept that we devised was skill *level*. Levels are not stages, because there is so much variability in each child's activities that children do not show ladderlike changes from one stage to the next at specific ages. What they do show is qualitative changes in skill organization, especially in their most complex activities. For example, at 2 and 3 years a girl represents the role of her mother as a collection or set of behaviors, such as [$^{JANE}_{MOTHER}$], and separately she represents the role of father as another set, [$^{WALTER}_{FATHER}$]. She can understand and act on each role separately, but she has difficulty representing the two roles in relationship, simplifying to one role at a time. At about 4 years of age, her understanding shifts dramatically, as she represents social role relationships for the first time, relating mother to father to understand their special parental and romantic relationship, [$^{JANE}_{MOTHER}$——$^{WALTER}_{FATHER}$]. Similarly, at this age she relates her role as friend to another child's role as friend to capture the relational meaning of "best friend" (Fischer, Hand, Watson, Van Parys, & Tucker, 1984).

The conceptions of specific skill levels grew from our efforts to determine where major qualitative changes in organization occurred by working extensively with protocols describing specific developing activities, some from our own observations and others from Piaget, Bruner, and other researchers. In the first skill development model based on these analyses, we found that the clearest changes in organization corresponded roughly with what Piaget (1936/1952, 1983) called primary circular reactions, secondary circular reactions, tertiary circular reactions, representations, concrete operations, and formal operations.

We found evidence for another level in the middle preschool years, which is similar to what Piaget and his colleagues called semi-logic (Piaget, Grize, Szeminska, & Bang, 1968) and which we call representational mappings. This mapping level marks a significant advance in negotiating social relationships in the family, as illustrated in the above mapping of mother and father roles that leads to understanding the special relationship of mother and father (Watson & Fischer, 1980; Watson & Getz, 1990). Another mapping skill that surges at this level is understanding self and other, as in the currently popular research on theory of mind (Frye, Zelazo, & Palfai, 1995; Leslie, 1987). Various descriptions and theories proposed other stages or substages, but for those we found less convincing empirical evidence of abrupt qualitative change from one step to the next (Fischer, Pipp, & Bullock, 1984).

Piaget's descriptions of each of these "stages" provided a good starting point but did not adequately capture the organization in the many examples that we examined. Gradually we invented a different way of describing the structures, which we introduced above in the skill diagrams for mother and father roles. This tool is based on the concept of skill defined in terms of a few simple kinds of relations among skill components—mappings (————), systems ($\leftrightarrow$), and systems of systems ($\Leftrightarrow$); brackets mark a distinct skill. The skill components are *sets*, not points, because they always include a number of adaptations of activities to a particular context. An example is the skill for the mother-father role relationship, [$^{JANE}_{MOTHER}$ ————$^{WALTER}_{FATHER}$], which involves relating two sets through a mapping. We will only sketch a few ideas from this analytic method here. A full explanation is available in other sources (Fischer, 1980b; Fischer & Farrar, 1987; Fischer & Bullock, 1994).

We also sought clearer, more explicit ways of defining levels empirically, ways of specifying the dramatic changes that we had seen in the many developing activities that we had analyzed. Eventually we found that discontinuities in growth curves, such as spurts and drops, provided an excellent empirical criterion for emergence of a new level, with clusters of spurts occurring at certain age periods. An excellent example is the growth spurts in vocabulary, sentence production, and pretend play late in the second year in most toddlers (Corrigan, 1983; Reznick & Goldfield, 1992), as illustrated for personal pronoun vocabulary for the Dutch child Tomas in Figure 12.1 (Ruhland & van Geert, 1998). Another is the spurts in understanding family roles, friendships, and self-other relationships (theory of mind) at ages 4 to 5 years.

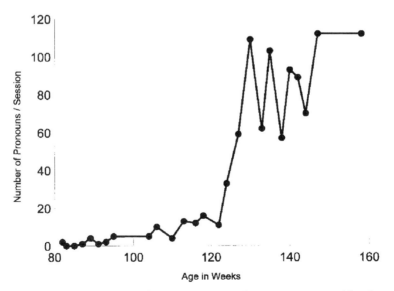

FIGURE 12.1. Spurt in personal pronoun use marking a new optimal level: Tomas. Source: Ruhland & van Geert, 1998

In describing the series of skill levels in infancy and early childhood, our main conscious metaphors were chemical structures (which inspired the skill diagrams) and building blocks. A characteristic of these kinds of structures is that smaller units become components of larger structures. In the same way each new level of skill involves combining two or more units from the prior level to form a qualitatively different kind of skill structure, as the isolated roles of mother and father at one level are combined to form the skill for mother and father in relationship at the next level.

The evidence pointed to a series of levels, initially seven that we could identify between 4 months and 12 years of age. We also found what seemed to be further structure within the series—a cycle of levels that we called a *tier*. The first hint of a tier came from the dramatic changes that occur late in the second year with the emergence of the level of representations. We hypothesized that a higher order of structure emerged at that level, similar to a new building block that can be constructed from simpler building components. With the emergence of such a new structure the cyclical building process of levels begins over again, starting once more with single sets and developing through relations among sets (mappings, systems, systems of systems). Figure 12.2 illustrates this *growth cycle* with the building-block metaphor.

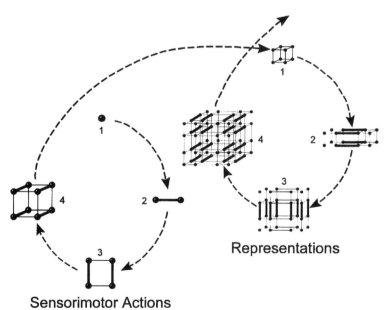

FIGURE 12.2. Cycle of levels and tiers. Numbers mark the four levels within each tier. Dark lines indicate the new relations formed at each level.

In forming the new building block at about age 2, children coordinate several systems of sensorimotor actions to form a new kind of skill—a single representation. For example, most 1-year-olds have an action system for manipulating a doll and another action system for walking themselves. With the emergence of single representations late in the second year, they coordinate those two systems to form a representation in pretend play: they move the doll in a way that represents its walking across the floor. Similarly, they coordinate action systems to be able to represent actions and perceptions in speech: they say "Me walk" as they walk across the kitchen. (Single representations typically involve an agent or object doing an action or having a characteristic, such as "Me walk" and "Big cookie.")

The hypothesis of tiers led quickly to generalizations predicting later and earlier levels. We predicted that moving through levels of skills for representations, children would eventually produce another new building block, abstractions (related to what Piaget [1957] called formal operations). The tier hypothesis produced the first general model predicting the further development of new levels and capacities beyond formal operations: starting with single abstractions, adolescents construct skills at levels of mappings, systems, and systems of systems from age 10 into adulthood (Fischer, 1980b). Predictions about these levels have been strongly supported in subsequent research (Fischer, Yan, & Stewart, in press; Kitchener, Lynch, Fischer, & Wood, 1993). Also, we predicted that in early infancy a tier of controlled reflexes leads to the emergence of sensorimotor actions at approximately 4 months of age (Fischer, 1980b; Fischer & Hogan, 1989). Empirical evidence about these earliest levels is encouraging but not yet substantial enough to be conclusive.

Transformation Rules for Developmental Steps

A key concept for analyzing how skills are constructed is transformation rules, which both specify change processes for specific skills and define steps in developmental sequences and scales. Careful longitudinal and microdevelopmental observation of developing activities, such as search (object permanence) and pretend play, showed strongly that skills developed through sequences of many small steps in each domain. When we analyzed their skills through detailed developmental sequences, children did not usually remain for long periods at one step. Even when spurts occurred, children moved rapidly through a series of steps rather than jumping instantaneously to the next level.

How could we describe, explain, and predict these steps? What was required was a relatively continuous scale or ruler involving qualitative changes of various types and degrees. Following analogies from chemistry and geometry and building on the focus on transformations in linguistics and structuralism (Chomsky, 1957; Piaget, 1968/1970b), we looked for ways that a skill could be transformed. We worked out the transformations required to explain steps in development and learning for specific developing skills, especially focusing on agency in pretend play (Watson & Fischer, 1977), self-recognition (Bertenthal & Fischer, 1978), object permanence (Bertenthal & Fischer, 1983; Corrigan, 1981; Corrigan & Fischer, 1985; Jackson, Campos, & Fischer, 1978), social roles such as mother-father, parent-child, doctor-patient, and boy-girl in stories and play (Fischer et al., 1984; Fischer & Watson, 1981; Van Parys, 1983; Watson & Fischer, 1980), and affective themes such as "nice" and "mean" in stories and interactions (Fischer & Pipp, 1984a; Fischer & Lamborn, 1989; Hand, 1982; Lamborn, 1986).

Four different rules portray most transformations of skills to create small steps within a level in a developmental sequence in a domain, and a fifth rule depicts the movement to a skill at the next level. The rules for substitution and compounding were immediately obvious in the developmental sequences that we saw: substitution involved substituting a slightly different object or event in an activity, such as having a bear replace a doll to act in the role of mother, $\begin{bmatrix} BEAR \\ MOTHER \end{bmatrix}$ replacing $\begin{bmatrix} DOLL \\ MOTHER \end{bmatrix}$. Compounding involved adding a new major component, such as coordinating a child role simultaneously with mother and father roles, $\begin{bmatrix} WALTER - JANE & - \\ FATHER & MOTHER \\ JOHANNA \\ CHILD \end{bmatrix}$, combining the simpler relationships.

The rule for shift of focus grew out of some struggles we had in distinguishing integration from mere juxtaposition of skill components. We eventually realized that it was not just a coding problem but a skill difference. This rule has turned out to be one of the most general and useful for explaining developmental transitions, occurring nearly universally in major transitions between levels that we and other investigators have studied (Fischer & Bidell, 1998; Goldin-Meadow, Nusbaum, Garber, & Church, 1993; Gottlieb, Taylor, & Ruderman, 1977). Children and adults routinely shift back and forth between two skills for doing a task, thus juxtaposing the skills, and through this process they move toward integrating them to form a new, more complex and sophisticated skill. For example, when faced with two dolls occupying the roles of mother/father (taking care of child) and wife/husband (focusing on their own relationship), 3- and 4-year-olds tend to confuse the roles badly, mixing up mother with wife and husband with father (Fischer & Watson, 1981; Watson & Getz, 1990). As they begin to master the distinction, they regularly shift between the role relationships rather than integrating them: $\begin{bmatrix} JANE & - \\ MOTHER \\ WALTER \\ FATHER \end{bmatrix} > \begin{bmatrix} JANE & - WALTER \\ WIFE & HUSBAND \end{bmatrix}$. A few articulate children even signaled such shifts by saying sentences such as "And then a long time later they were husband and wife."

Eventually children work through many transformations of these skills in a series of small steps until they can fully coordinate two skills at the next developmental level, which is called intercoordination, the transformation rule for full-level growth. A child can integrate, for example, mother and wife with father and husband in a single relationship, with each person occupying two roles simultaneously,

$$
\left[
\begin{array}{ccc}
\textit{WIFE} & & \textit{HUSBAND} \\
\textit{JANE} & \ll & \textit{WALTER} \\
\textit{MOTHER} & & \textit{FATHER}
\end{array}
\right]
$$

(Interestingly, the mastery of this role distinction seems to play a key role both in children's resolution of the Oedipus conflict in nuclear families and their adaptation to their parents' breakup in divorced families [Watson & Fischer, 1993]).

The final transformation rule is differentiation, which turns out to be not a separate transformation but a part of each of the other four transformations. In cognitive science, differentiation has been a hard nut to crack, with people arguing endlessly about whether differentiation precedes or follows integration (or coordination). We eventually found that the best answer is that the two are always together—two sides of the same coin, as Heinz Werner (1957) indicated. Whenever some kind of coordination occurs, such as compounding, intercoordination, and controlled shift of focus, differentiation is part of it. Likewise, any differentiation always involves a simultaneous coordination. Family roles illustrate this process. To coordinate mother with wife and father with husband, a child needs to differentiate the similar roles; and, likewise, to differentiate them, a child must relate them to each other by coordinating them.

Once we had carefully designed a system for assessing and analyzing the organization of activities, however, we faced two major challenges. First was how to move beyond merely asserting that *décalage,* or unevenness in level, is the rule in cognitive development: How can these variations be explained? Second was how to apply skill analysis to the full range of human activities—emotion, learning, context, culture, and social interaction as well as traditional cognitive tasks. Indeed, the second challenge turned out to help deal with the first one, explaining most cases of unevenness in development. The analysis of developmental variations naturally became the central task in our next decade of research.

☐ Early Growth of the Theory: Variations in Organization and Change

The 1980s marked a major transition in the history of developmental science. While Piaget, Freud, Vygotsky, Werner, and other founders of the field still had dominant influence, various forms of "neo-theories" came to dominate the landscape, such as neo-behaviorist, neo-Piagetian, and neo-Vygotskian, along with a central emphasis on specific tasks and domains rather than grand conceptions. Many researchers were not satisfied with merely learning and using classical theories but instead aimed to work out specific applications that typically were more modest in ambition than the grand theories, such as a specific developmental analysis of use of a balance beam (Siegler, 1981), or of domain effects on self-evaluation (Harter & Pike, 1984). This emphasis on specificity fit well with skill theory's emphasis on the specificity of skills and their relative independence across domains.

In this intellectual context, skill theory entered into its second major phase of development, a fruitful period after the publication of the 1980 article. During this period we expanded our research and theory to deal with a wide range of topics, published numerous articles about this expansion, and achieved several breakthroughs in dealing with variations in the organization of action and thought and in patterns of change. Publications involved extensive empirical research (Calverley, Fischer, & Ayoub, 1994; Fischer, 1987; Fischer, Hand, & Russell, 1984; Fischer & Pipp, 1984a, 1984b; Fischer, Shaver, & Carnochan, 1989; Kitchener & Fischer, 1990) as well as advances in developmental methodology for detecting change and variation in organization (Fischer & Bullock, 1981; Fischer, Pipp, & Bullock, 1984). Four topics played an especially substantial role in development of skill theory: contextual support, social grounding, emotions and unconscious processes, and brain-growth correlates of cognitive changes.

Contextual Support: Optimal and Functional Levels

The concept of contextual support, as well as the related concepts of optimal and functional levels, initially came from our research on the development of social roles. We assessed development in two contextual-support conditions, because researchers were always arguing about whether assessments should focus on spontaneous behavior or structured, evoked behavior. When we included both conditions, we consistently found different skill levels, even in the same child in assessments just a few minutes apart in virtually identical tasks. In various explorations between 1977 and 1985 we tried to eliminate the difference between conditions through simple changes in assessment conditions, but we found that the difference robustly remained. So long as there was a difference in contextual support (little direct support versus high support), virtually all children and adults showed consistently different upper limits on their skill, even in a narrowly defined domain.

High support involved priming the gist of a task—its key components—and then asking the person to perform the task on his or her own. Low support involved simply asking for a performance on the same task without any priming. These conditions consistently produced two different, stable levels, which we named optimal and functional levels, respectively. Daniel Bullock played a key role in our eventually recognizing the basic importance of this phenomenon—the fundamental role of context in skill (Fischer & Bullock, 1984; Fischer et al., 1993; Watson & Fischer, 1980). Context directly participates as part of a skill, just as physical objects support perception through their affordances (Gibson, 1979).

In an arithmetic study we tested optimal and functional levels for the first time with evenly distributed ages, which are essential for accurately assessing the shape of a growth curve (Fischer, Hand, & Russell, 1984). Malcolm Watson's dissertation research on social roles, for example, had not distributed ages evenly (Watson & Fischer, 1980), because the experimental psychologists on his dissertation committee insisted that ages had to be clustered into narrow age groups for analysis of variance. To our surprise and delight, with distributed ages we found sharply different growth curves for high versus low support: optimal level (high support) showed sharp discontinuities in growth at specific ages, such as jumps in skill level, while functional level (low support) showed no systematic discontinuities and commonly slow, smooth growth, as illustrated in Figure 12.3 for levels of development of abstract skills in adolescence and

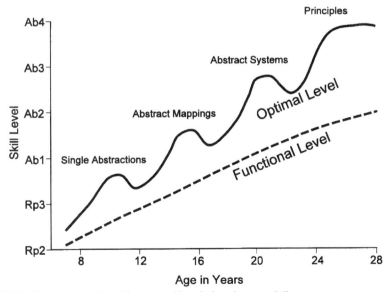

FIGURE 12.3. Optimal and functional levels for abstract skills.

adulthood. Testing this difference in many studies across many domains, we replicated it repeatedly.

From this work, the importance of good rulers and clocks for detecting the shapes of growth curves also emerged, because the shapes of growth curves can be detected only with decent scales and unbiased time sampling (Rose & Fischer, 1998). The finding of developmental range due to different social-contextual conditions was one of the most exciting discoveries we made because it went beyond describing *décalage* to showing a systematic basis for it in context.

The above research and thinking led to the concept of *developmental range*, one of the central concepts leading to further research on developmental variation and dynamic construction. *People's capacities are not fixed but vary across a broad range of levels from moment to moment*, topping out at an optimal level that appears primarily in situations with strong social-contextual support for complex understanding and acts as a dynamic attractor in skill development. Most activities occur well below that optimal level and show other kinds of limits, such as the functional level—the upper limit on skills in ordinary activity without any contextual support. It has not been an intellectually easy task, however, for researchers to appreciate the significance of the developmental range, even when they value Vygotsky's (1978) related concept of zone of proximal development. Most psychological and educational assessments give grossly inadequate portraits of people's skills because they assume one level of competence and ignore the developmental range and the several different upper limits for each person in each knowledge domain. In addition, most important processes of learning and problem-solving in children and adults take place in the variation in skill levels below optimal level (Fischer & Bidell, 1998; Fischer et al., 1993; Granott, Fischer, & Parziale, 2002).

Social Grounding

From the start, the goal was to find concepts and methods to analyze how behavior is fundamentally grounded in physical context and social relationships. That is why the concept of skill is foundational, and why skill level routinely varies across the developmental range and below it. That is also why we have continually studied children's and adults' constructions of social interactions and social roles, starting with Watson & Fischer (1977, 1980). The research on social-role development greatly facilitated our analyses of the social foundations of development, especially through pretend play, which powerfully combines cognition, social interaction, and emotion in one set of activities.

Children grow up in social relationships, and eventually by living in them and sharing them with the people in their lives, they come to represent the roles and interactions in play and language (Fischer et al., 1984; Fischer & Watson, 1981), as when 2-year-old Kara acts out the role of [$^{ME}_{MOTHER}$] and says "Kara is Mommy." The development of self-concepts and skills is grounded in the body and in relationships, as evidenced in studies with Bennett Bertenthal and Sandra Pipp (Bertenthal & Fischer, 1978, 1983; Pipp, Fischer, & Jennings, 1987; Pipp, 1990). The situations for analyzing self-recognition and self-representation skills were fundamentally interactional, with mother and interviewer being central components of the skills being assessed. The analysis of the social-contextual grounding of skills proved to be one of the most fruitful parts of skill theory, because of progress in analyzing both developmental variability and development of socioemotional relationships.

Emotions and Unconscious Processes

The work on social relationships relates naturally to emotions and unconscious processes, which are central parts of development and learning that we have integrated into skill theory. During the time that I was in Denver, a remarkable group of developmentalists (Joseph Campos, Susan Harter, Phillip Shaver, Robert Emde, and others) were helping to build the new functional/organizational approach to emotion and to bring emotion to the center of developmental science (Campos, Barrett, Lamb, Goldsmith, & Stenberg, 1983; Harter, 1986; Shaver, Schwartz, Kirson, & O'Connor, 1987). Working with them, we were able to formulate concepts and methods for analyzing how emotional organization participates in skill development and learning (Fischer, Shaver, & Carnochan, 1989, 1990). Children's skills involving family relationships, for example, are obviously permeated with many powerful emotions, including love, happiness, fear, anger, and shame.

The most important concept for analyzing emotions is *action tendency*—the bias or constraint that an emotion exerts on the organization of behavior (Frijda, 1986; Lazarus, 1991). For example, the emotion of anger brings with it a strong tendency to aggressive action and speech as well as a bias to blame someone. Action tendencies thus shape skills in immediate situations, and through repeated evocation over long periods, they shape developmental pathways.

Action tendencies and other parts of the functional approach to emotion helped us to describe and analyze how emotions shape particular activities and thus developmental pathways. Three essential components for analyzing the organization of emotions are valence (positive/negative or approach/avoidance—the most pervasive dimension of emotion—and also other fundamental dimensions such as arousal and self/other), action tendencies portrayed by emotion scripts, and grouping of emotions into conceptual families. With this synthesis of concepts of emotion into skill theory, we were able to describe many specific skill pathways that are shaped by emotions. For example, we began to describe a family of pathways for development of affective splitting and dissociation, including distinctive pathways for particular kinds of child maltreatment (Fischer & Ayoub, 1994; Fischer et al., 1997; Fischer & Pipp, 1984a). The emotion framework facilitated understanding an essential point about many pathways to psychopathology as well as normal emotional development: splitting and dissociation are not abnormal or pathological but are normal, active control processes that involve "unconscious" skills for keeping apart or dissociating broad classes of actions and thoughts shaped by emotions. In cases of extreme, abusive environments, they produce adaptations that are functional within the context of abuse but pathological outside it, as in patterns of hidden family violence and multiple personality disorder.

Brain Growth: Levels and Cycles

The discovery of developmental range, especially the distinctive growth curves for optimal level, also led to an important advance in relating brain and behavior development. We discovered that some growth curves for brain activity (electroencephalogram, abbreviated EEG) looked similar to cognitive growth curves, with shapes like the optimal level curve in Figure 12.3 (Fischer, 1987; Fischer & Pipp, 1984b). This discovery came from Sheldon White's suggestion that we examine the EEG growth data of Matousek and Petersén (1973): it turns out that the ages of brain growth spurts correlate closely with the ages for emergence of each optimal level between 1 and 21 years. These similar patterns could provide a way of relating brain and behavior development by analyzing common patterns in growth curves. As a result of these findings, I was bouncing off the walls with excitement for several days.

We began consulting with developmental neuroscientists, starting with a conference on relations between brain and cognitive-emotional development, held at the University of Denver in November of 1986 and organized by Kurt Fischer and Joseph Campos with funding from the Sloan Foundation. There we first met Robert Thatcher, who collaborated with us for ten years, teaching us much about development of the brain and analysis of the EEG. His findings of growth cycles for EEG coherence and power give further evidence for straightforward relations between cognitive and cortical growth curves. In this way we began the process of describing growth cycles of brain and cognition and searching for data to pin down the patterns. Reconceptualizing stages and levels in terms of growth cycles began with the tier cycles in Figure 12.2, which were first proposed in 1980. In our current efforts we continue to discover ways that cycles ground development and learning (Fischer & Bidell, 1998; Fischer, Yan, & Stewart, in press).

Putting Together All the Variations

By the end of the 1980s, we had enjoyed some success in unpacking sources of variation in human development by using a set of concepts and methods for developmental levels (sequences and synchronies), developmental range, social-contextual support, emotions, and brain functioning (Fischer, 1987; Fischer & Farrar, 1987; Fischer & Hogan, 1989; Fischer & Bidell, 1991). At the same time, we obviously needed new tools for analyzing the connections among the parts of human development.

One problem that illustrates this need is the *generalization* of skills: How can the range of generalization be analyzed and predicted? People often generalize skills from one task or situation to another, but predicting when generalization occurs has proved to be one of the most difficult problems in cognitive science. For example, 12-year-old adolescent Johanna comes to understand that her best friend feels neglected when Johanna forgets about her birthday, but her best friend is only one of the people she is close to. Predicting whether and when she will generalize that understanding to, say, her mother's birthday is difficult. Much research finds little evidence for generalization of classroom instruction, even from courses designed to teach generalizable knowledge (Detterman, 1993; Perkins & Salomon, 1989). Analysis of development provides a powerful window for understanding, predicting, and producing transfer, and the skill theory research of the late 1980s began this analysis: we are able (a) to predict sequences of generalization within a domain, (b) to separate generalization from concurrent development of distinct skills, and (c) to specify pathways of generalization driven by emotional experiences.

At the same time, skill theory could not predict and explain the full range of generalization across task domains in individual people. For instance, degrees of contextual support strongly affect range of generalization within a task domain, but predicting variations in individual generalization with support can be done only by combining multiple factors in a single model, not merely acknowledging their relevance. Research in the 1980s and beyond continued to show that skill theory tools can be used successfully to analyze specific patterns of skill organization and change, but dealing comprehensively with the pervasive variations in behavioral organization requires the use of dynamic systems concepts and mathematical models of growth.

☐ Later Growth of the Theory: Dynamics of Variation

The last decade has seen rapidly growing attempts to apply dynamic systems theory to human development and other parts of psychology (Bogartz, 1994; Case & Okamoto, 1996; Fischer et al., 1993; Fischer & Hogan, 1989; Port & van Gelder, 1995; Thelen & Smith, 1994; Vallacher & Nowak, 1994; van der Maas & Molenaar, 1992; van Geert, 1991). The common theme underlying all these efforts is analysis of the ways that many factors interact complexly over time in context to produce wide variation in action, thought, and development. Modern dynamic systems theory provides important tools for analyzing and understanding the complex organization and variation in real-life human development.

Although dynamic systems theory is deeply rooted in the systems theory of the 1950s and 1960s (von Bertalanffy, 1968), it goes well beyond those general, sometimes vague concepts to offer powerful analytic tools. Specific concepts such as self-organization, emergence, complexity, nonlinearity, attractor, and fractal combine with explicit mathematically sophisticated tools for analyzing and explaining complex variations, and they have been widely used in physics, biology, and industry (Forrester, 1961; Huckfeldt, Kohfeld, & Likens, 1982; Levine & Lodwick, 1992; Prigogine & Stengers, 1984; Zeeman, 1976). Piaget's (1975/1985) concept of equilibration is also relevant—how growth processes work together to produce relatively stable, long-term skills and knowledge built on activities (van Geert, 1998).

Skill theory concepts obviously demand dynamic analysis of development and learning, and dynamic systems theory provides not only an emphasis on analysis of variation but also powerful analytic tools and a focus on complex growth patterns such as that for optimal level in Figure 12.3. The dynamic systems perspective helps bring together the system for analyzing change in skill organization created in the 1970s with the many components studied in the 1980s that produce complex variations in action, thought, and emotion across domains. Following our collective nose, we found a remarkable match between skill theory and dynamic systems theory.

Modeling Dynamics in Competence

The banner year for this effort was 1992, when we formed a study group at the Center for Advanced Study in the Behavioral Sciences at Stanford to work together on applying dynamic systems theory to analysis of development. The core members of this group were developmental psychologists Kurt Fischer, Robbie Case, and Paul van Geert, with support from neuroscientist Robert Thatcher, developmentalists Katherine Nelson, Peter Molenaar, and Han van der Mass, cognitive scientist Nira Granott, statistician John Willett, and social psychologist Abraham Tesser. For the entire year we worked intensively to devise tools for modeling and measuring dynamic growth and development, including a series of specific mathematical models (Case & Okamoto, 1996; Fischer & van Geert, 1993; Fischer & Kennedy, 1997).

This study group had a profound impact on the development of what we now call *dynamic skill theory*. We learned how well the dynamic systems perspective complements skill theory concepts and methods. Melding the two produces a powerful framework, with blueprints and a tool kit for analyzing change and variation in the organization of actions, thoughts, and feelings in individuals and small groups, which we call ensembles (Fischer & Granott, 1995). We are engaged in building models for processes of growth and change and capturing important pathways of development and learning.

The first major product of our research along this line was a book chapter entitled "The dynamics of competence: How context contributes directly to skill" (Fischer et al., 1993), which was the first publication of ours that included the word "dynamics" in the title. Criticizing the traditional concept of fixed competence, we explained how immediate context contributes directly to skill level as evidenced in optimal and functional levels. Most important, we synthesized the many findings about developmental range and systematically explained the dynamic processes underlying development, including a sketch of a neural-network model. People act in medias res—in the middle of things in the real world, not merely as logical agents acting on objects rationally and without emotion.

Contrary to static conceptions, *people have no single fixed competence like the capacity of a drinking glass, but instead there is a dynamic range of competences.* People's activities vary widely from moment to moment up and down a developmental complexity scale (defined by skill levels) as a function of degree of contextual support, emotional match, and specific task demands of the moment. When contextual support changes, a person's level changes. The upper limit on performance (the competence) varies directly with support. Both human behavior and models of neural networks show this dynamic variation as a function of support. This was the beginning of our most successful dynamic analysis until that date and led to mathematical models of developmental range as a function of contextual support, task, domain, and experience with a situation (Fischer & Kennedy, 1997).

Context powerfully organizes development in many ways, and variation in support is only one part of context's effects. Differences in task and domain also powerfully shape developmental pathways. A useful model for such contextual factors, first formulated by Thomas Bidell, is the construction of a web, illustrated in Figure 12.4 (Bidell & Fischer, 1992). This metaphor has generated a number of useful analytic tools and concepts for describing developmental pathways, including their multiple, partly independent strands (Fischer & Bidell, 1998; Fischer, Yan, & Stewart, in press). The web highlights the separation of diverse domains (strands), the joining and dividing that can occur within a domain (along a strand), and the concurrent zone for discontinuous changes across many strands—all seen in Figure 12.4. Distinct strands represent separate task domains,

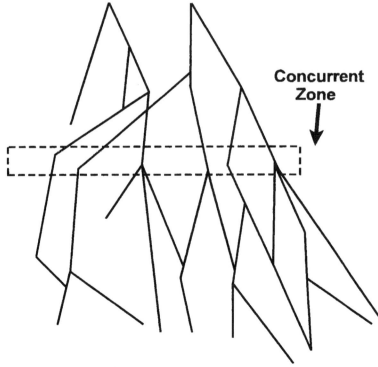

FIGURE 12.4. Constructed web of development: parallel, distributed strands and concurrent zone.

and the general separation of strands on the left and right reflect the encapsulation or dissociation of skill domains, such as private roles versus public roles, or spatial reasoning versus verbal reasoning. The box in Figure 12.4 indicates the concurrent zone for the emergence of an optimal level, marked by a cluster of discontinuities (spurts, drops, junctions, and forks).

Microdevelopment

The dynamic framework affirms the importance of microdevelopment, short-term patterns of change based on processes of learning and development. Dynamic analysis emphasizes both processes of change and the importance of analyzing the specifics of growth in individual people instead of through group means. Because growth is frequently nonlinear, group data can only be used when careful assessments are made to ensure that group means actually represent individual growth patterns. The themes of change processes and individual growth were both present in skill theory from the start, but the dynamic framework shows how central they are to the enterprise of understanding skill variation and change.

Skill theory actually began with microdevelopmental analysis, which was the topic of Kurt Fischer's thesis on learning in individual rats and pigeons in 1970. Our goal was to find a common framework for integrating microdevelopment with long-term growth (macrodevelopment), but many years of work on macrodevelopment intervened before Thomas Bidell and Nira Granott in the early 1990s led us to breakthroughs in concepts and methods for analyzing microdevelopment (e.g., Bidell & Fischer, 1994; Fischer & Granott, 1995). The short-term developmental changes found in these studies vividly demonstrated the dynamic nature of microdevelopment and the relation with macrodevelopment. Microdevelopmental studies have now become a critical resource for uncovering and explaining growth mechanisms underlying developmental variations, and they also provide ways to test dynamic skill ideas in everyday activities relating to learning and education.

When children or adults are faced with a task or problem they cannot immediately solve, such as working with a Lego robot or building a friendship with a new peer, they routinely lower their activities with the task down to a low level, as illustrated in Figure 12.5, and they rebuild their skills to fit the new task. They explore the task with simple activities that help them build a more adequate representation of the specifics of the task. This process is not a unitary march toward higher level skill but involves frequent drops to a low level to build and rebuild the skill, as shown in Figure 12.5 (Granott, 1994; Granott, in press; Granott, Fischer,

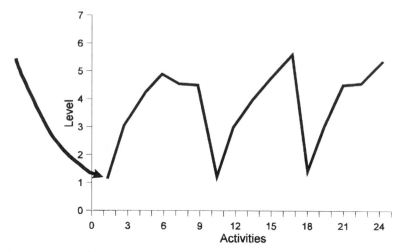

FIGURE 12.5. Backward transition to build and rebuild a new skill.

& Parziale, 2002; Yan, 2000). Animals learn through a process similar to people (Fischer, 1980a). In novel tasks, many rebuildings are required to achieve generalizable skill. Importantly, this constructive process is typically done in collaboration with peers or mentors, forming ensembles for learning and problem-solving (Granott, 1993).

An important microdevelopmental finding is that most tasks, even in educational settings, do not require people's optimal skill levels but can be effectively done at lower levels. In our microdevelopmental research to date, people seldom approach their optimal or functional levels, even when they show expert performance. When faced with a task, experts initially drop down to a lower level only briefly and then move up to the level required for adequate performance of the task, where typically their performance remains mostly steady. Novices, on the other hand, show highly variable skill levels, building and rebuilding the skill many times in order to move to a high enough, stable level of performance (Fischer, Yan, McGonigle, & Warnett, 2000; Yan, 2000). In this ongoing research, we seek to understand dynamic patterns and mechanisms of growth and variation and to build explicit dynamic models of these changes.

Diverse Developmental Pathways, Emotions, and Interactions

Emotions and close relationships are major contributors to the dynamics of growth and variation and primary influences in shaping pathways for both macrodevelopment and microdevelopment. Indeed, emotions *in* close relationships have especially powerful effects. Research has led to the discovery of many different pathways and to a questioning of traditional analyses that assume one common pathway for most people. The tools for skill analysis make it possible to analyze individual developmental pathways from a person's own viewpoint instead of forcing him or her into the viewpoint embodied in a standard model of development, such as science and logic (Piaget, 1970a), ego maturity (Loevinger, 1976), healthy interpersonal skills (Ainsworth, Blehar, Waters, & Wall, 1978; Kohut, 1971), or moral judgment (Kohlberg, 1984).

One common belief among behavioral scientists is that psychopathology involves retarded, fixated, or regressed development: people with narcissistic disorders, schizophrenia, autism, and many other disorders are said to be stuck at an early point along the normative developmental ladder to mental health. Our research challenges this belief. In research with abused children, adolescents, and adults, for example, individuals developed to the normative optimal level for their age when assessed from their own perspective. They showed an *idiosyncratic emotional organization of relationships*, but their skill level was not retarded, fixated, or regressed.

Many abused adolescents in our studies organize themselves in their relationships around the assumption that they are fundamentally bad, in contrast to the usual positive self-bias that accompanies most healthy development. With methods that can detect this distinctive self-organization, these adolescents show levels of skill complexity that are entirely normal for their age, with no developmentally primitive skills. From the dynamic skill perspective, most psychopathology involves distinctive developmental pathways, not primitive ones (Calverley et al., 1994; Fischer, Ayoub, Noam, Singh, Maraganore, & Raya, 1997). Dynamic skill theory provides tools for detecting and analyzing these distinctive pathways.

Both macro- and microdevelopment work mostly through social interactions, especially in close relationships. People interact and develop together in ensembles, not acting in isolation. Even when people act alone, their activities are grounded in close relationships and social supports. Skill theory tools work well in analyzing these growth processes, combining cognitive, contextual, social, and emotional factors. Nira Granott (1993, 2002) has shown how adult students spontaneously form small ensembles (dyads or triads) to solve new problems together, often working effectively as an integrated social unit that cannot easily be divided into separate individuals for analysis. Michael Mascolo has analyzed how mother and child play with a toy together to build skills as well as a relationship, as well as how adult couples act together in therapy to elaborate and hopefully mend difficulties in their relationships (Mascolo & Fischer, 1998; Mascolo, Fischer, & Neimeyer, 1999; see also Westerman, 1990) . We expect this new direction to become increasingly important in dynamic skill theory—unpacking the socioemotional roots of micro- and macro-development as well as the cultural construction of emotions and relationships (Mascolo, Fischer, & Li, in press; Fischer, Wang, Kennedy, & Cheng, 1998).

Synthesis of Many Components in Skill Theory

The greatest challenge of dynamic skill analysis is the same as the greatest challenge of analyzing human behavior: combining the many components in a way that (a) unpacks without dissecting and (b) simplifies and clarifies enough to help understanding rather than overwhelming it. In the chapter by Fischer and Bidell (1998) in the *Handbook of Child Psychology*, we present an overview of the dynamic structural approach to development that aims to present a number of concepts, tools, and applications coherently and clearly. Moving beyond the previous frameworks of skill theory, this new synthesis has several important features that articulate key components of skill theory with dynamic systems:

1. It is a *grounded theory* of development, interweaving concepts with methods for analyzing dynamic structures and requiring explication in terms of specific activities in context. Research designs, measurement tools, and data analysis techniques are all intertwined with the theoretical framework.

2. It moves beyond neo-Piagetian structuralism to *dynamic constructivism*, in which skill organizations vary dynamically according to specifiable growth processes and control parameters. Different from most dynamic systems approaches, such as Thelen and Smith (1994), dynamic skill theory begins its analysis with a wide variety of *developmental* changes in children's and adolescents' specific activities. Different from most neo-Piagetian approaches, such as Case (1991, Case & Okamoto, 1996) and Piaget (1983), it deals with development and *variation in real-life activities*, not focusing on logic, rationality, or unitary competence. It integrates analysis of growth processes with the dynamics of actions and tasks rather than focusing primarily on just tasks or just rational development.

3. Developmental *variations*, as in developmental range, micro-development, and pathways, are taken as critical resources for grounding developmental analysis rather than as random noise or measurement error.

4. Dynamical *concepts* are brought to the foreground, such as stability within variation, in medias res, collaborative construction, construc-

tive web, growth and transition processes, dynamic growth modeling, the organizing effects of emotions, and cycles of reorganization in the developing brain.

Over thirty years of development, dynamic skill theory has gradually taken its current shape. Still we are at the beginning of the intellectual journey of understanding human development in all its richness and diversity. Our new challenge is how to understand the broad spectrum of human development across different domains and through various levels. The newly established Mind, Brain, and Education program at the Harvard Graduate School of Education represents our latest effort to bring a multidisciplinary perspective to the enterprise. To understand the rich diversity of human development requires contributions from a wide range of disciplines, integrating cognitive science, neuroscience, anthropology, pedagogy, philosophy, linguistics, and many other disciplines.

☐ Dynamic Construction of Dynamic Skill Theory

Like the development of a child, dynamic skill theory was constructed dynamically over time, with multiple factors interacting within a coherent system in context to produce change and variation. The previous sections of this chapter have focused primarily on the concepts and methods of dynamic skill theory. To capture the dynamic construction process, we also describe development of the theory in terms of four metaphors based on acting with one's body: following our noses, opening our eyes, moving our legs, and holding each other's hands.

Following Our Noses

During our thirty-year journey of developing the theory, we repeatedly followed our noses: We pointed ourselves in a general direction and then groped forward, letting observations and interactions guide us toward a solution. We started with a strong, general sense of where we wanted to go—most broadly, understanding how people change in a wide and rich panoply of ways—but we did not know how to get there. Baldwin (1894) and Piaget (1936/1952) described this process of *groping* in child development, and it applies as well to scientific discovery. Good science relies primarily neither on deduction according to logical principles, nor on naked induction from observations, but on a construction that dynamically combines direction from both the scientist and the world observed. This is the process that the great nineteenth-century philosopher C. S. Peirce (1982–1993) called "abduction" (Hanson, 1961).

Early in the dynamic construction of skill theory, we had to follow our noses to build a system for analyzing change in the organization of action and thought. Grounded in concepts from Piaget, Bruner, Werner, and others, we explored ways of characterizing the development of specific activities in infants and children and gradually invented the system that was presented in the 1980 *Psychological Review* paper. Later when we were challenged by pervasive and complex variations in the organization of actions, thoughts, and feelings, we followed our noses again to find concepts and methods for analyzing the dynamics of variations. Key in all the successes of the thirty-year journey was the emergent process of groping and dynamic construction to produce concepts and methods grounded in people's developing activities and not fixed by one predetermined theory or method.

Opening Our Eyes

As we groped forward following our noses, it was essential to keep our eyes open, consistently finding and integrating new observations, insights, and tools into the existing framework so that we could better understand developmental processes. To achieve any success in the challenging task of understanding human development requires going beyond the one-dimensional theories that still dominate most of the developmental, educational, and cognitive sciences. We needed to stay open to seeing what developing children and adults showed us, and we needed to continually reach out to explore new ideas and methods from any relevant disciplines. Skill theory was invented in the 1970s and 1980s from concepts, findings, and methods involving cognitive development, learning, problem-solving, emotions, psychopathology, cultural similarities and differences, social relationships, ecological analysis, and other phenomena. Dynamic skill theory was formulated in the 1990s on the basis of concepts, findings, and methods involving change in dynamic systems, variations across and within cultures, attachment patterns, microdevelopmental analyses, neural networks, brain growth, biological growth cycles, and neuroscience. Openness to different ideas, observations, and methods made possible the long dynamic journey toward understanding human development in all its richness and diversity.

Moving Our Two Legs

So much work in the behavioral sciences focuses primarily on either theory or method, not on the connection of the two. To walk effectively, people need two legs. To do the best work, scientists need the two legs of theory and method together. Our research experience tells us that it is neither sufficient nor wise to rely mainly on one leg or the other to advance the study of human development. During our thirty-year journey of following our noses with open eyes, we have striven consistently to use both legs, matching and integrating both conceptual improvements and methodological advances in order to build the best explanations of developing actions, thoughts, and feelings. Along with essential concepts such as skill, developmental range, and dynamic growth, we have tried always to find or devise appropriate methods, such as task analysis, optimal and functional assessment, and dynamic modeling, respectively. Theory and method have been so closely intertwined in our research that every major advance has involved a combination of concept and method together to produce a more effective analytic system.

Holding Each Other's Hands

The enterprise of building dynamic skill theory never involved one person. There was always a group of us walking forward with our eyes open, following our noses, intensively and successfully collaborating in our journey. Despite American culture's emphasis on individual achievements, one person alone cannot capture the richness and diversity of human development. Scientific research by nature is a social construction process (Ochs & Jacoby, 1997).

We have had the good fortune to work closely with three major groups of collaborators. First, the formulation of skill theory has been significantly influenced by our mentors, including those we worked with personally and those we knew only through their writings, especially Piaget, Skinner, Freud, Bruner, Roger Brown, Fantino, Hebb, Jerome Kagan, Kohlberg, Harry Stack Sullivan, Vygotsky, Werner, and Sheldon White. Second, collaborations with colleagues have been essential to our progress, especially Joseph Campos, Robbie Case, Paul van Geert, Marshall Haith, Susan Harter, Karen Kitchener, Gil Noam, Phillip Shaver, and Robert Thatcher. Third, we have had the remarkable good fortune to work with a group of bright and diligent graduate students, some of whom have gone on to become colleagues and collaborators for many years. We learn from each other, inspire each other, and support each other! Students who have become long-term collaborators have included Catherine Ayoub, Thomas Bidell, Daniel Bullock, Roberta Corrigan, Nira Granott, Rebecca Hencke, Catherine Knight, Jin Li, Michael Mascolo, Samuel Rose, and Malcolm Watson.

In short, during our thirty years of research, we have been following our noses in active exploration, opening our eyes for constructive synthesis of new insights, moving our two legs of theory and method together, and holding each other's hands for long-term collaboration. The sweet fruit of our constructive collaboration has been dynamic skill theory. Time will tell how dynamic skill theory fares as it moves from its childhood into the adulthood we seek in the new millennium. Most important, we hope that dynamic skill theory will continue to help us human beings better understand how we develop in all our richness and diversity.

☐ Acknowledgments

We dedicate this chapter to the memory of our friend and colleague, Robbie Case, who died too young in the midst of a good, strong, productive life. Preparation of this chapter was supported by grants from Mr. and Mrs. Frederick P. Rose, Harvard University, and NICHD (grant #HD32371).

☐ References

Ainsworth, M. D., Blehar, M., Waters, E., & Wall, S. (1978). *Patterns of attachment: A psychological study of the strange situation.* Hillsdale, NJ: Erlbaum.

Baldwin, J. M. (1894). *Mental development in the child and the race.* New York: MacMillan.

Bertenthal, B. I., & Fischer, K. W. (1978). The development of self-recognition in infancy. *Developmental Psychology, 14,* 44–50.

Bertenthal, B. I., & Fischer, K. W. (1983). The development of representation in search: A social-cognitive analysis. *Child Development, 54*(4), 846–857.

Bidell, T. R., & Fischer, K. W. (1992). Cognitive development in educational contexts: Implications of skill theory. In A. Demetriou, M. Shayer, & A. Efklides (Eds.), *Neo-Piagetian theories of cognitive development: Implications and applications for education* (pp. 9–30). London: Routledge & Kegan Paul.

Bidell, T. R., & Fischer, K. W. (1994). Developmental transitions in children's early on-line planning. In M. M. Haith, J. B. Benson, R. J. Roberts Jr., & B. F. Pennington (Eds.), *The development of future-oriented processes* (pp. 141–176). Chicago: University of Chicago Press.

Bogartz, R. (1994). The future of dynamic systems models in developmental psychology in the light of the past. *Journal of Experimental Child Psychology, 58,* 289-319.

Bruner, J. S. (1970). The growth and structure of skill. In K. J. Connolly (Ed.), *Mechanisms of motor skill development* New York: Academic Press.

Bruner, J. S. (1973). Organization of early skilled action. *Child Development, 44,* 1–11.

Calverley, R., Fischer, K.W., & Ayoub, C. (1994). Complex splitting of self-representations in sexually abused adolescent girls. *Development and Psychopathology, 6,* 195–213.

Campos, J. J., Barrett, K. C., Lamb, M. E., Goldsmith, H. H., & Stenberg, C. (1983). Socioemotional development. In M. M. Haith & J. J. Campos (Eds.), & P. H. Mussen (Series Ed.), *Handbook of child psychology. Vol. 2: Infancy and developmental psychobiology* (4th ed., pp. 783–915). New York: Wiley.

Case, R. (Ed.) (1991). *The mind's staircase: Exploring the conceptual underpinnings of children's thought and knowledge.* Hillsdale, NJ: Erlbaum.

Case, R., & Okamoto, Y. (1996). The role of central conceptual structures in the development of children's thought. *Monographs of the Society of Research in Child Development,* *61*(5–6, serial no. 246). Chicago, IL: Society for Research in Child Development.

Chomsky, N. (1957). *Syntactic structures.* The Hague: Mouton.

Corrigan, R. (1981). The effects of task and practice on search for invisibly displaced objects. *Developmental Review, 1,* 1–17.

Corrigan, R. (1983). The development of representational skills. In K. W. Fischer (Ed.), *Levels and transitions in children's development. New Directions for Child Development, 21* (pp. 51–64). San Francisco: Jossey-Bass.

Corrigan, R., & Fischer, K. W. (1985). Controlling sources of variation in search tasks: A skill theory approach. In H. Wellman (Ed.), *Children's searching: The development of search skill and spatial representation* (pp. 287–318). Hillsdale, NJ: Erlbaum.

Damon, W. (Gen. Ed.). (1998). *Handbook of child psychology* (5th ed.). New York: Wiley.

Detterman, D. K. (1993). The case for the prosecution: Transfer as an epiphenomenon. In D. K. Detterman & R. J. Sternberg (Eds.), *Transfer on trial: intelligence, cognition, and instruction* (pp. 1–24). Norwood, NJ: Ablex.

Fischer, K.W. (1970, August). The structure and development of sensory-motor actions. Ph.D. dissertation, Harvard University, Department of Social Relations.

Fischer, K. W. (1972). Structuralism for psychologists. [Review of *An introduction to structuralism* (Basic Books, 1970), by Michael Lane]. *Contemporary Psychology, 17,* 329–331.

Fischer, K. W. (1975). Thinking and problem solving: Cognitive psychology. In K. W. Fischer, P. R. Shaver, & A. Lazerson (Eds.), *Psychology today: An Introduction* (3rd ed., pp. 120–143). New York: CRM/Random House.

Fischer, K. W. (1980a). Learning and problem solving as the development of organized behavior. *Journal of Structural Learning, 6,* 253–267.

Fischer, K. W. (1980b). A theory of cognitive development: The control and construction of hierarchies of skills. *Psychological Review, 87,* 477–531.

Fischer, K. W. (1987). Relations between brain and cognitive development. *Child Development, 58 ,* 623–632.

Fischer, K. W., & Ayoub, C. (1994). Affective splitting and dissociation in normal and maltreated children: Developmental pathways for self in relationships. In D. Cicchetti & S. L. Toth (Eds.), *Rochester Symposium on Developmental Psychopathology: Vol. 5. Disorders and dysfunctions of the self* (pp. 149–222). Rochester, NY: Rochester University Press.

Fischer, K. W., Ayoub, C. C., Noam, G. G., Singh, I., Maraganore, A., & Raya, P. (1997). Psychopathology as adaptive development along distinctive pathways. *Development and Psychopathology, 9,* 751–781.

Fischer, K. W., & Bidell, T. R. (1991). Constraining nativist inferences about cognitive capacities. In S. Carey & R. Gelman (Eds.), *The epigenesis of mind: Essays on biology and knowledge* (pp. 199–235). Hillsdale, NJ: Erlbaum.

Fischer, K. W., & Bidell, T. R. (1998). Dynamic development of psychological structures in action and thought. In R. M. Lerner (Ed.), & W. Damon (Series Ed.), *Handbook of child psychology: Vol. 1. Theoretical models of human development* (5th ed., pp. 467–561). New York: Wiley.

Fischer, K. W., & Bullock, D. (1981). Patterns of data: Sequence, synchrony, and constraint in cognitive development. In K. W. Fischer (Ed.), *Cognitive development: New directions for child development, 12,* 69–78. San Francisco: Jossey-Bass.

Fischer, K. W., & Bullock, D. (1984). Cognitive development in middle childhood: Conclusions and new directions. In W.A. Collins (Ed.), *Development during middle childhood: The years from six to twelve* (pp. 70–146). Washington, DC: National Academy of Sciences Press.

Fischer, K. W., Bullock, D., Rotenberg, E. J., & Raya, P. (1993). The dynamics of competence: How context contributes directly to skill. In R. Wozniak & K. W. Fischer (Eds.),

Development in context: Acting and thinking in specific environments (pp. 93–117). JPS Series on Knowledge and Development. Hillsdale, NJ: Erlbaum.

Fischer, K. W., & Farrar, J. (1987). Generalizations about generalization: How a theory of skill development explains both generality and specificity. *International Journal of Psychology, 22*, 643–677.

Fischer, K. W., & Granott, N. (1995). Beyond one-dimensional change: Parallel, concurrent, socially distributed processes in learning and development. *Human Development, 38*, 302-314.

Fischer, K. W., Hand, H. H., & Russell, S. (1984). The development of abstractions in adolescence and adulthood. In M. Commons, F. A. Richards, & C. Armon (Eds.), *Beyond formal operations* (pp. 43–73). New York: Praeger.

Fischer, K. W., Hand, H. H., Watson, M. W., Van Parys, M., & Tucker, J. (1984). Putting the child into socialization: The development of social categories in preschool children. In L. Katz (Ed.) *Current topics in early childhood education* (vol. 5, pp. 27–72). Norwood NJ: Ablex.

Fischer, K. W., & Hogan, A. E. (1989). The big picture for infant development: Levels and variations. In J. J. Lockman & N. L. Hazen (Eds.), *Action in social context: Perspectives on early development* (pp. 275–305). New York: Plenum.

Fischer, K. W., & Kennedy, B. (1997). Tools for analyzing the many shapes of development: The case of self-in-relationships in Korea. In E. Amsel & K. A. Renninger (Eds.), *Change and development: Issues of theory, method, and application* (pp. 117–152). Mahwah, NJ: Erlbaum.

Fischer, K. W., & Lamborn, S. (1989). Mechanisms of variation in developmental levels: Cognitive and emotional transitions during adolescence. In A. de Ribaupierre (Ed.), *Transition mechanisms in child development* (pp. 33–67). New York: Cambridge University Press.

Fischer, K. W., & Pipp, S. L. (1984a). Development of the structures of unconscious thought. In K. Bowers & D. Meichenbaum (Eds.), *The unconscious reconsidered* (pp. 88–148). New York: Wiley.

Fischer, K. W., & Pipp, S. L. (1984b). Processes of cognitive development: Optimal level and skill acquisition. In R. J. Steinberg (Ed.), *Mechanisms of cognitive development* (pp. 45–80). San Francisco: Freeman.

Fischer, K. W., Pipp, S. L., & Bullock, D. (1984). Detecting discontinuities in development: Method and measurement. In R. Emde & R. Harmon (Eds.), *Continuities and discontinuities in development* (pp. 95–121). New York: Plenum.

Fischer, K.W., Shaver, P., & Carnochan, P. (1989). A skill approach to emotional development: From basic- to subordinate-category emotions. In W. Damon (Ed.), *Child development today and tomorrow* (pp. 107–136). San Francisco: Jossey-Bass.

Fischer, K. W., Shaver, P. R., & Carnochan, P. (1990). How emotions develop and how they organise development. *Cognition & Emotion, 4*(2), 81–127.

Fischer, K. W., & van Geert, P. (1993). Modeling and measuring growth and development: Excerpts from the Group Report. *Center for Advanced Study in the Behavioral Sciences: Annual Report 1993* (pp. 39–44). Palo Alto, CA.

Fischer, K. W., Wang, L., Kennedy, B., & Cheng, C. (1998). Culture and biology in emotional development. In D. Sharma & K. W. Fischer (Ed.), *Socioemotional development across cultures. New Directions for Child Development, 81* (pp. 21–43). San Francisco: Jossey-Bass.

Fischer, K. W., & Watson, M. W. (1981). Explaining the Oedipus conflict. In K. W. Fischer (Ed.), *Cognitive development. New Directions for Child Development, 12* (pp. 79–92). San Francisco: Jossey-Bass.

Fischer, K. W., Yan, Z., McGonigle, B., & Warnett, L. (2000). Learning and developing together: Dynamic construction of human and robot knowledge. In J. Weng & I. Stockman (Eds.), *Workshop on Development and learning: Proceedings of an NSF/DARPA workshop* (pp. 50–59). East Lansing, MI: Michigan State University.

Fischer, K. W., Yan, Z., & Stewart, J. (in press). Cognitive development in adulthood: Dynamics of variation and consolidation. In J. Valsiner & K. Connolly (Eds.), *Handbook of developmental psychology*. Thousand Oaks, CA: Sage.

Fogel, A. (1993). *Developing through relationships: Origins of communication, self, and culture.* Chicago: University of Chicago Press.

Forrester, J. W. (1961). *Industrial dynamics*. Cambridge, MA: MIT Press.

Frijda, N. H. (1986). *The emotions.* Cambridge, England: Cambridge University Press.

Frye, D., Zelazo, P. D., & Palfai, T. (1995). Theory of mind and rule-based reasoning. *Cognitive Development, 10,* 483–527.

Gibson, J. J. (1979). *The ecological approach to visual perception.* Boston: Houghton-Mifflin.

Goldin-Meadow, S., Nusbaum, H., Garber, P., & Church, R. B. (1993). Transitions in learning: Evidence for simultaneously activated rules. *Journal of Experimental Psychology: Human Perception and Performance, 19,* 92–107.

Gottlieb, D. E., Taylor, S. E., & Ruderman, A. (1977). Cognitive bases of children's moral judgments. *Developmental Psychology, 13,* 547–556.

Granott, N. (1993). Patterns of interaction in the co-construction of knowledge: Separate minds, joint effort, and weird creatures. In R. H. Wozniak & K. W. Fischer (Eds.), *Development in context: Acting and thinking in specific environments* (pp. 183–207). Hillsdale, NJ: Erlbaum.

Granott, N. (1994). Microdevelopment of co-construction of knowledge during problem-solving: Puzzled minds, weird creatures, and wuggles. *Dissertation Abstracts International, 54*(10B), 5409.

Granott, N. (in press). How microdevelopment creates macrodevelopment: Reiterated sequences, backward transitions, and the zone of current development. In N. Granott & J. Parziale (Eds.), *Microdevelopment:Transition processes in development and learning* Cambridge, UK: Cambridge University Press.

Granott, N., Fischer, K. W., & Parziale, J. (2002). Bridging to the unknown: A transition mechanism in learning and problem-solving. *Microdevelopment: Transition processes in development and learning* (pp. 131–156). Cambridge, UK: Cambridge University Press.

Hand, H. H. (1982). The development of concepts of social interaction: Children's understanding of nice and mean. *Dissertation Abstracts International, 42*(11), 4578B.

Hanson, N. R. (1961). *Patterns of discovery.* Cambridge, UK: Cambridge University Press.

Harter, S. (1986). Cognitive-developmental processes in the integration of concepts about emotions and the self. *Social Cognition, 4,* 119–151.

Harter, S., & Pike, R. (1984). The pictorial scale of perceived competence and social acceptance for young children. *Child Development, 55,* 1969–1082.

Huckfeldt, R. R., Kohfeld, C. W., & Likens, T. W. (1982). *Dynamic modeling: An introduction.* Beverly Hills, CA: Sage.

Inhelder, B., & Piaget, J. (1958). *The growth of logical thinking from childhood to adolescence.* (A. P. S. Seagrim, Trans.). New York: Basic Books. (Originally published 1955.)

Inhelder, B., & Piaget, J. (1964). *The early growth of logic in the child* (G. A. L. D. Papert, Trans.). New York: Harper & Row. (Originally published 1959.)

Jackson, E., Campos, J. J., & Fischer, K. W. (1978). The question of *décalage* between object permanence and person permanence. *Developmental Psychology, 14,* 1–10.

Kitchener, K. S., & Fischer, K. W. (1990). A skill approach to the development of reflective thinking. In D. Kuhn (Ed.), *Developmental perspectives on teaching and learning thinking skills. Contributions to Human Development* (vol. 21, pp. 48–62). Basel, Switzerland: S. Karger.

Kitchener, K. S., Lynch, C. L., Fischer, K. W., & Wood, P. K. (1993). Developmental range of reflective judgment: The effect of contextual support and practice on developmental stage. *Developmental Psychology, 29*, 893-906.

Kohlberg, L. (1969). Stage and sequence: The cognitive developmental approach to socialization. In D. A. Goslin (Ed.), *Handbook of socialization theory and research* (pp. 347–480). Chicago: Rand, McNally.

Kohlberg, L. (1984). *The psychology of moral development: The nature and validity of moral stages.* San Francisco: Harper & Row.

Kohut, H. (1971). *The analysis of the self.* New York: International Universities Press.

Lamborn, S. (1986). Relations between social-cognitive development and personal experience: Understanding honesty and kindness in relationships. *Dissertation Abstracts International, 47*(8), 2959A.

Lazarus, R. S. (1991). *Emotion and adaptation.* New York: Oxford University Press.

Leslie, A. (1987). Pretense and representation: The origins of "theory of mind." *Psychological Review, 94*, 412–426.

Levine, R. L., & Lodwick, W. (1992). Parameter estimation and assessing the fit of dynamic models. In R. L. Levine & H. E. Fitzgerald, (Eds.), *Analysis of dynamic psychological systems: Vol. 2* (pp. 119–150). New York: Plenum.

Lewis, M. D. (2000, in press). The promise of dynamic systems approaches for an integrated account of human development. *Child Development.*

Loevinger, J. (1976). *Ego development: Concepts and theories.* San Francisco: Jossey-Bass.

Mascolo, M. F., & Fischer, K. W. (1998). The development of self through the coordination of component systems. In M. Ferrari & R. Sternberg (Eds.), *Development of self-awareness across the lifespan* (pp. 332–384). New York: Guilford.

Mascolo, M. J., Fischer, K. W., & Li, J. (in press). Dynamic development of component systems of emotions: Pride, shame, and guilt in China and the United States. In R. J. Davidson, K. Scherer, & H. H. Goldsmith (Eds.), *Handbook of affective science.* Oxford: Oxford University Press.

Mascolo, M. F., Fischer, K. W., & Neimeyer, R. (1999). The dynamic co-development of intentionality, self, and social relations. In J. B. Brandstädter & R. M. Lerner (Eds.), *Action and self-development: Theory and research through the life span* (pp. 133–166). Thousand Oaks, CA: Sage.

Matousek, M., & Petersén, I. (1973). Frequency analysis of the EEG in normal children and adolescents. In P. Kellaway & I. Petersén (Eds.), *Automation of clinical electroencephalography* (pp. 75–102). New York: Raven Press.

Ochs, E., & Jacoby, S. (1997). Down to the wire: The cultural clock of physicists and the discourse of consensus. *Language in Society, 26*, 479–505.

Parke, R. D., Ornstein, P. A., Rieser, J. J., & Zahn-Waxler, C. (Eds.). (1994). *A century of developmental psychology.* Washington, DC: APA.

Peirce, C. S. (1982–1993). *Writings of Charles S. Peirce.* Bloomington: Indiana University Press.

Perkins, D. N., & Salomon, G. (1989). Are cognitive skills context-bound? *Educational Researcher, 18*, 16–25.

Piaget, J. (1952). *The origins of intelligence in children* (M. Cook, Trans.). New York: International Universities Press. (Originally published 1936.)

Piaget, J. (1954). *The construction of reality in the child* (M. Cook, Trans.). New York: Basic Books. (Originally published 1937.)

Piaget, J. (1951). *Play, dreams, and imitation in childhood* (C. G. F. M. Hodgson, Trans.). New York: Harcourt Brace. (Originally published 1946.)

Piaget, J. (1957). Logique et équilibre dans les comportements du sujet [Logic and equilibrium in subjects' behavior]. *Études d'Épistémologie Génétique, 2*, 27–118.

Piaget, J. (1970a). *Genetic epistemology.* New York: Columbia University Press.

Piaget, J. (1970b). *Structuralism* (C. Maschler, Trans.). New York: Basic Books. (Originally published 1968.)

Piaget, J. (1983). Piaget's theory. In W. Kessen (Ed.), & P. H. Mussen (Series Ed.), *Handbook of child psychology. Vol. 1: History, theory, and methods* (pp. 103–126). New York: Wiley.

Piaget, J. (1985). *The equilibration of cognitive structures: The central problem of cognitive development* (T. Brown & K. J. Thampy, Trans.). Chicago: University of Chicago Press. (Originally published 1975.)

Piaget, J., Grize, J. B., Szeminska, A., & Bang, V. (1968). Épistémologie et psychologie de la fonction [Epistemology and psychology of the function]. *Études d'Épistémologie Génétique, 23.*

Pipp, S., Fischer, K. W., & Jennings, S. (1987). Acquisition of self and mother knowledge in infancy. *Developmental Psychology, 23*(1), 86–96.

Pipp, S. L. (1990). Sensorimotor and representational internal working models of self, other, and relationship: Mechanisms of connection and separation. In D. Cicchetti & M. Beeghley (Eds.), *The self in transition: Infancy to childhood* (pp. 243–264). Chicago: University of Chicago Press.

Port, R. F., & van Gelder, T. (Eds.). (1995). *Mind as motion: Explorations in the dynamics of cognition.* Cambridge, MA: MIT Press.

Prigogine, I., & Stengers, I. (1984). *Order out of chaos: Man's new dialogue with nature.* New York: Bantam.

Reznick, J. S., & Goldfield, B. A. (1992). Rapid change in lexical development in comprehension and production. *Developmental Psychology, 28,* 406–413.

Rose, S. P., & Fischer, K. W. (1998). Models and rulers in dynamical development. *British Journal of Developmental Psychology, 16,* 123–131.

Ruhland, R., & van Geert, P. (1998). Jumping into syntax: Transitions in the development of closed class words. *British Journal of Developmental Psychology, 16*(Pt 1), 65–95.

Shaver, P. R., Schwartz, J., Kirson, D., & O'Connor, C. (1987). Emotion knowledge: Further exploration of a prototype approach. *Journal of Personality and Social Psychology, 52,* 1061–1086.

Siegler, R. S. (1981). *Developmental sequences within and between concepts. Monographs of the Society for Research in Child Development, 46*(2, Serial No. 189).

Skinner, B. F. (1938). *The behavior of organisms.* New York: Appleton-Century-Crofts.

Skinner, B. F. (1969). *Contingencies of reinforcement: A theoretical analysis.* New York: Appleton-Century-Crofts.

Thelen, E., & Smith, L. B. (1994). A dynamic systems approach to the development of cognition and action. Cambridge, MA: MIT press.

Vallacher, R., & Nowak, A. (1994). *Dynamical systems in social psychology.* New York: Academic Press.

van der Maas, H. L., & Molenaar, P. C. M. (1992). Stagewise cognitive development: An application of catastrophe theory. *Psychological Review, 99,* 395–417.

van Geert, P. (1991). A dynamic systems model of cognitive and language growth. *Psychological Review, 98,* 3–53.

van Geert, P. (1998). A dynamic systems model of basic developmental mechanisms: Piaget, Vygotsky, and beyond. *Psychological Review, 105,* 634–677.

Van Parys, M. M. (1983). The relation of use and understanding of sex and age categories in preschool children. *Dissertation Abstracts International, 45*(2), 700B.

von Bertalanffy, L. (1968). *General systems theory.* New York: Braziller.

Vygotsky, L. S. (1962). *Thought and language* (E. H. G. Vakar, Trans.). Cambridge, MA: MIT Press.

Vygotsky, L. (1978). *Mind in society: The development of higher psychological processes* (M. Cole, V. John-Steiner, S. Scribner, & E. Souberman, Trans.). Cambridge MA: Harvard University Press.

Watson, M. W., & Fischer, K. W. (1977). A developmental sequence of agent use in late infancy. *Child Development, 48,* 828–835.

Watson, M. W., & Fischer, K. W. (1980). Development of social roles in elicited and sponta-neous behavior during the preschool years. *Developmental Psychology, 16,* 484–494.

Watson, M. W., & Fischer, K. W. (1993). Structural changes in children's understanding of family roles and divorce. In R. R. Cocking & K. A. Renninger (Eds.), *The development and meaning of psychological distance* (pp. 123–140). Hillsdale, NJ: Erlbaum.

Watson, M. W., & Getz, K. (1990). The relationship between Oedipal behaviors and children's family role concepts. *Merrill-Palmer Quarterly , 36,* 487–505.

Werner, H. (1957). The concept of development from a comparative and organismic point of view. In D. B. Harris (Ed.), *The concept of development.* Minneapolis: University of Minnesota Press.

Westerman, M. A. (1990). Coordination of maternal directives with preschoolers' behavior in compliance-problem and healthy dyads. *Developmental Psychology, 26*(4), 621–630.

Yan, Z. (2000). Dynamic analysis of microdevelopment in learning a computer program. Unpublished doctoral dissertation, Harvard Graduate School of Education, Cambridge, MA.

Zeeman, E. C. (1976). Catastrophe theory. *Scientific American, 234*(4), 65–83.

CHAPTER

Richard M. Lerner

Multigenesis: Levels of Professional Integration in the Life Span of a Developmental Scientist

Today, I label myself as an applied developmental scientist (note, *not* psychologist). Yet, when I began my study of psychology—in 1964, during my sophomore year at what was then Hunter College in the Bronx (and is now Lehman College), one of the senior colleges of the City University of New York (CUNY)—there was no field of professional activity called, or even a course in, applied developmental science (ADS). In fact, although I am certain I took an undergraduate course in child psychology, I cannot remember even thinking about the topic of development, in either an applied or basic manner, during my undergraduate years.

☐ The Genesis of a "Basic" Developmental Researcher

The first time I can ever recall thinking seriously about the concept of development was early in my first year of graduate school. In February 1966, I had entered the then relatively new Ph.D. program in psychology at CUNY, hoping to be a physiological psychologist. As an undergraduate at the Bronx campus of Hunter College I had taken two courses with Professor Charles A. Knehr. In both courses—Advanced Introduction to Psychology and Physiological Psychology—books by Donald Hebb (1949,

313

1958) were the core texts. I left undergraduate school enamored with Hebb's approach to psychology, which I interpreted as physiological psychology.

However, in graduate school—through the instruction of Elizabeth Gellert and, most importantly, Sam J. Korn—I learned that Hebb (1949) was actually presenting a theory of development, of how, through interactions between the organism and experience, the brain and, ultimately, behavior became organized. I began to understand that the process of development enabled the actualization of the potential for plasticity in brain organization and behavioral function that Hebb discussed (Lerner, 1976, 1984, 1986).

In addition, and although it took several decades for me to realize it, my exposure to Hebb was actually my first acquaintance with applied developmental science. Hebb had been a clinician during World War II. He had experiences with hospitalized soldiers who during the war had received brain injuries that resulted in substantial loss of tissue from the cerebral cortex. In addition, Hebb encountered younger (e.g., infant) patients who happened to be hospitalized (e.g., as a consequence of car accidents) with brain injuries corresponding to those of the older soldiers.

Hebb's experiences with these two instances of brain injury provided evidence that the same neurological insult had vastly different implications for behavioral and cognitive functioning, depending on the point in the life span when the injuries occurred (Hebb, 1949). Older patients, who had had more ontogenetic time to organize their brains (and to capitalize on their potential for plasticity through, for instance, redundantly organizing the neuronal bases of their intellectual functions) were able to demonstrate, upon recovery from their injuries, high-level performance (e.g., to receive an IQ score on an intelligence test that was several standard deviations above the mean). An infant with a corresponding injury never attained normal intelligence. This difference led Hebb (1949) to conclude that the infant's functional capacity was constrained because of the fact that injury occurred prior to the point in life when the potential for plasticity had been actualized (e.g., through redundant organization). Simply, the infant had less tissue with which to be redundant.

Hebb's evolving theory of organism-environment interaction in the service of the organization of behavior across ontogeny both informed and was informed by his clinical experiences. Although he did not specify the precise implications of his theory for treatment regimens for the differently aged patients, his discussion clearly implied that his theory was linked not only to different interpretations of their behavioral and cognitive capacities but also to contrasting prognoses and rationales for intervention (Hebb, 1949).

Hebb, then, may be one of the early examples of an applied developmental scientist. Applied developmental science is scholarship that seeks to significantly advance the integration of developmental science with actions that address the pressing human problems of individual, family, and community life besetting our nation and world. For instance, Fisher and Lerner (1994b, p. 5) define ADS as involving the use of theory, data, and methods from the study of human development in applications "related to normative and atypical changes and challenges facing individuals and families at all points along the life span." In addition, they note that a distinguishing feature of ADS is a focus on "how developmental theory, the developmental knowledge base, and developmental science methodologies can be directly used to promote the health and welfare of individuals in our society" and that ADS thus uses "a scientific focus to understand the complex interplay between human development and social intervention, looking at social intervention itself as a process of influence that must be studied" (Fisher & Lerner, 1994b, p. 5).

Accordingly, Hebb's use of developmental theory to benefit understanding of, and potentially interventions for, brain-injured people had implications for the health and development of these individuals. His work had considerable import for understanding normative development, and also for appreciating how individuality and experience interrelate in the organization of behavior and in the actualization of plasticity (Lerner, 1984, 1986). Indeed, interest in the nature of plasticity in human development is a concern for science, education, and policy—in fact, for any realm of social life pertinent to understanding how people's capacities develop and how this development may be enhanced. In short, a key, intended impact of applied developmental science is the enhancement of the life chances of the diverse individuals, families, and communities served by such scholarship. Hebb (1949), a major figure in the history of developmental theory (e.g., see Hunt, 1961; Lerner, 1976, 1986) was also an important early example of applied developmental science.

However, this connection between Hebb's theory and applied developmental science would not occur to me for more than twenty years! I now see Hebb as a developmental psychologist and—as I shall describe below—as an exemplar of a person working within a traditionally defined, basic science approach to development. And, at this point in my training, I was primarily concerned with understanding what development meant and with trying to prove myself as a person who—if he were able to get through graduate school (something my professors seemed far from certain I could do)—would be capable of making valued scientific contributions to the basic science field of developmental psychology.

Although I knew I had a lot to learn and was often overwhelmed by it, motivated by Sam Korn's gentle prodding, I was also growing in my intellectual excitement about what I was learning. Through studying Dale

Harris's (1957) classic edited volume *The Concept of Development*, I was exposed to some of the key philosophical issues involved in understanding development—for example, teleology, organicism, and the unity-of-science, or mechanistic and reductionist, perspectives (Nagel, 1957). In addition, this book introduced me to the ideas of Heinz Werner (1957), Robert Sears (1957), and—most important to me—T. C. Schneirla (1957).

As I grew to understand Schneirla's (1956, 1957; Tobach and Schneirla, 1968) ideas, I began to recognize that both he and Hebb (1949) were presenting compatible ideas about the character of organism-experience relations and about the ways in which these relations constituted the basic developmental process (Lerner, 1976, 1984, 1986). Moreover, one section of Schneirla's chapter in the 1957 Harris book gave me not only the basic idea to test in my dissertation, but also provided the frame through which I enacted more than fifteen years of postdoctoral research.

In a section of his chapter, a section entitled "Circular functions and self-stimulation in ontogeny" (1957, pp. 86–89), Schneirla explained that individuals are in relationships with themselves over the course of their development. On the basis of their characteristics of individuality, individuals evoke differential reactions in other organisms; these reactions provide feedback to the individual and constitute a significant portion of the experience that promotes the development of further individual distinctiveness for the organism. In essence, then, by influencing those who influence him or her, the person becomes a source of his or her own development (Lerner, 1982; Lerner & Busch-Rossnagel, 1981; Lerner & Walls, 1999). As such, the integration of action—the relation of the organism on the social context and of the context on the organism—becomes the focal process of development (Brandtstädter, 1998, 1999; Brandtstädter & Lerner, 1999a, 1999b).

For my dissertation, I used this idea of circular functions to frame a study of the role of individual differences in male children's and adolescents' body builds for their personality and social development. To understand the nature of the feedback that these youth might receive as a consequence of their physical individuality, I assessed the positive and negative social stereotypes that existed in regard to fat, average, and thin male body builds (Lerner & Korn, 1972).

Although the dissertation was eventually successfully defended, it is prophetic that a key objection of the CUNY psychology doctoral faculty to my proposal to do this research as a dissertation was that the topic was not *psychological* in nature. Although Sam Korn, who was my dissertation adviser and mentor, did not ever tell me which colleague or colleagues raised the objection to the proposed focus of the research, he did say that when the faculty met to discuss my defense of the proposal, one objection was that the topic seemed more sociological or anthropological than psychological.

At the time, given the perhaps understandable lack of objectivity by a graduate student interested primarily in completing his doctoral degree, I objected to and in fact dismissed this criticism. Had not Boyd R. McCandless (1961, 1967, 1970)—the then (founding) editor of the new APA journal, *Developmental Psychology*—not only discussed but in fact sponsored analogous dissertation research (see Staffieri, 1967)? However, in retrospect, there was a good point being made by this comment—at least insofar as what the traditionally personological approach to psychological development is concerned.

The larger theoretical significance of my extension of Schneirla's ideas to human development (Schneirla was a comparative psychologist whose research dealt mainly with army ants and kittens; Schneirla, 1956, 1957; Tobach & Schneirla, 1968) was that a personological analysis of individual development was incomplete. If one accepted the circular functions notion as a prototype of the relations between individual and context that comprised the basic process of development, then—in order to understand the nature of the feedback the individual child or adolescent received from the social context as a consequence of his or her characteristics of individuality—one had to understand the mores, values, attitudes, and customs that influence the society and culture of the individual at a given point in history. One could not, then, rely solely on psychology to obtain all the information necessary to understand the relation between the individual and the ecology of human development.

In the work I pursued after completion (in 1971) of my doctorate (see Lerner & Korn, 1972), I extended the empirical focus of my research to include not just body build but, more generally, physical attractiveness. In addition, I also considered the import of other characteristics of what I termed "organismic individuality" for child and adolescent development, that is, temperament and puberty (e.g., Lerner & Lerner, 1977, 1983, 1989). This research continued to be framed by an interest in circular functions and in the broader organism-context relational ideas of Schneirla, Hebb, and other scientists from comparative psychological backgrounds (e.g., Gottlieb, 1970; Lehrman, 1953, 1970; Tobach, 1981; Tobach & Schneirla, 1968) and from psychiatric and pediatric areas of medical training (e.g., Chess & Thomas, 1984; Thomas & Chess, 1977; Thomas, Chess, & Birch, 1968; Thomas, Chess, Birch, Hertzig, & Korn, 1963).

For instance, through the influence of psychiatrists Alexander Thomas and Stella Chess (1977), I explored the notion of "goodness of fit" as a way of understanding the positive or negative valence of the feedback a child might receive from parents, teachers, or peers as a consequence of the effect of his or her individual characteristics on them. For instance, if a child's temperament in regard to the rhythmicity, or predictability, of his or her sleep/waking cycles matched or was congruent with parental preferences, attitudes, or behavioral (work) schedules, positive parent-child interactions (feedback) would occur. Such relationships would constitute a "goodness of fit" and would provide the basis for healthy development. Alternative interactions and development would be likely to occur in the face of a poorness of fit (Lerner, 1983, 1989).

This line of work, which extended through the mid-1980s, proved the fear of the unknown CUNY faculty member or members correct. As I continued to conduct child and adolescent development research framed by the person-context relational model I have described, I found myself drawing more and more from disciplines other than psychology to understand the individual nature of development of the young people I was studying. Anthropology (e.g., Super & Harkness, 1981), sociology and history (Elder, 1974; Simmons & Blyth, 1987), psychiatry (Chess & Thomas, 1984; Thomas & Chess, 1977), and evolutionary biology (Gould, 1977; Lewontin, Rose, & Kamin, 1984) were among the disciplines that had ideas pertinent to person-context relations that, as I understood them, were relevant to the broad theoretical model of development that was beginning to occupy my thinking and writing. My work was substantially advanced by my good fortune in gaining an academic appointment at the Pennsylvania State University.

☐ The Genesis of a Developmental Systems Theorist

During the mid-1970s, I realized that the concept of development was not the exclusive province of any one discipline, including psychology. Instead, developmental changes among all levels of organization involved in the ecology of human life needed to be integrated in order to understand human development (e.g., Baltes, 1987; Bronfenbrenner, 1983; Riegel, 1975; Schaie, 1965; Tobach, 1981). Certainly, the human ecological theory of Urie Bronfenbrenner (1977, 1979) and the dialectical theory of Klaus Riegel (1975, 1976, 1977a, 1977b) were central in furthering my understanding of this idea. However, my understanding of this point was deepened and extended by my colleagues in the Department of Human Development and Family Studies at Penn State. The life-span developmental perspective being developed by Paul B. Baltes (e.g., 1968, 1983, 1987, 1997; Baltes, Lindenberger, & Staudinger, 1998; Baltes, Staudinger, & Lindenberger, 1999), by John R. Nesselroade (e.g., 1983, 1988; Nesselroade & Baltes, 1974), and by their colleagues, both at Penn State and around the world—for instance, Margaret Baltes (e.g., Baltes & Lerner, 1980), Orville G. Brim Jr. and Jerome Kagan (e.g., 1980), Glen H. Elder Jr. (e.g., 1974), David L. Featherman (e.g., 1983), David F. Hultsch (e.g., 1980; Hultsch & Hickey, 1978), Gisela Labouvie-Vief (e.g., 1982), Lewis P. Lipsitt (e.g., Reese and Lipsitt, 1970), Jacqueline V. Lerner (e.g., 1983), David Magnusson (e.g., 1988), Willis F. Overton (1973, 1998); Hayne W. Reese (1976; Reese & Overton, 1970), Matilda White Riley (e.g., 1979), K. Warner Schaie (e.g., 1965, 1983), Graham B. Spanier (e.g., 1976, 1979), and Joachim Wohlwill (e.g., 1973)—enhanced my appreciation of the dynamic, interlevel, and temporal character of human development.

My colleagues helped me understand that humans, and their families, communities, and societies, develop; they show systematic and successive changes over time (Lerner, 1998b). These changes are interdependent. Changes within one level of organization, for instance, developmental changes in personality or cognition within the individual, are reciprocally related to—integrated with—developmental changes within other levels, for instance, involving changes in caregiving patterns or spousal relationships within the familial level of organization (e.g., Lewis & Rosenblum, 1974).

Moreover, I understood more clearly that the reciprocal changes among levels of organization are both products and producers of the reciprocal changes within levels. For example, over time, parents' "styles" of behavior and of rearing influence children's personality and cognitive functioning and development; in turn, the interactions between personality and cognition constitute an emergent "characteristic" of human individuality that affects parental behaviors and styles and the quality of family life (e.g., Lerner, 1998b).

I recognized that these interrelations illustrated the integration of changes within and among the multiple levels of organization comprising the ecology of human life (Bronfenbrenner, 1979). Human development within this ecology involves organized and successive changes—that is, systematic changes—in the structure and function of interlevel relations over time (Ford & Lerner, 1992). In other words, I saw that the human development system involves the integration, or "fusion" (Tobach & Greenberg, 1984), of changing relations among the multiple levels of organization that comprise the ecology of human behavior and development. These levels range from biology through culture and history (Elder, Modell, & Parke, 1993; Gottlieb, 1997; Riegel, 1975, 1976, 1977a, 1977b), and include both the natural and the designed physical ecology as well. Indeed, the embeddedness of all levels of the system within history provides a temporal component to human development (Elder et al., 1993); makes the potential for change a defining feature of human development (Baltes, 1987); and, as such, assures that relative plasticity (i.e., the potential for systematic change across ontogeny) characterizes development across the human life span (Lerner, 1998a).

Given that human development is the outcome of changes in this developmental system, I concluded that the essential process of development for individual ontogeny involves changing *relations* between the developing person and his or her changing context (Lerner, 1998b). Similarly, for any unit of analysis with the system (e.g., for the family, studied over its life cycle, or the classroom, studied over the course of a school year), the same developmental process exists. That is, development involves changing relations between that unit and variables from the other levels of organization within the human development system.

Accordingly, I came to believe that the basic process of human development is a relational one (Lerner, 1976, 1978, 1991): development is a concept denoting systemic changes—that is, organized, successive, multilevel, and integrated changes—across the course of life of an individual (or other unit of analysis). Throughout the mid- to late 1970s and into the 1980s, I argued that a focus on process and, particularly, on the process involved in the changing relations between individuals and their contexts, was at the cutting edge of contemporary developmental theory and, as such, was the predominant conceptual frame for research in the study of human development (e.g., Lerner, 1976, 1978, 1979, 1982, 1984).

☐ Developmental Contextualism as an Instance of Developmental Systems Theory

I was not alone in drawing these conclusions. As I have emphasized, my colleagues were stimulating the development of my ideas. They did this through critiquing my work and by developing scholarship that, while converging with my ideas, represented independent, creative, and significant models of developmental systems (e.g., Baltes, 1987; Baltes, Reese, & Lipsitt, 1980; Brim & Kagan, 1980; Bronfrenbrenner, 1979; Elder, 1980; Featherman, 1983; Nesselroade & Baltes, 1974; Gottlieb, 1970, 1997; Overton, 1973; Petersen & Taylor, 1980; Tobach, 1981; Tobach & Greenberg, 1984). As a consequence, in the years between the mid-1980s and the end of the twentieth century, the conceptual and empirical efforts of scholars interested in relational, developmental systems notions of human development came to shape the core intellectual vision found in the preponderant majority of theoretically driven scholarly works about human development (Lerner, 1998a). For example, in at least seventeen of the nineteen chapters included in Volume 1 (*Theoretical Models of Human Development;* Lerner, 1998a) of the fifth edition of the *Handbook of*

Child Psychology (Damon, 1998), a model consistent with such a developmental systems perspective was forwarded.

Indeed, as evidenced by the theories presented in this volume of the Damon *Handbook*, contemporary theories stress that the bases for change, and for both plasticity and constraints in development, lie in the relations that exist among the multiple levels of organization that comprise the substance of human life (Ford & Lerner, 1992; Schneirla, 1957; Tobach, 1981). These levels range from the inner biological level, through the individual/psychological level and the proximal social relational level (e.g., involving dyads, peer groups, and nuclear families), to the sociocultural level (including key macroinstitutions such as educational, public policy, governmental, and economic systems) and the natural and designed physical ecologies of human development (Bronfenbrenner, 1979; Riegel, 1975, 1976, 1977a, 1977b). These levels are structurally and functionally integrated, thus requiring a systems view of the levels involved in human development (Ford & Lerner, 1992; Sameroff, 1983; Thelen & Smith, 1994).

The specific theoretical model that I have developed to represent these ideas—developmental contextualism (Lerner, 1998b)—is one instance of such a developmental systems perspective (e.g., see Lerner, 1998a). As in other developmental systems models, developmental contextualism promotes a *relational* unit of analysis as a requisite for developmental analysis: variables associated with any level of organization exist (are structured) in relation to variables from other levels; the qualitative and quantitative dimensions of the function of any variable are shaped as well by the relations that variable has with ones from other levels. Unilevel units of analysis (or the components of, or elements in, a relation) are not an adequate target of developmental analysis; rather, the relation itself—the interlevel linkage—should be the focus of such analysis (Riegel, 1975, 1976, 1977a, 1977b). Critically, when one recognizes that these linkages may involve relations among all the multiple levels of organization integrated within the ecology of human development, then the study of the development of organism-context relations is an analysis of the developmental system (Lerner, 1998b).

In short, for what is now more than a quarter century (e.g., see Ford & Lerner, 1992; Lerner, 1976, 1983; Lerner & Busch-Rossnagel, 1981; Lerner & Spanier, 1978; Lerner & Walls, 1999), I have been interested in understanding and advancing such developmental systems approaches to human development theories, in general, and in improving the instance of this approach to developmental theory that I have developed, that is, developmental contextualism (Lerner, 1986, 1991, 1995, 1996, 1998a, 1998b; Lerner & Kauffman, 1985). In the context of this work I have stressed that systematic and successive alterations in structure and function are defining features of developmental change (Ford & Lerner, 1992; Lerner, 1986, 1991, 1998a, 1988b).

Accordingly, I have called for moving the study of human development beyond the point of just promoting multivariate-longitudinal designs involving change-sensitive measures of intraindividual change. In addition, I have suggested that developmental contextualism would lead scholars to design research studies that involve:

1. Dynamic (fused) relations among the multiple levels of organization (Ford & Lerner, 1992; Tobach & Greenberg, 1984) involved in the ecology of human development;
2. the appraisal of levels ranging from the inner-biological, and individual-psychological, to the physical ecological, the sociocultural, and the historical; and here, concepts that stress the ways in which levels interrelate, or are fused—such as the "goodness of fit" notion (Thomas & Chess, 1977)—may be particularly helpful;
3. the individual differences (the diversity) that derives from variation (e.g., in the timing) of the interactions among levels; and, since researchers may not be expert in the culture and ecology of all the diverse groups of youth they study;
4. as necessary, a "co-learning" model for the design of research (and intervention) programs (Lerner, 1998b) since, to both understand the ecological role of theoretically relevant variables in the life spans of diverse people living in their varying developmental niches and to use such knowledge to test, through community-embedded interventions, the impact of such variables on developmental trajectories, collaboration should occur with the individuals whose lives are affected by these variables (e.g., Lerner, 1995; Lerner & Galambos, 1998).

The importance of co-learning rests on a key feature of developmental contextual theory and, more broadly, of action theoretical approaches to human development (e.g., Brandtstädter, 1998, 1999; Brandtstädter & Lerner, 1999a, 1999b; Heckhausen, 1999; Lerner & Busch-Rossnagel, 1981; Lerner & Walls, 1999), that is, the contributions of individuals themselves to their own development. Co-learning between researcher and research participant and/or between interventionist and program participant must occur because individuals have expert knowledge about the issues, assets, and risks affecting their lives. They have unique vantage points in regard to providing information about their goals and intentions, and about the actions they have enacted or will be likely to enact to pursue them (Brandtstädter, 1998, 1999).

Co-learning in research or intervention diminishes problems of "alienation" between researchers and participants (Riegel, 1975, 1976, 1977a, 1977b), and suggests that any quantitative appraisal of human development rests on a qualitative understanding of participants' life spaces and meaning systems. Through co-learning, such understanding is shaped at least in part by the participants' input. Thus, research and, especially, programs derived from such information are more likely to be valued and "owned" by and, therefore, efficacious in influencing the lives of people (Jensen, Hoagwood, & Trickett, 1999; Lerner, 1998b).

☐ The Genesis of an Applied Developmental Scientist

To this point I have described much of the beginning and early middle part of my career (I see myself, at this writing, now in only the late middle portion of my career). During these periods I had what may be a common view of the connection between the above-described ideas—my theoretical and empirical work—and the real-world issues of human development.

My idea of this connection is perhaps captured by the phrase "trickle-down relevance." That is, it was up to me and to other developmental scientists like me to do the basic scholarship about development. I believed (in a self-congratulatory way) that this was the really "hard" work, the work that required the best of the best to do. Other, less theoretically attuned and/or empirically rigorous colleagues could then be responsible for translating the "gems" I produced into actions that could directly affect the lives of children, youth, and families.

However, across the last twelve years (at this writing) I have moved away from the traditional conception of a basic researcher and defined myself as an "applied developmental scientist" (Fisher & Lerner, 1994a, 1994a; Lerner, Fisher, & Weinberg, 1997). How did this happen? Certainly, there were compelling conceptual reasons for this transition, or perhaps more accurately, this progression (Nisbet, 1980). Belief in the concept of co-learning would lead necessarily to forming collaborations with community members whose "learning" agenda may have more practical conceptions of importance than would be the case if learning were pursued only from the perspective of the theoretician or basic researcher. In addition, and certainly like many people who enter psychology as a profession, I was always motivated to help people as well as to understand them.

For instance, my above-described research in adolescent development proceeded at a time in history when children and adolescents in the United States and around the world were faced with historically unique challenges to their survival, health, and positive development (Hamburg, 1992; Lerner, 1995). For example, there exists an historically high level of comorbidity among problem behaviors, and this covariance is associated with more than two decades of high-level youth poverty in the United States (Huston, 1991; Jessor, Donovan, & Costa, 1991; Ketterlinus & Lamb, 1994; Lerner, 1995; Lerner & Galambos, 1998). Despite this level of risk facing American youth, however, I remained a traditional developmental researcher through the mid-1980s. It was not the plight of the millions of youth faced with diminished opportunities for positive lives that changed my direction. To be completely candid about the basis for the redefinition of my work, it was one young person who changed my direction:

> Justin came into my study. I was glad that he did. I was just removing the cellophane from the "warehouse" copy of my seventeenth book, the copy the publisher sends to the author as soon as a new book reaches the distribution center.
>
> "Hey, son, come here. I want to show you something." His five-year-old eyes widened and he rushed over to my desk. I suppose he thought it might be a new office gadget—a "toy" he could play with.
>
> "What do you have, Daddy?"
>
> "See," I said, proudly holding up the volume before him, my face beaming with a broad grin of self-congratulatory accomplishment, "it's my new book!"
>
> "Oh." He breathed a deep sigh, punctuated by a shrug of his shoulders and a grimace of disappointment.
>
> I was crushed that he took no joy in my accomplishment. A moment of resounding silence filled the room. He looked at my face, which was clearly saddened by his reaction. He seemed to grasp the meaning of my changed expression.
>
> Then, more as an explanation of his response than as a question, he asked, "Why do you write those things anyway? Do they ever help anybody?"

His questions led to an epiphany. In the moment that his words pierced the silence, an image, a glimpse of a possible future, burst before me.

> I saw a young man—my son years in the future—kneeling with a woman I imagined was his wife, in a dark attic, a tiny space illuminated by a single hanging light bulb. He had just opened a carton. He was, with his wife peering over his shoulder, staring at its contents.
>
> "Wait, I know what these are," he said, reaching inside the box. He pulled out a book covered in dust, and blew on its side and cover. "These are copies of the books my dad used to write." He paused, then breathed the same sort of sigh I had heard in my study. Then, aloud, but more to himself than to her, he said, "I remember all the time he spent on doing these . . . squirreled away on weekends and almost every night. I never got to spend as much time with him when I was growing up as I would of liked . . ." His voice halted and choked a bit. "He chose to do these instead."

I saw that this is what my work would come to, what it would mean to my son: missed opportunities to have spent time with his dad for the sake of books that would gather dust in an unknown carton in a dark attic. And all for what? My son would believe that I had helped no one, that all my time had been wasted. The result of all that I gave up to produce these books was dust and sad memories of missed opportunities.

I guess that as a result of this vision I could have had a Scrooge-like conversion, repudiated my "workaholic" ethic, and adopted a life focused solely on spending time with my son, his younger sister, and infant brother. But that is not the resolution I made at that moment.

I decided that, in some way, I would make my work of value to my son, to his siblings, to my family. I resolved to find a way, although exactly how would not become clear to me for several months, to recast my work so that my son could say that his dad mattered, that he had done more than produce the useless and pointless knowledge that Bob Dylan described in "Ballad of a Thin Man," that because of his work life had become better.

But better for whom? I was a scholar of child and adolescent development, an expert in the study of youth and families. Clearly, it seemed, I should contribute not only to better knowledge about youth development but, as well, to using that knowledge to make development better for young people.

"Okay, then," I thought. "This is what I'll do." This goal seemed certain. But how I would reach it did not.

The path this question took me on over the next two years was one that first involved coming to appreciate the implications of my own scholarship for application (Birkel, Lerner, & Smyer, 1989). My theory stressed that human development occurs through the bidirectional relationships individuals have with their physical and social world. One could test this theory by introducing changes into the contexts within which young people interacted; one could then evaluate whether these changes resulted in predicted developmental outcomes. I began to realize, then, that in the real ecology of human development these changes in person-context relations could be represented by programs or policies. These interventions into the course of life could be aimed at altering individual-context relations, at improving the quality and outcomes of individuals' development.

By using my ideas to design and assess the effectiveness of programs and policies, I could at the same time learn something about the adequacy of these interventions *and* about the theory of development from which such community-based actions derived. Within developmental contextualism, then, programs and policies represent theory-guided actions to alter youth-context connections in ways that promote positive developmental trajectories. Evaluation of the effectiveness of these applications of developmental science provide information about both the efficacy of such interventions and the basic, relational process of human development.

Simply, then, when applied developmental science is framed by developmental contextualism, basic and applied issues of human development merge. As a consequence, I realized I had a model that could result in scholarship that might do more than generate dust-producing volumes of theory and research. The model could lead to scholarship that would inform the program and policy development, implementation, and evaluation process. When I recognized these implications of my model, I realized that I could become an *applied* developmental scientist (Birkel et al., 1989).

The desire and commitment to become an applied developmental scientist required more than just a change in what I would now place in the foreground of my scholarship—an emphasis on serving youth and families directly through my scholarship, and in ways that they valued and defined as important. In addition, it would require a change in the substance of my research. Albeit perhaps a distinction without a difference or only a subtle change in emphasis, this alteration is to me a hugely significant one. I have altered my scholarship a focus on "understanding the basic, relational process *of* development" to "understanding the basic relational process *in promoting positive* development."

For example, my current research is not aimed primarily at elucidating the parameters of circular functions of goodness of fit but, instead, at using ideas associated with developmental contextualism to understand how relations between diverse youth and the multiple levels of the ecology of human development (e.g., families, peers, school, neighborhoods, schools, culture, public policies, and the physical environment) are associated with variations in positive and healthy ontogenetic change. The goal here is to identify those individual and ecological variables associated with the promotion of positive outcomes in youth (Lerner, 1995, in preparation; Lerner & Galambos, 1998).

To illustrate, within a project supported by the William T. Grant Foundation my colleagues and I are conducting a longitudinal study of African American male adolescent gang members from Detroit (Taylor et al., in press-a, in press-b). The study is not intended to document how these youth succumb to the violence, drugs, and other risks confronting them. Rather, through borrowing a term from Werner and Smith (1992), we are investigating the process of "overcoming the odds" that exist among these youth. We are seeking to understand the individual and ecological conditions that lead a small percentage of these youth to actually end up living positive lives for themselves, their families, and their communities.

Our goal, then, is to see if the model of those individual-context relations can be replicated so that we can bring such positive development to scale in a cross-validational sample of other gang youth. For example, we hope to work with Latino gangs in Detroit as well. Such a cross-validational effort in effect constitutes a program aimed at promoting positive youth development. If this intervention were to be successful, we would then use our results to engage the policy-making process, in the hope of bringing to scale and sustaining an instance of "best practice" in the service of youth. In essence, then, by using my theoretical and empirical work as an overall architecture for understanding human development and by applying such knowledge to promote positive development, I seek to find ways to apply developmental science in "real world" settings. I seek to enhance those connections between youth and contexts that promote positive development.

As I see it, the transition from basic to applied scholar has been seamless. This is because when a developmental contextual perspective is applied, there is no difference in the study of human development between basic and applied research. When one is seeking to alter, in theoretically predicted ways, the connection between youth and their contexts to promote positive changes, one is not only testing ideas about the basic, relational process of human development but is also using these ideas to institute actions aimed at improving the life chances of young people. In short, I believe that one can use developmental science as a frame both for doing scholarship and for promoting positive developmental outcomes in youth (Lerner, 1995, 1998b; Lerner, Sparks, & McCubbin, 1999).

However, as I have pursued my work as an applied developmental scientist I have learned that such efforts need to be embedded in other changes in the ecology of contemporary life in order to substantially alter the life chances of America's young people. I have learned that to pursue applied developmental science within the framework of the contemporary Western university system requires that the human development scholar extend his or her expertise to understand the nature of American higher education.

☐ The Genesis of a Reformer of American Higher Education

From a developmental systems perspective such as developmental contextualism, to best promote positive development all individuals, groups, and institutions in the context should integrate their resources. They should collaborate or form partnerships to promote positive development. This contention is based on the ideas that if the relations in the developmental system are the bases of human development, then it may be feasible to promote positive development by having individuals and institutions within the system act in a collaborative manner, combining their strengths to enhance the lives of youth.

However, one institution that has remained essentially at the periphery of providing its assets and resources to promote positive development among youth has been the university. Consistent with developmental systems thinking, then, I have conducted scholarship pertinent to the reform of higher education (e.g., Lerner & Simon, 1998a, 1998b). I have argued that ADS may be an exemplar of how university faculty may merge scholarly and community interests within the context of higher education institutions that are striving to become vehicles of community engagement, that is, institutions making value-added contributions to community life—as the community defines and values such contributions (Kellogg Commission, 1999; Spanier, 1999; Votruba, 1999a, 1999b).

In other words, ADS provides a key means through which "outreach scholarship" may be conducted (Lerner & Miller, 1998). Outreach scholarship involves the enactment of the knowledge "functions" of the university—the generation, transmission, preservation, or application of knowledge—in manners devised through community-university co-learning collaborations and thus in directions valued by all partners in the collaboration. By providing an intellectual context for integrating the voices and concerns of children, youth, and families with those of research-active scholars, ADS may become a key means through which scientists—and the universities that employ so many of them—may serve people.

In addition to making these arguments, I have tried to take actions consistent with them. I have worked for the past decade to build university-community partnerships promoting positive development. To create such co-learning collaborations, I have established applied developmental science centers at Michigan State University and Boston College in order to provide a unit through which communities can access universities *and* through which faculty, students, and staff can engage in outreach to communities. Now, at Tufts University, I am continuing this work, again trying to build co-learning partnerships with communities—collaborations wherein the values, the voice, and the vision of the community are equally as important as those of the scholars coming to the collaborative "table." In fact, I have learned that the perspective of the community may be more important when issues of program scale and program sustainability are considered (Lerner, 1995; Lerner et al., 1999).

To illustrate some of this university-community collaborative "outreach scholarship" pursued at these centers, I may note that I am working with the National 4-H Council to help them forge a vision of "community youth development," of positive youth development in a community context. 4-H is the largest youth-serving organization in this nation, with six million youth a year going through 4-H programs. Thus the potential impact of this work is enormous. In addition I am working with the International Youth Foundation, as a consultant on behalf of the W. K. Kellogg Foundation, to help them build principles of best practice in youth programming within each of the sixty countries with which IYF will be working over the next four years.

In addition to creating outreach partnerships, I believed that the university centers/institutes with which I have worked had to be vehicles for disseminating high-quality scientific information that also affects policies and programs. To reform higher education to the extent that community-collaborative partnerships serving youth and families are not only accepted but also highly regarded and rewarded (e.g., in terms of tenure and promotion decisions), centers conducting such work also must be both generators of and catalysts for significant scholarship pertinent to the application of developmental science.

Accordingly, much of my work directed at reforming higher education so that it becomes more involved with communities in support of positive youth development has involved the generation of outlets for ADS scholarship. Two illustrations of this work may be useful. First, Celia B. Fisher (Fordham University), Richard A. Weinberg (University of Minnesota), and I founded a journal, *Applied Developmental Science*, which publishes methodologically rigorous empirical work representing the use of ideas about development to promote positive outcomes in youth. Special issues of the journal are used to bring together policy makers, scholars, and funders to discuss issues that would advance the application of developmental science for policies and programs aimed at promoting positive youth development.

For instance, In Volume 3, Number 4 (1999), Senator Edward M. Kennedy keynoted a special issue on building university-community collaborations promoting positive developmental outcomes for youth and families. In addition to Senator Kennedy's article, there were articles by program officers from the W. K. Kellogg Foundation, by Peter Jensen, Kimberly Hoagwood, Edison Trickett from the National Institute of Mental Health, by Linda Thomson, special secretary for Child, Youth, and Families in the cabinet of the governor of Maryland, by Graham Spanier, president of Penn State University and chair of the Kellogg Commission on the Future of State and Land-Grant Universities, and by Lonnie Sherrod, executive vice president of the W. T. Grant Foundation.

As a second example of ADS dissemination efforts, I launched with

Kluwer Academic Publishers a scholarly book series called "Outreach Scholarship." At this writing, six books have appeared in the series and several others are in production. For instance, one book, edited by Chibucos and Lerner (1999), is entitled *Serving Children and Families through Community-University Partnerships: Success Stories*. The book is aimed at giving people who are in leadership positions and able to make decisions about marshalling resources for youth (university administrators, funders, legislators) easily accessible evidence about how higher educational institutions can collaborate in promoting community-valued, positive outcomes for youth. The book contains fifty success stories, from universities across the United States and from across the life span, that illustrate such collaborations.

A second book in the series is *Family Diversity and Family Policy: Strengthening Families for America's Children* (Lerner, Sparks, & McCubbin, 1999). The key aim of this volume is to offer a vision for developing in the United States a youth policy that both promotes positive outcomes in youth and advances civil society. A third book that has appeared in the series, *Social Change, Public Policy and Community Collaboration: Training Human Development Professionals for the Twenty-first Century* (Ralston et al., 1999), is derived from a conference that was held under the auspices of the American Association of Family and Consumer Sciences and the National Taskforce on Applied Developmental Science. The volume seeks to provide a model for building a new generation of applied developmental scholars, professionals who integrate the worlds of the academy and of the community in order to enhance the lives of diverse children and their families.

Together, the dissemination activities of the university centers, coupled with the applied developmental science research fostered by such units, serve as examples to universities and their faculty that theoretically predicated scholarship may meet high academic standards of funding and publication and, at the same time, develop in collaboration with, and serve the interests and values of, the diverse children, youth, and families of the communities within which universities exist. If all levels of the context of human development should be positively integrated in order to promote the healthy development of children, we cannot let higher education institutions—organizations with a special ability to generate, transmit, preserve, and apply knowledge (Boyer, 1990)—remain at the periphery of (or worse, be uninvolved in) efforts to enhance the lives of young people. ADS, when embedded in centers such as I have described, can serve as a model for and a means of university-community partnership. Such efforts can bring new meaning to Kurt Lewin's (1943) oft-noted observation that there is nothing as practical as a good theory.

☐ Conclusions

This chapter shows how my initial intellectual curiosity about the process of development has been gradually transformed into a central and abiding interest in how to apply my work in ways that "matter" for the diverse children and adolescents of my nation and world. The developmental systems theory that I have dubbed developmental contextualism has enabled me to view interventions into the life course—public policies and youth-serving programs—as (potentially) theory-guided ways of arranging relations between individuals and their ecological settings to promote positive life changes (Birkel et al., 1989; Bronfenbrenner & Morris, 1998). The evaluation of the efficacy of these policies or programs not only provides information about the adequacy of these interventions but also data that might elucidate the basic process of human development (Lerner, 1991, 1995, 1996; Lerner, De Stefanis, & Ladd, 1998).

Of course, I recognize that this account of the genesis of my scholarly career may be regarded as nothing more than an academic odyssey motivated by a perhaps offhand or overinterpreted remark by a very young boy to his father. However, if this history is an account of the genesis of what is a passionate and, as Rick Little (1993), president of the International Youth Foundation, would suggest is needed, an irrational commitment to improving the lives of youth, then it is one that was born from the love of a father for his son, and of that father's resulting hope that his son would remember him as having lived a life that mattered—to his own family and to the families of countless others. To matter to my son I set out on a path committed to helping others matter to the children and families across our nation and world.

☐ Acknowledgment

The preparation of this chapter was supported in part by a grant from the W. T. Grant Foundation.

☐ References

Baltes, M. M., & Lerner, R. M. (1980). Roles of the operant model and its methods in the life-span approach to human development. *Human Development, 23,* 362–367.

Baltes, P. B. (1968). Longitudinal and cross-sectional sequences in the study of age and generational effects. *Human Development, 11,* 145–171.

Baltes, P. B. (1983). Life-span developmental psychology: Observations on history and theory revisited. In R. M. Lerner (Ed.), *Developmental psychology: Historical and philosophical perspectives.* Hillsdale, NJ: Erlbaum.

Baltes, P. B. (1987). Theoretical propositions of life-span development psychology: On the dynamics between growth and decline. *Developmental Psychology, 23,* 611–626.

Baltes, P. (1997). On the incomplete architecture of human ontogeny: Selection, optimization, and compensation as foundations of developmental theory. *American Psychologist, 52,* 366–380.

Baltes, P. B., Lindenberger, U., & Staudinger, U. M. (1998). Life-span theory in developmental psychology. In R. M. Lerner (Ed.), *Theoretical models of human development.* Volume 1 of the *Handbook of child psychology* (5th ed., pp. 1029–1144), Gen. Ed., W. Damon. New York: Wiley.

Baltes, P. B., Staudinger, U. M., & Lindenberger, U. (1999). Lifespan psychology: Theory and application to intellectual functioning. In J. T. Spence, J. M. Darley, & D. J. Foss (Eds.), *Annual Review of Psychology* (vol. 50, pp. 471–507). Palo Alto, CA: Annual Reviews.

Baltes, P. B., Reese, H. W., & Lipsitt, L. P. (1980). Life-span developmental psychology. *Annual Review of Psychology, 31,* 65–110.

Birkel, R., Lerner, R. M., & Smyer, M. A. (1989). Applied developmental psychology as an implementation of a life-span view of human development. *Journal of Applied Developmental Psychology, 10,* 425–445.

Boyer, E.L. (1990). *Scholarship reconsidered: Priorities of the professoriate.* Princeton, NJ: The Carnegie Foundation for the Advancement of Thinking.

Brandtstädter, J. B. (1998). Action perspectives in human development. In R. M. Lerner (Ed.), *Theoretical models of human development.* Volume 1 of the *Handbook of child psychology* (5th ed., pp. 807–863), Editor in chief: W. Damon. New York: Wiley.

Brandtstädter, J. B. (1999). The self in action and development: Cultural, biosocial, and ontogenetic bases of intentional self-development. In J. B. Brandstädter & R. M. Lerner (Eds.), *Action and self-development: Theory and research through the life span* (pp. 37–65). Thousand Oaks, CA: Sage.

Brandstädter, J. B., & Lerner, R. M. (1999a). *Action and self-development: Theory and research through the life span.* Thousand Oaks, CA: Sage.

Brandstädter, J. B., & Lerner, R. M. (1999b). Development, action, and intentionality: A view of the issues. In J. Brandstädter & R. M. Lerner (Eds.). *Action and self-development: Theory and research through the life span* (pp. ix–xx). Thousand Oaks, CA: Sage.

Brim, O. G., Jr., & Kagan, J. (1980). Constancy and change: A view of the issues. In O. G. Brim, Jr., & J. Kagan (Eds.), *Constancy and change in human development* (pp. 1–25). Cambridge, MA: Harvard University Press.

Bronfenbrenner, U. (1977). Toward an experimental ecology of human development. *American Psychologist, 32,* 513–531.

Bronfenbrenner, U. (1979). *The ecology of human development: Experiments by nature and design.* Cambridge, MA: Harvard University Press.

Bronfrenbrenner, U. (1983). The context of development and the development of context. In R. M. Lerner (Ed.), *Developmental psychology: Historical and philosophical perspectives.* Hillsdale, NJ: Erlbaum.

Bronfenbrenner, U., & Morris, P. A. (1998). The ecology of developmental process. In R. M. Lerner (Ed.), *Theoretical models of human development.* Volume 1 of the *Handbook of Child Psychology* (5th ed., pp. 993–1028), Gen. Ed., W. Damon. New York: Wiley.

Chibucos, T. R., & Lerner, R. M. (1999). Serving children and families through community-university partnerships: A view of the issues. In T. R. Lerner & R. M. Lerner (Eds.), *Serving children and families through community-university partnerships: Success stories* (pp. 1–11). Norwell, MA: Kluwer Academic Publishers.

Chess, S., & Thomas, A. (1984). *Origins and evolution of behavior disorders.* New York: Brunner/Mazel.

Damon, W. (Ed.). (1998). *Handbook of child psychology* (5th ed.). New York: Wiley.

Elder, G. H., Jr. (1974). *Children of the great depression.* Chicago: University of Chicago Press.

Elder, G. H., Jr. (1980). Adolescence in historical perspective. In J. Adelson (Ed.), *Handbook of adolescent psychology* (pp. 3–46). New York: Wiley.

Elder, G. H., Jr., Modell, J., & Parke, R. D. (Eds.). (1993). *Children in time and place: Developmental and historical insights.* New York: Cambridge University Press.

Featherman, D. L. (1983). Life-span perspectives in social science research. In P. B. Baltes & O. G. Brim Jr. (Eds.), *Life span development and behavior* (vol. 5, pp. 1–57). New York: Academic Press.

Fisher, C. B., & Lerner, R. M. (Eds.). (1994a). *Applied developmental psychology.* New York: McGraw-Hill.

Fisher, C. B., & Lerner, R. M. (1994b). Foundations of applied developmental psychology. In C. B. Fisher & R. M. Lerner (Eds.), *Applied developmental psychology* (pp. 3–20). New York: McGraw-Hill.

Ford, D. L., & Lerner, R. M. (1992). *Developmental systems theory: An integrative approach.* Newbury Park, CA: Sage.

Gottlieb, G. (1970). Conceptions of prenatal behavior. In L. R. Aronson, E. Tobach, D. S. Lehrman, & J. S. Rosenblatt (Eds.), *Development and evolution of behavior: Essays in memory of T.C. Schneirla.* San Francisco: Freeman.

Gottlieb, G. (1997). *Synthesizing nature-nurture: Prenatal roots of instinctive behavior.* Mahwah, NJ: Erlbaum.

Gould, S. J. (1977). *Ontogeny and phylogeny.* Cambridge, MA: Harvard University Press.

Hamburg, D. A. (1992). *Today's children: Creating a future for a generation in crisis.* New York: Wiley.

Harris, D. B. (Ed.). (1957). *The concept of development.* Minneapolis, MN: University of Minnesota Press.

Hebb, D. O. (1949). *The organization of behavior.* New York: Wiley.

Hebb, D. O. (1958). *A textbook of psychology.* Philadelphia, PA: Saunders.

Heckhausen, J. (1999). *Developmental regulation in adulthood: Age-normative and socio-cultural constraints as adaptive challenges.* New York: Cambridge University Press.

Hultsch, D. F. (Ed.). (1980). Implications of a dialectical perspective for research methodology. *Human Development, 23,* 217–267.

Hultsch, D. F., & Hickey, T. (1978). External validity in the study of human development: Theoretical and methodological issues. *Human Development, 21,* 76–91.

Hunt, J. McV. (1961). *Intelligence and experience.* New York: Ronald Press.

Huston, A. C. (Ed.). (1991). *Children in poverty: Child development and public policy.* Cambridge, UK: Cambridge University Press.

Jensen, P., Hoagwood, K. & Trickett, E. (1999). Ivory towers or earthen trenches? Community collaborations to foster "real world" research. *Applied Developmental Science, 3,* 206, 212.

Jessor, R., Donovan, J. E., & Costa, F. M. (1991). *Beyond adolescence: Problem behavior and young adult development.* Cambridge, UK: Cambridge University Press.

Kellogg Commission on the Future of State and Land-Grant Colleges. (1999). *Returning to our roots: The engaged institution.* Washington, DC: National Association of the State Universities and Land-Grant Colleges.

Ketterlinus, R. D., & Lamb, M. (Eds.). (1994). *Adolescent problem behaviors: Issues and research.* Hillsdale, NJ: Erlbaum.

Labouvie-Vief, G. (1982). Dynamic development and mature autonomy: A theoretical prologue. *Human Development, 25,* 161–191.

Lehrman, D. S. (1953). A critique of Konrad Lorenz's theory of instinctive behavior. *Quarterly Review of Biology, 28,* 337–363.

Lehrman, D. S. (1970). Semantic and conceptual issues in the nature-nurture problem. In L. R. Aronson, E. Tobach, D. S. Lehrman, & J. S. Rosenblatt (Eds.), *Development and evolution of behavior: Essays in memory of T. C. Schneirla* (pp. 17–52). San Francisco: Freeman.

Lerner, J. V. (1983). The role of temperament in psychosocial adaptation in early adolescents: A test for "goodness of fit" model. *Journal of Genetic Psychology, 143,* 149–157.

Lerner, R. M. (1976). *Concepts and theories of human development.* Reading, MA: Addison-Wesley.

Lerner, R. M. (1978). Nature, nurture, and dynamic interactionism. *Human Development, 21,* 1–20.

Lerner, R. M. (1979). A dynamic interactional concept of individual and social relationship development. In R. L. Burgess & T. L. Huston (Eds.), *Social exchange in developing relationships* (pp. 271–305). New York: Academic Press.

Lerner, R. M. (1982). Children and adolescents as producers of their own development. *Developmental Review, 2,* 342–370.

Lerner, R. M. (Ed.). (1983). *Developmental psychology: Historical and philosophical perspectives.* Hillsdale, NJ: Erlbaum.

Lerner, R. M. (1984). *On the nature of human plasticity.* New York: Cambridge University Press.

Lerner, R. M. (1986). *Concepts and theories of human development* (2nd ed.). New York: Random House.

Lerner, R. M. (1989). Developmental contextualism and the life-span view of person-context interaction. In M. Bornstein & J. S. Bruner (Eds.), *Interaction in human development* (pp. 217–239). Hillsdale, NJ: Erlbaum.

Lerner, R. M. (1991). Changing organism-context relations as the basic process of development: A developmental-contextual perspective. *Developmental Psychology, 27,* 27–32.

Lerner, R. M. (1995). *America's youth in crisis: Challenges and options for programs and policies.* Thousand Oaks, CA: Sage.

Lerner, R. M. (1996). Relative plasticity, integration, temporality, and diversity in human development: A developmental contextual perspective about theory, process, and method. *Developmental Psychology, 32,* 781–786.

Lerner, R. M. (Ed.). (1998a). *Theoretical models of human development.* Volume 1 of the *Handbook of child psychology* (5th ed.), Editor in Chief: W. Damon. New York: Wiley.

Lerner, R. M. (1998b). Theories of human development: Contemporary perspectives. In R. M. Lerner (Ed.), *Theoretical models of human development.* Volume 1 of the *Handbook of Child Psychology* (5th ed., pp. 1–24), Gen. Ed., W. Damon. New York: Wiley.

Lerner, R. M. (2002). *Adolescence: Development, diversity, context, and application.* Upper Saddle River, NJ: Prentice-Hall.

Lerner, R. M., & Busch-Rossnagel, N. A. (Ed.). (1981). *Individuals as producers of their development: A life-span perspective.* New York: Academic Press.

Lerner, R. M., Castellino, D. R., Terry, P. A., Villarruel, F. A., & McKinney, M. H. (1995). *A developmental contextual perspective on parenting.* In M. H. Bornstein (Ed.), *Handbook of parenting: Vol. II. Biology and ecology of parenting* (pp. 285–309). Hillsdale, NJ: Erlbaum.

Lerner, R. M., De Stefanis, I., & Ladd, G. T. (1998). Promoting positive youth development: Collaborative opportunities for psychology. *Children's services: Social policy, research, & Practice, 1*(2), 83–109.

Lerner, R. M., Fisher, C. B., & Weinberg, R. A. (1997). Applied developmental science: Scholarship for our times. *Applied Developmental Science, 1,* 2–3.

Lerner, R. M., & Galambos, N. (1998). Adolescent development: Challenges and opportunities for research, programs, and policies. In J. T. Spence (Ed.), *Annual Review of Psychology* (vol. 49, pp. 413–446). Palo Alto, CA: Annual Reviews Inc.

Lerner, R. M., & Kauffman, M. B. (1985). The concept of development in contextualism. *Developmental Review, 5,* 309–333.

Lerner, R. M., & Korn, S. J. (1972). The development of body build stereotypes in males. *Child Development, 43,* 912–920.

Lerner, R. M., & Lerner, J. V. (1977). Effects of age, sex, and physical attractiveness on child-peer relations, academic performance, and elementary school adjustment. *Developmental Psychology, 13,* 585–590.

Lerner, R. M., & Lerner, J. V. (1983) Temperament and adaptation across life: Theoretical and empirical issues. In P. B. Baltes & O. G. Brim Jr. (Eds.), *Life-span development and behavior* (vol. 5, pp. 197–231). New York: Academic Press.

Lerner, R. M., & Lerner, J. V. (1989). Organismic and social contextual bases of development: The sample case of adolescence. In W. Damon (Ed.), *Child development today and tomorrow.* San Francisco: Jossey-Bass.

Lerner, R. M., & Miller, J. R. (1998). Developing interdisciplinary institutes to enhance the lives of individuals and families: Academic potentials and pitfalls. *Journal of Public Service & Outreach, 3*(1), 64–73.

Lerner, R. M., & Simon, L. A. K. (Eds.). (1998a). *University-community collaborations for the twenty-first century: Outreach scholarship for youth and families.* New York: Garland Publishing.

Lerner, R. M., & Simon, L. A. K. (1998b) The new American outreach university: Challenges and options. In R. M. Lerner & Simon, L. A. K. (Eds.), *University-community collaborations for the twenty-first century: Outreach scholarship for youth and families* (pp. 3–23). New York: Garland.

Lerner, R. M., & Spanier, G. B. (Ed.). (1978*). Child influences on marital and family interaction: A life-span perspective.* New York: Academic Press.

Lerner, R. M., Sparks, E. S., & McCubbin, L. (1999). *Family diversity and family policy: Strengthening families for America's children.* Norwell, MA: Kluwer.

Lerner, R. M., & Walls, T. (1999). Revisiting individuals as producers of their development: From dynamic interactionism to developmental systems. In J. Brandstadter & R. M. Lerner (Eds.), *Action and development: Origins and functions of intentional self-development* (pp. 3–36). Thousand Oaks, CA: Sage.

Lewin, K. (1943). Psychology and the process of group living. *Journal of Social Psychology, 17,* 113–131.

Lewis, M., & Rosenblum, L. A. (Ed.). (1974). *The effect of the infant on its caregivers.* New York: Wiley.

Lewontin, R. C., Rose, S., & Kamin, L. J. (1984). *Not in our genes: Biology, ideology, and human nature.* New York: Pantheon.

Little, R. R. (1993). *What's working for today's youth: The issues, the programs, and the learnings.* Paper presented at an ICYF Fellows Colloquium, Michigan State University, East Lansing.

Magnusson, D. (1988). Individual development from an interactional perspective. In D. Magnusson (Ed.), *Paths through life* (Vol. 1, pp. 3–31). Hillsdale, NJ: Erlbaum.

McCandless, B. R. (1961). *Children and adolescents: Behavior and development.* New York: Holt, Rinehart and Winston.

McCandless, B. R. (1967). *Children.* New York: Holt, Rinehart & Winston.

McCandless, B. R. (1970). *Adolescents.* Hinsdale, IL: Dryden Press.

Miller, J.R., & Lerner, R.M. (1994). Integrating research and outreach: Developmental contextualism and the human ecological perspective. *Home Economics Forum, 7,* 21-28.

Nagel, E. (1957). Determinism in development. In D. B. Harris (Ed.), *The concept of development.* Minneapolis: University of Minnesota Press.

Nesselroade, J. R. (1983). *Implications of the trait-state distinction for the study of aging: Still labile after all these years.* Presidential address to Division 20, Ninety-first Annual Convention of the American Psychological Association, August, Anaheim, California.

Nesselroade, J. R. (1988). Some implications of the trait-state distinction for the study of development over the life-span: The case of personality. In P. B. Baltes, D. L. Featherman, & R. M. Lerner (Eds.), *Life-span development and behavior* (vol. 8, pp. 163–189). Hillsdale, N.J.: Erlbaum.

Nesselroade, J. R., & Baltes, P. B. (1974). Adolescent personality development and historical changes: 1970–1972. *Monographs of the Society for Research in Child Development, 39,* 154.

Nisbet, R. A. (1980). *History of the idea of progress.* New York: Basic Books.

Overton, W. F. (1973). On the assumptive base of the nature-nurture controversy: Additive versus interactive conceptions. *Human Development, 16,* 74-89.

Overton, W. F. (1998). Developmental psychology: Philosophy, concepts, and methodology. In R. M. Lerner (Ed.), *Theoretical models of human development.* Volume 1 of the *Handbook of child psychology* (5th ed., pp. 107–189). Gen. Ed., W. Damon. New York: Wiley.

Overton, W. F., & Reese, H. W. (1973). Models of development: Methodological implications. In J. R. Nesselroade & H. W. Reese (Eds.), *Life-span developmental psychology: Methodological issues* (pp. 65–86). New York: Academic Press.

Petersen, A. C., & Taylor, B. (1980). The biological approach to adolescence: Biological change and psychological adaptation. In J. Adelson (Ed.), *Handbook of adolescent psychology* (pp. 117-155). New York: Wiley.

Ralston, P., Lerner, R. M., Mullis, A., Simerly, C., & Murray, J. (Eds.). (1999). *Social change, public policy and community collaboration: Training human development professionals for the twenty-first century.* Norwell, MA: Kluwer.

Reese, H. W. (1976). Conceptions of the active organism (introduction*). Human Development, 19,* 69–70.

Reese, H. W., & Lipsitt, L. P. (Eds.). (1970). *Experimental child psychology.* New York: Academic Press.

Reese, H. W., & Overton, W. F. (1970). Models of development and theories of development. In L. R. Goulet & P. B. Baltes (Eds.), *Life-span developmental psychology: Research and theory* (pp. 115–145). New York: Academic Press.

Riegel, K. F. (1975) Toward a dialectical theory of development. *Human Development, 18,* 50–64.

Riegel, K. F. (1976). The dialectics of human development. *American Psychologist, 31,* 689–700.

Riegel, K. F. (1977a). The dialectics of time. In N. Datan & H.W. Reese (Eds.), *Life-span development psychology: Dialectical perspectives on experimental research.* New York: Academic Press.

Riegel, K. F. (1977b). History of psychological gerontology. In J. E. Birren & K. W. Schaie (Eds.), *Handbook of the psychology of aging.* New York: van Nostrand Reinhold.

Riley, M. W. (Ed.). (1979). *Aging from birth to death.* Washington, DC: American Association for the Advancement of Science.

Sameroff, A. J. (1983). Developmental systems: Contexts and evolution. In W. Kessen (Ed.), *Handbook of Child Psychology. Vol. 1: History, theory, and methods* (pp. 237–294). New York: Wiley.

Schaie, K. W. (1965). A general model for the study of developmental problems. *Psychological Bulletin, 64,* 92–107.

Schaie, K. W. (1983). The Seattle Longitudinal Study: A 21-year exploration of psychometric intelligence in adulthood. In K. W. Schaie (Ed.), *Longitudinal studies of adult psychological development* (pp. 64–135). New York: Guilford.

Schneirla, T. C. (1956). Interrelationships of the innate and the acquired in instinctive behavior. In P. P. Grassé (Ed.), *L'instinct dans le comportement des animaux et de l'homme* (pp. 387–452). Paris: Mason et Cie.

Schneirla, T. C. (1957). The concept of development in comparative psychology. In D. B. Harris (Ed.), *The concept of development* (pp. 78–108). Minneapolis: University of Minnesota.

Sears, R. R. (1957). Your ancients revisited. In E. M. Hetherington, J.W. Hagen, R. Kron, & A. H. Stein (Eds.), *Review of child development research*. Chicago: University of Chicago Press.

Simmons, R. G., & Blyth, D. A. (1987). *Moving into adolescence: The impact of pubertal change and social context*. New York: Aldine.

Spanier, G. B. (1976). Formal and informal sex education as determinants of pre-marital sex behavior. *Archives of Sexual Behavior, 5,* 39-67.

Spanier, G. B. (1999). Enhancing the quality of life: A model for the 21st century land-grant university. *Applied Developmental Science, 3*(4), 199–205.

Staffieri, J. R. (1967). A study of social stereotype of body image in children. *Journal of Personality and Social Psychology, 7,* 101–104.

Super, C. M., & Harkness, S. (1981). Figure, ground, and Gestalt: The cultural context of the active individual. In R. M. Lerner & N. A. Busch-Rossnagel (Eds.), *Individuals as producers of their development: A life-span perspective* (pp. 69–86). New York: Academic Press.

Taylor, C. S., Lerner, R. M., von Eye, A., Bobek, D., Bilalbegović Balsano, A., Dowling, E., & Anderson, P. (in press-a). Positive individual and social behavior among gang and non-gang African-American male adolescents. *Journal of Adolescent Research.*

Taylor, C. S., Lerner, R. M., von Eye, A., Bobek, D., Bilalbegović Balsano, A., Dowling, E., & Anderson, P. (in press-b). Internal and external developmental assets among African-American male gang members. *Journal of Adolescent Research.*

Thelen, E., & Smith, L. B. (1994). *A dynamic systems approach to the development of cognition and action*. Cambridge, MA: MIT Press.

Thomas, A., & Chess, S. (1977). *Temperament and development*. New York: Brunner/Mazel.

Thomas, A., Chess, S., & Birch, H. G. (1968). *Temperament and behavior disorders in children*. New York: New York University Press.

Thomas, A., Chess, S., Birch, H. G., Hertzig, M. E., & Korn, S. (1963). *Behavioral individuality in early childhood*. New York: New York University Press.

Tobach, E. (1981). Evolutionary aspects of the activity of the organism and its development. In R. M. Lerner & N. A. Busch-Rossnagel (Eds.), *Individuals as producers of their development: A life-span perspective* (pp. 37–68). New York: Academic.

Tobach E., & Greenberg, G. (1984). The significance of T. C. Schneirla's contribution to the concept of levels of integration. In G. Greenberg & E. Tobach (Eds.), *Behavioral evolution and integrative levels* (pp. 1–7). Hillsdale, NJ: Erlbaum.

Tobach, E. & Schneirla, T.C. (1968) The biopsychology of social behavior of animals. In R. E. Cooke & S. Levin (Eds.), *Biologic basis of pediatric practice*. New York: McGraw Hill.

Votruba, J. C. (1999a). Implementing public policy education: The role of the university. In P. Ralston, R. M. Lerner, A. K. Mullis, C. Simerly, & J. Murray (Eds.), *Social change, public policy, and community collaboration: Training human development professionals for the twenty-first century* (pp. 117–120). Norwell, MA: Kluwer.

Votruba, J. C. (1999b). Afterword. In P. Ralston, R. M. Lerner, A. K. Mullis, C. Simerly, & J. Murray (Eds.), *Social change, public policy, and community collaboration: Training human development professionals for the twenty-first century* (pp. 141–145). Norwell, MA: Kluwer.

Werner, H. (1957). The concept of development from a comparative and organismic point of view. In D. B. Harris (Ed.), *The concept of development* (pp. 125–148). Minneapolis: University of Minnesota Press.

Werner, E. E., & Smith, R. (1992). *Overcoming the odds: High-risk children from birth to adulthood*. Ithaca, NY: Cornell University Press.

Wohlwill, J. F. (1973). *The study of behavioral development*. New York: Academic Press.

AUTHOR INDEX

SUBJECT INDEX